PENGUIN BOOKS

Successful Aging

Born in 1948 in New Jersey, Mark Novak completed his B.A. there at Rutgers University and received his Ph.D. in sociology at York University in Toronto. He has held teaching positions in sociology at York University, Laurentian University and the University of Winnipeg. In addition to numerous articles and studies for magazines and academic journals, he has previously published one book, *Living and Learning in the Free School* (1975). Active in several community senior groups, Mark Novak now lives in Winnipeg with his wife and three children.

SUCCESSFUL AGING

THE MYTHS, REALITIES AND FUTURE OF AGING IN CANADA

DR MARK NOVAK

Contemporary Family Issues

Penguin Books

Penguin Books Canada Ltd., 2801 John Street, Markham, Ontario, Canada L3R 1B4
Penguin Books Ltd., Harmondsworth, Middlesex, England
Penguin Books, 40 West 23rd Street, New York, New York 10010 U.S.A.
Penguin Books Australia Ltd., Ringwood, Victoria, Australia
Penguin Books (N.Z.) Ltd., Private Bag, Takapuna, Auckland 9, New Zealand

First published by Penguin Books Canada Limited, 1985

Copyright © Mark Novak, 1985
All rights reserved.
Typeset by Jay Tee Graphics Ltd.
Manufactured in Canada by Webcom Limited

Canadian Cataloguing in Publication Data

Novak, Mark W.
  Successful aging

Bibliography: p.
ISBN 0-14-007213-6

1. Aging. 2. Aged - Canada. 3. Gerontology.
I. Title.

HQ1064.C32N68 1986   305.2'6'0971   C84-099700-0

50,576

SUCCESSFUL AGING

For my Mother

CONTENTS

ACKNOWLEDGEMENTS

YOU CAN LEARN to swim in two ways. You can read about it and take classes in it or you can watch someone do it, then plunge in.

Each method has its good points. I learned about aging the second way. Before I had read much about the subject I decided to go out and talk to older people about what it is like to be old. Like the non-swimmer who learns by watching and doing, I did not have time to worry about whether I was learning the "right" way. I just tried to get my bearings and stay afloat.

Day after day I talked to older people on downtown streets, in small neighbourhood parks and in personal care homes. Often they invited me into their homes. They played music for me — hymns and popular tunes from the twenties and thirties. One man even put on a magic show. They opened themselves to me — a young stranger with a lot of questions and a tape recorder. Without their help I would know a lot less about aging and I could never have written this book. I refer to only some of them by name in the text, but they all helped shape the ideas here. I thank them all deeply for their kindness and patience.

I also owe a debt to the first professionals I talked to about aging. Yhetta Gold, former director of Age and Opportunity, Inc., in Winnipeg and now president of Canada's National Advisory Council on Aging, gave me a short course in the realities of aging. She showed me how deeply committed someone can be to the welfare of others. Dr David Skelton, then head of the Extended Care Unit at St Boniface Hospital in Winnipeg, taught me my first lessons about health care and the aged. More than anything else he showed me that geriatric medicine attracts a very special breed of doctor — one who knows basic medicine but also one who has compassion and love for the people he treats. I thank both these people for passing along to me their enthusiasm for working with older people.

Some people influenced my work at a distance. When I turned to writings on aging the works of Paul Tournier, Michel Philibert, Bernice Neugarten and Robert Butler struck me as sensible and well written. They still do. Robert Butler's award-winning book, *Why Survive? Being Old in America*, has served as an unsurpassable model for my own writing.

Closer to home, my dear friend and mentor Hans Mohr stands as a compass and guide to me in all my work. Whatever good sense I bring to my writing I credit to him. Likewise I thank my friend and colleague Leroy Stone, senior advisor to Statistics Canada. Leroy works hard to make census data available for people in the field of aging. He showed me the importance of population studies. If Canada ever decides to declare people national treasures, I would like to nominate Hans and Leroy for the honour.

Other colleagues have read, commented on or listened to my reports on successful aging. Neena Chappell, director of the Centre on Aging at the University of Manitoba, was one of the first people to see something worthwhile in my study of successful aging. I thank her for her early, much-needed support. Neena also reviewed the chapter on health care. Gloria Gutman, director of the Centre on Aging at Simon Fraser University, carefully read and commented on the chapter on housing. Leroy Stone reviewed the chapter on demography. Professors Charles Axelrod and David Cheal, good friends, were ready to listen when I needed to try out an idea. I would also like to thank the many researchers across Canada, some of whom I have mentioned in the text, who work so hard to improve our knowledge and understanding of aging. They have all helped make this a better book.

I owe a debt of thanks to people who worked behind the scenes to make this book possible. The Social Sciences and Humanities Research Council of Canada supported this research with two grants. The University of Winnipeg also supplied funds for the research. Without this support this book could not have been written. I also want to thank Ross McCormack, academic vice-president at the University of Winnipeg, and Sheila Armstrong and France Landriault at the Social Sciences and Humanities Research Council.

John Hofley and Doreen Smith, two gifted department chairpersons, encouraged me and helped me schedule time to prepare and write this book. Christine Bollenbock, my research assistant, saved me hours of time. She always managed to unearth the arcane source I needed on short notice. Also I thank Pat Doyle, research assistant, interviewer and co-worker. She taught me how to listen.

My editors Cynthia Good and David Kilgour at Penguin deserve more than thanks. Cynthia saw the possibility of this book in my first outline. Both she and David warmed to the topic of aging right away. Their belief in the project kept me going, and their comments made this a better book.

Mary Maione and Linda Gladstone deserve thanks and praise for typing drafts I couldn't read anymore. Without their patience and help it would have taken twice as long to finish the job.

Last, I would like to thank my family. Writing takes time. If I had known at the start how much time it would take, I might never have started. My sons Christopher, Jonathan and Sean and my wife Mona put up with an absentee father and husband. No time for games, no time to fix the faucets, only a few stolen moments from the typewriter for a Saturday night out. (Sean would check in daily to see how I was doing. ''Oh, only four more chapters to go,'' he would say. ''Then you'll have time for us.'' That comment always sent me back to work.) I thank them all for their patience and their love.

One person made this and all of my work possible — my mother. I thank her and love her more than I can say. I dedicate this book to her.

INTRODUCTION

WALK UP TO one of those wall sized maps at a big airport or university. If you are lost, the tangle of lines and jumble of names can make you more confused. But one little red dot and three words — ''you are here'' — can put the whole thing into perspective. With that bit of knowledge you not only see where you are, you can plan how to get where you want to go.

I think of this book as that little red dot. It is designed to give the reader some perspective on the jumble of myths and fears that surround aging today, to show how far we have come in creating a good old age and where we are going. I believe that we have come a long way and that we will do even better in the future. In short this book takes an unabashedly optimistic view of aging today.

Some people may not agree with this approach. They are convinced that it is necessary to show the horror and misery of old age before people will act to help older people. Some writers go out of their way to do this, even when the facts show that older people do better today than ever before in Canada's history.

Such sensational treatment of the subject of aging may scare us into changing the system. It can embarrass government into taking action or frighten people enough to make them save for their old age. But the guilt and fear engendered by it do not create lasting change. If you use these tactics long enough people become deaf to the problems you are shouting about. The issue eventually loses its currency and you are left where you started.

I think a different tactic makes more sense. First, let's look at the facts, at what we have done and at what still needs to be done. We can only move ahead to make things better if we know where we are now.

In each chapter of this book I begin with the facts on a single issue — health, housing, income, etc. In most cases I use data gathered by Statistics Canada, government agencies and researchers throughout the country. Few people will dispute the figures, but numbers alone do not tell the whole story: someone has to give them meaning. Not everyone will agree with my interpretations of statistics. In every case I explain why I think my version of the facts makes sense. Interested readers are encouraged to go back to the original sources I have cited if they want to review the facts for themselves.

After a survey of data I describe the system that gives rise to them — the health care system, the housing system, the pension system, etc. — and how it serves older people today. I then show how the system is changing to meet the new and changing needs of older people. Finally, at the end of each chapter I look at where we are headed, given what we know about aging today.

As you'll see, older people today live much better lives than most of us believe. Canada today has one of the best health and welfare systems in the world. To the old it offers a web of health care options, programs to improve incomes, a wide range of housing and rent support programs and recreation and education schemes in every part of the country.

These programs have their faults. Some people are not covered by them, some people do not get enough support, some people do not know about them or cannot use them because they live in isolated areas. But the programs *do* exist, and they can — and will — be improved.

To maintain the momentum of positive change we all need to know more about aging. Already the press and other media have begun to pick up on this need. Newspapers, magazines and television regularly run special features on old people and aging. They carry stories about the growing population of older people. They have raised the question of how we will pay for the medical care and pensions older people need. By now, almost everyone has thought a little — sometimes too little — about pensions, RRSPs and retirement. And many people have begun to worry about how they will care for their aging parents.

Despite the new concern about aging, people still do not know much about it. Many of us hide from the thought of aging, and much of what passes for knowledge turns out to be half-truth and myth.

In this book I want to look at the realities of aging today and show that old age brings more than problems: it also brings new challenges and new opportunities.

Canada today has the resources to create a Utopia for the elderly. We have the money and the know-how to create a model of old age, and we have begun to move in this direction. Not just the elderly but all of us will gain from these changes. The young will have the pleasure of seeing their parents and grandparents well cared for. And all of us will know that we can look forward to the same decent treatment when we get old.

Mark Novak
Winnipeg, 1984

1

COMING OF AGE
IN CANADA

Our Attitudes to Aging

Peege is the grandmother of a middle class family — a father, mother and three teen-aged grandsons. She has been in a nursing home for eight years. She is blind. She wears a catheter tube. And she is confused.

A film about Peege[1] opens with a Christmas visit from her family. As we ride with them in the car to the home it becomes clear from their conversation that this may be their last trip: Peege is dying.

I can't relate in words the shock of seeing her. She wears a colourless dress. She sits slumped over in her chair, held up by straps across her shoulders. Her grey hair lies matted across her forehead. Now and then her tongue lolls out of the corner of her mouth. A tray sits bolted to the chair in front of her. Her hands lie on the tray like two lumps of dough.

Peege confronts us with our worst fears about aging: the nightmare of senility; the terror of dependence on strangers; the fear of being weak and helpless; the horror of dying alone. The film's director heightens these fears through the use of flashbacks. In each one Peege grows older, but it is still difficult to see this "thing" in the chair as the same woman whose life one watches unfold.

Everyone who sees this film prays, I'm sure, that they won't end up like Peege, yet we seem so powerless in the face of aging, and, as this film shows, time and fate can play such cruel tricks.

But do people really fear aging? Aging means living, and we're doing that all the time. "Aging isn't so bad," someone once said, "when you consider the alternative." What people do fear is powerlessness, weakness, dependence and, of course, death. Old age, according to psychiatrist Robert Butler, "reminds us of our own mortality. It demands our energy and resources, it frightens us with illness and deformity. . . ."[2] When we think of aging all these fears come to mind. For most people aging means what it did for Lou Andreas-Salomé nearly a century ago when she called it "life on the wrong side of the ladder."

This image of aging appears again and again in studies on attitudes to old age. One American study, for instance, found that 61% of the adults interviewed believed that people 65 years old "repeat themselves in conversations;" 86% saw 65-year-olds as "set in their ways" and "conservative;" and 81% thought 65-year-olds "like to think about the good old days."[3] Many other studies have found similar negative attitudes to the elderly.[4]

I've found this attitude in my own talks with students and friends. For instance, I once asked each of my students to interview an older person they thought was aging successfully to find out what it was like to age well.

As I gave out the assignment I could see one student glaring at me. His head shook from side to side as he took down what I said. When I finished, he spoke out. "I'm sorry, Professor," he said. "I'm sure you believe what you're saying about many people living a good old age, but I don't know anyone who is. And I'm not sure I believe there is such a thing as good aging."

"Do you know any older people?" I asked.

"Yes, I do," he said. "My mother-in-law is an old woman. And she's in a nursing home. There's my father-in-law — he's depressed, lonely and bored. I don't know where I'm supposed to find all the happy, successful older people you're talking about.''

''Why don't you try where you work? Contact someone who's just retired and see how they're doing.''

He agreed, rather reluctantly, to try, and we left it at that. The following week I got a call from him.

''Well, how's it going?'' I asked.

''I'm not sure. I've just finished my seventh interview. I've seen five men and two women.''

''Seven? Why so many?'' I asked. ''I only told you to interview one.''

''Well,'' he said, ''I began with a man who just retired from our plant. He told me he was enjoying retirement — just got back from a trip to Europe with his wife. He was getting active in local politics again. And he said he felt great.

''I thought that sounded too perfect, so I contacted another one of our retirees. I got about the same story. He suggested I talk to a friend of his . . . and now I'm on my eighth case. All of them seem to be enjoying old age. I plan to do two more to round it out to ten.''

''You know, if you really want some bad cases I can tell you where to find them,'' I said. ''You can go down to Main Street to some of the rundown hotels, or you can go to a nursing home to talk to some sick people.''

''Oh, I know that,'' he said, ''but those people would be exceptions. They're not typical of older people today.''

Until he went out and looked for himself, this student had assumed that all old people were decrepit, sick, miserable and lonely. The tragedy is that he isn't alone in that belief. Many people carry around a bundle of stereotypes and rigid ideas about aging. When I gave out the above assignment, one of my young students said that he didn't know any old people at all. I told him to go home and ask his parents for some names. When he came back with the assignment done, I asked him where he had found the old person he'd talked to. ''Oh, he's our neighbour. He lives two doors down. I just never thought of him as old. He's always out working in the yard or coming back from somewhere in a jogging suit.''

Not everyone who ages well takes trips to Europe or wears jogging suits. There are many ways to enjoy old age. But when we think of old age most of us still think of it as a time of misery and suffering.

The following exercise may help put the matter in perspective. Allowing yourself one minute, list the ten most serious problems you think older people face today. When you are done, time yourself for another minute. This time list what you consider to be the ten best things about old age.

Most people complete the first list with no trouble: problems seem to come to mind right away. But I have found that some people cannot even think of three good things to say about old age in one minute.

Somewhere on your list of problems I expect you have the following items: lack of money, a sense of loneliness, poor health, the feeling of being useless and bored. You may have other problems listed as well, such as housing or health care. These items show up on almost everyone's list — usually near the top.

The fact that these few points appear so often suggests one or two possible conclusions. Either these really are the most serious problems older people face and we all recognize this fact, or we are all brainwashed to believe certain things about old age, especially about the kinds of problems older people have.

As for the first possibility — it's true. These problems all point to basic needs of older people, they must be met before a good old age is possible. In the absence of a basic income, decent health, a sense of belonging and good self-esteem, a good old age simply isn't possible. Aging, like any experience in life, is not a healthy process when it occurs in conditions of severe need. But do older people in general suffer from these problems? Do they lack the basics in life? Is old age as harsh a time as we imagine?

A Harris poll conducted for the American National Council on

Aging showed that older people themselves don't report these as their most pressing problems. This study suggests that to a large degree we project our own fears and doubts onto old age.[5]

The Harris organization asked older people what they considered to be "very serious problems." They then asked a sample of the general public what "very serious problems" the elderly faced. The public often had a more negative view of later life than older people themselves.

For instance, 62% of the public thought money was a "very serious problem" for the older person, but only 15% of the older people thought so. Sixty percent of the public thought loneliness was a "very serious problem", while only 12% of the elderly agreed. Fifty-one percent of the public listed poor health. Only 12% of the elderly did. Harris then went a step further. He compared general feelings of life satisfaction to see if the old enjoyed life less than the young. Using *The Life Satisfaction Index Z,* developed by Robert Havighurst of the University of Chicago, he found that older and younger people report about the same degree of satisfaction.

Studies in Canada support Harris's work. They have found high life satisfaction common among older people. Milton Orris, in a study done in 1970 in Saskatoon, found that 72% of older people thought their income was adequate.[6] Sociologist Daniel Koenig and his co-workers at the University of Victoria studied a sample of 730 older people in British Columbia. They found that "most of the senior citizens surveyed reported a basic satisfaction with their life as a whole, as well as with all aspects of life about which they were asked. . . ."[7] Most of them were pleased with their housing, for instance, and four-fifths were pleased or mostly satisfied with their health.

In 1979 sociologist Herbert Northcutt at the University of Alberta studied life satisfaction in a group of 440 Edmontonians. He found that older people more often than younger people said that they felt no pressure in life. As pressure went down life satisfaction went up, so the old people in his study showed a higher degree of satisfaction with their lives than did the young. Based on these feelings he concludes that "old age looks far more attractive than stereotypes suggest."[8]

Of course it could be that older people just don't like to complain. Or they may not see something as a *very* serious problem, even though it would be for a younger person. They may have different standards of judgment.[9] One man I know lives on a basic Old Age Security and Guaranteed Income Supplement from the federal government — about $500 a month. He lives in a small but clean one-bedroom apartment in a government subsidized housing block. He says that he buys fewer books now and goes to the public library more often. He uses his car less and travels more by bus. You or I might feel pinched in his position, but he laughs at his good luck. He feels that he has never had it so good. To him a guaranteed income for the rest of his life is like a dream come true. To understand this you have to know that he nearly starved to death during the Depression.

Some older people may have hidden their problems from Harris and other researchers, or they may have said what they thought the researchers expected them to say.[10] Still, the fact remains that people don't know much about aging. What they do know is often biased or wrong.

Erdman Palmore of Duke University devised a quiz to test people's knowledge of the facts of aging, including "basic physical, mental, and social facts and the most common misconceptions about aging."[11] He found that undergraduate university students who took the quiz answered only 65% of the questions correctly. Even graduate students in human development missed 20% of the answers. And all the groups he studied (including faculty members, who missed 10% of the questions) showed a negative bias toward aging in their answers. This negative attitude shows up not just in questionnaires but in everyday life too.

One recent morning I was riding the bus downtown. At one point the driver stopped for a red light and I saw two teenagers — a boy and a girl — begin to run for the bus from about half a block away. The light turned green, but the driver saw them and waited until they boarded.

The boy got on the bus first, and he sat down in the first seat facing the aisle. The girl came up behind him, a few seconds later, winded and panting from the run.

"Whew," she said as her foot hit the first step, "I must be getting old." She pulled herself up the steps, huffing and puffing. When she put her money in the fare box she said it again, this time to the driver but loud enough for everyone to hear, "Boy, I must be getting old." She said it a third time as she sat down next to her friend.

No one on the bus appeared to think anything was strange, no one seemed to notice what the girl had said, no one was shocked or surprised or annoyed. But what if she'd spilled her change as she got on the bus, and the driver had to wait for her to pick up her money? Imagine if, after she had collected herself, she'd said, "Boy, I'm acting just like a cripple," or, "Gosh, you'd think I was a clumsy Ukrainian!"

People on the bus would have been shocked and perhaps outraged. Yet no one batted an eye when she likened herself to an old person. She easily blamed her own problem — the fact that she couldn't run half a block without getting winded — on aging. She used a stereotype of old age to excuse her own weakness, and in doing so she subtly scapegoated the elderly.

To the extent that no one responded or even seemed to take offence at what she said, all of us gave tacit support to her prejudiced remarks. People showed no sign of surprise at what she said because, I suspect, they silently agreed — consciously or unconsciously — that old age makes people weak, slow and troublesome.

Robert Butler calls this kind of stereotyping "ageism." "Age-ism," he says, "reflects a deep seated uneasiness on the part of the young and middle-aged — a personal revulsion to and distaste for growing old, disease, disability. . ."[12] "Age-ism, like racism and sexism, is a way of pigeonholing people and not allowing them to be individuals with unique ways of living their lives." Through ageism, younger people subtly cease to identify with their elders as human beings.[13]

By scapegoating the elderly we pin the blame for our own weaknesses on others. In other words, we project certain traits onto old people and somehow imagine we don't have these traits ourselves. Scapegoating is an easy way to avoid self reflection; more dangerously, it provides grounds for maintaining a distance from, or even hostility toward the other person who shows traits such as slowness, illness or senility.

Even the best intentions sometimes coincide with ageist beliefs. A supervisor from a nearby nursing home once came to talk to one of my classes about aging, bringing with her a tray of slides to show us what the home was like. At one point in her talk she came to a slide that showed an elderly couple in wheelchairs holding hands. "Aren't they cute?" she asked. "They met at our home last year and they just got married. We think they're just adorable."

Suddenly hands shot up around the room. "That's a pretty condescending thing to say, don't you think?" one student said. "You wouldn't say that about two middle-aged adults who'd just got married. You wouldn't call them *cute* or *adorable*, would you? Those are words you use for children."

Just as decrepit health and senility are considered "appropriate" to old age, love and romance are not. By denying old people the right to enjoy positive experiences like love without being dismissed as "cute," we distance ourselves still further from them.

Simone de Beauvoir, in her book *Old Age*, on aging through history, also found ageism common among younger people. "When young people, particularly girls, are asked about their future," she wrote, "they set the utmost limit of life at sixty. Some say, 'I shan't get that far: I'll die first.' Others even go so far as to say 'I'll kill myself first!' "[14]

Louis Harris sums up this view:

> To put it bluntly, the portrait of the mature citizens drawn by those who have not reached maturity is that of unalert . . . narrow-minded, ineffective, sexually

finished old people rolling away in poor health, without proper medical care and without enough money to live on. . . [This view is] a flat and unmitigated libel and downright lie.[15]

It seems that older people have to put up with narrow-minded attitudes. When they get the chance to speak up, they say they resent these attitudes. A study conducted by the Ontario Advisory Council on Senior Citizens reports older people's feelings in their own words.

One woman says that after retirement:

Store clerks . . . were more frequently calling me 'dear' and telling me not to forget my parcel or my handbag and to watch that step. . . .

On the job, I drove in the daily rush-hour traffic and the weekend highway stream for thirty years. Now if I plan to go over twenty-five miles or if a few snowflakes appear, I hear concerned remarks: 'Surely you're not going to drive. Why not take a bus or taxi?'[16]

The Council reports that many of the people interviewed felt frustrated, hurt and angry with this kind of unfair pigeon-holing.

"Is the age of 65 the day you become a different person?" one person asked. "[It seems] you join the group of human beings that are set apart. Alive but not living . . . I find it hard to understand the sudden change . . . because only yesterday I was one of you. . . ."

Myths and Realities of Aging

How do we develop such a lopsided view of old age?

Partly, as I have said, it comes from ignorance. In general, we don't know much about old age today: what it offers or what problems older people face. Until just a few years ago aging wasn't even discussed in our schools and university courses on human development barely touched on it. These courses concentrated on childhood and adolescence, and when they turned to look at later life (usually in the last week of the term), they focused on marriage, child-rearing and retraining for work in middle age.

Psychologist Erik Erikson's work provides us with a good idea of how much emphasis people gave to aging in the 1950s. Erikson deserves credit for being one of the few people ever to propose a picture of the entire life cycle, and he has produced many studies of adulthood in recent years. But in his 1950 study of "The Healthy Personality" and later in his famous essay on "The Eight Ages of Man," Erikson showed the bias of his time. Of the fifty pages he devotes to the whole life cycle, he gives only the last one and a half to old age (and, indeed, only the last four pages to adulthood).[17]

Things have changed since then. Courses on aging have begun to spring up and research on aging has increased dramatically. In 1981, for instance, the Social Sciences and Humanities Research Council granted over $1 million to the study of aging. But most of this new interest and knowledge has not filtered down to the general public. Most of us were brought up at a time when aging was still treated as a chronic disease, something you got and had to tolerate.

Today the older person still has to swim upstream against a current of negative stereotypes — nearly all of them untrue or only partly true. What follows is a list of a few of these common beliefs — and the facts that show how wrong they are.

Myth #1: Many people believe that most older people are sick and are locked up in nursing homes.

Fact: Actually, only a small number of older people live in nursing homes — about 6% of Canadians over 65. Even among those 85 and over, only 14% live in institutions of any kind — including hospitals and mental hospitals.[18]

Most older people are well. The National Center for Health

Statistics in the U.S. reports that 80% of the aged are healthy enough to engage in normal activity.[19] And the Canada Health Survey reports that 62% of people over 65 experience no limitation of their major activities due to poor health.[20] Most older people go about their daily lives with little or no dependence on the health care system.

Myth #2: Many people believe that old age means senility and feeblemindedness.

Fact: Older people do suffer from mental distress, perhaps more than the population as a whole. Jon and C. Davis Hendricks write, "when all the forms of psychopathology experienced by the elderly both in and outside institutions are tallied the proportion of elderly who may be suffering serious mental distress could easily range from 25 to 60 percent."[21]

But this is a catch-all figure. It includes organic as well as functional problems. It includes people who suffer from social problems, stress and role loss. It includes those who may have spent most of their lives in mental hospitals.

Other estimates are more moderate. When it comes to emotional problems, for instance, "the best estimate," the Hendrickses say, "is that somewhere between 10 and 15 percent of the older population has emotional problems of sufficient magnitude to require mental health attention." And Palmore says that in a "series of eight community surveys . . . the prevalence of psychosis (of all types) . . . ranges from 4 to 8%."[22]

There is a wide range between the worst and best estimates of mental health in old age, but when most people use the word senile they don't care much about statistics. They aren't using a technical term: they use the word as a put-down. Someone is supposed to be senile when they become forgetful, or when they talk a lot about the past. A middle-aged woman, for instance, forgets her keys. Her daughter says, "Mom, you must be getting senile." They both laugh and Mom rolls her eyes.

In fact, recent research shows that mental ability can actually improve with age. Psychologist D. Bromley, for instance, reports that vocabulary, information and comprehension scores on intelligence tests "show little if any decline . . . with increasing age after early maturity and there are many reasons for supposing that performances in them improves at least up to middle age (and possibly later for well-educated people with verbal interests)."[23]

Other abilities also improve. Paul Baltes, K. Warner Schaie and their colleagues found that crystallized intelligence — verbal comprehension, numerical skills, inductive reasoning, skills most people learn in school — *improve* with age. Visualization — the ability to find figures in a complex ground — also increases. On these measures, they write, "we see a systematic *increase* in scores for the various age groups, right into old age. Even people over 70 improved from the first testing to the second."[24]

Patients who show signs of "senility" show a different pattern of loss. "The senile condition," Bromley says, "is not so much an exaggeration of normal old age as a disturbance of it."[25] In other words sudden or severe mental loss in old age is not a normal event: it can be traced to some illness or disease.

In spite of some declines in mental activity "most normal people in old age do not appear to be mentally confused, and they manage the routine affairs of every day life without evidence of intellectual deficit."

Myth #3: All old people are alike. You become a certain type of person when you reach a certain age.

Fact: Aristotle expressed this myth over two millennia ago when he wrote that the old

> are sure about nothing and under-do everything. . . .
> They are cynical . . . distrustful and therefore suspicious of evil. . . . They are small-minded . . . cowardly
> . . . [and] are too fond of themselves. . . . They are
> continually talking of the past. . . . Their passions have
> slackened, and they are slaves to the love of gain.[26]

That has been the view of aging off and on for at least twenty-five centuries. But people over 65 are as different from one another as they are from people who are younger. Most people don't know this, not even people who work with the aged.

A social worker I know found this out one day when she started work at a nursing home. During her first week on the job Mr McGivens, a new patient, arrived. He was a 67-year-old victim of a mild stroke, and although in most respects he was well, he was confined to a wheel chair. The social worker wanted him to feel at home, so when she found out he liked stamp collecting she wheeled him over to Mr Lavery. He liked stamps too, and she was sure they would become friends. Then she went off to do some other work.

When she returned after a few minutes she found them sitting silently looking into space. What had gone wrong? Nothing, except that the two men had nothing in common apart from stamp collecting. Other than that, they had no interest in one another. Furthermore, although they looked alike to the social worker, they were actually twenty years apart in age. They were separated by a generation gap.

Most experts now talk about at least two groups of old people — the young old (55-75) and the old old (75 +). But the terms apply more to life-style than to age. The young old have retired from work but remain active and healthy. They live in a stage of life that the French call "the third age." It comes after adulthood, "the second age," and before physical decline and frailty, "the fourth age." The old old live in the fourth age, a time of poor health and special medical and social needs.[27] Gerontologists also recognize that older people differ in several other ways. Some people retire, others continue working. Some are married, others are single. Some are widowed, some divorced. Health, race, ethnic background, sex and social class, as well as a lifetime of experience, all give a special shape to later life. Rather than making us more alike, old age seems to accent our unique personalities and habits.

Myth #4: Middle-aged children abandon their aging parents.

Fact: Family relations are not what they once were. Though we long for the good old days of the big three-generation family, the fact is that in the past the nuclear family was also the rule. Yet things were different then, in that families lived in neighbourhoods or related households. Today it is rare to be related to a neighbour. Instead "contacts (are) carefully maintained, but increasingly separated from the daily business of life, becoming instead 'social,' in the colloquial sense." Still, "most older people in America never become totally isolated. The great majority lived near their children and grandchildren, and visited frequently."[28]

A review of studies done in Britain shows that: "Only a very small percentage of elderly Britons are old and alone . . . the largest majority of older people remain in close contact with their children and the rest of their families." Studies show that more than half of all old people have contact with their children every day. And another quarter meet with their children at least once a week. Most people, the studies show, "exchange services, live in the same locale and have regular interaction between the generations."[29]

In Canada 65% of people aged 65–74 live in families with a spouse or with unmarried children. Even past age 75, 60% of men still live with their families, though the figure for women drops to 25%.[30] In times of need older people still turn to the family for support. When an older person falls ill or needs money, it is the family that most often comes to his or her aid.[31]

Myth #5: Old age brings physical decline and suffering. Old people can't do the kinds of things they used to do or want to do.

Fact: Changes do take place in the body as a person ages. Senescence — the decline in the body's ability to respond to stress — increases by about 1% yearly from the age of 30 onwards. But in any given age group individual performances vary. Physical strength, for instance, does tend to decline in old age. Studies of various kinds of muscular strength show a decline of

15% to 46% compared to young adulthood.[32] Dr Jordan Tobin writes, in a report on blood sugar metabolism, that, on the average, performance decreases with age. Blood sugar is metabolized more slowly in older subjects. But, he says, "we do have some 60-year-old subjects who perform as well as the average 20-year-old."[33]

Many functions remain almost unchanged when a person is in an unstressed state. They are only affected when one faces sudden stress from the environment. So, even though scientists can measure a certain change in the body's functions, this does not mean these changes will affect a person's behaviour, life-style or life satisfaction.

In men, for instance, sexual functioning tends to slow up as they age. It takes more time and physical stimulation to arouse a man as he ages.[34] The interval is also longer before he can perform again. But these changes in sexual performance don't necessarily lead to a decrease in the enjoyment of sex.

Dr Alex Comfort, best known for his books *Joy of Sex* and *More Joy of Sex* has also written on old age. He says "that compared with, say, running ability, these changes are functionally minimal and actually tend in the direction of 'more miles per gallon' and greater, if less acute, satisfaction for both partners."[35] Comfort goes on to say that most people give up sex for the same three reasons they stop riding a bicycle: (1) they think it looks silly; (2) they have arthritis and can't get on; (3) they don't have a bicycle.

All the scientific evidence shows that the body has a reserve capacity. It may lose some of its strength as it ages, but most bodily systems have enough in reserve to allow people to carry on their lives without much change into late old age. In most cases when changes take place as we age — changes not caused by a specific disease — they take place gradually over many years. Consequently most people adjust to them without much trouble.

Myth #6: Older people run a high risk of getting mugged, robbed and defrauded by criminals.

Fact: News stories often promote the idea that the elderly suffer more from crime than other age groups. But the statistics don't support this myth.

The figures show that older people run less risk of victimization than the general public.[36] "The elderly," sociologists Jon and C. Davis Hendricks say, "are victimized about one quarter as often as younger adults — except for purse-snatching and the like where the rates are identical."[37] Studies in the U.S. have found that even older people in inner-city neighbourhoods run the same risk as other people in the same parts of town.

Older people do, however, run a high risk of fraud. A Winnipeg police pamphlet called "Protection for Senior Citizens" lists a range of schemes from "The Pigeon Drop" and "The Bank Examiner," to consumer frauds, home improvement deals and retirement estate scams. But again, the statistics show that "attention is greater than the rate." In a study done in the U.S., researchers found that "the elderly are no more likely to be duped than others," they just have fewer resources to fall back on when it happens.[38]

That may explain why elderly people fear crime more than other age groups. Harris, in a 1981 study of aging in the U.S., found that 25% of people over 65 thought crime was a very serious problem for older people.[39] In some studies, as many as 50% of older people say they fear crime.[40]

No one knows how to protect older people from crime or how to ease their fears. An American study showed that even a lower rate of crimes against the elderly does not reduce older people's fear. "Even the reporting by the media, or by neighbors, of a single violent or non-violent crime against an elderly person may . . . arouse or heighten the level of fear among the elderly population, not only in the neighborhood where the event took place, but also across community, regional and national boundaries."[41]

This leads to a surprising conclusion. News reports make the crime rate against the elderly seem higher than it is, and they make older people seem more oppressed and preyed upon than they are.

This heightens older people's fears and adds to the myth that old age is a time of weakness and failing ability to care for oneself.

Social Roots of Bias against the Elderly

None of these facts or figures will make our fears about aging go away, but they can help put our fears in perspective. Someone like Peege, for instance, is not just old. She is also ill, very ill — on the verge of death. And a lot of what we see in Peege we put there ourselves.

To a large degree Peege is the product of her environment. She has been abandoned by her family out of their fear and sense of helplessness. Even when they visit her, you can feel the guilt and fear in the air. No one goes near her. No one touches her. No one holds her. They seem afraid of her, as if she were contagious. The people around her perceive her through their own terror. And so much of what is worst about aging comes from this fear of growing old.

"The things which make oldness insupportable in human societies," Alex Comfort says, "don't at all commonly arise from consequences of the biological aging process. They arise from 'sociogenic aging'. This means, quite simply, the role which society imposes on people as they reach a certain chronologic age."

This role can be improved, but it will only change as people begin to drop the negative stereotypes and fears they have about aging. Today people are bombarded by them daily from every direction.

A recent study of birthday cards, for instance, found that one half of the cards contained negative messages about aging. Some of them were even hostile. One card read:

> Roses are red, violets are blue. One thing makes me happy . . . I'm younger than you.[42]

The cards in general saw the loss of youth as a loss of physical attraction, a decline in ability and skill and a loss of interest in sex and the ability to perform.

Another card read:

> Birthday Greetings. You're at an age when you should give up half your sex life . . . which half will it be, talking about it or thinking about it?

The writers concluded that while the cards may not cause ageism, they reflect non-humorous popular stereotypes of aging and "reinforce ageist ideas."

In 1975 Dr Patrick Babın of the University of Ottawa studied age bias in the textbooks used in Ontario public schools. He reviewed 1,719 texts or 96.8% of all the texts used. The books, he says, play up the limitations of old age. Pictures contained in them tend to portray older people as poor.[43] One text told students that many Canadian senators were past retirement age, but instead of emphasizing their active role as leaders of society, it stated that their "most active and fruitful years [were] behind them."

Dr Babin reports that all the texts he studied show a "lack of specific reference to older people (including women). . . . The bias by omission," he says, "might be dominant."

Studies of advertising have found this too. A study of 6,785 ads found that only about 6% had any elderly people in them at all and of the 17,838 people in these ads only a little over 3% were elderly. (The elderly make up about 10% of the population.) These people weren't treated negatively in the ads. Instead, as the writers of this article suggest in the title, "Approaching Invisibility," the elderly are conspicuous by their absence.[44]

A detailed study of TV dramas showed that on television, too, the old are underrepresented. One study looked at all dramatic programs on all three major networks in the U.S. for one week in the fall of each year from 1969 to 1978. The total sample of prime-time shows and weekend daytime shows contained 1,365 programs and these were analysed for the way in which 16,688 characters were portrayed. The researchers found that only a little over 2% of all the fictional characters were 65 years old or over.[45]

They also found that more older characters were treated with disrespect than any other age group. When they compared men with women, they found that more older women were treated badly than older men. Likewise, more older women were seen as ''bad'' than middle-aged women, and more older women were seen as unsuccessful than successful. Seventy percent of the men and 80% of the women studied were not held in high esteem or courteously treated.

Does this have an effect on the people who watch these shows? When they compared attitudes to the elderly with the amount of TV watched, the researchers found that in a study of 600 sixth and ninth grade students, TV viewing did not lead to any positive views of aging. Not only that, but the more TV a person watched, the more negative the person's attitude. Heavier viewers saw old people as ''unhealthy, in worse shape financially, not active sexually, closed-minded, not good at getting things done, and so on.'' They concluded that ''heavier viewing makes a consistent negative contribution to the public's image of the personal characteristics of the elderly, and the quality of their lives.''

Prejudice and stereotyping can also produce in the older person the exact kinds of negative behaviour people expect to find. Social scientists call this the self-fulfilling prophecy: if people think something is so, it often becomes so just because of their belief. Think of what happens when there is a run on the banks. People believe that the banks are failing (though this may not be so) and, as a result, they rush to take their money out. Because so many people withdraw their money, the banks do fail. People thereby bring about the very condition they feared.

The power of self-fulfilling prophecy among all ages is apparent in the work of Robert Rosenthal and Lenore Jacobson, two psychologists who wrote about it in their study, *Pygmalion in the Classroom*.[46] They took a group of grade school students and assigned them randomly to two classrooms. The teachers of one group were told that their students were late bloomers — they could be expected to bloom in the class that year. The other group's teachers were told nothing.

Rosenthal and Jacobson found that when teachers expected the students to do well, they did in fact "bloom" that year. Their grades were higher than those of the students in the classroom where teachers expected nothing special. The teachers' expectations, it seems, brought about the difference in grades. When they expected the best they very often got it, but when they expected nothing they got that too.

This is one of the points the film *Peege* makes so forcefully. When the rest of the family leaves, Peege's eldest grandson stays behind. He moves closer to her, puts his arms around her neck and brings his head up to hers. "Somewhere inside there," he says, "is the grandma I used to know." And he believes what he says.

At this moment Peege starts to revive. She moves closer to her grandson, her blind eyes look in his direction, she answers his questions and she recalls, in simple words, the past life they shared together.

When her grandson finally leaves she is no longer the vegetable she was at the start of the film. In the last scene, as the car drives away, the camera comes back to focus on Peege's face — she is smiling.

Peege is a dramatic film, and when I show it to students I always leave the lights low for a few minutes after it's over. I have often wondered why people cry at the end. I used to think they were sad, but now I see that this isn't so. This film shows that even in what looks like the worst illness some spark of life remains.

Peege gives us hope, but something more too. She confirms something we always knew, that what we were seeing wasn't really Peege, it was something she had become, a role she was playing — one that her family and the life in the nursing home had forced her into.

Her family feared her and hated to come to see her. They felt uncomfortable, and Peege knew it. So she behaved just as they expected her to — like a confused, senile old woman. She gave them what they expected, not a thing more.

Her grandson, though, came with a different point of view. He neither prejudged nor pitied her. He took her for what she was — sick, lost and tired, but also the grandmother he loved. And he showed it by touching her and reminding her she was still a person to him. By believing Peege was still a person, her grandson couldn't make her walk again or heal her; he simply knows she is sick and accepts it. Perhaps that is the message here: we need to know and accept the limits of old age, but we also need to know its possibilities.

Today, we need to change our expectations and our attitudes to old age — for the sake of older people and for the sake of our own old age. "Very distorted stereotypes have grown up around old people," the National Council of Aging stated in its first annual report:

> And these stereotypes remain to be challenged. . . . It is important for the public to regard these years as a period when intellectual, cognitive, affective and social development can be maintained and extended. The stereotypes can only be destroyed if replaced by a more positive and more accurate conception.[47]

Alex Comfort says this too, in his book *A Good Age:*

> We can't take the pain out of the fact that humans aren't immortal or indefinitely disease-proof, or that illness accumulates as we age. We can, however, wholly abolish the mischievous idea that after a fixed age we become different, impaired or non-people.[48]

First, he says, we have to reject this idea for ourselves. And then we have to stop imposing it on older people.

Changing Attitudes

Some changes in our attitudes to aging seem to be taking place.

The first studies made of attitudes in the late 1950s and 1960s all revealed negative conceptions of aging.[49] Even studies of children showed this. One study of 355 students from Grade 3 to college found that the older the adult the less pleasant the image for the student. This suggested that negative attitudes toward the elderly began in childhood, and also that they would be unlikely to improve.[50]

Later research showed a different trend. Selzer and Atchley in a study of children's literature, for instance, did not find the clear growth of negative stereotypes with age that other researchers found.[51] And another study of 1,000 children in Grades 6, 8, 10 and 12 found that in their order of preference these students preferred young people first, middle-aged people last and older people second. The researchers say these children "do not share the allegedly general negative attitude toward old age." Instead they tended to think of the older person as a "loving grandfather type who had time for grandchildren."[52] These studies and others suggest that negative attitudes to the elderly are not set once and for all in childhood. Perhaps negative attitudes and stereotyping of the elderly grow in middle age when people begin to fear their own aging.

Other studies show that the kinds of information and contact one has with the elderly will shape one's attitudes. Watching a lot of TV programs in which the elderly are shown little respect may lead someone to adopt that attitude himself. But researcher Susan Green found that when people worked with the elderly they believed fewer negative stereotypes about the old. People who had frequent, non-intimate contact with the elderly had a more positive attitude.[53] As more and more people move into old age this kind of distant contact will become more frequent and negative stereotypes of old age may begin to disappear.

Also, in a recent study of television, Robert Atchley found less negative stereotyping and prejudice than in the past.[54] He found that more shows today tell the positive side of aging. Shows like *Over Easy*, for instance, point to a trend in public acceptance of old age. Atchley also found that, at least in dramatic programs, television today has begun to respond to changing times. It seems, he says, ''to be moving toward more representative and accurate portrayals of mature adults.''

Historians who have looked at attitudes over time have found that old people have a better image today than in the past.[55] And at least one historian, David Hacket Fischer, sees this as a trend that will continue into the future. Ageism will decrease, he says, as North American society moves to a point where it treats people as individuals rather than members of a category. Just as racism and sexism have been attacked and at least publicly rejected, so, he says, ageism will erode in time.[56]

All of this research and these changes in society point in a positive direction. But I think the most powerful single effect on our attitude to the aged will come from the changing population of old people themselves.

If in the past old age meant poverty and sickness, now we need to rethink this time of life. We know, and as I will show in subsequent chapters, that older people today are healthier, better educated, more active and better off financially than ever before. And these people will play a more active role in the life of society.

More than anything else they will force us to change our image of old age. The stereotype of the decrepit nursing-home patient or the wise old farmer will no longer fit. Gerontologists have already begun to speak about ''The New Old'' and a ''New Age for Aging.''[57] These people are members of the first generation to feel the effects of a great change in the pattern of aging and in the structure of Canadian society.

2

CANADA COMES OF AGE

The Geriatric Boom

George Burns worked for years as straight man for his wife Gracie Allen until she retired. "Hell," George says, "I was too young to retire. When I was sixty-five, I had pimples. So I played Vegas with a line of girls and found out I could do an act by myself. And here I am [at 80] starting another career by myself in the movies."[1] Now, several years and many movies later, George Burns is a superstar.

Just before his death Henry Fonda won an Academy Award for his role in *On Golden Pond* as a bitter old man who mellows through his relationship with a young boy. The film contained no sex scenes, no violence and no special effects, yet it played to pack houses and to people of all ages throughout the country.

My local Chuckwagon Steakhouse gives senior citizens a 10% discount on their meals. At the cash register you can pick up a free copy of the latest *Senior Citizen News* to read with your dinner. Today older people can get discounts on everything from train fares, travel tours and hotels to theatre, ballet and movie tickets.

What do George Burns, Henry Fonda and my Chuckwagon Steakhouse have in common? Taken singly they may not seem related. But they all point to a basic change in our society. The Canadian population is getting older, and as a result more people have become aware of aging and old age.

Today there are more older people in Canada than ever before. In 1981 2.3 million people or 10% of the population was over age 65.[2] Statistics Canada figures also show that the older population is growing faster than the population as a whole. Since the turn of the century the total Canadian population has increased fourfold from about 5.5 million people in 1901 to 23 million in 1976. In that same period the population 65 and over has increased more than sevenfold — nearly twice the rate of the population as a whole.

Projections show that this group will keep on growing in the future. The Department of Health and Welfare projects a rise in the proportion of the elderly population to 12% by 2001. And by 2031, when the baby boom generation settles into old age (and barring major changes in birth, death and international migration rates), one Canadian in five will be 65 years old or over.[3]

Some people have called this rapid growth in the older population the "geriatric boom." And though this label makes the change seem more sudden than it is, it points to the powerful effect population lag will have on Canadian society. Just as the baby boom brought massive change — schools sprang up like dandelions on a suburban lawn, and the youth culture of the 1960s rocked the value systems of the establishment — so the geriatric boom will reshape Canadian life. It will force us to rethink our ideas about retirement; it will make us change our assumptions about work; and it will demand economic planning and new services to meet the needs of an older population.

Projections show, for instance, that in the future older people will occupy more hospital beds and require more medical services. Also, more people than ever before will be drawing government pensions, and since they will live longer they will collect their pensions for a longer period of time. They will also require recreation facilities and new educational opportunities. These changes and others raise a basic question that planners and government officials have begun to ask: Can Canadian society afford to meet the needs of this large group of people?

Today in Canada the social security system costs 14% of Canada's GNP, or $32 billion annually.[4] If the population of older people doubles in the next 50 years as expected, will people be willing to pay out 20% or more of the country's income to care for older people? Or will resentment lead to a backlash? Some writers see an increase in political and social conflict over this issue.[5] Victor Marshall, associate professor at the University of Toronto, warns of "increased potential for generational conflict."[6]

The popular press has picked up on this issue. The cover of the January 17, 1983 issue of *Maclean's*, for instance, shows a picture of a woman at four stages of life — from middle life to old age. In the first picture she has dark hair, smooth skin and she wears a bright smile. In the next picture grey streaks appear in her hair. In the third picture wrinkles show up in her skin, her hair has turned greyer and she no longer smiles. In the last picture her hair is all grey, her face is very wrinkled. Her eyes look out in a vacant stare. She is frowning.

This cover portrays the image many people have of old age. It shows that the change from middle age to old age is a change from happiness to misery and suffering. But the article's title takes this image of aging one step further. It tells us that we have more to fear than just a miserable old age for ourselves. It says we also need to fear "The Coming Crisis of Old Age" — a society-wide crisis that will come about as Canada's population gets older into the next century.

The woman on the cover looks depressed, according to the article, because society is unprepared to help people age today. And so aging has become (or will become) more than a personal misery. It will become a *social* crisis. "With the current lack of action," Val Ross writes in her article, "the greying of the baby-boom generation will almost certainly transform today's quiet tragedies into tomorrow's noisy crises."[7]

What form would this crisis take? It might start out with problems in our social security system. The United States already faces this sort of crisis. In early 1983 the American social security system faced bankruptcy. The system was paying out more money than it was earning, and the deficit was growing each year. The system was barely rescued by emergency legislation, but the solution will cost taxpayers more money. It will increase the national deficit, and yet does not guarantee that the system will be solvent when today's middle-aged workers retire.

A *Newsweek* story on social security summed up the problem in a picture on the cover showing the generations of man standing in a human pyramid. At the top, on a plank of wood, sat a large group of older people. In the middle stood a group of middle-aged people grimacing from the weight. At the bottom sat a small number of young people being crushed from above. The visual message was clear: the large number of older people in society today and in the future will become an increasingly cruel burden on younger generations.

Several years ago a columnist for the Washington Post, David S. Broder, thought the government was already doing too much for the elderly. "America's public resources," he said, "are increasingly being mortgaged for the use of . . . the elderly. The benefits being paid to them are rising faster than any other major category of federal spending, and the taxes being levied — mainly on their children . . . are also going up faster than any others."[8]

Some writers in Canada wonder if we can afford to take action that will put off a crisis. "Popular discussion of the future income prospects of Canada's older population," demographer· Leroy Stone says, "is marked by gloomy forebodings that the 'national bank' will be broken by a combination of over-generous welfare programs and an explosion of older population growth caused by the aging of the post-war baby boom."[9]

The popular concern about the increased number of older people typically pits the old against the young. The Science Council of Canada, for instance, calls an older population of between 13% and 15% "a significant social burden."[10] Statistics Canada, in a popular report, tells us that old age creates problems, and these problems "are the nation's concern."[11] Without saying so, these comments seem to represent the older generation as a public nuisance, a drain on society's resources.

Ronald Blythe, in his book *The View in Winter*, comments on this tendency to blame older people for living so long. "The old," he says, "have been made to feel that they have been sentenced to life and turned into a matter of public concern. They are the first generations . . . of old people for whom the state, experimentally, grudgingly and uncertainly, is having to make special supportive conditions."[12]

But Blythe goes on to remind us that the aging of our population is not due only to older people living longer. "We rarely add," he says, "that any blame for an imbalance must be shared by the young for not having babies. . . ." And, we might add, also by the immigration system that regulates the number of younger people who come to Canada. The large number of older people in Canada today exists for more than one reason and each individual older person is only one piece in this puzzle. To understand the current aging of Canada's population we need to look at the social forces that have changed Canadian society over the last 100 years.

The Roots of Change In Canada

Most people think of aging as something that happens to *people*, but societies age too. Demographers define a society as old if more than 7% of its population is over 65 years of age. A young society, they say, is one in which less than 4% of the population is over 65.

By this standard, Canada was a young society only a century ago. In 1881, for instance, only 4% of Canada's population was 65 or over.[13] At that time Canada had a population distribution like that of the developing nations today. The population was relatively stable, the birth rate was high, but the death rate was also high. This meant there were a large number of young people and only a small number of older people in the country. When graphed the population looked like a steep pyramid with a wide base and a pointed peak at the top.

During the last one hundred years Canada has undergone a demographic transition from a young to an old society, a change that has taken place in all the developed nations around the world. It generally takes place in two stages. First there is a decrease in the *death rate*: more people live longer. Then as the nation industrializes the *birth rate* falls: fewer people are born. This decrease in births completes the transition. When the birth rate drops, the proportion of older people climbs.

This change is evident in our own population figures. From 4% in 1881, the older population (65 +) grew to almost 7% by 1941, and to more than 10% today. This makes Canada an old nation by world standards.

In addition to the changes in death and birth rates, one other population shift has helped Canada come of age — *immigration*. Each of these changes is worth examining in turn.

Immigration

Immigration has played an important role in increasing the size of our older population. By 1981, for instance, a large proportion of Canadians over 65 were foreign born, and the 1981 Census reported that "the older population was more likely than the younger population to speak a language at home that was neither French nor English."[14]

Many of these people came to Canada in the early years of this century. Between 1901 and 1911, for instance, one and one half million people arrived in Canada — as many people as in the previous forty years combined. In that ten-year period immigration accounted for 44% of Canada's total population increase.[15] This group accounts for 7% of the elderly today. A still larger group entered Canada between 1919 and 1929. They make up 8% of the elderly today.

These immigrants did more than increase the number of people in Canada. They also changed the face of Canadian society since, for the first time, a large mass of people came to Canada from Europe outside the British Isles. Leacy says that Canadians of "other European" origin jumped from 37% of the European-born population in 1881 to 43% of the same population in 1911.[16]

Today, the Science Council of Canada estimates that foreign-born Canadians constitute as much as 20% of Canada's older population,[17] and estimates project that that proportion will grow in the years to come.[18] While the immigrants of the early 1900s will die off, those who came to Canada during the 1950s (as large as the wave of 1901-1911) will add to the older population by the year 2000.

Death Rate

At the end of his television essay, "The Drive for Power," scientist Jacob Bronowski asks an unsettling question: "Where would a man like me be," he asks, "where would you be, if we had been born before 1800?"[19]

The answer is simple. If you are over 30 years old, you would almost certainly be dead.

Before the industrial revolution life expectancy was low. Sociologists Jon and C. Davis Hendricks say that military records from 1350 to 1500 show that at least 20% of soldiers in Europe died violently, and only 25% of those who went to war lived to age 50. The aristocrats lived the longest. Still, at age 20, in 1550, a British aristocratic man on the average could expect to live less than thirty more years. By 1700 that figure had risen to only thirty-two more years. The same was true for all the European ruling families.[20] Halley's study of Breslow, Poland in the 1600s took the "common people" into account: it showed a normal life expectancy of only a little more than 33 years.[21]

Not only war, but famine and, above all, disease routinely killed off large numbers of the population. Historian Fernand Braudel says that "Plague occurred in Amsterdam every year from 1622 to 1628 [the toll: 35,000 dead]. . . . Plague struck London five times between 1593 and 1664-5, claiming, it is said, a total of 156,463 victims." Things improved in the eighteenth century, but even then a plague in Toulon and Marseilles killed off half the population of each city.[22]

Few people survived into old age. Historian David Hacket

Fischer says that in North America before 1800, only about 15% of the population lived to age 60 and only about 10% to age 70. By the start of this century, though, life expectancy began to improve. In the United States in 1900 over 56% of the population lived to age 60 and over 40% to age 70. In 1960 over 86% of the population was living to age 60 and almost 80% to age 70.[23]

The same trend holds true for Canada. From 1921 to 1971 the death rate in Canada fell from 13.3 to 8.4 (deaths per 1000) for males and from 12.4 to 5.2 for females.[24] This meant that the Canadian population was growing, and more people — especially women — were living into old age. There were at least three causes for this decline: first, improvements in medical care; second, better living conditions; and third, a better environment in general.

Most experts agree that, of these three, medicine played the smallest role.[25] This may come as a surprise: in the last few years the media have played up medical advances that keep people alive longer — heart surgery, pacemakers, miracle drugs. This gives the impression that medical technology and treatment gave rise to longer life expectancy.

But when it comes to the diseases of adulthood today, medicine has done little to lower the death rate. The death rates due to arteriosclerosis and cancer, for instance — two of the major killers in later life — continued to rise steadily from 1921 until 1970. Deaths in Canada due to cardio-vascular and renal diseases increased by about 50% from 1921 to 1961. And only in the last few years, since 1970, has a drop taken place in ischaemic heart disease. Medicine may have played a role here, but no one knows for sure.[26]

Even when medicine has played a role in decreasing the death rate for adults, it often came on the scene late. Chemotherapy for the cure of tuberculosis, for instance, became common only in 1947. But the decline in the death rate of TB victims began much earlier. McKeown shows that the death rate in Europe from TB began to decline as early as 1838.[27]

Studies of other diseases reveal this same pattern. Bronchitis, influenza and pneumonia (once known as "the old man's friend") have all decreased as causes of death. But the death rate from pneumonia, for instance, began to fall steadily from 1900 on, even though chemical treatment only began in the 1940s. In general, McKeown says, "effective clinical intervention came late in the history of the disease, and over the whole period of its decline the effect was small in relation to that of other influences."

It seems less surprising that medicine played a small role in decreasing the death rate when one observes medical practice up to the twentieth century. In the nineteenth century, when the death rate had already begun to drop, doctors still employed practices like bleeding and cupping — methods used by Galen in ancient Greece.

Lewis Thomas, writer and chancellor of the Sloan-Kettering Cancer Institute tells about a typical treatment for rheumatic fever in the late nineteenth century. He quotes from a medical text of 1854 by John Forbes, the "Physician to the Queen's Household."

> 'In its early stage,' Forbes wrote, 'acute rheumatism is speedily and effectively relieved by . . . bleeding, purging, salines with antimony, liluents and abstinence [abstinence meant a diet without meat]. . . .'
>
> When rheumatic fever failed to respond to moderate bleeding — that is, the rapid removal by lancet of ten to fifteen ounces of blood — the patient should be bled some more, as much as necessary, up to two quarts, in order to achieve blanching of the body, nausea, faintness, and a palpable weakening of the pulse: in short, the manifestations of shock. If this did not work, antimony and calomel were combined and given by mouth in doses sufficient to produce vomiting and diarrhea.[28]

Tuberculosis was handled in much the same way, except that more blood was drained and for a longer period of time, "for as many months as the patient survived."

The biggest change in death rates came not from special technologies but from improvements in the general standard of living. Where medicine extended life, it did so by bringing into medical practice new tools — like scissors, soap and insecticides — that the industrial revolution made available to nearly everyone. This often made an enormous difference in patients' chances of survival.

For women, for instance, this meant a dramatic decrease in death rate during the child-bearing years. A study of the first gynaecologist, I. Semmelweis, shows that in 1848 he decreased deaths "from puerperal fever by a factor of 15 just by using antiseptic procedures."[29] And mathematician Jacob Bronowski says that, "probably the iron bedstead saved more women from childbed fever than the doctor's black bag, which was itself a medical innovation."[30]

In Canada maternal mortality decreased more than a hundredfold in fifty years — from 5.8 deaths (per 1000 live births) in 1930 to .06 in 1981.[31] And the life expectancy for women at birth increased from 62.1 years to 77.2 years during this time.[32]

Other changes in the standard of living, such as clean underwear, soap, coal for heat and glass in the windows all helped people to stay healthier.[33] Also, improved housing and more efficient treatment of water and sewage increased resistance to disease. As the standard of living rose, the virulence of disease — and so the death rate — declined.

"Good food, air and water," Ivan Illich says, "play the decisive role in determining how healthy [people] feel and at what age [they] tend to die."[34] A higher quality environment reduced the death rate for all age groups. Better nutrition and fresher, more varied foods simply made for stronger people. But more than any other group, children benefited from these changes.

Better living conditions and immunization have led to a decline in childhood diseases over the past one hundred years. McKeown reports that in England and Wales the death rate from measles declined from 1150 per million children in 1850 to nearly zero in 1960.[35] In Canada, scarlet fever and diphtheria also show a steady decline as causes of death from a rate of 47 (per 100,000) in 1921 to a rate of only one death (per 100,000) in 1981. Smallpox no longer shows up at all in Canada as a cause of death.[36]

As a result of these changes, during the fifty years from 1931 to 1981 the infant mortality rate in Canada fell from 96 to 10.8 (deaths per 1000 live births) for males and from 76 to 8.4 for females — a decrease by a factor of 10 for both sexes.[37]

To get an idea of what this change means, you have to compare it to the past. In the past infant mortality was staggering. "In the Beauvaisis in the seventeenth century," historian Fernand Braudel says, "25 to 33% of new-born children died within twelve months; only 50% reached their twentieth year."[38] As late as 1900, Morton Puner says, 20% to 40% of all children born died in the first year.[39]

Historian Terry Copp reports that in 1891 infant mortality accounted for 43% of Montreal's total deaths.[40] And at the turn of the century, sociologist George Torrance says, "Montreal, Winnipeg and Vancouver came to vie among the worst cities in the world in health conditions . . . diseases such as smallpox, typhoid, influenza and tuberculosis took a fearful toll."[41] Alan Artibise, in a study called *Winnipeg: An Illustrated History*, says that in 1904-05 there were more deaths from typhoid in Winnipeg "than any other major North American or European city . . . coupled with extremely high infant mortality and general death rates."[42]

Today a better environment and higher standard of living mean that 98% of all children born can expect to live through infancy; 90% can expect to live to age 50; 66% to age 70; and 40% to age 80.[43] This gives Canada — along with Sweden, Denmark, Norway and the United States — one of the highest life expectancies in the world. Today the average life expectancy at birth for a Canadian is about 70 years for men and over 77 years for women — a gain of twelve years since 1931.[44]

Birth Rate

We don't usually think of the birth rate as a cause of population aging. Yet the decrease in the birth rate, especially since the 1960s, is the *primary* cause of population aging in Canada.

Canada's crude birth rate has decreased (with some important fluctuations) throughout this century. In 1900, for instance, the rate was about 30 children born per 1000 population, a rate equal to that of countries like Colombia and Guyana today. By 1935 it had dropped to about 20, and by 1974 it had fallen to an all-time low of 15.4.[45]

On the average, women are having fewer children today than in the past. In 1921, for instance, the average rate was 3.5 children per woman. In 1968 this average was only 2.4 children, and Statistics Canada forecasts an average of only about 2.2 for 1981.[46]

This has led to a sharp drop in the number of young people in Canada. Between 1976 and 1981, for instance, the population of young people 0-17 years old decreased from 7.3 million to 6.8 million or from 32% to 28% of the population — a 4% decrease. The number of children under 15 showed a 7% decrease.[47] Statistics Canada projects a further decline in the younger population into the next century. If projections are right, the younger population will fall to less than 20% of the total population. (In this same period it is expected that the middle-aged population will remain the same, while the older population will grow to about 20%.)

Several changes have led to the fall in the birth rate.

First, in the past high infant mortality led people to have many children because as few as half of them survived. Today, nearly all children survive to adulthood, and so the birth rate is lower.

Second, people have more choice today about when, or if, they will have children. The figures show this clearly. The greatest decline in birth rate is among mothers under 20 years old. Abortion as well as birth control have made it easier not to have an unwanted child.

Third, a new attitude toward children has developed in the last few years. Married couples do not take for granted the fact that they will have children. Some couples have even come to see children as an expensive luxury, a "super pet." They are something people choose or choose not to raise, like goldfish or schnauzers.

Even those couples who choose to have children often opt for smaller families than in the past. A couple in my neighbourhood, Joanne and Bob McGill, offer a good example of this trend. They have been married nearly ten years. They put off having children until Joanne completed graduate school and finished her law degree.

Now she works full time as a lawyer. They had their only child, a girl, two years ago when Joanne was 32, and they don't plan to have any more children. She has just started to move up in her law firm, and Bob needs to focus on his research as a provincial biologist if he wants to get his next promotion.

The McGills also illustrate two other trends. First, the changing role of women has changed attitudes to having children. Women like Joanne stay in school longer and tend to go to work when they finish school. In 1956 women accounted for less than 25% of the labour force, but by 1970 they accounted for about 45% of all workers.[48]

Second, women are delaying marriage and child-rearing to later in life.[49] Kelly Peterson, an 18-year-old university student, speaks for this new ethic. "I can't imaging having kids until I'm at least 30," she says. "I've got my schooling to finish. Then I want to travel and have a career. And if I get married I want to spend a few years alone with my husband before we have kids."

Careers, education, inflation, the cost of raising children and for some people an uncertainty about the future have all led couples to opt for fewer children. Of course, differences show up according to social class or region: lower-class and working-class couples may still have more children than upper- and upper-middle-class couples. But the general trend to fewer children exists. In every social class people have more choice today, and they are often choosing not to have children.

There is one other reason for the jump in the older population due to a change in birth rates: the baby boom.

As I noted earlier, the decrease in birth rate has not been steady through this century. The rate went down each year until the mid-1940s, then shot up again. This increase in births continued into the 1960s, then suddenly dropped off. It was the single most dramatic change in the Canadian population in this century.

This baby boom generation will have an impact on the aging of Canada's population into the next century. Demographers call this the "pig in a python" effect. On their charts the baby boom looks like a big bulge (the pig) in the middle of otherwise slim-sized age groups (the python). As it moves through the population over time some people die off and this bulge gets smaller (the python is digesting the pig). But with today's low death rate this bulge won't shrink very much as the baby boomers age.

Instead, somewhere around the year 2006, this generation will hit old age like a tidal wave, much as it hit the school system in its youth and the job and housing markets in middle age.

By 2031, Statistics Canada projects that while the younger population (0-17) will have decreased by 16% from 1976, the older population (65 +) will grow by 211.7%. This will create the largest group of older people in Canadian history.

"By 2026," John Kettle writes, ". . . the median age will be forty-three, half the electorate will be over fifty, [and] a fifth of the population will be over sixty-five. . . ."[50] These people will make new demands on social services and will reshape Canadian society.

The growing size of Canada's older population today, as you can see, is not due only to older people living longer. Population aging has its roots, to a significant extent, in immigration decisions made by past generations of Canadians. In part it is due to Canada's development as a wealthy industrial society. And finally, recent decisions about family size made by young and middle-aged couples play a part in helping Canada's population to age.

One note of caution. This overview makes it look as if all of Canada has aged at the same rate. This isn't true: only Ontario and New Brunswick have roughly the same proportion of people over 65 as Canada as a whole (9.7% for Canada; 10% for Ontario and New Brunswick). Northern Canada has a population more like that of the developing nations. It has a high proportion of young people and few elderly (Yukon 4%, Northwest Territories 2% over 65).

Prince Edward Island, Saskatchewan and Manitoba, on the other hand, are old provinces. They have elderly populations higher than the national average (Prince Edward Island 12.2%, Saskatchewan and Manitoba 12% over 65 in 1981).[51]

Even within the provinces the age of the population differs in cities and small towns. Some small urban centres in Saskatchewan, for instance, have populations containing 14-15% over the age of 65 — a rate equal to that found in countries like Sweden and West Germany today. By the year 2001, projections estimate, 21% of the population of Saskatchewan will be over 65 and 11-12% over 75.[52] Canada as a whole will not likely reach that level until the middle of the next century.

Still, even with these differences between regions, the trend toward an older society holds. And as we shall see, this change will affect both individual Canadians and the structure of Canadian society.

Changing Patterns of Aging

There is no one way to grow old. Older people come from different backgrounds; they bring many different interests with them into old age; they have different skills and talents and different needs. But most older people today have one thing in common: they are all part of the first generation of what British writer and researcher Ronald Blythe calls ''full-timers'' — people who expect to live a long life.[53] What will this new trend mean for Canadians and Canadian society? Let's look at some of the most dramatic changes taking place.

The Old Old

In the future there will be more people over 65 than ever before, but more people will also live into late old age. A man who is 60 years old today can expect to live an average of 17 more years, a woman 23 more years. This means that people entering old age today can expect one-fifth to one-quarter of their life to lie ahead of them. Old age has become a much longer period than ever before. In 1981, the population over 80 made up 19% of the group 65 and over. By 2001 it will grow to 24%.[54] The group over 85 will grow even faster. In 1951 the number of persons 85 years and over per 100 persons 65 years and over was 5, as compared with 8 in 1981.[55] This is the fastest growing group among the elderly.

Betty Havens, Manitoba's provincial gerontologist, showed that people in late old age (80 and over) have different needs than younger old age groups (between 65 and 79 years old). The older age groups (85 +) show a higher need for basic household maintenance, food and clothing. Their health care needs also grow as they age.[56] An example will show why.

Mrs Arthurs is as frail as a bird. She lives in Golden Gate Lodge, a modern high-rise nursing home. I met her for the first time in a downtown park after a caretaker told me about her. He said to look for "a little white-haired lady in a bikini." The image of an old woman in a skimpy bathing suit intrigued me, so I returned the next day.

When I spoke with Mrs Arthurs she told me she wore her bikini (actually a halter and short skirt) so that she could get the sun on her hip. It soothed her arthritis.

Last winter, she said, she'd lived in her own home by herself, her husband having died five years ago. At age 81 she still cooked, cleaned and shopped for herself — with the help of her son, who kept in touch daily. Then one night she had a near fatal accident.

"It was late at night," she said. "I got up to turn up the heat. I got out of bed and then I must have fell. I can remember lying there. I could feel myself getting colder and colder, but I couldn't get off the floor. I wanted to get up, but I didn't have the strength. I lay there all night. In the morning I could hear the phone ringing. Ringing and ringing. It must have been my son Tom. When he found me the next day he said I was just like a chunk of ice.''

''The doctor said it was a slight stroke . . . a slight stroke.''

After that she needed nursing care for a few months. She needs almost no medical care now, but she is still frail and could relapse at any time, so she can't live on her own. Last spring her son sold her home and she now lives in a small room on the fifteenth floor of the Lodge. Mrs Arthurs will probably live in that room (or, if her health gets worse, in one of the heavy care rooms on the first floor) for the rest of her life.

People in late old age like Mrs Arthurs will create special problems for social planners and government in the years to come. This group, for instance, shows more health impairment than the general population.[57] And those 75 and over show the highest proportion of disabilities among those 65 and over. In addition, this group places the heaviest demand on institutional health-care services. Figures show that one in four people will be institutionalized in old age. But ''only 2% of older people 65–69 are institutionalized. The rate increases to 14% for those over 85 years.''[58]

The cost of caring for this group will go up as its numbers increase. Mrs Arthurs's room, for instance, cost $48.20 per day in 1983. The provincial government paid $30.50 of that total. The rest came from her government pension and savings. Community care programs would be cheaper: in the future, we will have to invent new ways to meet the old-old person's needs.

Women

Within Canada in the past fifty years women have gained most in life expectancy. In 1931 the life expectancy for a 60-year-old woman was 78, in 1961 it was 81 and today it is 82.

A recent study in the U.S. shows a decline of 22% in death rate for women 65 and over between 1966 and 1977. Men over 65 show a smaller decrease of only 14.5%. Women over 85, though, show the greatest decline — over 28%.[59] Canada shows this same trend.

Between 1921 and 1976 the death rate of Canadian women aged 70–74 decreased by 50%. Men showed only a 10% decrease during this period.[60]

As a result of these changes the proportion of older women in the population has grown. Until the mid-1950s older men outnumbered older women. At the turn of the century there were 105 men to every 100 women over the age of 65. This ratio has dropped throughout the century. By the 1960s women had begun to outnumber men; and by 1976 there were only 78 men to every 100 women over 65. At the ages of 75 and over there were only 65 men left in the population for every 100 women.[61]

This gap between the number of men and women in the older population widens each year. In the years to come the ratio of men to women will continue to be unequal, especially in late old age. By 2001, projections say, there will be 1.5 women to every man in Canada over the age of 65.[62]

Widowhood

A longer life for women has brought a greater chance of widowhood. For a man or a woman, loss of a spouse comes as the greatest shock in old age. One study rates widowhood as one and one half times more stressful than institutionalization, twice as stressful as the loss of a close family member and nearly five times as stressful as retirement.[63]

But this shock has a greater effect on the lives of women than men. For one thing, men tend to remarry in later life; women tend to stay single. This may be because there are more women for men to choose from in old age; also, men can more easily marry younger women. In our society an older woman who marries a younger man faces social disapproval. A man gets a wink and a pat on the back.

In 1981 76% of older men (65 +) were married, but only 40% of older women. Only 14% of men were widowed, compared to 49% of women.[64] For a woman, then, widowhood will probably mean a sudden and permanent change in her life before late old age. One woman I spoke with called the loss of her husband "devastating." A year after his death she still found herself in limbo. Another woman turned to alcohol and pills to cope with her loss: she eventually needed professional counselling and Alcoholics Anonymous to help her find a new meaning in life. Most people will need some support from family, friends or a professional counsellor to help them through.

Ethnic Background

Many older people who migrated to Canada 40 or 50 years ago still hold on to their language and customs. Statistics Canada reports that in 1981 11% of people over 65 spoke a language other than English or French at home.[65] This group as a whole will grow larger in the future. People over 65 come from many ethnic backgrounds. Each of these sub-groups has unique needs.

The size and closeness of an ethnic group, for instance, affects the kind of informal and formal supports older people can draw on as they age. People from a Jewish background, for instance, tend to live near one another in large cities. "Religious and geographic concentration," sociologist Linda Gerber says, "undoubtedly encourages ethnic group cohesion and institutional completeness."[66] This community offers a wide range of social and cultural resources to its members.

Chinese older people also have a community. One study found that some older Chinese women would rather live alone in Chinatown than with their children in the suburbs. The women said they liked to shop in the neighbourhood. They also found it easy to talk with other residents, and they liked the chance to meet people with the same culture and background.[67]

Other groups have no community to belong to. Many Estonian men, for instance, came to Canada alone and never married. A study of this group in Toronto found that 68% of them had no families. Because they form a small group they also have no community resources to draw on. The study predicts that they will need more social services than other groups in the future.[68]

Different groups need more or less from non-family sources. Older British people, for instance, tend to live on their own; older

Italian people live with their children. Older Hungarians seldom live with their children; older Polish people usually do. Different groups also use institutions at different rates. This may have to do with family values about caring for the elderly, but it also has to do with the average age of the group members. The Chinese population in Canada, for instance, includes a high proportion of people over 85 years old: they also have the highest rate of institutional use.[69]

Most of the older people in these groups came to Canada in their 20s and 30s. They grew old in Canadian culture. But a new group of immigrants — the Portuguese and Vietnamese, for instance — have come to Canada in old age. And they have special needs.

For a start, they need language skills. They also need to learn about the Canadian health, welfare and social systems. And they need to meet other people from their culture. Senior centres in Winnipeg have begun to look for staff who can communicate with these older people and help them adjust to Canadian life. Also, a Core Area Initiatives Program has started English-as-a-second-language classes for older immigrants.

Both new and recent immigrants make the older age group the most diverse in the country. And they pose special challenges to the social service system now and in the future.

The Young Old

The young old, gerontologist Bernice Neugarten says, live vigorous and healthy lives. Members of this group can be any age. An 80-year-old man in good health who golfs and swims would be young old.

"It's the young-old," Neugarten writes, "who are helping to make this an age-irrelevant society."[70]

These people often want to keep on working after age 65. They also want more recreation facilities and more education. In Winnipeg, for instance, a high school found itself with too few students in its typing classes. It opened the classes up to adults and over 100 older people showed up to enrol for twenty available places.

Vera Akins, a woman I spoke with, serves as a model for the

young-old way of life. Vera started to work for her degree after her husband died.

At 70 she is tall and thin. She lives with her teen-aged foster daughter in a small, one and a half storey, wood frame house not far from downtown. I visited Vera because she said she was enjoying a good old age and I wanted to know what that meant to her. We sat and talked in her living room.

"Until five years ago," she says, "Saturday nights meant 'Hockey Night in Canada.' My husband and I watched the game together every week. I'd knit and he'd sit beside me." Shortly after he retired he died of a sudden heart attack. That was about five years ago.

She went through a bad period after that. She stayed home a lot, brooding. Then she tried the traditional grandmother role. She babysat for her granddaughter while her daughter-in-law went to work: "But the baby slept all day and what was I supposed to do?" It took her about a year to begin to pull herself together.

She decided to get out and do something. She went back to school and got her high school diploma, then enrolled in a summer course in psychology at the local university. Now she's gone back for the fall term to work on her bachelor's degree.

She spends part of every day at the university. Most of the time she is in classes, but when she's not you can find her in the coffee shop with her classmates, in the library getting ready for her next exam or at a foreign film festival on campus.

"I used to like knitting," she says. "But now I want to participate in things. I'm learning more about the world and about people, and it's opening up my mind.

"I don't think it matters if I ever get a degree, but what does matter is learning. That's what's important to me. I have a bump of curiosity and I want to find out about things."

Today she's more active than ever. She sees this as a time of opportunity, a chance to do things she could never do before.

People like Vera want to stay in the mainstream of society, but the current bias in favour of retirement at 65 has forced them out. To overcome this bias, schools, recreation programs and job bureaus have sprung up to help older people remain active. They also help to challenge the myth that older people can't work or contribute to society after 65.

All these services for older people — job bureaus, schools and counselling services — cost money. Also, every older person — sick or healthy, rich or poor — receives federal Old Age Security payments. And many people get a supplement as well. With more people living longer, these costs will soar.

The question remains. Even if older people stay healthy and active, will the sheer number of older people in Canada create a crisis as some people predict? Or will Canada be able to adapt to an aging population?

The Changing Shape of Old Age

Before we panic about a coming crisis of old age, it makes sense to ask what people mean when they talk about a crisis. Consider Canada's future prospects when compared to other nations. What changes will they face in the years ahead? And what changes will take place in the world as a whole?

First, the entire world population is aging today. In 1950, according to the U.N., about 200 million people in the world were over the age of 60. By 1975 that population had grown to 350 million. And projections estimate that there will be 1 billion people 60 + by 2025. This population will have grown 224% in about fifty years, while the total world population will have grown by only about 102%. So by 2025 the world population of the elderly (60 +) will be about 14% of the total world population.

But population aging does not take place at the same rate in every country. In the year 2000, for instance, about 18% of the population of the developed nations will be over age 60.[71] By this standard the percentage of older people in Canada will not be very large when compared to other developed nations.[72] In West Germany, for instance, more than 15% of the population is already over 65. In England the figure is more than 14%, and in France more than 13%. Canada will not reach these levels until at least the next century.

The developing nations of Africa, South and Central America and Asia, though, face a sharp and sudden change in their populations. In some cases the developing nations will double their populations of people aged 60 and over in the next forty years. In South Asia the older population will grow 174% in only twenty years (from 1980–2000). And in Japan the older population is expected to grow from 15 million people in 1980 to 33 million by 2025 — or from 12.7% to over 25% of the total population in forty-five years.[73]

By the year 2000 60% of the world's elderly will live in the developing nations, and by 2025 that figure will climb to almost 75%. For these poorer nations, without resources or the social machinery to meet older people's needs, these changes will be devastating. At the U.N. World Assembly in 1981 and at an international seminar in Paris in 1983 representatives of the developing nations discussed the problems their people face.

They spoke about entire villages that age almost overnight as the young people move to the cities for work. They talked about the lack of communications, transportation, supplies and services for the elderly in rural villages.

They also pointed out that the number of older persons in their cities will increase. But these cities often have neither the social services nor the economic resources to help the elderly poor.

They spoke about the migration of older workers, who return home after working in neighbouring countries. These workers are often expelled from countries where they have worked during their middle years: they return to their native countries with no work, no skills, no pensions and the prospect of growing old in poverty.

Even where social security systems exist they often don't help the aged. *The Globe and Mail* reported the following story:

> After 35 years as a farm laborer, Feliciano Rodriguez has retired. The Peruvian Social Security system is giving him a pension equivalent to 10 cents (U.S.) a

month. All is not lost, however. . . . He gets an extra 2
cents a month because he is married."[74]

A look at these nations helps put Canada's own "crisis" in
perspective. We live in an affluent society. We have the government and social machinery in place to deal smoothly with changes
in our population. We have time to plan and create an aging
society that could serve as a model for the rest of the world.

The "sudden" crisis of population aging in Canada is, in fact,
more a matter of a sudden awareness of aging. The aging of
Canada's population is certainly not a sudden or unexpected
event. The statistics show clearly that the Canadian population has
been aging for more than a century.

True, Canada's population will grow older. But even though
the numbers and percentage of older people will increase over the
next fifty years, the rate of increase will not be any more dramatic
than has been seen in the past fifty years.

Also, the over-all dependency ratio — the measure of the non-
working to working segments of society — will not change very
much in the years to come. Frank Denton and Byron Spencer of
McMaster University reported that while the ratio of people 65
and over in the population to those 20-64 will nearly double from
1976 to 2031, the number of young people will decline. When they
combined these projected changes in the young and old populations, they found that this led to "a somewhat *lower* overall
dependency ratio for the remainder of this century and through
the first decade of the next, as compared with 1976, and then a
pronounced increase in the following two decades or so." In spite
of this increase, they say that in 2031 the over-all dependency ratio
will be no higher than in 1976.[75]

Dependency is a complex issue and numbers don't tell the whole
story. Demographic changes tell us little about the economic
burden of an older population.[76] One recent study, for instance,
estimates that an older person costs three times more in social services than a younger person, so the increase in the number of older
people may cost society more even if the younger population

shrinks. But more work needs to be done before we will know the actual costs of an older population.

In countries like Sweden and Norway, for instance, over 14% of the population is now over 65. But they have not faced crises due to their aging populations. They have tax structures similar to Canada's and good programs to serve older people. As the Science Council of Canada says, "it can be done"[77] — and done without social upheaval.

Of course, the state of the economy and future birth rates will alter the effects of dependency. With a strong economy more services for the elderly may not be felt as a burden. And a higher birth rate would mean more young people to support the older population. But, even if birth rates stay the same, demographers Leroy Stone and Susan Fletcher remind us that the large baby boom generation will affect the population for only twenty years or so.[78]

In the end, dependency and the supposed burden of an older population have more to do with our way of thinking about aging than with the numbers of older people. The calculation of dependency, for instance, assumes a traditional retirement age of 65. It assumes further that people 65 and over will depend on the middle-aged worker for support.

But today older people have begun to question the retirement age of 65. In the U.S. the mandatory retirement age has been raised to 70. And in Canada, provinces like Saskatchewan and Manitoba have no legal retirement age. This means we need to change the common assumption that the age of 65 signals the start of dependence on others.

Our government has already moved in this direction. In its *Report on Aging* to the United Nations World Assembly on Aging in 1982 it recognized the typical older person's "undiminished capacity" to work and to contribute to society.[79] Today many older people still work full or part time, some because they need the money, some because they love their work, others just to keep busy. Future projections of labour force participation indicate a rise in participation rates in the next century. If Canada as a whole moves in the direction of later retirement or a flexible retirement age, and if at least some of the people 65 years old choose to keep on working, then the real dependency ratio will be lower than projected.

All this suggests that, as John Myles and Monica Boyd, sociologists at Carleton University, say, "alarmist exercises in futurology . . . have produced more oversight than insight."[80] "Taken together," Denton and Spencer say, "[projected population changes] would seem to suggest that overall there will be no 'crisis' associated with the expected general aging of the population, as some have suggested."[81]

The Challenge of An Aging Population

This doesn't mean that Canadian society won't have to change to meet the challenge of an aging population. Institutions connected with education, work, housing and health care will all have to change their structures as the population ages. Canada is not free of problems related to aging. Some of the poorer provinces (Prince Edward Island, Manitoba, Saskatchewan), for instance, have a high proportion of the elderly. Those middle-aged people who live in these provinces will have to bear the cost of more services to the elderly — and they may be least able to afford those costs. Also, many of the problems of aging affect women more than men. As we'll see, women suffer financially more than men as they age, and this worsens for women the older they are.

All these problems are real. They must be dealt with. Our current systems need to be monitored and improved. Recent government guidelines that limit wage increases to 6% and 5% for the years 1983 and 1984, for instance, have been applied to Old Age Security payments. This limit will put a pinch on the already strained budgets of many older people.

As I write this, the federal and provincial governments have begun to battle over health care fees. Several of the provinces have begun to allow extra billing by doctors as well as hospital user-fees. These fees threaten to create a two-tier medical system — one supported by public funds and another elite system for those who can pay the extra costs. It also threatens to discourage older people, who may not be able to pay the extra fees, from getting the health care they need.

Changes like these need to be watched and criticized where necessary, and existing programs should be reviewed constantly. New programs will have to be set up to meet new needs as the population ages. All this can and should be started now.

The transition to the next century can be smooth, gradual and carefully planned. We know most of the facts and have a pretty good idea of what needs to be done. Whether we act on this information or not is another matter. That will depend on the average citizen knowing what lies ahead, knowing the options to planning their own old age and speaking out on the issues to the government.

Lois Wilson, a former moderator of the United Church, once said that the Chinese write our word for crisis as two characters: "dangerous opportunity." I think this idea gives the right slant to the "crisis" of aging in Canada today. Aging implies some danger, but it also offers us a challenge — one we can anticipate and meet as we move into the future.

HEALTH CARE FOR AN AGING SOCIETY

Good Health Is More Common than You Think

Bea Carruthers is a 73-year-old widow who speaks enthusiastically of her studies in massage, yoga and holistic health.

"I've done deep breathing, of course," she says. "Tai Chi and yoga, foot massage and meditation — a little bit of everything. I'm very keen on exercise for the elderly. I swim every day. That's why I chose this apartment. There's a pool right nearby."

"Don't people think you are a bit odd," I ask, "with all this yoga and massage?"

"Oh, yes," Bea says. "They think I'm crazy. My sister, who's 82, and a couple of her friends have been introduced to foot massage, but my own friends won't let me touch them."

Her friends may think she's crazy, but Bea may be more normal than many of us believe. A few years ago, before I learned about Seniors' Liberation, I went to speak to a stress management class for older people at the local Y. I arrived a few minutes late, and when the group leader met me outside the door and hustled me into the room, I looked around in shock. About thirty older people were scattered around the room lying on the floor.

I must have looked surprised, because I heard the group leader whisper, "It's okay. They just decided to practise their yoga postures while they waited."

I was astounded. At that time I thought healthy older people were as common as whooping cranes, and I wasn't the only one with that idea. In his 1975 poll for the American National Council on Aging Louis Harris found that 51% of the general public thought old people suffered from poor health.

Even some doctors think of aging as a disease: if you live long enough, you get it. They feel there's not much they can do for their older patients. Social workers and counsellors call people like Bea the "well elderly." They see healthy older people as special, abnormal. Sickness is the norm.

At a recent health conference in Minneapolis I saw how often people lump old age and sickness together. Looking over the schedule to see what sessions I might go to besides my own, I found that there were meetings on physiotherapy, intensive care treatment, senility, time management for hospital administrators and so on. As I looked down the list it came to me that this wasn't a *health* conference at all. It was a *sickness* conference. Nearly all the sessions dealt with how to treat sick older people.

Granted, the people who came to the sessions worked in hospitals and nursing homes. They wanted to learn how to give the best care to their patients. But I found that these workers, who saw only sick old people, took it for granted that all old people were sick. The conference only reinforced this idea.

We should know better. Good health in old age is more common than we think.

Louis Harris's poll in the U.S., for instance, found that only 21% of older people reported that health was a very serious problem for them.[1]

In Canada a recent health survey found that 80% of people 65 and over live with no health service support, or with only periodic care. And only 53% of all people over 65 reported that they had seen their doctors three times or more in the previous year. (About the same proportion of parents reported this much contact with a doctor for children under 5, and about 35% of the population as a whole said they saw a doctor this often.)[2]

Though 75% of older people say they have at least one chronic health problem, most older people think of themselves as healthy. A U.S. study found that "even among 80-year-olds living in the community, one half said their health was good."[3]

This does not mean that sickness isn't a part of old age. Older people do suffer from chronic illnesses more than the young. They report more problems as they age. And the old old, or frail elderly, often require the services of the health care system in order to survive. As the older population grows in the years ahead, older people will make more demands on health care services. And the old old, the fastest growing group over 65, will need special care. Politicians and planners worry about the future costs of health care because they see a growing number of older people who will need help.

They don't often see two other things. First, more people like Bea Carruthers and other young-old people will come into old age in good health. They will also stay healthy longer than old people in the past. Second, projections of soaring costs often assume that we will use the same services in the future that we use today. The truth is that as Canadian society ages our system will change. It has already begun to happen.

Before we look at this change and at the health of older people in the future, we should examine the cause of all this concern — the health care system today.

The System Today

The Cost of Care

In 1976 there were more than 1,400 hospitals in Canada, 38,000 doctors and 350,000 other health care workers. About one person in 56 worked in this system. In other words, Canada had one health care worker to serve every 50 people.[4]

In 1976 Canadians spent $13.5 billion on health care, or 7% of the Gross National Product (GNP), up from 6% in 1965.[5] This came to an average of almost $600 per person, about $200 more (not counting inflation) than the 1960 figure.

To give you an idea what this means, compare Canada to Britain — one of the few countries with broader coverage. Britain spent only $160 per person in 1976 for medical care, or 5.4% of its GNP. Canadians now spend proportionately more money on health care than any other country except the U.S. (and possibly Sweden and the Netherlands).

Where does all this money go? The largest share of the health care dollar pays for hospitals, the next largest for doctors and the next for prescription drugs. Canadians spent six and a half times more money (in constant dollars) on prescription drugs in 1971 than in 1956, three times more for doctors and two and a half times more for hospital care.[6]

In 1971 we spent $1.5 billion on hospital costs, or twice as much on hospitals as on doctors and more than three times more than on prescription drugs. By 1976 fully $6 billion or almost half of our national health care bill went to hospital costs (up from 20% in 1920 and 40% in 1973). That came to about $110 a day for each patient (up from $36 a day in 1966).[7]

Not only have costs for health care soared, but experts predict that they will rise even higher in the years ahead. Economists Frank Denton and Byron Spencer project "substantially higher health care costs, both per capita and as a percentage of the gross national product" into the next century.[8] They see costs rising to as much as 9% of the GNP in the future (from 7% today).

Still, even with rising costs, a recent survey showed that 84% of Canadians believe they get good value for their tax dollar from the health care system. The study indicated that we feel more positive about health care than any other government service.[9]

There's good reason for this feeling. Canada has one of the most complete government-sponsored health care systems in the world. Today 99% of Canadians have coverage of costs for doctors' services, hospital treatment, out-patient and extended care services.

Provinces like Manitoba also cover costs for nursing homes, home care and prescription drugs.

The system has not only eased the cost of health care for individuals. It has also made it easier for all people to get the care they need. For instance, differences in access to doctors' services by region and income have gone down. Social class differences in the use of services have decreased, and the system has relieved the fear of poverty that comes with long-term illness.[10] This means a lot, especially to older people. "I give thanks for our health care plan," one retired school principal told me. "I don't have to worry about being financially ruined if I get sick. And I don't have to worry about being a burden on anyone else."

An older person — or anyone with a chronic illness — in the U.S. might not be so lucky. Writers James Bennett and Jacques Krasny report that more than 10 million people in the U.S. have no private or public hospital insurance. Public funds, they say, pay only 40% of the nation's health care costs: the rest comes from individuals' income or savings. These costs result in an estimated 50,000 personal bankruptcies a year.[11]

For all these reasons Canadians can feel good about the system they have. And even as costs go up in the years ahead, they will probably pay the bill and count themselves lucky. But the question of costs too often hides a more important question, one that all of us should ask, whether we are buying a $13.95 pair of tennis shoes, a $13,000 car or a $13 billion health care system. What do I get for my money? What will I get if I spend more? And how well does this item meet my needs?

The Causes of Higher Costs

Some people argue that our system wastes fortunes of money. In the late 1970s, for instance, health care costs grew at a rate of 15% per year. When critics look at these figures they say that costs have gone out of control. But Professor David Coburn of the University of Toronto says that cries of alarm don't mesh with the facts. "In fact, health expenditures have been kept within reasonable balance," given inflation and the increased use of the system.[12] Researchers Bennett and Krasny looked beyond per person costs. They compared the cost of health care to Canada's GNP, and their findings support Coburn's. They found that from 1971 to 1975 the amount of the GNP spent on health care dropped one tenth of a percent. Based on this figure, they say that "Canada's health care . . . system is relatively well managed."[13]

Why have costs gone up then? Rising doctors' fees, rising cost of complex treatments, more tests to diagnose disease, rising hospital costs and increased use of the system have added to the cost of health care. One Canadian in six now goes into a hospital for treatment each year, "the highest rate in the Western world." And each year one in two Canadians goes to a hospital emergency outpatient clinic.[14]

Canada also has an aging population. And older people make heavier use of the health care system than the young. In a recent study Denton and Spencer found that health care costs follow a pattern by age. Costs at birth and in infancy run high. They drop off to age 10, then gently rise to age 30. After that costs rise steeply into middle and old age. Health care for a 70-year-old costs three to four times more than for a 10-year-old.[15]

Statistics Canada reports, for instance, that hospital case rates (the number of discharges reported by hospitals) and average length of stay increase with age.[16] From the age of five on, the case rate goes up steadily. People 65 and over show three times the case rate of those under 15. Those 65 and over also stay in hospital longer than the general population — two and a half times more "bed-days" a year.

A task force study in Ontario found that the elderly use health care services twice as much as the general population, suggesting that 13% of the population (most of them elderly) use 30% of all Ontario Health Insurance Plan (OHIP) services.[17]

As Canadian society ages, this pattern will show up across the country. Already Quebec reports that the elderly receive twice as much medical treatment as 15-24 year olds, and a study of the Saskatchewan system says that the elderly, who will make up 12%

of the population by 1985, will use 28% of medical services and 46% of all hospital-days in that province.[18]

By 2001, researchers J. Clarke and N. Collishaw say, the 65-and-over age group will make up 11% of the population of Canada, and they will account for 42% of all hospital patient-days.[19] All the existing research shows that older people demand more from the system than the young. Higher costs reflect this change in health care needs, but also a difference in the kinds of illness that an older population has. Older people suffer more from chronic long-term illnesses than young people do.[20]

Throughout this century the danger of acute illness has decreased. From 1931 to 1969, for instance, the crude death rate for influenza, bronchitis and pneumonia decreased by 64%. For tuberculosis it decreased 97%, while for the childhood diseases diphtheria, whooping cough, measles and scarlet fever it decreased 99%.

During this same period cardio-vascular and renal diseases increased by 33%, cancer by 49%. In 1977 diseases of the heart and blood vessels caused more hospitalizations than any other illness.[21] And as our population has aged the rate of cardio-vascular incidents or strokes has increased.[22] In Canada stroke patients now account for 20% of all hospital in-patient days (the number of days all patients spent in hospitals in a given year), and this figure will likely go up in the years ahead. Ironically, longer life expectancy, the triumph of modern society, has led to an epidemic of chronic illness.[23]

This same rise in chronic illness shows up in the rates of non-fatal illnesses. Today 40% of older people report that they have arthritis and rheumatism, 28% hypertension, and 20% limb or joint disorders. But only 10% of the general population report arthritis or problems with their limbs and joints, and only 6.5% report hypertension.[24]

An increase in certain chronic illnesses adds to rising costs because they cost so much to treat. Blood dialysis, for instance, costs $5,000 to $10,000 a year at home, $15,000 to $20,000 a year in the hospital. Cancer and heart disease, two common illnesses of old age, also add to the rising costs of health care. Between 1965 and 1975 hospitals added 60% more staff to care for these patients, and costs for drugs, X-ray film and supplies rose by 80%.[25]

Alzheimer's disease — an organic disease of the brain — shows up in middle and old age. It is the most common form of senile dementia. One American estimate suggests that Alzheimer's victims cost between $25 and $26 billion a year in care, and more cases show up every year.[26] A closer look at Alzheimer's shows why costs run so high.

Alzheimer's begins when a person in middle or old age shows irritability, loss of initiative, increased anxiety, hyperactivity and memory loss. Fran Jeffries's mother came down with Alzheimer's in her 70s.

"We first noticed the change," Fran says, "when Mom got lost driving over here one day. She was 72 and she's lived in this city all her life. She lives about fifteen minutes away and she used to visit us every day.

"One day she drove around and around in her neighbourhood, but she couldn't remember any of the landmarks or street names. She drove like that for two hours. When she finally got to our house she looked white as a sheet. She decided not to drive anymore.

"She got worse over the next two years. She'd watch a TV drama but she couldn't follow the story. I'd show her a map of the city, but she couldn't understand it. She'd get angry at me for not explaining it clearly."

Another case also involved the use of a car. Bill Hargrave could still drive, even five years after doctors diagnosed him as an Alzheimer's victim. But he no longer had a driver's licence, and his family kept the keys hidden.

One day he took the keys from his wife May's purse. He drove almost to the U.S. border before the car ran out of gas. He ran the battery down trying to start the car, then walked to the nearest farmhouse. He had a two-day growth of beard and wild eyes. The woman who owned the house called the police. The police traced the car and called May at 2:00 a.m. to come and get Bill. Two weeks later May at last admitted she couldn't care for Bill at home anymore. She decided to put him in a nursing home.

Like Bill and Fran's mother, all Alzheimer's victims steadily get worse. They lose speech and motor control, become socially maladjusted and disoriented. Many of them wind up in institutions where they may need care for fifteen years or more.

Problems in defining the disease make it difficult to say how many people have it. Reports vary from "a minority of institutionalized cases"[27] to 27%.[28] One researcher estimates that 20% of women patients in geriatric wards and 8% of men have the disease.[29]

One thing is sure: no one knows the cause of the disease or how to treat it. Donald Price, researcher and neuropathologist at Johns Hopkins University, says, "There is no effective therapy." Another researcher calls the prognosis "hopeless." Cases tend to accumulate in chronic and geriatric wards.

All chronic diseases present the same problems: people suffer with them for years, they get worse even with care and no cures exist.

These two changes — the increase of older people and the increase of chronic illnesses — have led to a shift in the types of health care services people need. But the present system is not designed to deal with chronic illness, and this mismatch between illness and treatment only adds to the rising costs of care.

The Limits of the Health Care System

We can and will pay more for health care in the future, but will spending more money buy us better health? Here are some recent findings:

1. The cost of health care in Canada increased by 1.75% of the GNP from 1931 to 1961. Life expectancy went up in that time by eight years. From 1961 to 1971 costs again went up by 1.75% of the GNP, but life expectancy rose only one year.[30]

2. Though health care costs quadrupled from 1960 to 1976 — from $125 a person per year to almost $600 a person per year — Canada had no fewer cases of long-term illness in 1978 than it had in 1950.[31]

3. Today older people spend more time in health care institutions — hospitals and nursing homes — than ever before. Over 8% of Canada's older population live in institutions — one of the highest rates in the world.[32]

The rises in costs have not created more health. Some critics of the system, such as sociologist George Torrance, go so far as to suggest that the structure of the system itself lies at the root of rising costs and increased rates of illness.[33]

First, Torrance says, the system "medicalizes" problems. In the past, for instance, people worked out psychological problems for themselves. Now they go to a psychiatrist. Second, the system makes health care the source of corporate profits. Nursing homes are sometimes owned by large corporations and are run for a profit. This encourages more use and development of these services. Finally, the system leads to overspecialization. The older person has to make the rounds from the GP to the back doctor, to the podiatrist, to the X-ray technician. Sometimes older people collect a cabinet full of pills on the way, and these pills can lead to more health problems.

Dr Cal Spencer of Winnipeg's Westwood Hospital makes this point in a story about one of his patients, a woman who complained of tiredness, memory loss and wild mood swings. When he asked her to bring him all the drugs she had at home, she appeared with a shopping bag full of them, a small mountain of pills, tablets, powders, ointments and creams. Dr Spencer took her off all medication: her symptoms disappeared.

Dr Spencer makes the point that the woman had "the best specialists" treating her problems. But, he says, older people often have special needs. For instance, they may have more than one illness at a time. Their illnesses may result in odd symptoms: a heart attack can show up as confusion, with no chest pain. Older people may also take longer to recover from acute illnesses. A doctor may have to work with a counsellor and a social worker to get an older patient back into the community.

This becomes clear when older people spend a long time in the hospital. It isn't enough to cure the illness. They may need social or psychological support too. In one case an older woman came into an extended care ward after she broke her hip. Until the accident she had lived with her daughter and son-in-law, but when the time came for her to move back home the family didn't want to take her. They said they couldn't cope with her medical needs. The woman became depressed and needed counselling. Her family also needed professional help to deal with their guilt. In the end she went into a nursing home.

A counsellor or social worker who works on a team with doctors and nurses can help to deal with social problems before they become crises, but too often medical care takes place in a social vacuum. Not all doctors understand the complex needs of the older person. Geriatrics ranks low among medical specialties. The profession rewards specialties — like surgery — that can bring about miraculous cures. In general, medical schools train doctors mostly in acute care. In 1974, Marc Lalonde, the Minister of Health and Welfare, reported that only one hundred doctors in Canada specialized in physiological medicine and rehabilitation, a ratio of one in 200,000. In the future, Lalonde predicted, there will be an even greater shortage of doctors to care for older people.[34]

Hospitals, too, gear themselves to intensive treatment, high turnover and curative medicine. But as our population has aged, hospital staffs have found that "an increasing proportion of their beds are filled by patients for whom they can provide little active medical treatment."[35] This clash between the values of the medical staff and the kinds of illnesses they have to treat can cause problems.

Sociologist Joan Eakins Hoffman studied stroke patients in a general hospital. Stroke or CVA (cerebro-vascular accident) comes on suddenly, when an embolism or blood clot cuts off the blood supply to the brain. A person can wake up and not be able to get out of bed, or may collapse suddenly. Though a stroke can kill a person, more often it disables him for a long time — sometimes for the rest of his life. "Some CVA patients," Hoffman writes, "are left with only minimal incapacity, but for many others the classic sequel is hemiplegia or paralysis of one side of the body. Varying degrees of aphasia, or the loss of the neural capacity to speak, are also common."[36]

Recovery from a stroke takes many months. In the meantime, once the hospital staff stabilizes the patient's body functions, they can do little but wait. "Beyond a thorough 'workup' on admittance, the administration of a few drugs and a half-hour of physiotherapy a day," Hoffman says, "the average stroke patient receives little treatment while in the hospital."

Hoffman found that the hospital's orientation to high turnover led the staff to resent stroke patients. They held a "widespread belief that 'nothing can be done' to help [the patients]."

"*There isn't much you can do* after the first day or so after the stroke," one intern told her. "I mean you can't reverse CVA. The hospital is mainly interested in getting them out of here." A nurse gave a more personal response: "Strokes are so mopey. They're always depressed. There just isn't anything you can do for them."

I saw this attitude when I visited my father in the hospital two weeks after he had suffered a stroke. He had healed a lot by then, but I got a clue about his condition from my family. "It's hard to visit," an uncle told me. "He's out of touch a lot." "I came for an hour," a cousin said, "but after five minutes, I said everything. You won't want to stay more than an hour."

They were right: it was a hard visit. But not for the reasons they gave. Since I lived 2,000 miles away I had not seen my father in over a year. He had changed a lot since then. His face looked puffy, his skin grey-white. The stubble of his beard grew in patches, and his salt and pepper hair had turned white. He was extremely weak.

I got used to his changed looks, and we even tried a short walk across the room. He held on to my arm and we shuffled along, pulling the IV bottle beside us. "See, I'm getting better every day," he said. "I can walk better now." He still had some spirit left, and I enjoyed just sitting with him.

The worst part of the visit came later. I watched as a nurse came in to check my father's temperature.

"Well, how are you today, Mr Novak?"

"Feeling better," he said. "This is my son, he's a college professor."

"How nice. Now open up, I want to take your temperature."

She put the thermometer in his mouth, then began to feel around his wrist for his pulse.

"I can't seem to find your pulse," she said to herself, but loud enough for me to hear. "Maybe if I try over here." She moved her hand. Still no luck. She tried again in another spot. "I guess I'll let one of the other nurses try later," she said in frustration.

Then she took the thermometer out of my father's mouth and wrote the reading on a clipboard.

"I'll be starting dialysis again on Monday," my father said in a soft voice. "They say. . ." He stopped. She hadn't heard him and was already on her way to the next room.

The demands of an acute care hospital don't allow the staff much time to get to know a patient. A report for the Greater Vancouver Hospital District found that older people in hospitals often feel lonely and lost. The report recommended that someone in the hospital take on the role of "listener," but everyone seemed to think that it should be someone else's job.[37]

During a visit with my father a nurse came by to say hello. She said her name, but my father didn't remember her: she looked hurt and moved on to the next bed. "So many nurses," he said to me.

Yes, I thought, so many nurses and so many doctors, so many friends and well-wishers, and they all wanted something from him that he couldn't give. The nurses, the doctors, all of them wanted him to get better, but he couldn't manage it. He couldn't even put up a good front. And none of them seemed to see *him*: they saw a broken body, someone who didn't smile much, who spoke too slowly.

"Do you want to go home, Dad?" I asked.

"Yeah, but they say I can't yet. Soon. Maybe next week."

We sat in silence. Then I got up to go. I kissed him goodbye.

When I got to the door I looked back one last time. He had his head down on the table in front of him, the way we used to rest our heads at recess in grade school. He was sleeping.

I looked at him and I thought "Let him go home. Please, let him go home."

Of course the doctors and the hospital wanted to get him home too. "We need the beds," one resident told Hoffman in her study. "There are a lot of people who need these beds more than CVA's."[38]

Unfortunately, my father — and many like him — couldn't leave until he had somewhere to go. My mother was past 70 herself and couldn't help him out of bed or give him his insulin shots. Until he got stronger and the doctors could provide him with some home help or get him into a nursing home, he had to stay where he was.

Hoffman found that stroke patients often remain hospitalized for months. A shortage of nursing home beds and not enough home services leaves them stranded. Dr Colin Powell, head of geriatric medicine at Winnipeg's St Boniface General Hospital, told *The Winnipeg Free Press* that "At any given time now we have about 50 people in here who are waiting for placement in personal care homes, and they wait for eight or nine months because of the shortage of facilities in the community."[39] An Ontario task force listed this as a major health care problem, and projected fewer services in the future.[40]

These problems call for change in the use of money for health care. With an aging society we need more institutions that fit the older person's needs. We also need chronic home care programs to keep people out of institutions when we can. This would free up acute care beds; it would also cost less. Even more important, it would give people the kind of care they want and need as they get older.[41]

Changes in the System

The Nursing Home[a]

Nursing home care costs only about one quarter as much as hospital care (in 1982 about $200 a day per patient in a hospital, but only about $55 a day in a nursing home). They offer a relatively cheap alternative to hospitals. They also offer long-term care and special programs for older patients.

But even if nursing homes save us money and serve special needs, few people want to live in one. To most people they bring to mind the horror of dependence and death.

Some recent writing supports this view. In the U.S., Claire Townsend wrote an exposé of nursing homes called *Old Age: The Last Segregation*. She detailed the horror of nursing home life: insensitive staff, confused older people who wander around without supervision and the use of drugs to keep patients quiet.

Daniel Jay Baum calls nursing homes in Canada *Warehouses for Death*. "The aged in institutions," he says, "may survive in body, but this does not mean that they survive in mind and spirit."[42] When people move into nursing homes, for instance, they lose many of their rights. At one home I visited the staff keep patients'

[a]I use the term nursing home here to cover three types of non-hospital institutional care. The Manitoba government defines them as (1) Personal Care Level II: the person needs nursing care for 2 hours or less a day over a long period of time; (2) Extended Care Level III: the person needs continuing nursing care for 3 to 5 hours a day; (3) Extended Care Level IV: heavy nursing care, mostly for bedridden people.

Sometimes an institution will offer only one type of care, but often one home will give all levels of care. A person will then move from one type of care to another as their health gets better or worse. In this section I describe people placed in Personal Care Levels II and III.

personal liquor supplies in a locked office: the patients have to ask staff for permission to have a drink. Baum says that often, "Residents cannot leave the home without notifying and, in some cases, obtaining the approval of the administrator. If the administrator considers it necessary he or she is empowered to confine the resident to bed using restraining devices."

Research shows that even where care is good, institutional life itself causes problems. Researcher Robert Kahn found that withdrawal was the most common pattern of illness in institutions. People sit and stare into space. They don't respond to questions, or if they do respond they just say "I don't know." Many of these cases are labelled "brain-damaged," but Kahn found that the same "brain-damaged" person who won't respond to a doctor's questions about her illness will answer a nurse a few minutes later. Kahn traced this kind of withdrawal to the low demands of institutional life. He found that about 40% of all institutionalized older people showed "excess disability." He found that they lived *down* to the expectations of the institution.[43]

This often happens, despite the best intentions of the staff. Mrs Grazia, 75, came into Deer Park Lodge with a mild stroke. After some time she could get around on her own. She could shop downtown, walk by herself in the park, visit her family. But because she might black out again and because she was still weak, she couldn't go home.

In Deer Park she got the care she needed. In some ways, however, the care was too good. She no longer had to cook, clean, change the linen or make her own bed.

"I used to make my bed," she told me. "Then one day I forgot to do it. I went downtown to shop at the Bay and when I got back the bed was made. 'How nice,' I thought." She never made the bed again.

Now her bones feel stiff. Her joints ache from lack of use. She may find that one day soon she *can't* make her bed even if she wants to.

Institutional life can lead to a sense of uselessness and to depression. It can also produce strange behaviour. Psychologists call this "institutional neurosis."

I saw this while visiting a home with my class last fall. We got to the home in the late afternoon, toured the building, then talked to the patients.

One thing puzzled me. I saw people lined up in wheelchairs along the hall. "Why are they sitting there?" I asked a nurse. "They're waiting for supper," she said. "They start to gather in the halls at about 3:30. It's like that every day."

Dinner didn't start until 5:30. I asked one woman why she was there so early. "I come here to be bored," she said. These people had nothing else to do, so two hours before dinner they got ready to go downstairs. Down in the dining room I saw the same thing. people got to their places a half hour before dinner, even though they had reserved seats.

I doubt that any of these older people would wait that long in the lobby of a restaurant, or that the staff would take a wait like that for granted anywhere else. But here, no one thought it was odd. Life in an institution has its own tempo, and it shapes people to its own demands. That's why most of us are so frightened by nursing homes and want to avoid going into one.

Still, nursing homes have a role to play in health care for older people. The nursing home can give a person a place to recover after hospitalization. It can solve the problem of how to get the older person to and from a doctor for treatment in the winter in rural areas. It may also be the only way some people can get the care they need if they live far from a hospital.

Given the choice, most people want to stay in their own homes, but not everyone does best at home. Cope Schwenger, professor in the Department of Health Administration at the University of Toronto, says that "the older person may be much worse off, even more 'institutionalized' in a certain sense, if bedfast or housebound and with few available home care services."[44] And if an illness goes on for a long time it can destroy family life. "The slogan, 'Keep the old folks at home,'" Professor Schwenger says, "can be a cruel and onerous message to some elderly persons and their relatives." Beyond a certain point, he says, "it is no longer fair to older people, their families, or to the community to sustain the psychological, social, or financial cost of home care.'' At that point the nursing home makes sense.

The nursing home also makes sense if a person needs a special kind of care or more intensive care than a family can give. At their best nursing homes give the older person types of care they wouldn't get at home.

I talked to Win Lindsay about this side of nursing home life. Win is a former standards officer for personal care homes in Manitoba. She just retired to part-time work, and now she spends most of her time speaking and consulting with groups of professionals across the country.

For the past ten years Win has designed programs to meet nursing home residents' needs. She has also worked with staff to develop their helping skills. Win calls herself a ''life enrichment counsellor.''

''I do a lot of work with staff attitudes,'' Win says. ''The staff often don't see what's in front of them. They have to be shocked to really see what's there.

''Their patients are people — not just a thing to be washed or put to bed, but an individual who is going to bed at night. Staff have to learn to treat people as people.''

Win designed a program called *LEEP* — Life Enrichment for Extended Care Patients — for the confused, frail elderly. ''LEEP is a program for people who don't respond at all,'' Win says. ''They are withdrawn, they hallucinate, they don't engage with their environment. Generally the diagnosis for people like this will be 'organic brain syndrome' or 'massive CVA.' They are people who don't respond to any kind of therapy now being used. They are rejects, all of them, from all the other programs — reality orientation, remotivation centring, retraining — all these things. These are people you can't reach. I don't think you can make them better. But you can change their life experience.''

Win decided to work within the limits of the system. She didn't ask for more staff, and she didn't expect that overworked nurses would suddenly spend a lot more time talking to withdrawn patients. Instead she designed a bare bones program, one that she could put in place right away.

"When we looked at the staff time we had per person — beyond nursing care — we found that each patient could get 21 minutes per week of extra contact. We divided the time into three periods of seven minutes each."

With travel time to and from the person that left only four minutes to talk with the person — not much, but more than these withdrawn people got before the program.

Because these people didn't respond, most of the staff and the families of these people had given up on them. But the LEEP workers don't expect a response. The people can never fail in this program, and the staff don't feel frustrated. Win says the LEEP program makes no demands. "We talk as if they'll answer, but we don't expect a response or a big change in the person."

The program takes patience. "Not everybody can do it," Sheri Reed, a LEEP worker, told me. "There's no reward. And often nobody else sees what happens during the program, even though we write up reports. People think when you put someone on a program, they are going to start eating again, or start doing something drastically different. That doesn't often happen."

A few cases do respond, sometimes right away. Mr Chisholm, for instance, was a hostile resident. He had no medical problem, but his health got worse and worse. He stopped eating or talking to people. He had to be strapped in a chair so that he wouldn't hurt himself.

"He'd just sit there and every once in a while you'd see a jiggle at the top of his face," Sheri says. "That was all." He showed no interest in anything. When he was awake he would shake in his chair; otherwise he slept.

"So we put him on the LEEP program as a last resort," Sheri says. "I went to see him and I explained who I was. I told him I'd come three times a week.

"The first day I held his hand and he shook mine. He didn't respond very much. He watched, especially my lips. After a few visits, I noticed that his attention span was increasing. I could talk about things and he'd respond and bring up subjects. He started to take more interest in things around him.

"One day he said, 'I'm not afraid to die.' I thought maybe he wanted to talk about dying, and when I went to see him next that's what he wanted to do. He saw that I was afraid. And he began to take an interest in convincing me about life after death . . . that it wasn't so bad.

"I think he responded because at last someone was interested in *what* he had to say. Now he's demanding to see someone in authority to get him out of the chair. The nurses all feel that if he'd been left he would have died."

Sheri concedes that Mr Chisholm is an extreme example, but he does prove that there is hope. Another case shows a more typical response. Mrs Grabowski has no specific ailment, but she has given up on life. The staff have kept her alive by feeding her. She won't do anything for herself, won't even speak. Each day they prop her up in a chair for a little while. Her eyes always look unfocused and she drools a lot. "She's been on the LEEP program for a year," Sheri says. "But in the last month I've noticed some change. She's now trying to talk, but nothing comes out and she gets frustrated, so she starts shaking.

"There was one day she was trying to talk. I was trying to get her to say something, and I would say, 'That's okay, I'm going to listen. You can just keep trying to tell me something.' And, 'it's okay if you can't get it out. I'm still going to come back.' (You have to keep reassuring them.)

"She got more and more agitated and I didn't know why. I just felt the frustration of it. I was just about to leave — the four minutes were up — and she had an accident. *That* was what she'd been trying to tell me.

"It was really upsetting, because she was trying — finally — and I didn't know what she wanted. It was frustrating for both of us, but at least she was trying."

"With the LEEP program," Sheri says, "you give them a choice. You're there, and if they want to communicate you give them the option. Often, when they're being bathed or fed, they have no choices: you're going to feed them, and that's it. But this is just a friendly visit. They know you're going to come back no matter what they do, no matter how they look, whether they talk or not.''

"That's the key to the program's success," Win says. "You simply accept the people as they are. Sometimes you'll discover a person who responds. Not always, but sometimes. But even if they don't respond, I think their life is a little enriched by what we do."

The LEEP program is only a beginning, and it serves a small group of people. Of the 8% of older people in extended care institutions, Win says "only two or three out of a hundred are candidates for LEEP." But the program points the way to a new philosophy of health care. Even when a cure isn't possible, we can still make life better for the older person.

Other programs are also being influenced by this philosophy. Some homes, for instance, have a room that couples can use when they want to sleep together. Most homes arrange dances for patients, and wine and cheese parties. Some homes regularly invite dance groups and choirs to perform, and others show current movies once a week.

One home I know arranges visits of high school students who bring their pets in for visits. The program has been a big success. The older people love the animals, and the animals give the young and older people something to talk about.

Still, nursing homes, as good as we make them, are a last resort. They cost a lot, and people don't want to go into a home unless they have to.

Home and Community Care

Everyone — government, doctors, nursing home staff and older people themselves — agrees that we should keep people out of institutions when we can. And yet today more people live in institutions than ever before. On any one day in 1976, almost 8.5% of Canadians 65 and over lived in institutions, compared to only 7% in 1962. Some provinces have even higher rates. In Alberta nearly 10% of older people live in some kind of institution, and this figure doesn't include people who live in semi-institutional "lodges." Manitoba, Ontario and Saskatchewan have rates of about 9% each. These are some of the highest rates in the world. England in 1971, for instance, had only 5% of its older people in institutions. And the U.S., from 1973–77, had only 6.3%.[45]

The Science Council of Canada offers some reasons why we have such high rates. As already noted, our long winters and the long distances between older people and hospitals sometimes make institutional life the only way for people to get the care they need. Also, the complex equipment needed to treat illnesses sometimes makes hospital care the only choice.

But "one of the main factors (that accounts for high rates of institutionalization)," the Council reports, "is that in Canada home care services were *not* insured simultaneously with hospital and institutional care (as was done in Great Britain under the National Health Service)."[46] This made it cheaper for the person to go into an institution than to stay at home. It led to a building boom for nursing homes, and it retarded the growth of home care services.

The lack of home care services also creates a vicious circle. It forces more people into institutions. This makes for long waiting lists, which government and private corporations use as an excuse to create more nursing home beds. This draws money away from home care, so more people have to go into institutions. This makes for long waiting lists. . . .

To lower the rates of institutionalization we need more alternative services to supplement institutional care for older people. A report in Ontario, for instance, judged that one patient in ten could leave the hospital "*if* there were adequate outpatient services."[47] And the 1982 Canadian Government Report to the U.N. states that many people go into hospitals "because of social rather than medical needs." Social services, the report says, should aim to "help older persons continue to live in their own homes for as long as possible."[48]

Sweden, where 15% of the population is over 65, has led the way in home care services, and it shows what can be done. In the early 1970s there were 50,000 home helpers in Sweden. That meant 47 helpers for every 1,000 older people. Each helped two to three older people for five or six hours a week. It has been estimated that in 1969 more than 100,000 older people who got this kind of help were able to stay in their own homes.[49]

In a report called *Programs for the Aged in Europe*, Lola Wilson described a "cleaning patrol" program in Stockholm. It provides an insight into the Swedish approach to home care.

"Briefly," she says, "a patrol consists of a station wagon outfitted with the necessary supplies and equipment to do a complete heavy cleaning job in a house or apartment." First, two workers clean out clothes closets and drawers. They remove drapes and get the place ready for a heavy cleaning. Then two workers follow with a carload of cleaning equipment to do the job. Finally two more workers come in afterward to shop for freezer goods, to can food, to bake and mend.[50]

As far as I know no program as elaborate as this exists in Canada, but most provinces now offer a wide range of programs to help a person stay in the community. These programs differ from province to province, but they include counselling, diet advice, nursing help and supplies. The Ontario Advisory Council on Senior Citizens has tried to promote more of these services. A report called *A Guide to Community Support Services* lists some of the programs that now exist in the province.

Dial-a-Dietician: People can get information about diet and nutrition by making a free telephone call. Two cities now have this service.

Nursing Care: the Victorian Order of Nurses or the St Elizabeth Nursing Organization can help an older person who needs part-time nursing care.

Day Hospitals: these offer rehabilitation, physiotherapy and after-care to discharged patients. Older people get meals if they stay for a whole day.

These programs and others like them can help a person to stay at home and still get the care they need.

Each province today also has a medical home care program. Many older people don't need major treatment to stay well. Instead, as Daniel Baum says, they need "checkups and care for aches and minor troubles."[51] Paramedical people and nurses can often meet the needs of older people in the community. In Ontario a member of the provincial health plan (OHIP) can get free care. This includes nursing, physiotherapy, homemaker help and Meals On Wheels.

Until 1981 Ontario provided these services only to people who could be rehabilitated, and even then a person could only get eighty hours of free homemaker services. The program did not serve those who needed long term or chronic home care. Finally in 1981 a chronic care program was established. It offers forty hours a month of free homemaker service, for as long as a person needs help, as well as the other services listed earlier.

Other home care programs across the country include speech and occupational therapy, shopping help, handyman and visitor services.

John Rankin, 95, for instance, lives on his own in a senior citizens' high rise. An orderly comes in twice a week to bathe him, a housekeeper comes in once a week to clean the apartment and a homemaker cooks him supper twice a week. Without these supports he would have to move to a nursing home.

In another case a nurse visits a diabetic man once a week to help him prepare his insulin shots. She doesn't give him the injections. She just checks on dosages and organizes the insulin needles so that he remembers to take them. A housekeeper also comes in to keep the place clean. Without this help he too would need nursing home care.

The provinces also offer adult day care. People can come to a nursing home or hospital for the day, get a chance to meet other people, take part in crafts programs and receive medical treatment if they need it.

Sometimes even a simple service like a day care centre with no medical treatment can help a family keep a sick person at home. John Gilchrist developed Alzheimer's disease five years ago. He wanders around the house all day, from the front to the back door, trying to get out. His family had to put key-operated dead bolts on both doors, but occasionally someone forgets to put a key away or leaves one in the lock, and John gets out. Jean, his wife, and their teen-aged sons spend hours trying to find him when he escapes.

"When he stops wandering," Jean says, "he falls asleep. Then he's up all night. He turns on the stove or gets into the food. One time he mixed the macaroni in the honey. Another time he filled the toilet with oranges. I had to call a plumber to get them out."

John's family loves him. They want to care for him at home as long as they can, but Jean finds herself tied to the house all day. And sometimes he keeps her up all night, so she feels too tired to do anything. Her social life has begun to shrink and she's edgy and tense.

She finally went for help to the provincial social services department, which now send a housekeeper in to watch John two days a week. This gives Jean time to run errands, visit friends for lunch or go to Alzheimer's Society meetings.

Jean also found a day care program for John at the Saint Aidan's Clinic. This gives her (and her sons) a break. It also gets John out of the house. The program gives him some stimulation, and Jean thinks this has improved his mental ability and made him easier to care for at home.

Some nursing homes also offer a small number of beds for short term stays — a weekend to a week. A family can leave a sick older person while they take a holiday or just to get a break from the pressure of daily care.

These programs make good sense in an aging society. First, they stretch the health care budget. A study done in Saskatoon found that home care cost only 14% of institutional care, in Newfoundland it was reported that home care cost only 11% of institutional care. A report from Ontario estimated that it cost $6,800 in

1978 to keep a patient in an extended care institution, while home care for a person in that year came to only $53.87 — a little more than $1 a week.[52]

Second, these programs give older people the kind of service they want. One woman summed up this feeling for the Ontario Advisory Council on Aging. "Every senior citizen should stay in his accustomed surroundings as long as possible," she said.[53]

And yet the health care budget still favours institutions. In 1980-81 the federal government gave over $700 million to the provinces, most of it for institutional care. In 1978-79 the provinces spent over $920 million on special care in homes for the elderly. But in that same year in Ontario the home care and support services budget came to "less than a quarter of that spent just on extended care."[54]

The Science Council of Canada has called home care the "most significant future development in health care delivery."[55] And sociologist John McWhinnie lists more home care as a top priority for the Canadian health care system.[56] Yet, before we can have better home care we will have to make a greater financial commitment to these programs.

Prevention

So far I've done what I've criticized others for doing: I've focused on sickness. There's no other way to talk about the system. Although we call it a health care system it's actually a sickness-treatment system. It serves people who are already sick, and it focuses on curing disease. In 1974, Minister of Health and Welfare Marc Lalonde said that $7 billion a year (about 2/3 of the money spent on health care at the time) went to treat existing illnesses.[57]

A look at the illnesses people have in Canada today shows the limits of this approach. The 1978 Canada Health Survey studied the health of over 23,000 Canadians in 12,000 households in 100 areas throughout the country. The report listed the most common problems people reported. They include chronic diseases like hypertension, mental disorder, limb and joint problems, arthritis and rheumatism. These problems disable the most people and lead to the heaviest use of the system.[58]

But spending more money on hospitals, doctors' fees, nursing homes or home care won't do away with these problems or create better health. A "classical cure for chronic disease is a vanity. . . . Once chronic disease is diagnosed, it usually results in the death of the individual."[59] At best the health care system can alleviate symptoms, ease pain and extend life.

"The only real 'cure' for chronic diseases," according to Statistics Canada, "is prevention through environmental or life-style change. The task of contending with the causes of chronic disease is predominantly a societal one, not a medical one."[60]

As early as 1974 Marc Lalonde recognized the social sources of illness. In a report called *A New Perspective on the Health of Canadians* he proposed to include the social causes of illness in a broad concept of health care — the "health field." The health field takes into account the health care system; it also includes the improvement of human biology, the environment and a person's life-style as ways to better health. Within the health field the health care system is *one* way — but not the only way, or even the best way — to improve health. The other components of the health field are worth examining one at a time.

Scientific Research
Scientific research may account for the biggest improvement in health in old age in the future. Dr Lewis Thomas uses typhoid, polio and pulmonary tuberculosis to show how this could happen. Until science isolated these diseases, he says, treatment took place in expensive hospitals and sanitoria over months and years. Now that we know the cause and can treat the diseases at their roots, the sanitorium is obsolete and the diseases have almost disappeared.[61]

In the same way a scientific breakthrough into the causes of diseases like Alzheimer's, diabetes, heart disease, cancer or stroke would improve health in old age. Organ transplants and artificial organs could also help people live healthier and longer lives. According to Thomas, "we would still age away and wear out, on about the same schedule as today."[62] But, he says, scientific breakthroughs would put an end to the diseases that grind away and cause people so much suffering late in life.

More scientific knowledge about disease — its causes and cures — would also lower the costs of health care. Costs soar when we don't know the cause of an illness: then we have to use expensive corrective measures like open-heart surgery to treat disease. The more we know about diseases and the human body the more directly we can act to treat and prevent illness. There are no miracle cures in sight, but progress in medical research is being made every day.

Social Environment

Our social environment affects our health. Consider the following research findings.

Tension and stress can cause illness. Research shows that a "sense of urgency, time pressure, tensions, repressed aggressiveness, and hostility" create a high risk of heart attack."[63] In some ways our culture promotes these feelings. It even rewards the competitiveness and overwork that cause them.

Food packagers add chemicals to our food. Industry pollutes water and land. Advertising promotes unhealthy foods and drinks. This abuse of our environment and our bodies continues, even though some experts believe that as many as 75% of cancers come from environmental irritation.[64]

The work place can also cause illness. Lung diseases, cancer, silicosis, asbestosis and hearing loss make up a short list of work-related diseases of which we are aware.

These diseases may be the hardest to eradicate. For one thing they strike slowly. Their effects often don't show up until years later. Statistics Canada, for instance, reports a 1974 study of illness among uranium miners. Twenty-four years had passed before anyone made the link between the miners' health and their work.[65]

Only a change in public awareness about the causes of illness can lead to a change in the social environment. Public pressure on government and industry, for instance, can lead to better working conditions and higher environmental standards. The success of anti-smoking lobbies in cities across the country shows a growing awareness of problems. Changes here will come slowly, but they must come if we want to enjoy good health in old age.

Life-Style

Our health care system, biological research and environmental change are all forces outside us which can improve our health. But good health in old age also depends on a person's habits and life-style — especially the way the person lived in middle age.

Dr Victor Heinrich, director of the Extended Care Unit at Winnipeg's City Hospital, pointed this out to me in a slide presentation. One slide shows half a dozen male patients sitting in wheelchairs in a semi-circle.

"Do you notice anything strange in this picture?" Dr Heinrich asked. I looked, but saw nothing unusual. "They all have cigarettes in their hands," he said.

Sure enough, above each man's hand I could see a trail of smoke.

"Cigarette smoking cuts down blood circulation," said Dr Heinrich. "And that's why these men had their legs amputated. Yet they went back to smoking even before they left the hospital. If they live long enough, these men will probably be back for more surgery."

Some of them won't live that long. Recent research shows that smoking accounts for much of the difference in life expectancy between men and women. These men not only risk more illness, they also increase their chances of dying sooner.

"Self imposed risks," Marc Lalonde writes, "and the environment are the principal or important underlying factors in each of the five major causes of death [car accidents, accidents, heart disease, respiratory and lung diseases and suicide] between age one and seventy."[66] Sixty percent of all deaths can be traced to life-style or environment.[67]

One recent study at the Harvard Medical School shows that

while a healthy life-style and good habits do not lengthen a person's life after age 70, they can improve an older person's well-being.[68] Many of us have begun to see this link and have changed our habits. People have become more conscious about calories and fat in their diets; companies now produce low-calorie, low-sodium TV dinners; and the diet drink market has begun to boom. Also, more people now exercise to keep fit.

The Federal Government has promoted this kind of change in life-style. The Department of Health and Welfare increased its funding of life-style programs by 278% between 1969 and 1974. This funding rose from the lowest to the second highest amount given to health care programs (after health care organization).[69]

One program supported by the government has caught on with older people — Participaction. Billie Lucas directs the St Vital YMCA's Participaction program in Winnipeg.

"I've got one policeman," she says. "He was a speed cop, a motorcycle policeman for twenty-five years. He got arthritis, and he could hardly hobble when his doctor sent him to us.

"Now he can jog for about forty seconds. He walks fast the rest of the time. Last year he played golf all summer. He started with nine holes and by summer's end was playing eighteen. He didn't come back here until they closed the golf course."

Billie tells this story with gusto, but it's only one of many success stories. Seven years ago, with no experience in teaching older people to exercise, Billie began an experiment at the Y. "We started with fifteen people," she says, "and so far this year we've signed up about 215.

"Each year the program has grown until now it's the largest exercise program for older people in Canada. We've got people who've been here for six or seven years for the program, and they're still coming back. So there must be some good in it. Last Monday I had seventy-five people in the gym. And they'll come out every day."

The program offers no frills — no bingo, cribbage or coffee breaks, no crocheting or crafts, just a good physical workout that members can attend up to five days a week.

The 45-minute program starts with stretching and a slow warm-up exercise — like picking imaginary apples. Then there's some walking with a jump-and-clap routine thrown in, working up to jogging, and finally some work on the mats — toe touches, bending and twisting. After that it's time for the pool and a sauna.

During the program Billie works in some talking, and a few jokers in the crowd usually moan and groan at the right moment to get a laugh out of everyone. The atmosphere is relaxed, non-competitive and friendly. People come, I found out, to socialize as well as to exercise.

Billie is a model for the program — slim and flexible, dressed in a bright red track suit. She brings a spark of energy to what might otherwise be a tedious work-out. Above all, she believes in what she's doing.

"Well, I figure that this program has proved itself," she told me. "It's been running now for seven years. It's multiplying all the time. It's proved itself all the way through as far as I'm concerned. You know, it could go on the market."

In order to help spread the word Billie has written a book that describes her program. It contains a summary of the exercises she believes are best in her work with older people. "People can do their exercises at home or alone," she said, "they just need to read and find the right type of exercises. My main objective is to get as many people as I can involved in bettering themselves when they get old."

Research supports Billie's belief that exercise can lead to a better old age. Herbert DeVries, professor at the University of California and a pioneer in research on exercise for older people, says that good nutrition, relaxation and physical fitness all lead to "positive good health in old age." He has found that exercise helps people stay mobile, energetic and in better spirits.

In one study of people about 70 years of age, DeVries found the reverse of the stereotype that old age leads downhill. He showed that people can improve their physical condition through exercise. Men in their 60s and 70s in the study reached a level of fitness equal to that of an unconditioned 40-year-old. He also found an added bonus to the exercise: people said they felt more relaxed when they finished. ''The good news,'' he says, ''is that our daily habits — our life style, if you please — appears to be much more important to our good health than anything anyone else could do for us. . . . To a very great extent we now control our own health and destiny.''[70]

We moan about the high cost of health care and we endlessly repeat the statistics about illness in old age, but there is something morbid in this concern with illness. Changes in life-style, improvements in the environment and better health care systems have all led to better health in old age. Today Canada not only has a bigger older population than ever before, it also has the healthiest older population ever — possibly the healthiest in the world. It may take some time for this to sink in, but most older people live healthy lives well past the age of 65.

The Future

Most experts predict better health in old age in the future. First, people are healthier in childhood and middle age today than in the past. Many older people today suffer from the effects of past illnesses.

Vera Akins, for instance, had an acute infection of the middle ear when she was seven years old. She lost the hearing in her right ear, and now she has to sit on my right as we talk so that she can hear me clearly. Andrew Carlyle, now 69, picked up a bug in India during World War II. Now he suffers from bouts of dysentery and mild fever two or three times a year. Dee Allison, 68, walks with crutches. She was born with two disjointed hips. Only the muscles in her legs hold her up, and as she's grown older, these muscles have become weaker. Soon she will have to risk a dangerous operation to reset her legs. The alternative is to use a wheelchair for the rest of her life.

Today, few children suffer from acute infections like Vera's.

Future groups of older Canadians will, we hope, have no war injuries to carry into old age. And today a doctor would have fixed Dee's legs before she began to crawl. In the future people will come into old age in better health. And they'll stay healthy longer.

Second, the health care system of the future will help older people cope better with the illnesses they have. We may not be able to cure all illnesses in old age, but we can help people live more satisfying lives.

Institutions will improve as they break down the barriers between patients and the community. They will do this in two ways. First, they will bring people in and, second, they will get patients out.

Staff from the Rest Haven home, for instance, meet with a patient's family before admission. They go over the home's rules and regulations. "But," Mrs Jackson, Rest Haven's director, says, "we also try to establish rapport with the family. We want to give them a feeling for how we operate. We try to alleviate their fears about 'putting their relatives away.'"

The Rest Haven staff also makes it clear that the family plays a part in the health care program. The staff tells the family they expect them to visit, and Rest Haven has a family room where families can meet in private in a living-room setting. "We'll also provide snacks or meals at cost for family visits. Families can order salads, cheese platters and fruit for a Sunday luncheon or dinner. These parties encourage families to come."

Rest Haven also gets patients out. The staff takes patients shopping. They go bowling. And they are planning to start a swimming program. They also take healthier patients on summer picnics and bus tours.

When we can in the future, we will also help people stay active, independent and in the community as long as they want to. Larger, more flexible home care programs will make this a reality.

Third, more education will lead to better health. People know more today about how to prevent illness, about the habits and lifestyles that lead to good health.

An example: Robert Carter and his wife, both in their early 70s, lead active lives. He retired from medical practice five years ago and now works for half a dozen community agencies as a volunteer. His wife set up a weaving shop in their basement. She also works as a volunteer at a local hospital. In the winter both of them take extra care to avoid falls when they go out. They're not fanatics about this, but on icy nights, for instance, they may decide to cancel a social visit. "I know the statistics on broken hip bones at my age," Dr Carter says, "and I'm not going to take any unnecessary chances." As more people learn the facts about aging, like the Carters, they'll take better care of themselves as they age.

Fourth, more people will take part in active health promotion programs. Five years ago Creative Retirement Manitoba, an education centre for older people, held its first reflexology (foot massage) course. The classroom seated about thirty people, but when Peter Weir, the teacher, arrived he found sixty people crowded in the room and into the hall outside. Creative Retirement has found that more and more people want to stay healthy as they age. Its program now includes courses in massage, holistic health, tai chi, yoga, nutrition and preventive care.

This knowledge also reaches other older people who don't take the courses. Bea Carruthers visited her niece last year in Kingston, Ontario, and went for dinner to the local minister's house. After dinner the minister mentioned a cramp he had in his leg, and Bea had him take his shoes off right there. She gave him a foot massage, then she showed him how to do it himself.

Finally, the social environment has improved. Fewer people live in poverty today than in the past, and social services now exist for people in need.

This will create a healthier old age for more people.

Still, some people in Canada aren't as healthy as they could be. And it will take more than a better health care system to improve their lives. The Canada Health Survey, for instance, linked the quality of life, emotional health and physical health to a person's income and education: "It is clear that people of lower income groups and lower levels of education do not enjoy the same level of health as those Canadians of higher social and economic status.''[71]

Research may cure diseases. Exercise and diet may keep us fit. But they cannot take the place of good housing, a meaningful role in society and a decent standard of living. These conditions are all basic to good health. And better health in old age in the future will come about as we make improvements here.

HOUSING: HOUSES OR HOMES?

Living Arrangements

Val Rogers, 65, a former nurse, lives in a middle-class neighbourhood. Professors, doctors and accountants live here. The
smaller homes have three bedrooms, larger ones perhaps four or
five. As I arrive to visit Val on a cold December day, I see that she
lives in a large house set back from the street.

I ring the bell and a woman in her 30s opens the door. Behind
her, a golden retriever with a bandaged paw stares at me.

"Does Val Rogers live here?"

"Yes, but Mom's across the street. She'll be right back. Are you
Professor Novak? She's expecting you. Come in. Would you like
some coffee?"

While she goes to get the coffee I looked around. On my right is
a big dining room with oak-beamed ceilings, a dark mahogany
dining room set in the middle of the room. Plants hang in front of
the window. Up the stairs, straight ahead, I see a man working at a
desk. The living room is on my left. All the downstairs rooms have
twelve-foot ceilings. Golden-oak trim frames the doorways and
windows. In the living room is a bay window and a fireplace of old
brick that runs to the ceiling.

Past the living room I see a heated sun porch, a fresh Christmas tree brushing the ceiling and nearly filling the room. A Tonka truck and a Simon electronic game along with boxes and wrapping are spilled out into the living-room. The decor, the smell of coffee and the warm carpet under my feet create a magic warmth.

A few seconds later Val dashes in wearing a charcoal sweater and dark slacks — no coat or hat. Snowflakes cling to her hair. She leads me into the living room, where we sit down near the fireplace. A few minutes later her daughter brings us coffee.

"What a beautiful house," I say. "I see you live with your daughter. Do you have a room or a suite for yourself upstairs?"

Val's eyebrows rise. "This is *my* house. My son upstairs has come back home so he can finish university. My daughter moved back home in September when her marriage broke up. They live with *me*."

I feel like a fool. I had assumed that Val's daughter had taken her in, not the reverse. Val keeps this big house, she tells me, "as a haven for the kids. Someplace they can come back to when they need it."

I also discover that this house serves another purpose. It gives Val a chance to play the role of mother and caregiver to her children. This house gives more than shelter: it serves as a focal point for Val's family life.

Like Val, many older people say their homes improve their lives. A home allows them to do more and to be more. "I love my home," one woman said simply in a letter to the Ontario Advisory Council on Aging. "I live alone," another woman said, "but I am never lonely. I like baking, and my door is always open to visitors. I am never too busy to make them a cup of tea with a scone and black currant jelly."[1]

At home people express their personalities through their plants, pets and mementoes. In every older person's home I visit I see pictures of children, grandchildren, husbands and wives. People attach meanings to their furniture. "That dining room set," one 78-year-old woman told me, "belonged to *my* grandmother. I wouldn't part with it for the world." Even the house itself can give a person a sense of security. When Vera Akins's children wanted her to move in with them after her husband died, she refused. "This is my house," she told them, "I own it. I paid for it. And this is where I'm going to stay."

A home can also serve a practical purpose. It can help a person to remain active and in good mental and physical health. And it can help the older person stay in touch with others.

Not everyone needs a house to call home. Many older people live in apartments. Some live in developments for senior citizens. Others live with their children. Still others live in retirement villages, mobile homes, rooming-houses, hotels and communes.

No one housing design can meet the needs of all older people. After all, people differ according to their social class, ethnic group, sex, habits, personality and age. "The longer people live," gerontologist Bernice Neugarten says, "the more different they become."[2]

A good system of housing will meet the different needs of older people. It will give them variety and a range of options to choose from. But what does the system offer today?

The System Today

Older people today value their independence more than anything else. They want to stay out of institutions, they don't want to live with their children and they prefer to live alone rather than depend on anyone. From 1971 to 1976 the number of older people heading their own households went up by almost 4% a year, even though the older population went up by only 3% a year.[3] "The desire to remain independent in a home of one's own choice," Professor Alan Backley told a 1980 conference at the University of Toronto, "is overwhelming."[4]

Today three-fifths of people 65-74 years old live in private households with their spouses or unmarried children. Even past the age of 75, 65% of men live in these kinds of settings. Because of widowhood, women tend to live alone or in collective dwellings.

Still, only 9% of people over 65 live in any kind of ''collective dwelling'' — a hotel, nursing home, rooming house, lodge, motel or institution.[5]

Some people even risk their lives to keep their freedom. A few years ago Klinic, Inc., a Winnipeg community health centre, set up an outreach program for older people. Klinic hired a group of medical school students to survey the health needs of older people in the neighbourhood. They went from house to house on each block, locating the residences of older people, and then assessing the health needs of the older people they found.

One house looked deserted. Through the front door window the students could see newspapers piled to the ceiling. No one could get in or out. They saw no light inside, so they went next door. Most of the neighbours said that they thought the house was deserted, but one neighbour recalled seeing someone go into the house through the rear basement stairway.

The students went back, knocked on the basement windows and the back stairway door until they heard shuffling inside. The door opened a crack and a thin voice asked who was there. An old woman had answered. After fifteen minutes of talk, the students persuaded her to let them in.

The house stank. Old newspapers littered the hallway stairs and living room. The woman kept a dozen cats that roamed the house. She lived in the kitchen, using the stove to heat the room in the winter.

She could hardly walk. She had an arthritic back and couldn't bend over to cut her toenails. The nails had grown so long that they curled around and dug into the flesh under her toes. At first she wanted nothing to do with the students. ''I don't need no welfare,'' she kept saying. After a lot more talk, the students convinced her that they could help her.

First they cut her toenails so that she could walk. Later they returned with some food. Then they followed up with a medical check-up and regular visits.

This old woman refused to move into better housing. She wanted to live with her cats in her own house. The Klinic team respected her decision, but they knew she didn't have to risk sickness and death to do it. With some outside help — house-cleaning once a week, daily Meals on Wheels and a check-up now and then — they knew she could stay on her own with much less risk.

At their best, programs to help older people do what this Klinic team did. They help a person to live the way the person wants to. Canada's system of housing does a pretty good job of meeting this need. A whole network of options and programs help older people live in the kind of housing they choose.

Most older people today live in three kinds of housing: their own houses, apartments and "collective dwellings" — Statistics Canada's term for nursing homes, guest homes, hotels and institutions. Each of these options has its own problems and rewards.

Owning a House

We bought our house from an older friend. He and his wife had decided to move to Victoria. They'd had enough of Winnipeg's raw winters and short summers and wanted a piece of the good life on the coast.

They aren't alone. Both Victoria and Vancouver have high proportions of older people — over 17% for Victoria and 11.5% for Vancouver.[6]

Still, most Canadians don't move when they retire. Most people want to stay in the neighbourhood and town in which they worked and raised a family. And they often want to stay in their own house. A 1982 Household Facilities and Equipment Survey in Canada showed that three-quarters of all men and half of all women 65 and over own their own houses. Among people 80 and over 56% still own their own houses. Three-quarters of older homeowners own single detached two- or three-bedroom houses.[7] And 60% of people 65 and over had paid off their mortgages. This figure jumps to 95% for people over 80.[8]

Not only do older people tend to live in their own houses, most of them take good care of the houses they own. Only 12% of homeowners 65 to 79 years old said their houses needed major repair. Three-quarters of them said their houses needed only regular maintenance. People over 80 did even better: 77% of them said their houses needed only regular maintenance, and only 10% said their houses needed major repair.[9]

This does not mean, however, that older people don't need help to keep their houses. People who live only on the basic government pension, for instance, often feel strapped. One man told the Ontario Advisory Council that he needed a new furnace and an outside paint job. "These two would cost at least $1,500," he said, "which is impossible."[70]

The federal government and the provinces have moved to help people like this man stay in their own houses. They now offer a wide range of programs to help older homeowners — from grants to loans to tax rebates. In 1974, for instance, the federal government began a Residential Rehabilitation Assistance Program (RRAP). It offered loans of up to $10,000 to help people improve run down housing. By May 1981 it had loaned $118 million for house repairs. The government forgave close to 90% of the loans to those 3,400 older households with low incomes.[11]

Older people can also get help from their provincial government to keep their houses in good shape. Alberta has the Alberta Pioneers Repair Program, which grants up to $2,000 to people who earn less than $13,500 a year to make repairs, restorations or improvements to their houses. Nova Scotia offers up to $3,000 in forgiveable loans for house repairs. The province also runs a Home Emergency Repair Program that grants up to $2,000 for emergency repairs.

Many provinces also offer tax rebates for older homeowners. Saskatchewan, for instance, gives older people a school and property tax rebate and a $50 tax credit. Manitoba allows older people to defer property taxes until they leave their houses. Ontario gives a property tax credit through the income tax system.

These are just a few of the programs offered by different levels of government, but they give some idea of the assistance for older people who want to stay in their own houses.

Apartment Living

Yet many older people can't stay in their houses as they get older, even with government aid. They find it too hard to clean and care for a house. Dr Gloria Gutman, director of the Gerontology Centre at Simon Fraser University, found in one study in British Columbia that almost one older person in five who moved into a senior high-rise did so because they had "difficulty looking after their residence."[12]

But she also found that many older people want to live in an apartment. Forty-four percent of the people in the same study who had moved into a high-rise said they had done so because they wanted freedom from the responsibility of maintaining a home. A large majority of the people who moved (62.9%) said they felt very satisfied with their lives today. With an apartment, they have less to worry about if they travel or go to a summer cottage. They also have someone to shovel the walk and fix a leaky sink.

People with no financial limits can choose from a wide range of apartments on the market. They can pick someplace near a bus route and shopping, a one- or two-bedroom apartment with a balcony and a view. But people who rent apartments tend to have less money than homeowners. Owners had average assets in 1976 of $73,000, renters only $14,000. Owners had $16,000 in liquid assets, renters less than half that.[13]

Since World War II, government has answered the need for low-cost housing by building new apartments. From 1947 to 1980 the federal government loaned or insured loans of $215 billion to build 140,000 apartments for older people. Most of them were built in the 1960s and 70s. Nearly as many self-contained apartments were put up under the National Housing Act from 1971-76, for instance, than in the twenty-five previous years.[14]

Ontario alone has built over 80,000 family and senior units since the 1960s at a cost of $2 billion. The waiting-list for senior housing in the province dropped from 19,000 in 1974 to 500 in 1980.[15]

Alberta spent $62 million in 1979-80 to build housing for older people. In March of 1980 the province had over 6,500 self-contained apartments for older people — some of them designed for people in wheelchairs. The province has already begun to build

3,500 more. Older people in Alberta also have highest priority for all low-rent bachelor and one-bedroom apartments.[16]

What's it like, living in senior citizens' housing?

Pete and Rose MacMillan live in a subsidized housing block in Winnipeg. Until he retired they lived in a big house on a double lot on the river. Then they sold their house, bought a mobile home and headed south to Florida. After two years they found themselves missing their children and grandchildren, and they moved back. They didn't have much income apart from Pete's small pension, so in 1976 they moved into a government-subsidized housing block, where they have a one-bedroom apartment. A couch, two chairs, a television, a coffee table and a bookcase fill the living room. A small dining-room table sits behind the couch near the kitchen. You'd have to move some living room furniture to seat four people. Pete uses the table as a desk during the day.

The kitchen is a slit between the refrigerator and sink on one side and the stove and countertop on the other. If two people stood back to back in the narrow space, their bellies would touch the counter on either side.

The MacMillans' four-poster bed fills up their bedroom. The bed comes up to the dresser on the opposite wall with just enough space for a person to squeeze through. A small bathroom is next to their bedroom.

The apartment reminds me of graduate student housing built in the early 1970s — clean, small and no frills.

Pete and Rose moved here because they had to: they didn't have much money, and they had no other choice if they wanted a rent subsidy. But in the past few years some provinces have begun rent-subsidy programs. People can use these subsidies toward rent on any apartment they choose. This allows older people to choose a bigger apartment outside senior citizens' housing if they want to.

In 1980 Ontario, for instance, spent $250 million to subsidize rent for people over age 60. Manitoba spent $5 million in 1979-80 to subsidize rent for people over 60 with low incomes. Most of the other provinces, along with the federal government, also offer aid to renters with low incomes. These programs keep a person's rent payment at or below 25% of their income.[17]

Collective Housing

Not everyone can, or wants to, live on their own in a house or an apartment. In 1981 20% of women 75 and over, and 13% of men, lived in collective dwellings — hospitals, hotels, rooming-houses, mental hospitals, nursing homes, etc. Women make up the largest group in collective dwellings, most of them in nursing homes. These people either never married or have no family to turn to, and their numbers in nursing homes increase with age.[18] Past the age of 65, 73% of men and 79% of women who live in collective dwellings live in special care institutions like nursing homes. This figure jumps to 80% for both sexes after age 75.[19]

Terms for nursing homes differ across the country. Manitoba calls them personal care homes. Personal care homes give four levels of care: Level 1 or hostel-level care — houskeeping and meals for people with a slight disability; Level 2 or personal care — two hours or less a day of nursing care; Levels 3 and 4 or extended care — three hours or more of nursing care a day. Most homes offer some of each type of care.

Ontario uses different terms: homes for the aged give one and a half hours or less of nursing care a day; nursing homes house people who need one and a half to three hours a day of care; chronic care hospitals house people who need more than three hours of care daily.

These fine distinctions work best on paper. "Virtually all beds in the Metro [Toronto]-run homes [for the aged] are extended care," Salem Alaton writes, "sometimes with residents needing over three hours a day of care. . . ."[20] Likewise, chronic care hospitals often house people who are well enough to move into nursing homes: a shortage of beds forces patients to stay in hospitals longer than they need to.

Here I use the term nursing home to mean personal care homes as Manitoba defines them or homes for the aged and nursing homes in Ontario. Private companies run some of these homes. Churches or service groups like the Lions Club run others.

The provinces set standards and inspect the homes, but nursing homes vary in the quality of care they offer and in their attitude to the patients. "A seven-month *Globe and Mail* investigation in 1981," writer Salem Alaton says, "found these homes to range in quality 'from excellent to appalling.'"[21]

At one home in Manitoba run by a private company, workers tell me that nurses slap patients or wheel them into closets to get them to "co-operate." Some people say that more of this sort of abuse goes on in profit-run homes. But even here, homes differ. At another home I know of, also run for profit, the head nurse fired a worker on the spot for shoving a patient. The worker filed a complaint with the union, but the company that owned the home stood behind the head nurse and refused the worker severance pay. It fought the union and won.

Professor Barry McPherson says that quality of care mostly depends on whom the nursing home is accountable to. When a patient pays the bills or when family pays the bills and visits often, quality of care goes up; when the government pays the bills and a patient gets few visits, quality of care drops. "Not surprisingly," he says, "people with good economic resources and a supportive family tend to enter institutions that provide a higher quality of health care and whose personnel demonstrate greater concern for the residents."[22]

Church-run homes have the best reputation. The Calvin Home, a church-run home in Winnipeg, treats patients like family. "On the night shift," Grace Hopkins, the head nurse, says, "everyone who gets a pill gets a hug — and everyone gets some kind of pill." It may sound hokey, but it works. "Touching," social worker Bruno Gelba says in an article on human bonding, "plays a very important role in creating a trusting and caring relationship." Older people, he says, often don't get enough human contact. They are moved, changed and bathed, but are seldom touched in a caring way.[23] The best homes go out of their way to make patients feel worthwhile and loved in spite of their institutional settings.

As our population ages, more and more people will need nursing home care. In Ontario and Manitoba, for instance, all nursing home beds are filled all the time: a person often has to wait up to a year to get into a home. This backs patients up in chronic and acute-care hospital beds. When this happens, costs soar. Chronic care in an Ontario hospital cost $109.97 a day in 1983 — about $40,000 a year. Acute care cost more than twice as much or $230.11 a day — almost $84,000 a year. Nursing home care cost only $42.35 a day in Ontario in 1983 — about 60% less than chronic hospital care.[24]

Still, nursing home care isn't cheap, and it is not the answer to the housing needs of many older people who need health care. Experts speak of the need for a continuum of care, with options ranging from chronic care hospitals to what Manitoba calls guest homes. Here an older person who needs little or no nursing care can receive some supervision — either a standby nurse in the home or one who visits a few times a week — and meals and cleaning help. In guest homes residents have more freedom and responsibility than in nursing homes. They clean their own rooms, bathe and care for themselves.

Guest homes free up nursing home beds. They also cost less than institutional care. Salem Alaton says that care for *ten residents* at one guest home in Toronto costs only $5,150 a month (or $515 per person), compared to $1,270 a month for *one patient* in a nursing home bed and $3,300 a month for *one patient* in a chronic care bed.[25]

Here, again, standards differ from home to home. Until a few years ago, older people in these homes lived under the worst conditions. In a case in Manitoba, one man looked after fifty-four people in four different homes. People signed their pension cheques over to the owner. In return they got their food — macaroni and cheese (light on the cheese), luncheon meat sandwiches and watery canned soup. The rooms were bug-infested. People who couldn't make it to the washrooms lay in their own filth. They received no health care, seldom left the house and sometimes never left their rooms. The province finally closed these homes down as fire traps.

Today in Manitoba, the provincial government sets standards and licenses guest homes (homes for the aged). The worst places have been closed or cleaned up, but the Association for Residential Care Homes in Manitoba admits that homes still range from ''good (to) mediocre to substandard.''[26]

Owners of these homes claim that they don't get enough government support to pay the bills, and some homes have closed for lack of funds. One owner of a Montreal guest home went on a hunger strike to protest the lack of money in his province. ''Like everyone else,'' Conrad Lemay said, ''we have bills to pay and it is very close to the point when we won't have any money left to pay them.''[27]

If the government doesn't fund these homes, older people suffer: many of them have no place else to go. When the Manitoba government threatened to close one home in 1981, for health violations, the tenants protested. ''This is my home,'' Kathy Stenson, 74, told Deborah Reed of *The Winnipeg Free Press.* ''It [the closing] is separating us. . . .''[28]

For all their drawbacks these homes play a role in housing older people. They take in people who can't live on their own but who aren't sick enough to go to a hospital or nursing home. Without guest homes, about three hundred people in Winnipeg alone would have to move into nursing homes or hospitals.

Houses, apartments and collective dwellings of all sorts form a grab-bag of housing choices for the older person. But even with these options not all older people can live the way they want to. There are problems with the system, and they must be solved.

Changes in the System

A good housing system offers the most options. It should help older people find and afford the kinds of housing they need. But today the rising cost of living and changes in city life make it hard for many older people to live where they want to. When the Ontario Advisory Commission on Aging asked older people about their housing problems, respondents put the cost of housing at the top of their list. In 1978, for instance, older families spent more than 50% of their total income on food and shelter (the average Canadian family spent only 33%).[29]

Homeowners

Homeowners, one might think, would have the least trouble with housing. They have higher incomes than people who live in apartments and more money in assets. They have equity in their houses and they enjoy the comfort of living in the same neighbourhood they have lived in for years. They receive government help to make repairs, and they get tax rebates.

Still, some older homeowners have trouble paying their bills. Half of all older homeowners live in houses built before 1940. Only 20% own houses built after 1960.[30] They own large homes — 85% of them are single-family detached — that cost a lot to heat and maintain.[31]

High taxes can also make a house too expensive to keep. In cities like Toronto and Vancouver, older neighbourhoods have begun to attract young urban professionals who buy up old houses and renovate them. These changes drive taxes up, and older people only reap the benefits of higher equity if they sell. That time comes sooner, rather than later, if they can't pay their taxes.

The government has programs that help — homeowner repair grants, loans and tax subsidies. But these programs don't always give enough relief to people on fixed incomes. A Canada Mortgage and Housing Corporation (CMHC) study in 1982 found, for instance, that 33% of elderly homeowners in cities had difficulty in paying their housing costs. Half of their expenses for shelter went to pay utilities.[32]

The government could expand its shelter allowances to include older homeowners as well as older people who rent. But these then become income subsidies to a select group of older people, and, says Professor Albert Rose of the University of Toronto Faculty of Social Work, we may have gone too far with subsidies already. "There has been, if anything," he says, "a degree of concern which may have been influenced more by sentiment and 'ancestor worship' than by a rational examination of the devotion of large quantities of scarce resources to older individuals and couples than to families. . . ."[33]

A program known but ignored in Canada would help give older people enough income to stay in their houses, and it wouldn't cost the government a cent. Experts call this a reverse-annuity mortgage (RAM).

Economics professor Yung-Ping Chen wrote about RAMs in the early 1970s in a study called "Unlocking Home Equity for the Elderly"; Dr Robert Butler reported on them in his study *Why Survive?* in 1975. So the idea of a reverse-annuity mortgage has been around for some time. But what are reverse-annuity mortgages? And how do they work?

Reverse-annuity mortgages allow older people to unfreeze the money tied up in their houses. Most older people own their homes outright, so they have large assets on paper, but they live cash poor. Housing may be worth a fortune, but inflation can make it hard for an older person to pay the gas or water bill. Jane Bryant Quinn, in a 1981 *Newsweek* story on reverse mortgages, writes that "It's like living in a bank vault, dead broke."[34]

Two types of reverse mortgages exist. In the most common plan, an older person takes a loan from a bank using the house as security. Then he or she buys a lifetime annuity from an insurance company. The company pays back the bank loan with interest each month and pays the older person a set amount to live on. (The federal government calls this a Reverse Annuity Model [RAM].)[35] This plan gives the older person the most security. The insurance company agrees to pay the annuity for the rest of the person's life, and the owner can stay in the house as long as he or she wants to.

The plan does, however, have some drawbacks. The interest paid to the bank varies each month with interest rates. When the rates go up, the interest payments eat into the annuity the older person gets. Some firms in the U.S. no longer offer these plans because with high interest rates the older person gets very little.

A further problem is that even if interest rates remain steady, people who need added income the most get the least money. The plans pay back a fixed amount each month for life, based on the homeowner's age and sex, so a 63-year-old widow who has no other income would get less than a 63-year-old man, with a pension, because she has a longer life expectancy. Bartel and Daly, a Canadian investment firm, suggests that these plans only make sense for people over the age of 69.

Also, RAMs count as income in Canada. The annuity payments change a person's tax status, and in some cases people can lose their federal or provincial pension supplements because they make too much money from RAMs.

A second type of plan gets around some of these problems and might work better in Canada. The government calls this type of plan a Rising Debt Model (RDM). With an RDM, older people can take a loan for up to 75% of their house's value. The loan gets paid out to them in fixed monthly instalments over, say, ten or fifteen years. At the end of that time, if the house has gone up in value, the owner can get a new loan for the increased amount. If not, he or she has either to pay back the loan each month or to sell the house to pay the loan and use any profits to find a new place to live.

This plan will not appeal to people under 70 who want to live in their houses until they die. But it may appeal to Canadians more than the RAM. With an RDM the debt grows over the years as money is paid out to the house owners: the interest and principal only come due at the end of the contract. Furthermore, the government counts money from an RDM as a loan, not income, so a person with a federal or provincial pension supplement won't lose his or her benefits.

"Reverse mortgages," according to one government report, "appear to offer a possible mechanism to assist the aged, both in keeping their homes and improving their financial status."[36] Economists Henry Bartel and Michael Daly write in a paper for the Economic Council of Canada that, "faced with the rising costs and consequent financial strain of home ownership, the very act of parting with an interest in their home, through a reverse mortgage, may generate the income to financially enable senior citizens to remain there for the rest of their lives.''[37]

These kinds of plans work well in Britain and France, and have begun to catch on in the U.S. A non-profit company, the San Francisco Development Fund, began an experiment with different types of reverse mortgages in April 1981. It geared its plan to low-to-moderate income homeowners in Marin County, California. Five other communities will soon try reverse mortgage programs.

The U.S. has also tried a sale/leaseback program. In this plan owners sell their houses to investors for about 70% of market value. The investor pays 10% in cash and the rest out over ten or fifteen years. The investor gets a bargain on the house, but has to pay taxes and maintenance costs. In addition, the investor buys a deferred annuity to assure a lifetime income to the seller after the mortgage is paid off.

''The seller may stay in the house as long as he likes, at a rent guaranteed to rise more slowly than his retirement income. In effect, the seller gives up the future appreciation of the property in return for lifetime occupancy at an affordable rent.''[38]

At the moment, none of these plans have taken hold in Canada. And if we want them here, the government will probably have to help get them in motion. First, in Canada people can't deduct from taxable income interest paid out to the bank by an RAM. In the U.S. and in Britain they can. People stand to gain less from RAMs here. Second, as mentioned earlier, RAM annuity payments count as income in Canada. They are taxed and sometimes put people over their pension supplement minimum income. Third, people tend not to know much about these plans here, and they may be reluctant to get into something so new.

The government could do a few things to help establish these plans in Canada. It could exempt these annuities from income; it could make RAM interest payments tax deductible; it could educate people about these plans, and also set guidelines and enforce rules to protect older homeowners from fraud.

Reverse mortgages alone won't solve all the financial problems older homeowners face. For one thing, older homeowners had an average of only $35,000 in equity in 1982, which means that reverse mortgages alone won't cover their housing costs. But along with tax credits and government aid for repairs, the Canada Mortgage and Housing Corporation (CMHC) predicts that reverse mortgages would help "the affordability problems of elderly owners . . . decrease significantly."[39]

Renters

Renters also face high costs for housing. They pay more for housing than owners even though they generally have less money. Renters on the average in 1976 had incomes of about 75% that of homeowners, but owners spent an average of only $1800 on housing, while renters spent $2300.[40] In 1978 a fifth of renters 65 and over paid more than 40% of their income for shelter. The CMHC uses 25% of income as a standard. By this standard almost half of all older people who rent apartments live in unaffordable housing.[41] Single renters in 1978, many of them widows, paid more for rent than any other group.[42]

Rising oil prices drive rents up, as do higher interest rates. Poor people can move into subsidized housing, but a middle-class person on a fixed income, in an apartment, often has no alternative but to pay more.[43]

Jessie Fuller, 78, faced this problem. She had to move from her high-rise apartment because the owners of the building turned it into a condominium. She didn't want to buy the apartment, and couldn't afford to in any case, so she moved. After she had settled into her new apartment she found out that when her lease ran out the owners planned to turn this building into a condominium too. This time she decided to fight. She circulated a petition and organized her neighbours. They fought the developers' plan in city council and won.

The developers will try again, and next time they may win. Then Jessie will have to pay or move. She's not poor, but each year she and other middle-income older people have to use more of their income for rent, forcing them to make cuts in their standard of living.

In 1971 a group of older people in Winnipeg decided to combat rising rents by building their own apartment complex — Stafford Gardens.

"When I came to Winnipeg sixteen years ago," Mrs Livia Gary says, "I was seventy years old. I moved into an apartment but soon found the rent rising faster than my income. I moved, but again found the rent too high."

At an Age and Opportunity (A & O) convention in 1970, she became interested in the issue of housing for seniors, particularly in the idea of older people planning and owning their own apartments. A & O staff encouraged her to start her own housing corporation, and at the age of 75 Mrs Gary became the director of Canada's first housing corporation run by and for older people.

To get the kind of housing she wanted she had to fight a two-year battle, often against the very people who were supposed to be giving her advice. "We fought, from the day we started, to get what we wanted," she says. "We worked to get it and we're still working."

When she found, for instance, that the Manitoba Housing Authority had a rule stipulating that single seniors living alone must live in bachelor suites, she fought for bedrooms. Now 65% of the suites in her apartment block have bedrooms. She also fought for carpets and even for safety rails in bathrooms.

"When we were building this place," she says, "I said: 'I'm building a place for myself.' And I still feel that I built this place. . . . This is ours. Anything that's wanted, we pay for it. It isn't somebody doing something for us, it's us doing it ourselves."

Today residents in this complex don't have to worry about being gouged on their rents. Rent increases have stayed on a par with increases in the Canada Pension Plan. In terms of their rent, they are just as well off today as they were ten years ago. (In 1980, a one-bedroom suite rented for $157 per month.)

Two years ago Mrs Gary and her corporation built a second

apartment complex. "Any group," she says, "can get together and build their own — and they can build what they need."

Alice Thompson, a 75-year-old Calgarian, would agree. She's the past president of the Elder Statesmen, "a group of old people who organized to design, build and manage housing for the elderly."[44] Mrs Thompson faced some of the same problems Mrs Gary faced — cramped housing, high costs, housing in run-down inner-city neighbourhoods.

Mrs Thompson began building six-plex apartments designed to give older people the kind of housing they wanted. Ian McDougall, an architect, advised the group. "He found that the elderly dislike ground floor apartments, want to leave a building without being seen by gossips sitting in a front lobby. . . . In individual units, he planned more cupboard and storage space for the accumulation of long lives. He lowered shelves, raised electrical outlets and provided bathtubs with safety bars and a handy cord-pull alarm."

Like Mrs Gary, Mrs Thompson found that older people can get what they want if they work together and fight for it.

Collective Dwellings

Some people can't fight for themselves: they're too old, too sick or too powerless. They are a small group (about 5 per 1000 people over 65) but they often need the most help. They live alone, in poor health, in rooming-houses and hotels in the worst parts of the city. Sociologists call them SROs (single-room occupants).

As part of a television report on aging two years ago I went with a cameraman to talk to some of these people at the Aurora, a dilapidated hotel in the downtown core of Winnipeg.

The lobby was dark, much cooler than the street outside. The coolness settled on my skin like a damp towel. More than anything the lobby stank — a combination of beer, sweat and vomit.

John sat on a bench near the front desk. I didn't see him at first. He blended in with the colourless lobby, sitting staring into space, a tweed cap on his head.

"Can we interview you for TV?" I asked.

We settled on a fee of one dollar. John's face is creviced so deep that it shrinks inward away from itself. His left eye is all white, rolled permanently up into its socket. His body gives a single message: he wants to create the smallest possible target. He sits with his legs crossed, his arms folded in front of his chest and his shoulders hunched forward. He looks like an emaciated boxer against the ropes in the fifteenth round. He just wants to finish the fight.

John rents his room by the month. He lives on bologna sandwiches from the hotel coffee shop and drinks in the local bars. About the cost of living he says, "It's too much."

From the tangle of his criss-crossed arms and legs a finger points and wags as he speaks. He speaks hoarsely, half in a whisper, partly so the desk clerk won't hear him, partly out of sheer exhaustion.

"He's not supposed to open pension cheques," John says. His finger points to the clerk at the front desk. "He's not allowed."

"He opens your pension cheques, does he?"

"Yeah, he gets the cheque from the postman. He looks to see how much. In the winter he cashes the cheque. He takes a commission — five dollars. He takes next month's rent too. He's not supposed to take next month's rent. I'm not finished with this month yet. It's not right."

It's not right. It's not legal. As John speaks, the hotel manager keeps walking between us to hear what he's saying. John's angry, but he can't do anything. He's barely surviving.

In 1982, Independent Television in Edmonton aired a report called "Sunset on Skid Row," which looked at the old men who live in Edmonton's Boyle Street community. On 95th Street the crew went into a rooming house, a burned out building that houses drug dealers, outcasts and old men no one else will take. Local social workers won't go into the building after dark.

There they spoke with George, a "psychiatric case," who had had his right leg amputated a few years earlier. Now his left leg had swollen to twice its normal size and had turned green. He refused to go to a hospital, because he was afraid the doctors would cut that leg off too. He'd rather die of gangrene than lose his independence.

Then there was Peter, who got Meals on Wheels — his only hot food. He received one meal a day but said that one meal could last him three or four days.

There was a man, an alcoholic, who was slowly committing suicide by drinking shaving lotion: his liver was double its normal size. Another man had spent his $400 pension cheque on liquor in three days.

How many men live like this? In 1976 Wendy Zink Smith conducted a study of men in Winnipeg's Main Street area. On the basis of census data she judged that about 350 single men over the age of 45 rent housing on or near Main Street. And single men, she pointed out, constitute 72% of men 65 and over.[45] This older age group, she found, "dominates the age structure of the area," and she predicted that with a growing older population the size of this group would increase, as would their problems.

Most of these men live in the hotels and boarding houses on Main Street. They have low incomes. They spend their time in the bars and pool halls along the strip. And they eat — when they eat — in small restaurants and coffee shops.

Most of them have lived this way all their lives. When they were young they worked for the railway, or in logging and mining camps in the North and West. Some of them served in the Canadian forces. During the Depression they travelled around the country to find work, and when the Depression ended they never settled down to a middle-class life.[46]

Peter, an 88-year-old Winnipeg man, told me that he had immigrated to Canada in 1926. His brother got him a job as a cook for the CNR, and during the '30s he worked on the railroad. Later he worked as a camp cook in Shiloh for the army.

"Money," he said, "comes and goes. I made good money when I worked. When the jobs ended sometimes I had no money for two, three months. I spent whatever I made."

Now he lives in a Main Street hotel along with other similar men. He gets clothes from his brother's wife and family, who also take him home for supper once in a while. But few of these men have this kind of close contact with kin. Those who do have relatives — some still have wives — rarely see them.

They live here because they have problems with alcohol or because they can't cope with normal work and family life. Main Street accepts the way they act. These men change addresses often, but they seldom move out of the Main Street area. A study of skid row in Toronto found the same pattern.[47]

In the late 1970s the city of Winnipeg began to destroy many of the buildings on Main Street. In 1977, for instance, the inner city lost 178 rooming house rooms. Between 1972 and 1979 developers tore down about 400 units.[48]

A group of people led by Yhetta Gold of Age and Opportunity, Inc., became concerned about this trend and set out to create more housing for old men in the inner city. With support from CMHC they gutted and rebuilt a rundown Main Street hotel called Jack's.

It cost $595,000 to rebuild Jack's, not counting architects' fees, legal fees and the cost of the building. In 1977 it opened as a senior citizens' hotel. The sign in the window today reads: "Board and Room for Senior Citizens. Also available — meals by the day, week or month." Jack's shows what can be done to create liveable housing for even the most destitute older people.

I visited Jack's on a winter day in 1984. It sits across the street from the Lighthouse Mission and Jimmy's Food Market and two doors down from the Epic theatre ("U Have to Be 18 to Enter"). The stainless steel front doors and the heavy wood benches bolted to the concrete tell you that this is a tough neighbourhood.

A half-dozen men sat on a bench to my right past the office and front desk. They all looked up when I came in. I found out later from Pat, the recreation director at Jack's, that these men have a strong sense of territory: they know everyone in the hotel and they don't like strangers.

"Is Pat around?" I asked.

"Back there," one man said.

Pat sat by herself at a card-table in the open recreation room on the first floor. The room held a pool table, card-tables, a shuffleboard game and, at the back, a colour television and a Franklin stove. She was the only woman in the place. Only two women had ever stayed at Jack's. "I'd rent to one," she said. "But they get the picture pretty fast. They feel out of place."

Pat took me on a tour. We rode the elevator along with two tenants — a short man with a full white beard and a floppy hat and a big man with suspenders and a beer belly. We stopped at the top floor. There was a smell of urine in the stuffy hallway.

The architects had left the old plaster walls, a foot thick on the ground floor, and painted them a cream colour. They had changed the windows from the light shaft to double pane aluminium. Each room has a freshly-painted ruby red door with a silver metal room number on it.

Pat showed me one of the rooms. It held a bed, a desk and a chair.

"8 by 10?" I asked.

"More like 6 by 9," Pat said.

The room had no closet. Six feet off the floor a piece of woodwork with hooks held an array of trousers and shirts.

"The rooms at the front are bigger," Pat said, "but most are like this. That's one of the problems. The men say they'd like to have closets."

Each floor has two toilets, one at each end of the hall, a bath and a shower. Each floor also has a closet with a mop, pail and broom in it. The hotel expects each man to take care of his own room. The fourth floor also has a laundry room with washing machines, dryers and a colour television so the men can watch TV while they do their wash. There is no charge for the machines.

"Do the men use them?" I asked, pointing to the washers.

"Not much, I'm afraid. You have to keep after them about keeping themselves and their rooms clean.

"Once a week they get fresh sheets and towels delivered to their doors. Then you have to get after them to change their sheets. Some do, some don't. I go through all the rooms on Monday each week and give 'em heck."

The basement houses Jack's cafeteria. The men pay by the

month for their room and board (three meals a day). For room and board in 1984 the men paid a minimum of $332 a month, leaving even the poorest of them about $200 a month to spend. Men who earned more money paid a higher rate according to their income.

The CMHC has praised the idea of a cafeteria and "board" for tenants. Too often men on the strip wind up broke and hungry by the twentieth of the month. At Jack's they pay for room and board in advance, thus ensuring "that these old men spend a portion of their monthly income on food, as well as drink."

The menu at Jack's changes each day on a four-week cycle so the men get variety. At breakfast they have toast, juice, eggs and coffee (there are bacon, sausage, eggs and pancakes on Sunday). For lunch they get soup, a sandwich, a piece of cake or pie and a piece of fruit. For supper they get meatloaf, shepherd's pie or corned beef, potatoes and a vegetable, coffee and cake. They get milk at each meal, and can eat all they want.

How does Jack's compare to other housing options for these men? At Jack's in 1979 the men on the average paid 62% of their income for room and board. The CMHC evaluation study of Jack's found that only the Salvation Army offered a cheaper option — an average of 45% of income for room and board. The men, however, say they don't like the Sally Ann, where they have to live in dormitories with no privacy. They complain that people steal their things, that their dorm-mates are too dirty, and that the Salvation Army puts more limits on when they can come and go.

Men in rooming-houses in the same area spent about 71% of their income on room and board, and at one nearby hotel men spent 78% of their income on basics — 16% more than they paid at Jack's.

The study concluded that "the men residing at Jack's are 'better off' with respect to rental costs, than their counterparts who are living in non-subsidized accommodation. . . . [Food] costs are high, but when they are compared to those for the hotel, the rooming house, and the bachelor apartment, Jack's emerges as the most affordable form of accommodation."[49]

But cost doesn't measure the full benefit of living at Jack's.

When Yhetta Gold and her group designed Jack's they tried to create a high quality of life for the tenants, not just inexpensive housing. For instance, they encouraged an "informal alarm system": if a man didn't show up for a few meals, other tenants would check on him. Too many times in local hotels "guys died and weren't found until the smell bothered others."[50]

This system works well. Men will tell Pat if someone has been missing for a few days. She in turn watches for anyone who seems sick or who needs help. Jack's also has a twenty-four hour maintenance man on duty. He locks the front doors at 5:00 p.m. Each man has a key so that he can come and go as he pleases, but the locked doors keep outsiders from drifting in.

The men also receive help in caring for themselves if they need it. When they move in, for instance, Pat helps them recover from any illnesses they have picked up living in run-down rooms.

"It takes quite a while to get them up to a decent standard," she says. "I help them get glasses, hearing-aids. I work them up to it slowly."

Not all the men want Pat's help, and they are free to refuse it, but after a while they come to trust her. They rely on her and the other staff in a hundred little ways. She helps them set up bank accounts and manage their money. On the bulletin board near the elevator a sign reads: "Income tax preparation Feb. 27, 9:00 a.m., downstairs." Pat has arranged for someone from the income tax bureau to help the men fill out their forms.

Someone works in the cafeteria to help the men who can't carry their own trays. Pat arranges for a barber to come in every two months to give the men haircuts. She sponsors New Year's and Christmas dinners and a summer picnic in the local park. Last year 32 out of the 42 tenants turned out for the picnic.

Do the men like living at Jack's? They tend to move in and stay, and this says a lot about how much they like it there. In 1979 the tenants at Jack's had lived in their previous residences for an average of 2.6 years. Almost half had stayed less than a year, and almost three quarters had stayed two years or less.

In 1983 half of Jack's tenants had lived there more than three years, and of the ten people who left Jack's that year only four left by choice. Two abandoned their rooms and two moved to another place.[51] In other words most of the men who live in Jack's don't want to leave. For many of them this will be their last home before they go to a hospital or nursing home to die.

The CMHC study of Jack's concluded that Jack's is a successful project and that it meets an obvious need. It also recommended the building of more places like Jack's for ''down-and-out'' men.[52] Other cities have begun to think of similar housing for older men. Judy MacDonald of the Saskatchewan Housing Corporation visited Jack's in 1981 to report on its design. Regina has begun to design a Jack's-style hotel, and in 1984 housing planners from Montreal, Calgary and Edmonton visited Jack's to study how it works.

Older men like Jack's tenants make up only a small part of the older population, but the hotel can teach us about housing older people in general.

First, Jack's shows that different types of older people define their housing needs differently. You or I might not want to live at Jack's, but it suits its tenants just fine. It feels, looks and smells like an old hotel, and that's the idea. The CMHC study of Jack's found that '''oldness' is important to the men who live there.''

''The men who live at Jack's,'' the report says, ''like living there despite the small, stuffy rooms. . . . As one old guy said, 'Living in an old building which has been modernized is simply a continuation of what I've always been doing'''[53] The report went on to say that ''the attempt should be made to incorporate this characteristic oldness into the hotel-boarding-house model,'' and it even suggested furnishing hotels like Jack's with used furniture so that they would feel ''old'' from the start.

At Jack's the men feel no pressure to reform or live up to someone else's idea of how they should live. It is their place. They pay their rent, and they come and go as they please. Jack's meets their need for independence, while at the same time providing ''recreational opportunities, friendship, familiarity, security, comfort — elements that are difficult to quantify, but which are important for the quality of life. . . ."[54]

Second, Jack's pays its own way. The tenants pay the mortgage, recreation costs and upkeep through their rent. In a time of government restraint Jack's shows that a program for older people in need can carry itself without ongoing government aid.

Third, Jack's shows that housing can help people create informal social networks. Most older people want to stay in their own homes and neighbourhoods. They often rely on friends and neighbours to help them when they need something, and they help their neighbours in return. Jack's encourages the building up of mutual support and networks, as did Stafford Gardens.

Sociologists and planners agree that as our population ages, informal networks will become more and more important. They make good economic sense and even better social sense. These networks create a community for every older person, and this leads to high life satisfaction.

Jack's also serves as a model for a new kind of housing for older people. The Canadian Council on Social Development calls it "Enriched Elder Persons' Housing" (EEPH). EEPH "is concerned with the elderly persons' total environment — as an integral part of shelter. It is the link between the other two options: Self-Contained Housing and Personal Care Home."[55] This type of housing points the way to design for the future.

The Future

As people get older they find it harder and harder to live alone.

Betty Havens, Manitoba's provincial gerontologist, found that shelter needs were high or moderately high for men and women among all age groups of older people. She found that the need for household maintenance and help with food and clothing went up for women with age.[56] But even when services exist, she says, older people often can't get to them. A 1975 Winnipeg housing survey, for instance, found that out of eleven items, people ranked the need for a bus-stop near their home as number one. They ranked a grocery second.[57] Betty Havens found that the highest need for both men and women is "the need for resources to be more accessible."[58]

This need will grow in the next few years. By 2001 people 80 years old and over will make up almost a quarter of all people over 65 (they made up 19% in 1980). And we know that after the age of 80 "ability to live alone drops sharply."[59] If we want to help older people stay independent in the future, we'll have to plan for it.

Professor Albert Rose says that tenants who move into senior citizen housing in their sixties will often stay in these apartments until they have to move to a nursing home. At the end of their lives they'll need more and more help to stay on their own. "So-called senior citizen buildings," he writes, "will become homes for the aged."[60] Housing managers will have to provide support for their tenants, and planners should build this support into housing project designs.

Professor Gloria Gutman, who studied housing needs in the Vancouver area, says that many people in retirement housing want and need on-site services. Contrary to some people's beliefs that provision of housekeeping, meals, medical and recreational services will promote excessive independency and disengagement, she argues that the availability of such services leads to a more active social life, with more "dressing up" and "getting out" than before.[61]

Most public housing built since 1960 lacks these services. A Canadian Council on Social Development study, *Beyond Shelter*, found that in 1970 90% of self-contained apartments for seniors lacked any staff who worked more than ten hours a week. People often couldn't get to community services: in 55% of the developments studied people couldn't walk to a medical clinic, and in 46% of the developments people couldn't get to a shopping centre. Sixty percent had no homemaker service, 80% had no food-shopping service and 63% had no meal delivery service.

People also lacked recreational facilities and opportunities.

Eighty-six percent of developments had no group leadership service, only 10% had a senior centre on-site and 33% lacked access to a beauty shop. People rely on their residence for social, physical, emotional, mental and spiritual stimulation, but few buildings meet these needs.[62]

When the Lions Club of Winnipeg built its third senior apartment building — Lions Place — it set out to avoid these mistakes. It planned for the future needs of the tenants.

Lions Place opened in August 1983. It cost $14.35 million to build. It has eighteen storeys — sixteen for apartments and the first two floors for recreation and meeting space. There are 255 one-bedroom units (no bachelor apartments), 16 two-bedroom suites and 16 suites for disabled people. In all there are about 350 tenants.[63] None of these facts give a feel for the design of Lions Place. If Jack's is the Volkswagen of public housing (dependable, but basic), Lions Place is the Lincoln Continental.

When you come in from Portage Avenue you enter an open two-storey sunlit foyer. A hotel-style front desk stands in front of you. Hanging plants filter the light from a glass-enclosed walkway above. On the right, stairs ascend to the second floor balcony overlooking the entry hall. Further to the right, potted ferns and small trees are set alongside lounge-chairs in front of floor to ceiling windows that look out onto the street. Behind this lounge stretches over 5,000 square feet of lounge space with card-tables, soft chairs for reading or relaxing and more plants. At the back of the lounge stands a two-storey humidified greenhouse where tenants can take classes in gardening and care for their own plants. To the left from the front desk past the building's three elevators, the east wing houses a beauty salon, a craft shop, a convenience store, an extension of the public library and space for a small geriatric clinic with examination rooms.

On the second floor there is another recreation area about one-and-a-half times the lounge downstairs. This includes a coffee shop, an exercise area, a glass-roofed walkway, a carpet bowling alley, an arts and crafts room and a billiard room. The exercise area includes a whirlpool, sauna and changing rooms. The second floor also holds a kitchen and a dining room that seats 150 people, a meeting room for up to 90 people and a multi-purpose room for 170 people. Finally, there is a wood-panelled theatre with a full stage, dressing rooms and projection booth.

Each of the upper floors has a laundry room with washers and dryers (free to tenants), a lounge and a tub room for people who need help bathing. The builders carpeted the bedrooms and living-rooms in each suite. The kitchens and bathrooms have resilient flooring. Tenants can control the air-conditioning and heat in their own suites. Each suite comes with a refrigerator and stove.

Lions Place looks and feels like a simple but well-equipped hotel. How do you build a luxury high-rise for older people in a time of government restraint when the CMHC no longer has an interest in senior housing? And when the government only allots 200 new senior suites a year to the entire province of Manitoba?

"You negotiate," Jake Suderman says with a smile.

Jake Suderman is Winnipeg's Svengali of senior citizen housing, turning empty lots into luxury high-rises for older people. He now manages three buildings for the Lions Club of Winnipeg — Lions Gate, Lions Manor and Lions Place. And he is a master at outmanoeuvring bureaucrats and goading politicians into action.

"We started out with $80,000 from the Barbara Bell estate," Jake says. "I didn't know Mrs Bell knew about us, but one day I got a call from her trust fund manager. He said she had left Lions Manor (our second building) all this money for capital projects. When I heard about the money I thought we should build a new building, and that's how it got started."

He convinced the Lions Club board of directors of the benefits of the plan, then found some property for sale a block from Lions Manor. He negotiated to buy for about $1 million. Then he went to the CMHC to arrange a loan. The Winnipeg Lions Club runs some of the best senior housing projects in the country, and the CMHC knew they would get high-quality housing for their dollars. They approved the plan.

Lloyd Axworthy, federal MP and former provincial MLA from the Winnipeg core area, also supported the project. Lions Place soon became a part of the Winnipeg Core Area Initiative Development Plan. The federal government allowed the Lions Club to build a 287-suite building by giving it suite allotments not used by other provinces.

With the basic plan approved Jake started a new round of negotiations, this time over the size of the suites and the amount of lounge space. "What you can build," he says, "is dictated by land cost. The CMHC allows $3,500 per suite, and then so many square feet for amenity space. Sometimes you have to embarrass them into changing the rules. I said, 'You're going to build three hundred apartments with *three* lounges? You're kidding? You're going to build a morgue here.'

"In the end, we got the lounge space we wanted. And we got bigger apartments — the smallest one-bedroom has 515 square feet. The two-bedroom apartments have 725 square feet. We have twelve empty rooms in the building just for future use as tub rooms, and space downstairs for a small geriatric clinic."

Once the project was underway the City of Winnipeg put $700,000 into the building, the Lions Club raised $1 million and the Winnipeg Foundation donated $100,000 for furniture and supplies. In the end the CMHC backed a mortgage for over $13 million. The tenants' rents along with a government subsidy cover the mortgage costs each month.

A one-bedroom suite at Lions Place costs a maximum of 25% of a person's monthly income. The lowest rent came to $325 in January 1984. If this equalled more than 25% of a person's income they could apply for a provincial subsidy of up to $140 a month to make up the difference. No one pays more than $450 a month, no matter what their income.

But luxury doesn't come cheap. Even the highest rent doesn't cover the cost of an apartment each month. To break even, Jake Suderman says, Lions Place would have to charge $700 to $800 a month. Government subsidies cover the difference between what the tenants pay and the cost of running the building. Lions Place tries to keep a mix of income groups to pay the expenses and keep the subsidy low, but no matter how you look at it it costs the taxpayers a lot of money each month. What can justify this cost?

For one thing, expenses cover more than the cost of the mortgage. Lions Place has a three-member full-time staff to organize volunteers and programs for the tenants. The staff runs arts and crafts programs, physical fitness programs, day trips, guest lectures, theatre productions, gardening classes and discussion groups. (A Canada Works grant pays for another worker who runs special programs for male tenants — a weekend shopping junket to the U.S., for instance, or a recent garage sale auction that raised $3,100 for future program expenses.) These programs keep people physically and psychologically fit. They have at least one person on staff who can deal with medical and other emergencies, twenty-four hours a day.

The managers, staff and programs at Lions Place make all the difference between good and bad housing.

"Tenants like their suites and the design of the building," Jake Suderman says, "but more than anything else they like the staff. In their old apartments they only had a landlord or maybe a family that didn't care much for them. Around here we say, 'We're here just for you.' They know they can approach us. We get them involved — like in the auction or in the annual tea. And we make them feel at home. We let them have something to say."

Lions Place also has plans for the future. They may cost money now, but they'll pay for themselves later. Lions Place tenants now average about 75 years of age, but as they get older their needs will change.

"When you first open a building, you have to take only the healthiest people because of all the construction and change. But most of these people will live here until they die or get too sick to live alone. That's why we have twelve tub rooms in the building. They're empty now, and the CMHC doesn't like to guarantee mortgages for empty rooms. But they're set aside so that as people get older the staff can help them bathe. We may as well build them now: we know we're going to need them."

Jake says that many buildings for older people don't have enough space, and he advises groups or towns planning new buildings for older people to leave space in them for expanded services. He says they need space for a common dining room, for medical treatment and also for special programs.

Jake built Lions Place with these future needs in mind. As people get older they may not be able to cook for themselves in their own suites. Then the dining room on the second floor — a luxury now — will meet a basic need for many tenants. Lions Place also has 16 two-bedroom units, an expensive extra, but these suites allow families — two sisters and a brother, or a mother and daughter — to live together and care for one another as they age. The two-bedroom suites help maintain informal support networks.

Jake also wants to set up a closed-circuit TV channel that will broadcast Lions Place events to people who can't get out. He has already bought $4,000 worth of video equipment to tape field trips and tours.

All these plans and designs cost money now, but in 1983-84 the Manitoba Health Services Commission spent $134.6 million on nursing home care, a figure that will rise each year (it was less than $120 million in 1982-83). Through good design and planning, Lions Place will help people stay in their own apartments as long as possible, and this will save taxpayers money in the long run.

Ontario, for instance, has just invested $30 million in a home-care program for Toronto. The program helps people stay at home at about half the cost of nursing home care. A Canadian Medical Association task force report predicts that keeping people at home could save Canadian taxpayers more than $6 billion a year by 2020. But home care and enriched settings like Lions Place do more than save taxpayers' money. They help older people remain active, involved and independent as long as possible, and that's something you can't put a price on.

Lions Place has one further future goal that makes the most sense of all. In the neighbourhood around the building, 14% of the population is over 65 — about 5,000 older people in all. Ten buildings like Lions Place couldn't house all these people, so Lions

Place has set up an outreach program to help older people in the neighbourhood stay in their own homes. The government agreed to the two floors of recreation and lounge space partly for this reason.

The Lions Club has set aside a quarter of a million dollars for this outreach program. First, with the help of local churches the outreach program will survey the 5,000 older people in the neighbourhood to assess their needs.

Second, once Lions Place knows what local people need, it will set up programs to serve them. For instance, the Lions Place dining room will offer meals to non-tenants at a low cost. For people in the neighbourhood who can't get out, the kitchen will prepare Meals on Wheels. Lions Place will open all its recreation and cultural programs to non-tenants. The geriatric mini-clinic will allow older people in the neighbourhood to get treatment and check-ups without a cross-town trek to the doctor.

Third, Lions Place will offer services like lawncutting, painting, plumbing and home maintenance so that people can stay in their own homes. People need all of these services already. "For every service provided," Professor Albert Rose says, "there could be 10 additional units of service. . . ."[64] These services will become more vital in the future, but through careful planning Lions Place will be ready to meet increased needs.

Today most older people still rely on their families for support.[65] The parents of the baby boom, who come of age in the next twenty or thirty years, will have children to help them, but in the next century, when the baby boomers themselves grow old, that family support will decrease. Young parents today have fewer children; many people have none at all. By 2011 older people will feel the effects of the "baby bust," and they will need new types of support to take the place of the family.[66]

Some new options have sprung up already, mostly in other countries. Australia, for instance, offers "Granny Cottages" to older people. The government sets up a modular portable cottage for a parent on a son or daughter's property. When the older person dies or moves to a nursing home the government takes the cottage away. This allows children to care for their parents as long as they can.

Holland has housed 15% of its older people in adapted houses in which one-bedroom apartments are equipped with alarms connected to a central desk in the lobby. Older people can live on their own with the assurance that they can get help if they need it. Holland plans to house 25% of its older people in this way by 1985.[67]

In England, the Abbeyfield Society helps homeowners find roommates. By 1979 the Society had helped set up 700 houses for older people.[68] In the U.S. there is a similar program called "Share-a-Home": older people with big houses share them with other seniors. In Florida, groups of older people form into families, hire a manager and staff to help with food shopping, housekeeping, laundry and transportation.[69] These groups offer older people the chance to form caring communities and maintain their independence as long as possible.

Seniors in Canada have also tried home-sharing. Programs exist from coast to coast, and studies show that they work well. A report on home-sharing in Dartmouth, Nova Scotia, for instance, concludes that the program "has been successful in matching seniors and others to live together in comfortable, economic, human living conditions."[70] A report on another program, this time in Ontario, concludes that "home sharing can successfully include a number of variables such as age, sex, location, financial and social status."[71]

Maggie Kuhn, Gray Panther leader in the U.S., takes home-sharing a step further. She suggests "intergenerational shared living" to take the place of an extended family. Single people of all ages — old and young — live together in a house and share the costs of food, heat, lighting, home repairs, rent and even a car. This helps both older people on small budgets and young people just starting out in careers. Older members have someone to rely on if they need help, and young people get "comfort, advice, and a sense of 'survivorship' and stability."

The Gray Panthers in the U.S. have set up a special project fund to develop intergenerational housing alternatives. In Seattle, Washington, for instance, they help run "a home — or apartment — sharing counseling referral service." From 1978 to 1980 this program paired about 200 people. It also offers advice and aid to home-sharers after they move in together. In Boston the Gray Panthers bought and renovated a group of houses, then rented them at low rents to matched and screened older people.

Shared living, Maggie Kuhn says, can help widows or frail older people stay in their homes, maintain their houses and pay expenses. And it helps some people stay out of nursing homes. More than anything else, she says, it allows people — older and younger — to share with one another in a family setting.[72]

Older people, according to a recent government report, "want variety of kinds of housing ranging from single family dwellings and apartments to institutional living and the like. Some seek neighbourhoods offering multi-generational living; others prefer to live with their peer groups."[73]

Above all older Canadians need options and resources so that they can choose the kind of housing they want. The number of choices is growing every day.

PROVIDE, PROVIDE: PENSION PLANS

A Need for Pension Reform

Vic Watson is 76. His wife died a year ago and now he lives by himself. In 1980 Vic received $384.16 a month from the Canada Pension Plan and Old Age Security. He added $100 from his savings each month, which brought his monthly income to less than $500, or about $6,000 a year. Statistics Canada set the low income cut-off for 1980 at $5,822, so by government standards Vic lived just above the poverty line. I visited him to learn what it meant to be old and poor.

Vic has a large one-bedroom apartment with a balcony on the eleventh floor of a suburban high-rise. He brewed us some coffee that he blends for himself at the Bay, and while we waited for it I looked out the living-room window at the river and the big park beyond it. "On summer mornings," Vic says, "I like to get up early. I sit on the balcony and watch the sun come up. Sometimes I lie here nude on the living-room floor and soak up the sun."

For that luxury he spents $250 — almost half his monthly income — on rent. That doesn't leave him much. "I could live downtown in a cheaper place," he says, "but I'd face three brick walls, and then what would I have?"

Instead Vic makes the rest of his money go as far as it can. He has an apartment-sized freezer in his kitchen. He buys meat on sale, freezes it and uses it weeks later when prices have gone up. He showed me half-a-dozen packages of New Zealand lamb chops that he had bought in the summer when prices were low. He also buys cheap cuts of meat, like chuck, and trims them himself.

Vic enjoys life, but since he retired he has had to scale down his pleasures. Now he focuses on the little things. He mixes his own spices, blends his own teas and even pickles his own tomatoes. He insisted I try one, even though it was only ten in the morning.

Like Vic, older Canadians may not have a lot, but they don't go hungry or roam the streets. Today a combination of government pension plans and services create a safety net for even the poorest older people. This safety net ensures that most older people live above the poverty line.

In general for older people, demographers Leroy Stone and Michael MacLean say, "we don't get the impression of major inadequacy of incomes relative to expenditures. . . . Indeed, for the large cities in 1974 [there is] . . . a tangible margin of excess. . . ." They go on to predict that in the year 2000 older people's incomes will increase again by about 35% for men and 39% for women.[1]

Louis Harris's poll for the National Council of Aging in the U.S. supports this prediction. In 1981 he found that older people didn't report any more financial worries than the young. Median household incomes, he found, did drop with age, but 47% of those 65 and over did not agree that older people were worse off today than in the past. And of those older people with the lowest incomes (under $5,000 a year) 36% said finances were hardly a problem at all. "Despite significant age differences in household income," Harris says, "elderly Americans . . . are no more likely than younger Americans to feel financially strapped."[2]

In 1981 Tom Atkinson of York University asked 3,000 Canadians about life satisfaction and found that people over 65 in Canada report higher life satisfaction than any other group. "As people get older," he writes, "they rate the quality of life higher.

Income doesn't seem to influence their ratings. They feel at ease with their lives."[3]

Some studies go a step further. They show that older people have more financial stability than the young. Professor David Cheal, sociologist at the University of Winnipeg, has spent three years studying family gift-giving patterns. Most people, he says, assume that the very old (along with the very young) get the most help from others. This may be true when it comes to government pensions or health services, but it's not true within the family.

Cheal went to the Statistics Canada Consumer Expenditure Survey. He found that, in the family, money flows *from* older *to* younger people throughout the life cycle.[4] The young, he found, get more from middle-aged and older people, but "adult children received more tangible aid from their parents than they gave."[5] Even as income drops in old age gift giving only drops off slightly. "The elderly in Canada in fact incur relatively large financial *losses* in their interpersonal transactions."[6]

Income, however, is not the only element in the typical older person's finances. As Professor Cheal shows, many older people have savings that add to their income. He found, for instance, that while average total wealth decreased after age 64, liquid assets, like savings, did not. They reached their peak in old age, and older people tended to give this money away. "Many old people are relatively better off than earlier analyses had suggested . . . [and] many of the aged in North America have significant economic resources available for their own use and for transfer to others."[7]

Older people also have other resources besides savings. The Economic Council of Canada reports that in 1971, for instance, 75% of older men and 55% of older women owned their own homes, often free of mortgage. Those who live in apartments often receive rent subsidies. Older people also get discounts on travel and theatre tickets, and most communities offer free recreation programs for seniors. Taking this all together, researchers Stone and MacLean say, would raise older peoples' total average income by at least 30%,[8] and even this probably underestimates total income: other sources of income include non-cash benefits like subsidized health care costs and housekeeping services.[9]

Today older people in general have more financial freedom and security than ever before. You only have to go back to the 1960s, Stone and MacLean say, to "conclude that the welfare of older Canadians was dramatically enhanced from around 1967 to 1976."[10] So why do many of us believe that old people live in poverty? Some people, in fact, still do. Not all older people have extra money or even enough to live comfortably, but they don't complain. Like Vic Watson, they say they could live on less if they had to, but they have to work hard to stay afloat.

Inflation, for instance, has taken a big bite out of everyone's budget. The poorest older people on fixed incomes feel the pinch most. Last year Vic Watson had to sell his car because it cost too much to run. Now he travels by bus at the senior citizen discount rate. He also had to stop buying records. "I love music," he says. "It's a big part of my life, and I miss getting the records I want. Now I go to the public library and I tape whatever I can get."

Many older people today find themselves in Vic's bind. One woman told the Ontario Advisory Council on Senior Citizens that "with the high cost of living, food, heating, etc., [the government pensions and my small savings] are inadequate to provide for [my] needs."

Another woman said that she and her husband lived on $600 a month in 1978. "Half this goes into rent, utilities, phone, gasoline," she said. "The other half takes care of personal needs — food, gifts, dental care, prescriptions, clothing, travel, car repairs." This doesn't leave anything at the end of the month for savings or unexpected expenses.[11]

Certain groups are hit harder than others. People with little education, those who live in smaller urban areas, people who speak neither French nor English and blue-collar workers all have lower than average incomes in old age. So do single people (those who are widowed, divorced, separated or who never married).

In 1975, for instance, 62% of single men and a staggering 71%

of single women over 65 had incomes below the Statistics Canada low-income cut-off, compared to 27% of elderly couples.[12] In 1981 the poverty line for a single person in a large city was $6,521. That year 57% of older people had incomes under $2,000.[13] The National Council of Welfare also reports that in 1980 one-third of all poor single people in Canada were 70 years old or over.[14]

The fact is that while income has risen for older people in general, the income security system needs to do more for certain groups. Clearly something needs to be done: (1) to keep all older people out of poverty; (2) to make sure that the poorest people — women, the very old and single people — get special help to raise their incomes; (3) to ensure that all of us in the future will have a decent standard of living.

Labour, business and government all agree that the system needs to change, but at the moment no one can agree on what a better system would look like. The Canadian Labour Congress, for instance, wants a stronger government pension plan, one that would ensure retired workers 75% of their pre-retirement income.[15] Private industry, on the other hand, wants stronger private pension plans which would make more money available for investments. The government doesn't know what it wants.

Minister of Health and Welfare Canada Monique Begin said in 1981 that "The Government of Canada has not made a decision as to which of the many options it will select."[16] In its 1982 Green Paper on pensions the government called for still another study on pensions — a Parliamentary Task Force — before it would act to change the system.

So, for the moment, pension change hangs in limbo. Oddly enough, many Canadians don't even know this debate over pension reform is taking place.

"For most Canadians," wrote Barbara Amiel in a 1981 article in *Maclean's,* "the pension debate has been taking place somewhere in the stratosphere. . . . Though the outcome affects the lives of everyone, rarely has an issue of such universal concern been treated for so long as a universal yawn."[17]

A recent Gallup Poll, for instance, showed that people are more concerned with job security and working conditions than with pensions. "To date," Mrs Andrea Vincent, President of the Association of Canadian Pension Management, told *The Globe and Mail*, "there doesn't seem to have been a mandate from the employees to force greater changes [in the system]."[18]

One woman, a 27-year-old fashion buyer in Toronto, told Barbara Amiel that, "I don't want to think about making ends meet when I'm 65, I've got my career, rent increases and facing 30 on my hands now. Spare me old age."

Many people would like to forget about old age, but few of us can afford the luxury of ignorance. The facts tell us that most people today will live many years past the retirement age of 65, and the only thing that stands between them and a sharp drop in living standard will be how they plan for retirement now. A look at the system will show what plans need to be made.

The System Today

I recently took an informal poll to see how much people know about Canada's pension system: I asked students in my day and evening classes if any of them could tell me how the system works. These people ranged in age from 18 to over 70, with an average age of 35. Most of them worked — some part-time. They have more education than most people, and they either have middle-class incomes or come from middle-class families.

Of the 200 people I asked, only three said that they knew how the government system worked, and only a half-dozen of those who had pension plans knew the details of how they worked.

I don't pretend that this is a scientific study of Canadian society. Other groups likely know more about their pensions and about the system. I've met Veterans Affairs Department caseworkers, for instance, who know every comma and sub-paragraph in the pension laws. But I suspect that most people, like my students, know almost nothing about the pension system.

Before we look at the system's limits and see how it should

change, we need to know how it works. Here is a brief picture of the system today.

Government Transfers

Canada's pension system resembles a pyramid with three tiers. Government transfer programs — the Old Age Security (OAS), the Guaranteed Income Supplement (GIS) and the Spouse's Allowance (SA) — form the base or first tier of the pyramid.

Transfer payments are the public-bus system of pension plans. The federal government pays for transfer benefits as city governments pay for buses — with tax revenue. You don't need to be a plan member or even a taxpayer to receive benefits. These programs offer no frills, but like the bus system they make sure that everyone — especially the very poor — can get from place to place.

Those transfer payments make up the biggest share of older people's incomes today. In 1981 transfers made up 30% of older married couples' incomes, 32% of single males' total incomes and 43% of single females' total incomes.[19] More than half of all the pension income of retired people in 1975 came from transfer payments.[20]

People with the lowest incomes depend on transfers most. Older people who had less than a grade nine eduction in 1980 had the lowest incomes among the elderly (about seven thousand dollars a year on average, or slightly above the poverty line). Transfer payments made up about two-thirds of their income (51% for men, 72% for women).[21]

In 1984 the government paid Old Age Security benefits to almost 2.5 million people — over 99% of all people 65 and over. The OAS goes to everyone, no matter how much income they make from other sources. John Palevich, who lives on Edmonton's skid row, gets the same benefit as a retired corporation president. Some people don't know this: one former economics professor I know found out only after he retired that he was eligible for OAS benefits.

In the second quarter of 1984 the OAS came to $266.28 a month per person. (OAS rates, are fully indexed to the cost of living and are adjusted four times a year. In 1983 and 1984, however, the government capped rises in OAS payments to 6% and 5%.)

To supplement the OAS for the poorest of our old people, the government began the Guaranteed Income Supplement program in 1967. It goes tax-free to older people who have no income other than the OAS. GIS payments also go up quarterly with rises in the cost of living.

People either get full or partial GIS payments based on a yearly income test. The maximum GIS payment in 1984 came to $267.33 a month for a single person (or a married person whose spouse doesn't get the OAS or Spouse's Allowance), and $412.22 for a couple. In 1984, therefore, a single person received a maximum of $533.61 in both GIS and OAS payments, or about $6,400 a year. Each person in a married couple got $472.39 or $944.78 a month for two, a little more than $11,000 a year.

One final program makes up tier one — the Spouse's Allowance (SA). The government added the SA in 1975 to help low-income couples. This program pays a maximum amount equal to the OAS and the maximum GIS at the married rate to a GIS pensioner's spouse who is between the ages of 60 and 64. In 1984, this came to $472.39 a month.

Before 1975 both people in a marriage had to live on one OAS/GIS payment. Now they get the full couple's amount each month. A surviving spouse continues to receive SA payments even after the GIS pensioner dies: when the survivor reaches 65 he or she then gets an OAS/GIS pension, and the SA payments are discontinued. About 90% of SAs go to women.

In January 1984 the government paid out about 1.3 million GIS and SA supplements, more than one for every two OAS pensioners. Without GIS and SA benefits more than half of all older Canadians would live below the poverty line. One quarter of all people who receive the GIS (304,000 people) are so poor that they get the full amount.[22]

In addition to these federal transfers, most provinces have set up provincial supplement plans — Nova Scotia, Ontario, Manitoba,

Saskatchewan, Alberta, British Columbia and the Northwest Territories. These programs help the poorest people on the GIS. In Ontario 46%, and in British Columbia 51% of older people have incomes low enough to entitle them to provincial supplements. In 1978 Ontario guaranteed a single older person $319.17 a month — $58.11 more than OAS/GIS payments. A couple was guaranteed $638.34 — $140.34 more than their combined OAS/GIS payments. Manitoba guaranteed a couple $585.28 a month, British Columbia $634.34 a month.[23]

The CPP/QPP

The Canada Pension Plan (CPP) and the Quebec Pension Plan (QPP) form our pension system's second, smaller tier.[a] The government designed these plans, implemented in 1966, to pay benefits to all Canadian workers. Contributions to the CPP by employees who earned over $1,600, employers and self-employed people came to $3.2 billion in 1982.

The government set up the CPP for two reasons: first to ensure that all workers will save something for their retirement at age 65; and second, to ease the burden of transfer payments. In the fiscal year 1981-82 the plan paid out $245 million in benefits to about 1.5 million people.[24]

The CPP/QPP combine two plans: a savings plan and a transfer plan. Today, workers are required by law to pay 1.8% of their wages into the plan (up to a maximum of $538.40 per year for 1984), and their employers pay a matching amount. Self-employed people pay 3.6% of their incomes.

This money goes to the worker's credit, and the pension a worker receives when he or she retires depends on how much he or she has paid in, as reflected in the following cases of two self-employed workers.

[a]When the federal government set up the CPP, provinces were permitted to opt out and set up their own plans. Quebec took this option. The QPP differs from the CPP in some details — for instance, it invests its money differently and pays slightly different benefits — but in most ways it mirrors the CPP.

Joan Dakin made over $35,000 in 1984 as an accountant. She owns her own firm, so she pays the full 3.6% of her income into the CPP herself. In 1984 she paid 3.6% of $18,800 (the Year's Maximum Pensionable Earnings [YMPE] $20,800, minus $2,000, the year's basic exemption) or $676.80 into the plan. If her income stays above the YMPE, and if the CPP rules don't change, she will receive, when she turns 65, as a yearly pension 25% of the average YMPE for all the years she paid in.

Peter Wierzbowski drives a cab which he owns himself. He made $15,700 in 1984 and paid 3.6% of this amount (minus $2000 for the year's basic exemption) into the CPP, or $493.20. When he retires, if his income remains below the YMPE over the years, he'll get back 25% of his average income for the years he paid in.

The government designed the CPP/QPP plan to help people keep up their pre-retirement living standard. Unlike the OAS, which pays the same amount to everyone, the CPP will pay Joan Dakin a bigger pension than Pete Wierzbowski when they each retire. (Joan will also have paid more into the plan while she worked.) This makes the CPP look like a savings plan — what you get out reflects what you put in — but it's also like a transfer plan. The money you pay in doesn't go into an account for you alone: it goes into a fund to pay the pensions of retired plan members today.

When you and I retire we will get back an amount related to how much we put in, but the money will come from workers' payments at that time. Those workers, in turn, will get their pensions from the next generation of workers, and so on. This spreads the risk of saving for retirement among society as a whole.

Private savings, for instance, can decrease in value over time, or people may find that they haven't saved enough to last them their lifetime. The CPP acts as a buffer against these risks. It promises that you'll get back some set amount when you retire — for life.

The CPP has some other good points. First, it covers all workers, so no one who works will enter retirement without some CPP benefits.

Second, the plan moves with workers when they change jobs, a feature experts call "portability." In a fluid job market this can make the difference between having a pension or not.

Third, the plan offers immediate vesting, which means that both workers' *and* employers' contributions are locked into the program from the start. Workers keep all the money (their own and their employer's contributions) in their account even if they move from one employer to another.

Fourth, it promises to replace a certain pre-set amount of pre-retirement income for life, up to 25% of earnings on which contributions have been made.

Fifth, the plan treats men and women the same. Private pension plans, as we'll see, often discriminate against women.

Sixth, the CPP offers survivor and disability benefits to everyone, a vital point in a society where men marry younger women, where women have a greater life expectancy than men and where most women have no pensions of their own.

Seventh, and not least, the CPP is indexed to the cost of living. It goes up with rises in the Consumer Price Index, so a person will not fall behind each year as they would with a fixed-income pension.

Private Pensions, Savings and Work

In Canada the OAS/GIS and the maximum CPP make up 40% of older couples' total retirement income, and 43% and 50% of older single men's and women's incomes respectively. Benefits came to $11,284 for a single person in 1984 or $1,384 above the poverty line for a single person in a city of half-a-million people or more.[25] At best, the government estimates that the OAS/GIS and CPP cover only 40% of a middle-class person's average pre-retirement income.[26] The middle class worker therefore has to look to private pension plans and savings to make up the difference between government pensions and pre-retirement income. In private pension plans employers and employees pay equal shares. The employees get pensions based on how much they and their employers have put in. It sounds good, but in 1980 only 39.7% of all workers belonged to a private pension plan.[27] In 1981 private pension benefits made up only 16% of single men's incomes, 13% of older couples' and 9% of single women's.

Most people, as you can see, can't expect much help here. Instead many people rely on savings to make up for lost pre-retirement income. Income from private savings and other investments made up about 30% of older people's incomes in 1981, second after transfer payments as their major source of income.[28]

Savings will continue to play a role in most people's retirement plans. The government, for instance, has encouraged savings through Registered Retirement Savings Plans (RRSPs). Investors can save up to $5,500 a year tax-free in an RRSP and pay tax on the money only when they take it out in retirement. This defers taxes to a time when they will have a lower income — and so a lower tax rate. The number of RRSPs "have skyrocketed," a *Maclean's* article reports, "from 248,000 . . . in 1971 to about 2 million in 1980.[29] Canadians have now saved over $20 billion in RRSPs.[30]

Finally, some older people work. In 1981 earnings made up 15% of couples' incomes and 9% of single males' incomes, but only 5% of single females' incomes.[31]

All these plans and programs along with earnings from work should guarantee a decent old age for all Canadians, but they don't. Too many older people still suffer a sharp loss in income and a shocking change of lifestyle when they retire. Almost every tier and subsection of the system fails to do its job in some way.

The Limits of the System

"A retirement income system should perform two essential tasks," according to a report by the National Council of Welfare. "The first is to ensure that all elderly persons are assured a minimum income. . . . The second is to maintain a reasonable relationship between an individual's income before and after retirement."[32] Canada's pension system does neither.

The facts sound frightening:

Today, half of all older people make so little money that they need GIS payments to bring their incomes near the poverty line.

Sixty percent of single older people — mostly women — live below the poverty line.

The CPP replaces only a fraction of middle-class workers' incomes when they retire.

Most Canadians have no private pension plan, and those who do stand little chance of getting a full pension.

Almost everyone except the very rich and the very poor faces a drop in living standard after retirement.

As I said, each tier of the system fails in some way. It is worth examining them one at a time.

Government Transfers

Old Age Security payments in the second quarter of 1984 came to $266.28 a month. At the same time the GIS/SA came to a maximum of $267.33 a month for a single person (or someone married whose spouse was not receiving the OAS and SA) and $412.22 a month for a couple.[33] Still, the OAS/GIS/SA program doesn't keep all older people out of poverty. In 1980 raises in payments at last brought all older couples above the poverty line, but payments to single people still left them in poverty.

In 1984, for instance, a single person got a maximum OAS and GIS payment of $533.61 a month or $6,403.32 a year. But the National Council of Welfare low income estimate for 1984 for a single person in a large city came to $9,900, or more than one-and-a-half times the OAS/GIS payments.[34]

The federal government has pledged to raise GIS benefits ''as soon as economic conditions permit,''[35] but ''it will take another $730 million to bring all of our senior citizens once and for all out of poverty.''[36] Given the federal deficit, a national debt of $97 billion and a weak economy, this will take some time.

The GIS program also has a cruel twist to it. Some poor old people work to raise their income and then find themselves in a double bind. The federal government reduces the GIS by $1 in the next year for each $2 a person earns that year, and a person who gets a provincial supplement will lose the other $1 for every $2 they earn. This results in a 100% "taxback," so a poor older person gets nothing for work up to the amount equal to his or her GIS and Provincial Supplement.

The taxback scheme also discourages work in another way. It takes money from the older person's income *next* year for money earned *this* year. For many older people this means that when they work they risk a cut in income in the following year if they get sick or can't find a job.

These rules not only discourage older people from working, they also help keep them poor.

The CPP/QPP

Most people will agree that even with its limits our system today offers older people more social security than in the past. Until the 1920s, for instance, before any retirement plan existed, researcher Kenneth Bryden writes that "poverty among the aged was acute, widespread, and chronic."[37] Today's system at least helps all older people stay close to the low-income cut-off, but it doesn't do as well in helping people maintain their pre-retirement income. Half of all retired people currently face a 5% drop in living standard, a third face a 15% drop and a sixth face a 25% drop.[38] Part of the blame for this drop in income rests with the Canada Pension Plan.

The pension system in Canada began in the 1920s as a plan to help the poorest among older people. It assumed that most older people would take care of themselves in old age by saving for their retirement or continuing to work. The government designed the CPP in the 1960s to fit this ideal. "The benefits," the government said in its 1971 White Paper on Income Security, "have been designed to provide substantial protection and at the same time not to be so generous as to discourage the provision of private protection."[39]

But the CPP does not give "substantial protection" to most people. For many older people today — those who retired before 1966, for instance — it offers no protection at all. Even for those who do receive CPP benefits, the CPP does not pay enough.

In March 1977, for instance, more than ten years after the plan started, the maximum CPP payment came to $171.61 a month, men on the average received only $87.28, women $62.95.[40] Widows got only 60% of their husbands' pensions.

In 1984 the maximum total OAS and CPP came to only $7,845.36 a year, or more than $2,000 below the poverty line for a single person living in a city of over half-a-million people. And people who get GIS benefits lose $1 of their GIS for each $2 they make through the CPP. For the poorest older people this cuts CPP benefits in half.

Clearly these low CPP payments will not replace much of the average person's income. The CPP, former Minister of Health and Welfare Monique Begin says, "only protect[s] people from want."[41] For the average person a private pension plan or private savings will have to make up the rest.

Private Pensions

How well do private pensions help people maintain their standard of living in old age? Monique Begin called the private pension system "scandalous." "For most people," she told the Alberta Council on Aging in 1981, "there simply isn't any income from personal retirement savings and company pensions. The shortcomings of the private pension system have been singled out time and again by major studies."[42]

What are these shortcomings?

First, only 40% of Canadian workers have a private pension plan. Compare this to West Germany where 65% of workers belong to private plans, France (80%) or Sweden (an impressive 90%).[43] In Canada part-time workers, seasonal workers, those who work for small businesses and at low-paying jobs have no private pension. In other words the poorest people have the least chance to establish a pension.

Second, outside the civil service, few pension plans index payments to make up for inflation. At present rates inflation will cut a pension in half in nine years, so people on a fixed pension — even a good one — become poorer each year.

A senior chartered accountant I know retired on what looked like a generous pension two years ago. He sold his house in Toronto and moved to a luxury apartment in Victoria. Each year since then he's watched his pension shrink. This year he had to go back to work as an accountant, doing the books for a small pizza chain. He doesn't like the work and hadn't planned to work again, but he needs the money to maintain his life-style. Someone who can't work or possesses a less saleable skill has to sit by and watch his or her income drop.

Robert O'Connor worked as the registrar for a provincial university for twenty-six years. He and his wife planned for retirement. "We took steps to reduce economic problems as far as we could," he says. "We paid off our mortgage, we bought a new car — anything so we could go into retirement as well-equipped as we could."

Still, a drop in their living standard came as soon as he retired. "When I was working, I'd say to my wife, 'Well, come on, where will we go for dinner?' Now we don't go out to eat as much. And when we do go, it's more likely we go to Bonanza with discount coupons than to our favourite steak house.

"We don't talk about it much, but we've faced a lowering of our social standards. We can't say, 'Let's go back now and look at Scotland.' We merely say, 'Let's renew our subscription to *Britain in Pictures*.'

"One of the problems when you retire is to build up a small nest egg, but even relatively fortunate people like myself often watch it disappear. Six weeks ago we had to put a roof on our house — $900. Last week our washing machine broke down. There we had to dip into our bank account. The time is coming when it's not imprudent to contemplate almost the virtual exhaustion of our savings."

A third problem with private pension plans is that few people ever collect a full pension. The Canadian Labour Congress estimates that only 4% to 10% of those who belong to private pension plans ever collect their full pension.[44]

Even though more people belong to pension plans today (39% vs 31% in 1960), this doesn't mean that more people will have private pensions in the future. Many people don't stay with a firm long enough to collect full benefits; a firm may go bankrupt or move out of town; a person may fall sick and have to quit work before retirement. Almost anything that breaks a person's work career will cut into or wipe out a pension.

Two other problems face people who pay into private pension plans. First, most plans do not have early vesting, which means that the employer's share of the worker's fund belongs to the worker: both shares remain locked in the fund. Early vesting locks the money into the plan after a short time — say, two or three years. That way workers are guaranteed at least some pension from the company when they retire. Today, however, many plans vest contributions only after ten years or when a person reaches the age of 45. Few people put in enough time with one firm to have their money vested: better jobs, lay-offs, boredom all lead people to change jobs often.

Second, most plans have no portability: people can't take their pensions with them when they change jobs. This means that even if the whole labour force can belong to private pension plans, as long as workers change jobs often as they do today, only a small number of people will ever collect a pension. When workers leave a company they get only their share of their pension fund, sometimes with no interest. The employer's share stays in the fund, so each time a person changes jobs they lose half their fund and have to start again.

Late-vesting and non-portability affect women the most. In her report *Women and Aging*, Louise Dulude reports that in 1974 95% of women workers belonged to private pension plans that did not have full-vesting until a person had worked for the company ten years or more. But, she says, 75% of women aged 22-44 change jobs at least every five years. As a result few women ever collect a pension.[45] The employers' shares of their payments, which they never get, subsidize the pensions of workers — mostly men — who stay with the company. Many other rules work against women too. A look at the income status of women in old age exposes the worst injustices of the pension system in Canada today.

Women and the System

"To be old and female," the Canadian Council on Social Development reports in its *Fact Book on Poverty*, "is the best combination to ensure being poor in Canada." Former Minister of Health and Welfare Monique Begin told the Croll Commission that in 1975 two-thirds of unmarried women 65 and over (or about 400,000 people) lived in poverty.[46] She went on to report that while women make up 60% of the group 65 and over, in 1976 three times more women lived in poverty than men.

"After a lifetime spent taking care of their spouses and children," the National Council of Welfare says, "these women who had no opportunity to become financially self-sufficient are now abandoned by the generation that benefitted most from their work.[47] "The retirement income system has failed," the Croll Commission concludes, "and the failure is especially dismal with elderly women."[48]

Why do men have much better incomes than women in old age? And why do so many older women live in poverty? First, the private and public pension systems discriminate against women — openly and in hidden ways. Second, women in general hold lower-status jobs and earn less than men. And third, women get fewer fringe benefits than men — benefits like good pensions. Their low retirement incomes reflect these biases.

Professors Pat and Hugh Armstrong wrote about this in their classic study, *The Double Ghetto*. Their work showed two clear trends.

First, "in every occupation listed, [women] received lower incomes than their male counterparts." Among chefs and cooks, for instance, a woman's income came to only 57.5% of a man's, among typists and stenographers only 54%, and among sales clerks only 42.3%. "The average income of women with paid work was less than half that of men in 1971."[49] Ten years later, in 1980, the same inequality existed. Single men over age 15 made an average of $16,659 that year, single women only $8,101.[50]

Lower pay means lower pensions, and this fact alone would account for why women have lower incomes in old age than men. But few women ever collect a pension, and this has to do with the kinds of jobs they hold.

The Armstrongs found that women get channelled into work that pays poorly, demands the least skill and has the least prospects for getting ahead. Women, for instance, hold over 90% of all jobs as stenographers and typists, personal service workers (baby-sitters, housekeepers, etc.), graduate nurses and telephone operators. They hold over 75% of all jobs in the garment industry and food services.[51] The nearly three-quarters of variety-store sales clerks who are women receive the "lowest average wages in retail trade." These women serve as a "reserve labour army."[52] Industry uses them when and *if* it needs workers, then fires them when work slackens off, thus effectively preventing them from building up solid pension funds.

Also, women often work for small firms with no pension plans. Only 27% of women who work belong to a private plan (compared to 40% of the general working population), and almost half of these women work for the government or crown corporations. In private industry, Louise Dulude says, only 15% of women have private plans.[53] The Croll Commission estimates that the average income of all women 66 and over from private pensions in 1975 came to $370 for the year. For those who got pensions the average rose to only $1,976 a year.[54]

Many private plans, Dulude says, simply exclude women. In 1974 400 plans — about 3% of all plans in Canada — excluded women: 47 had separate plans for women, 93 restricted women from joining and the rest existed in male industries.[55]

Some plans use a more subtle approach. For instance, a plan will only cover certain jobs — jobs that women don't hold — or will only cover people earning above a certain income. Low-paid female workers tend not to be covered.

In 1977 23% of women worked part time, often because they were raising a family at the same time. In most such cases they would not be able to join a pension plan.

Some plans set out different rules for women and men. Fourteen hundred plans (almost 10% of all plans) allowed women to join only after age 25 (men could join after age 21). Twelve hundred plans forced women to take their benefits at age 60 (men didn't have to retire until 65).[56] Because she works fewer years than her male co-workers, a woman gets a smaller pension from these plans.

It is obvious that private plans don't favour older women, even when they've worked a lifetime and paid for their benefits. The Canada Pension Plan doesn't do much better. Most people agree that the CPP pays too little to too few people. The maximum CPP benefit in 1978 came to $2,333, but only 18% of women 65 and over outside Quebec got this much. New female members of the plan in 1976 got an average of $972 for the year, but any of these women who also received GIS payments lost $1 from their GIS for each $2 they got from the CPP.

The CPP sets the same rules for joining and for retirement for both sexes, but like private pension plans the CPP bases its payments on a worker's past income. Because women earn less than men on the average, the CPP carries this unfair treatment into old age.

The CPP also works against women who raise families. It bases benefits on ''average earnings'' — a figure based on the years a person *could have been* working between the ages of 18 and 65. This excludes years when a person can't work due to a disability. Theoretically, then, a person with no disability *could* have worked forty-seven years.

The plan allows a person to deduct the worst seven (or 15%) of those years, leaving forty years of work. The plan divides forty into the person's lifetime income (the total they earned over their best forty years) to arrive at "average earnings." A person who spends more than seven years earning a low income will find those years counted as part of their lifetime earnings, thus lowering their CPP pension.

Most women who raise families take more than seven years off from paid work. A woman with one child, for instance, will work outside the home an average of only twenty-five of a possible forty-seven years.[57] She will therefore have twenty-two years of low income, but she can drop only seven, so her lifetime earnings will include fifteen years of zero or low income because she stayed at home. She not only loses work time — time when she might have paid into a private plan or saved some money for her retirement — but also has a lower pension based on a lower figure for her "average earnings." In 1981 single older women got only 7% of their income from the Canada Pension Plan.[58]

Widows make up the largest group among women over 65, and of all women widows benefit least. In 1975 54% of widows aged 55-64 lived in poverty. The figure rose to 66% for widows over 65.[59] "After fifty years or so of unpaid, faithful service," the National Council of Welfare says, "a woman's only reward is likely to be poverty."[60]

Some people call widowhood the "double whammy." If being old and a woman combine to give a good reason for poverty in old age, Louise Dulude says that "to be old and a widow is an even better one." The vast majority of widows "struggled to survive on incomes incapable of providing the most basic necessities to anyone anywhere in Canada . . . [living in] financial circumstances, that the word 'poor' is too weak to describe."[61]

In 1970 56% of all single women 65 and over lived below the *rural* poverty line, even though 80% of them lived in high-cost cities.[62] In 1979 more than two thirds of older single women had cash incomes too low for them to live on their own.[63] Eighty-one percent of these women in 1975 had no private pension plan, and if you subtract the money these women got from their OAS, "at least one third [of them] had no personal income at all."[64]

What about their husbands' pension plans? Can widows count

on benefits from their husbands' plan to keep them out of poverty? Rarely.

Only 44% of private plans pay survivor benefits to widows. This raises the odds against a widow getting a pension to as high as five to one.[65] Even worse, only 10% of the married men who have these plans take up the survivor-benefit option for their wives.[66] Instead they opt for higher benefits in the short run.

My own university's pension plan shows how even a good plan can leave a woman poor in old age. At a meeting last spring our union leaders praised our pension plan as one of the best, but I wondered about its survivor benefits. "What happens if I die before I retire?" I asked. "What benefits will my wife get?" They looked surprised by the question. None of them knew the answer until someone in the audience said, "If a member dies before retirement, his or her spouse gets back only the member's contributions to date — not the university's share — and no survivor pension."

In other words our spouses have no survivor benefits to count on unless we live to retirement. If I die at 64, even though I'll have paid into our plan for almost forty years, my wife will get no pension. She won't even recover the university's contributions to my plan. That is what a *good* plan offers.

Well, you might say, "What about insurance? She'll get a good insurance payment." For most widows private insurance policies offer little help. On average death benefits from private insurance policies in 1977 came to about $4,000. "That," the National Council on Welfare says, "would just about cover the cost of a first-class funeral."[67]

Again, the CPP doesn't do much better. Less than 45% of widows between 50 and 64 got any CPP benefits in 1977. Those who did averaged less than $96 a month or less than $1,200 a year, in 1978.[68]

Unless the system changes many members of the next generations of older women (those 55 and under today) will also fall into poverty. "A woman now 55," a recent government report says, "will probably be better off than the 80-year-old woman [today], though only marginally so, by the time she reaches age 65." Only about a third of women now aged 55-64 work for pay, and those who work will get only small CPP benefits. The average woman has no pension. Even if her husband has one, his plan probably pays no survivor benefits. "This will result in a severe decline in her income and she will have to rely on a survivor benefit from the CPP/QPP, Old Age Security, and the Guaranteed Income Supplement if, as is likely, private savings were not large."

A younger woman in her thirties today will do better, but, given the way the system works, not much better. More women work today than ever before, so more women will spend most of their younger years at paid work, but unless the labour market changes a woman will likely work at a low-paying job, often part time. If she leaves work to raise a family she will lose a chance to pay into a private pension plan. "She too will probably have serious difficulties in retirement."[69]

Only pension system reform — for instance, an end to private pension rules that discriminate against women and better public and private pension plan survivor benefits — will help women today. The government has proposed these and other changes to the system, sparking what some people call "The Great Pension Debate."

Changes in the System

In 1982 the federal government released a Green Paper called *Better Pensions for Canadians*. The paper proposed changes that will solve many of the system's worst problems. Let's look at the proposed reforms one at a time.

Private Plan Reform
Private plans have failed the worst and need the most reform. First, they have to ensure portability. People change jobs often today, and pensions should go with them from job to job.

The government proposes to allow a new tax-assisted retirement fund — the Registered Pension Account (RPA). The worker and employer would both pay into the RPA, but an RPA would belong to the worker. The account would go with him or her wherever he or she worked, and all payments would be locked in until retirement. This would ensure more and better pensions for all workers.

It would help women most of all. For instance, it would allow small businesses (where women often work) to pay into an employee's pension plan, and it would not penalize a woman for changing jobs or for being laid off.

Second, the government calls for full vesting of private pension funds after only two years. Again this will help people who change jobs often: they will be able to keep all their pension savings when they move to a new job.

Third, private pensions should have indexed benefits that go up with the cost of living.

Business balks at the cost of this proposal. But, Monique Begin says, this attitude amounts to "robbing the old to pay the young."[70] Since people pay into pension plans at higher rates due to inflation, and pension plan investments earn higher dividends due to inflation, older people should have their pensions pegged to the rising cost of living. Robert Crozier of the Conference Board of Canada agrees. Why, he asks, can society "afford to pay a retired pensioner $5,000 a year in terms of a fixed basket of goods and services today, but cannot also afford to pay him the same fixed basket of goods and services 10 or 15 years later?"

In those ten or fifteen years, he says, society's wealth increases and we all make more money. We expect annual salary increases that match or exceed inflation, but we keep the retired person from getting these increases to take more for ourselves. "The transfer of real income from the old to the young would certainly be looked upon as a particularly vicious form of robbery if it took place in the open and not secretly under the cover of inflation."[71]

Fourth, the government says workers should have a stronger call on a firm's assets when a company goes bankrupt. This would reduce the risk of losing a pension when a company closes down.

Fifth, the government wants an end to unfair treatment of

women. All the changes I've listed so far will help women get better private pensions (indexing, for instance, will help women because they live longer than men on the average and so they suffer more from inflation), but the government also suggests other reforms to help women. The Green Paper recommends that there be one plan for all employees, regardless of sex. This would put an end to unfair rules like forced early retirement for women or longer waiting times before women can enter a plan.

The government also proposes a change in rules covering a marriage break-up. Today pension credits do not count in most cases as family assets: if a marriage breaks up, the husband's pension all goes to the husband. Private pensions under the new rules would ensure a split of pension credits to each spouse in the case of a break-up.

Private plans would also have to ensure a pension to the last survivor in a marriage: this would come to at least 60% of the full benefits. Also a widow would receive this pension even if she remarried.

Finally, the government also plans to set new higher contribution limits for RRSPs and pension payments. This would allow women who go to work late in life to save more money for their retirement in fewer years.

Public Pension Reform
The federal government has also proposed a series of changes in the Canada Pension Plan. First, it proposed an increase in the Yearly Maximum Pensionable Earnings (YMPE) to equal the Average Industrial Wage (AIW). Now the YMPE comes to only about 80% of the AIW. With the new scheme, people could pay more into the CPP, and get more out when they retired.

Second, it proposed to allow women who take time off work to raise a family to drop these years from their work record. (The QPP already allows this.) This will give women who work a higher CPP pension when they retire.

Third, the Green Paper proposed credit-splitting of CPP

benefits among both spouses. Each spouse would get half the pension benefits paid by the plan. Now credit-splitting applies only when a marriage breaks up, but it could also apply "when the younger spouse reaches 65, when either spouse dies, or when a non-earner spouse . . . becomes disabled."[72] Credit-splitting would spread retirement benefits over the lives of both spouses.

This change would help homemakers. The government has not yet found any other way to include homemakers in the CPP that is "free of important shortcomings." If the plan includes homemakers, the government says, payment rates could double, and people with low incomes might not be able to pay these rates. Instead, along with credit-splitting, the government proposes better survivor benefits. The surviving spouse, whether a contributor or not, would get his or her share of the CPP pension and 60% of the deceased spouse's pension. A widow would thus "receive 80% of the CPP benefits that were coming into the household before the death of the spouse."[73]

These changes would create more income security for all Canadians in old age. And "if these proposals were implemented by all governments," the Green Paper says, "the prospects for today's women after retirement would brighten considerably."[74]

Will these proposed changes become part of a new pension system? And if so when will they come into effect? Douglas Frith, head of the Parliamentary Task Force on Pensions, has said that change will come slowly. Professor Leroy Stone agrees. He predicts that policy change will take place only when powerful interest groups either favour or don't oppose change. Government, he says, is looking "for a safe level of 'inter-group consensus' before taking action on any controversial issue. . . ."[75]

Professor Stone studied the views of important interest groups to see where they stood on pension reform and found high consensus on some issues, but little on others. A wide range of groups from both labour and business favour credit-splitting, pensions for part-time workers, portability, vesting of employer pension credits and a child-care drop-out rule for the CPP (now approved by all provinces). If Professor Stone is right, the government will make these changes, at least for private plans.[a]

His study, however, goes on to show that some issues are complicated by a lack of consensus. Powerful groups still disagree with the plan to allow homemakers to pay in to the CPP, and with the ideas that private pension plans should index benefits to the rate of inflation, that private plans should cover all workers and that the CPP (and QPP) should expand to pay up to 50% of the average industrial wage. No one can assume that any of these proposals will come into effect as long as so many groups disagree.

The last item — an expanded CPP — may prove the hottest issue of all. Some groups, like the Canadian Labour Congress (CLC) and the National Action Committee on the Status of Women, want a stronger CPP: the CLC has called for a public pension plan that would pay up to 75% of workers' pre-retirement wages. Businesses and some provinces disagree. They want more money channelled through private pensions and savings. The Royal Commission on the status of pensions in Ontario, for instance, backed a rise in pension benefits but suggested that this increase should come through more and better private plans. A bigger public plan, most critics say, will take money away from the private sector. It could damage the economy, lead to higher inflation and undo the effects of higher CPP benefits.

Each side in this debate has some arguments in its favour. Proposed changes would double CPP benefits, but they would also double the amount of money people pay into the plan. This will give the federal government control over a vast amount of money.[77] Since 1966, for instance, the CPP has logged a surplus of $23 billion. The federal government has had control and use of this

[a]He cautions, though, that "no predictions should be made at this time about pension reform proposals that require federal government negotiations with provinces when key provinces have yet to declare their real positions (e.g. in the cases of all proposals that involve the Canada Pension Plan).[76]

money, money that people could not spend or invest in the market place. A stronger CPP will put even more money in the federal government's hands.

Also, a stronger CPP cannot replace private pensions. Even with the higher CPP rates proposed in the 1982 Green Paper most middle-class Canadians will still need some private pension income to maintain a pre-retirement standard of living.[78]

The problem, of course, is that the private pension system has such a poor record. It hasn't given people a fair chance to collect a pension; most plans don't match the rate of inflation; and they offer poor survivor benefits. The CPP has already solved all these problems, and above all a stronger CPP will help women — the majority of older people. It will also help people in the lower middle class who cannot save for retirement. The universality of the CPP argues for a stronger federal pension system.

How will this "great pension debate" turn out? Probably with a compromise. The government has always looked to private pensions and investments to fill the gap between a middle-class living standard and government support. It took this view when it started the CPP in 1966, and the model echoes the ideal of self-sufficiency that goes back to the first Canadian public pension plan of 1927.[79]

In its Green Paper, for instance, the government recommends a "balance" between private and public support in old age,[80] and it will use the current pension debate to find a system that strikes this balance. What does the idea of balance mean in practice?

For one thing it will mean more governmental control over private pension plans. If these plans expand to offer more benefits, the federal government will have to supply money to them for the first thirty years or more so they can offer benefits and also build up a pool of funds.[81] Also, the government will have to set standards and rules to ensure portability and vesting and to see that private plans serve their members better than they do today.

The reforms brought in by the Pension Commission of Manitoba give an idea of what reform might be. As of January

1985, in Manitoba all private pension plan benefits must be vested and locked in after five years of service. In case of a marriage break-up credits must be split between the two people. Part-time employees must have the option to join their company plan.

The revised Manitoba Pension Benefits Act also requires equal pensions for women who make the same payments to plans as do men. No plan, according to the Commission, can discriminate against an employee on the basis of his or her sex.[82]

All the proposed changes in private and public pension plans will also mean one other thing: pensions will cost more money.

The federal government estimates that reform will cost about $2 billion a year (in 1982 dollars); private industry reckons the cost at about $3.4 billion a year.[83]

What will this mean to you and me?

Just maintaining CPP benefits at 25% of the Average Industrial Wage will require a rise in rates to about 9% of our earnings by 2030 (from 3.6% today). Employers will pay for half of this increase, but this will still cost us each about $300 a year. Better private plans will cost about 1% more of our pay, or an average of about $125 a year. A better program for women (better survivor benefits, etc.) will raise costs about 0.7% of our pay or about $80 a year. The total will come to about $500 a year in take home pay.[84]

Will Canadians agree to pay this much (or more) for better pensions? Are we willing to save now for the future? And will the next generation be willing to pay more for our pensions in the twenty-first century? The current pension debate raises some dark issues.

In the end, writes Barbara Amiel, "much of the dispute between government and the private sector stems from a genuine disagreement over what Canada can afford in social as well as in economic terms." All of us want bigger pensions, but we will have to make do with less now to get more in the future. If we don't plan and save now, Amiel warns, we "have to oblige a future generation to pick up the tab for [our] retirement benefits."[85]

What will the future bring?

The Future

Pension reform will give new retirees better pensions, but some people have begun to ask whether the system will be able to meet the demands of a larger older population. Between 1976 and 2021 the number of old people in Canada will double, and experts predict a rise in transfer payments in those years of 250%.[86]

These figures have led some writers in the media to predict that the CPP will go broke in the near future. An article in *Quest* magazine offers a taste of this media scare. Diane Francis called her story "Ottawa's Pension Blues" and subtitled it "The Country's Largest Nest Egg Could Be Going Broke." She wrote that mismanagement of pension funds, a growing national debt and a growing population of older people have created a "fiscal time bomb."[87] Already, she said, OAS/GIS payments "are becoming a crushing burden," costing Ottawa in 1984 "$10 billion, or one out of every seven dollars spent."

The CPP, she predicted, will cost even more. In 1983 the CPP earned about $5.4 billion dollars in interest and contributions. It spent (in payments and administration costs) about $3 billion. That left a surplus of $2.4 billion, but this surplus will soon disappear because each year more people demand pensions from the CPP and more people earn full pension benefits. Also, with high unemployment fewer people pay into the plan. Inflation has driven CPP benefits up. Lower wages (due to wage restraints) mean smaller payments into the plan by workers. All these trends will drain the CPP surplus. If pay-outs keep going up and income keeps shrinking, the plan will use up its surplus in twenty years. Will the CPP go bankrupt?

Most serious students of the CPP say that the plan will not go broke. The government can do a number of things to keep the plan solvent. First it can begin to use the interest on the CPP surplus, now $23 billion, to pay benefits. As long as the CPP has run a surplus, the provinces have borrowed the extra money and used it for public works programs and social services. Right now, for instance, Ontario alone owes the plan over $12 billion, Alberta over $2 billion and B.C. over $3 billion.[88]

The federal government can demand that the provinces begin to make interest payments on their loans as of 1985. This money plus contributions would fund the plan until 1995. With this scheme, the CPP will still not be dipping into the $23 billion surplus that the provinces owe.

Second, in 1995 (or before) the government can raise CPP contribution rates. All projections for the future of the CPP include a rise in rates at least by the first decade of the twenty-first century if the current benefit system and contribution rates remain the same. This rise in rates along with provincial interest payments will carry the plan into the next century.

A rise in rates should come as no surprise. When the government set up the CPP in 1966 it knew that it would have to raise contribution rates in twenty years or so.[89]

And the CPP today faces no problems as long as people pay a bigger share of their income into it. Here, again, we have a number of options. The government can start a flat rate change in the mid-1980s that would increase rates to about 7% from today's 3.6%, or it can wait ten or fifteen years until about 1995 and raise rates to about 9%.

Frank Denton and Byron Spencer see ''no approaching 'crisis' in connection with the operation of the Canada and Quebec Pension Plans.''[90] And they see no tax revolt by the middle-aged. The projected rise in rates will still not equal the rates Europeans and Americans pay today. In the early 1980s Americans paid about 6.5% of their wages to their Social Security program — Canadians pay only 1.8%. Swedes paid 7% and West Germans 8% of their pay to their systems. These countries show no signs of economic collapse or revolt due to these payments.[91] They show that people can and will pay higher rates, either in taxes or through payroll deductions, to get better pensions.

How we feel about the rise in rates in the future will also depend on the Canadian and world economies. A strong economy, with higher salaries and lower inflation, will make paying higher rates easier, and those rates will not have to increase as much. A weaker economy will cause everyone to feel the pinch of higher pension rates: today some European countries have had to pull back on their pension programs. But this is due to national and world economic recessions and not to a middle-aged revolt against helping the old. In the end a strong pension system — given the average life expectancy today — makes sense for all of us.

Professor John Myles of Carleton University offers three other reasons why Canadians will support a stronger pension system.

First, he says, "the elderly are the *elderly parents* of the younger generation of producers." Without state support the young would have to care for their parents themselves. Younger people will prefer to "pool their risks" through a central pension system.

Second, he says, the middle-aged have a self-interest in supporting a strong pension and social security system for the elderly. They will be old soon themselves.

Third, without a sound pension system older workers will work longer. This will decrease the number of jobs open to the young, so the young have a stake in seeing that the old have a good reason to retire.[92]

A strong pension system serves all our interests — not just the older person's. It will give all of us more options as we age. But it will also force us to take new responsibility for our retirement. For many people this will mean learning about pensions for the first time.

A 1979 study in a Toronto suburb found that 41% of the women questioned "had no idea of the type of pension they could expect to receive at age 65," and even among the "well-informed" the study found their knowledge "very sketchy."[93]

The National Council of Women has called for an education program "to impress upon women the importance of providing for their own economic independence. . . ." Given the longer life expectancy of women and the fact that they tend to marry older men, this makes good sense. The Council goes on to say that "all individuals must look ahead to their own future. . . ."[94]

"If you don't plan ahead, if you don't ask questions," one woman told Barbara Amiel, "you're up a creek. No one is going to look after you in your old age but yourself."

This woman had worked as a copy writer for Eaton's for twelve years until she was fired. Then "I discovered part of my pension contributions were locked in," she says, "giving me the prospect of a pension of $47.66 a month when I reached 65. Well, I screamed and yelled, but there was nothing to be done." In the end she took out what she could and put it in an RRSP.[95]

Cases like this come up again and again. The National Council of Welfare says that each of us should know the basic facts and options involved in pensions, and we should use this knowledge to shape our pension plans to meet our own needs.

Government may hold the key to pension reform in the coming years. Both public and private pension programs will bend to new rules the government will set out.[96] But these rules will only affect your retirement, they will not determine it. Your retirement will still be yours. You will have to look out for your own interests. And the sooner you start, the better.

6

PLANNING RETIREMENT

Is There Life After Work?

I started teaching when I was 25. I had two problems then: how to get through a twenty-six week year with fifteen weeks worth of material, and how to look older than my students. As far as I can remember, the thought of retirement never crossed my mind. I don't even recall my father talking about his retirement at the time.

I knew I paid into a pension plan, but I didn't know how much, and I had no idea how much I would get when I retired. I doubt that more than a handful of my fellow faculty members knew either. It didn't seem to matter: we were young.

Recently the university held its first pre-retirement seminar and about a third of the faculty showed up — most were between 40 and 60 years old. I wondered what had happened. Why the sudden interest in retirement?

I came to a simple answer. We had all grown older. Aging experts say that aging is like being on an escalator: you get on at birth, and no matter what else you do you keep on moving. The average age of a faculty member at my school went from 35 to 42 years from 1973 to 1983, and a large majority of the faculty are now between 35 and 50 years old. We now see retirement as a real issue, something we ought to know about.

Now, long before people retire they have to start making choices. They have to think about how much money they will need when they retire, the kind of life-style they want to live, where they want to retire and what they might like to do with their free time. Retirement used to mean an end to work. Now it means the start of a new phase of life. What you do in retirement will depend to a large degree on how you prepare for it.

The stories of three professors at Canadian universities show that people need to prepare for retirement long before they leave work or they will face some hard knocks.

The first professor had worked at the university full time for twenty years when, at 65, she found herself forced out of work. Her union contract stipulated that all workers had to retire at 65. But she turned out to be more stubborn than anyone had expected. She asked the dean for an office so she could go on with her research work. He told her he had no spare offices; the teaching faculty took up all the space. He had no room for retired professors, and that was that.

The professor, however, did not give up. She looked around until she found an old broom closet on the top floor of an old building. She went back to the dean and said she'd found an office. When he heard about the broom closet he said she could move in — but that the university would not pay to fix it up.

She went to the maintenance staff and told them about her new office. The men there took up her cause. They found some old planks for book shelves and an old chair, and they used some left-over paint. Some students came to help too. They cleaned out the closet, and then the maintenance crew came in during their spare time to paint the walls and put up the shelves. They even found an old desk that fit in the new office. Since it had no windows, they cut a hole in the door and put in a screen for fresh air.

At last the professor moved her books and papers into her new office and threw a party in the hall (her office could only fit two people sitting knee to knee). She invited students, her fellow faculty members and even the dean, who came and ate cakes and shook his head at what she had done.

This professor still can't teach, but she does go on with her research. Since retiring she's become a world-recognized expert on seventeenth-century French drama and Canada's foremost expert on church stained glass. She does some of the most original research and writing on the latter subject, and she supervises a graduate student at the University of Toronto, who will carry on with her work. Right now, though, she works in her office whenever she's not in France doing research or travelling in Canada to look at stained glass windows. You can find her there most days talking with students who visit her or laughing over some joke or story she has just told one of her colleagues down the hall.

The second professor wasn't forced out. He opted for early retirement at age 60 after working hard for twenty-six years as an administrator. He had built up a continuing education program from nothing to a staff of twenty-four offering hundreds of courses. He thought of staying on for the money, but when it came time to retire he was ready to leave.

He doesn't have as much money as he might have if he'd stayed at work, but he has the freedom to do things now that he couldn't do before. After he retired the local bishop ordained him an Anglican priest, and now he visits people in nursing homes, counsels people who can't get out to church and conducts services for groups of older people. He's glad he retired. Apart from wishing he had more money, he wouldn't have it any other way.

The third professor didn't opt out, nor was she forced out: she won out. When told that retirement was mandatory at age 65, she said, "No, I don't want to leave. I'm healthy, I'm able and I do a good job. I won't go." She took her university to court.

She based her claim on her province's Human Rights Act, which stipulates that no employer may refuse to continue to employ a person solely on the basis of age. In 1981 she won her case. "The act," the Judge said, "[intends] to prohibit discrimination in employment against its adult citizens of whatever age.'' But the university still wanted her to leave, and it appealed the case. She won the appeal and now works happily and productively as if she were still young and 64.

Every story should have a moral, and these stories have three. First, *plan your retirement*. Each of these professors backed into retirement without any advance plans.

The first professor was lucky that she worked in a small university where she knew people, and where people liked her. Without that support the university would have thrown her out. The second professor was lucky to have enough public pension money (along with his wife's pension) to get by on. A few years ago, with smaller public pensions, he would have faced a sharp drop in income. The third professor was lucky that she lived in a province with strong human rights legislation. In 1984 in most provinces a person couldn't appeal age discrimination at work after age 64. Her case would have held up only in Quebec and Manitoba. In other provinces the third professor would have had to join the first professor in the broom closet.

Second, *choose your retirement*. None of the professors knew their options until the last minute, and then they had to scramble to create a decent retirement. Everything we know about retirement suggests that you should know in advance what you can do, what you want to do and how much you will have to do it with. This will take some thought and research. And if you are married, you will want to talk this over with your wife or husband. But then you should begin to make some choices about retirement — and make them now. The sooner you begin, the more options you will have when you retire. Even if you change your mind later on, it is better to have at least looked at the choices available.

Third, *take an active approach to your retirement*. Take some action. Make a choice. Check on your company pension plan to see what you can expect. If you work as a homemaker look at what will happen if your husband dies. Start to set up the economic, personal, career and work structures that will give you the retirement you want. Your co-workers will find themselves in the same boat.

And some changes — like changes in your union contract — come about faster if you and your co-workers get together.

Before you can begin to choose the retirement that is right for you, you need to know some of the facts. A lot of what we know or think we know about retirement is wrong or clouded in myth.

People don't get sick and die when they retire.

Carol Chesler came into class in the middle of the year with a sad story.

"Remember Mr Arnold?" she asked.

We all nodded. Carol had told us about him during a talk she had given on successful aging. He had retired from his job at the post office as a letter carrier about six months earlier and was spending his days at home. He got up late, read the newspaper, listened to the radio and went on short walks. Was he bored? No. He told Carol he felt content not to have to work. He had had a hard job, and he was glad to sit at home and relax.

Everyone remembered him. At the time we thought he lived a pretty dull life, but some people report high life satisfaction in retirement even though they don't do much. And while most of us would have done more with our time, we accepted Mr Arnold's life-style as his choice.

"Well," Carol went on. "I just found out he died suddenly last week at home. He had a heart attack and that was it. Can you imagine that? He only finished work six months ago. And now he's dead."

We all nodded, as if we had known it would happen. It's inevitable, isn't it? You retire, life loses its meaning and if you don't kill yourself first you die of a heart attack. "Everyone," gerontologist Robert Atchley says, "seems to know people . . . who carefully planned for retirement only to become sick and die within six months after leaving their jobs."[1] That is the common picture of retirement.

But does reality fit this picture? The latest research doesn't support this myth at all. Gordon Streib and Clement Schneider of

Cornell University studied 2,000 workers and found "little evidence to suggest that health declines at retirement. "There was no greater decline in health among retired people than among workers the same age."[2]

Researcher Susan Haynes and her co-workers found the same thing in a study of 4,000 workers in the rubber tire industry. They found that only poor health *before* retirement accounted for deaths five years later.[3] And Robert Atchley, in a study of 3,500 retired schoolteachers and telephone company workers, found that 83% of them liked retirement. Few among them said they felt depressed or dissatisfied.[4]

No matter what their job, Atchley says, "I have yet to encounter an occupational group for which retirement is related to a decline in self-reported health. It is true that many people expect retirement to adversely affect health, but very few realized their expectations."

Some people retire because they are sick and are unable to work anymore. A recent Canada Department of Health and Welfare Retirement Survey found that 34% of men and 38% of retired women workers reported bad health as the single most important reason for retiring.[5] Retirement did not cause their sickness: they brought bad health with them into old age.[a]

People don't have trouble adjusting to retirement.

We talk all the time about the Protestant Work Ethic and how people become addicted to work.

A report on the White House Conference on Aging in 1960 summed up this idea: "Retired persons find difficulty in filling time with leisure activity and have feelings of guilt when they do because their lives have been lived in a world that made a virtue of work."[7]

When they retire we expect people to fall into a deep depression at the loss of their jobs. Recent research punches some big holes in

[a]These figures may overstate the amount of illness among older workers. James Schulz, economist, reports that people sometimes use poor health as an excuse to retire because it sounds better than saying they don't want to work anymore.[6]

this balloon. Studies show that two-thirds of *all* retired people have no problems adjusting to retirement, and of those who have problems only about 7% of this group say that they miss their jobs.[8]

Most people adjust to retirement with little or no trouble.[9] And the earlier people retire, the more they say they like it.[10]

Dr Robert Wasylenki of the Clarke Institute in Toronto studied one hundred older teachers who retired and one hundred who kept on working. He found almost no difference in the levels of stress in these two groups. ''Only a small minority don't do well,'' he says, ''about 10% for whom work was the main source of identity in life.'' Doctors and executives can feel this most. Blue-collar workers often enjoy retirement.[11]

People want to retire.

Given the chance, some people want to keep on working after 65. Today two-thirds of older men and women who work on Canada's farms work past the age of 65, 21% of farmers work past the age of 70. They make up 90% of all primary workers over age 70 in Canada.[12]

Since the turn of the century, however, more and more people each year have retired. In 1921, for instance, 33% of Canada's older people worked for pay. By 1976 this figure had dropped to only 12%.[13] From 1971 to 1981 the number of male workers over 65 dropped from one worker in forty to one in fifty, and in 1975 90% of men over age 71 were retired.[14]

Some of them had to retire because their companies or union contracts forced them to, but today only 29% of men say they left work because they had to. Another 29% left because they wanted to. They had other things they wanted to do, and they saw retirement as a reward for a lifetime of work. In short, 70% of retired workers would have left work even if they could have stayed on.[15]

''The evidence shows that as one gets older, the desire to continue working is clearly not as strong as it was once thought to be by many sociologists.''[16] Most people stop working as soon as it is financially possible.

If most people want to retire and face no problems when they do so, why do people fear retirement? And why have these and other myths about retirement sprung up? A look at the system today will show why.

The System Today

Mandatory Retirement

Rev. John Wong felt bitter and angry when his church asked him to retire. "At age 65," he says, "you're no longer needed. You're no longer important. It doesn't matter what you were in your active years. You're nothing now in the church. You don't have a place there."

Rev. Dr Wong's father had worked as a lay priest in the Chinese community on the West Coast, and he had taken up his father's work when he became an ordained minister. He had spent his life in the church, derived his sense of self-esteem from his work and without that he felt like nothing.

Even when the church asked him to stay on part time after he retired, he felt used. "Once you retire," he says, "they don't base your pay on your experience or on how much you know. I heard the person interviewing me say, 'Well, you know, there is really no standard for paying retired people.' In other words, 'we'll pay you what we decided to pay you. And you can take it or leave it.'"

Mandatory retirement forced Rev. Dr Wong to give up for no reason other than his age a career he loved. People like Rev. Dr Wong often find it hard to adjust to retirement. Given the choice, they would prefer to go on working.

"The higher the level of occupation and the more absorbing the work," Bernice Neugarten says, "the longer people stay in it. That's because their self-concept gets built into being successful at work, and they find it hard to draw a line between work and play."[17]

Statistics Canada reports that in 1981 23% of people in the work force over 65 worked as managers and professionals, and they make up 21% of the over 70 workers, about the same percentage as workers 55-64 years old. The number of workers in clerical jobs, processing and construction jobs decreases dramatically with age. "About four in five older workers, are in categories where higher education has afforded them the opportunity to keep professional and managerial jobs, or perform as self-employed workers, or to pursue careers in self-employment. . . ."[18]

More than a third of men with university degrees, for instance, stay in the labour force past age 65. But only about one man in nine with less than a grade five education still works.[19] People with more education have more choice about working after 65 if they want to, and they often choose to go on working. But mandatory retirement rules force many of them out of work.

These rules aren't based on the law. No law forces a person to retire at 65, no statute requires people to leave work at a certain age. But, as one government report concludes, "mandatory retirement at 65 is practised by government and educational institutions, and employers in general follow this policy."[20] A worker who wants to stay at work often has no choice.

In 1984 only two provinces — Quebec and Manitoba — make it illegal to discriminate against someone on the basis of age. The federal Human Rights Bill (Bill C-72), while making it illegal to discriminate against someone on the basis of sex or race, specifically exempts compulsory retirement from its anti-discrimination provisions. The Canadian Council of Social Development says this "virtually establishes the practice as an acceptable norm."[21] When you reach 65 an employer can look you in the eye and tell you you can't have a job because you are too old.

Yet a 1975 Canada retirement survey found that about a third of the people surveyed opposed compulsory retirement.[22] And in 1981 Louis Harris found that a vast majority (90%) of the American public opposed compulsory retirement. They agreed that "nobody should be forced to retire because of age, if he wants to continue working and is still able to do a good job."[23] Canada's Croll Commission put it this way: "Forcing people to retire at age 65 or some other artificial age limit, particularly when they had inadequate income, or discriminating against people in employment because they are no longer young are clearly objectionable on social grounds. They are no more justifiable than discrimination because of religion."[24]

All of this will change when the new Canadian Charter of Rights comes into force in 1985. It will outlaw discrimination on the basis of age as well as sex and race. But a number of false beliefs support the idea that workers should quit at age 65, and even if the law changes, these beliefs may put unfair pressure on older workers to leave work.

First, some people argue that older workers don't work as well as younger workers. This myth justifies forced retirement as a good business practice. It assumes that the older worker is incompetent, even though studies show that the majority of older workers can work as effectively as younger workers.

"When speed of reaction is important," researcher Erdman Palmore of Duke University says, "older workers sometimes produce at lower rates, but they are at least as accurate and steady in their work as younger workers." Moreover, older workers' output tends to *increase* with age. They "perform at steadier rates from week to week than younger workers do."[25] They also have less job turnover and take time off work less often than younger workers.[26]

Older workers also have fewer accidents than younger workers. "A study of 18,000 workers in manufacturing plants found that workers beyond age 65 have about one-half the rate of nondisabling injuries as those under 65. And older workers have substantially lower rates of disabling injuries."[27]

Some people argue that older workers become outdated. They don't keep up with the latest information and technology. But older workers can, and do, learn new things: they just need more time and more repetition to learn something new.[28] Retraining programs at work can keep older people up to date and on their jobs. Given the productivity of older workers, this makes better business sense than forced retirement.

Second, some people support compulsory retirement because they say it fits the system of work rules and pension plans today and creates an efficient way for employers to get rid of obsolete workers. With a fixed retirement age, you don't have to justify why you fire people when they get old. You fire everyone at 65, then hire back the people you want to keep.

But this system creates a second class of workers — older workers who have no right to appeal discrimination on the basis of age. They work only at their employers' pleasure. A fixed retirement age leaves all the cards in the employer's hands. After 65 the worker has no right to demand fair treatment on the job.

On this ground alone compulsory retirement should end — no matter how smoothly and efficiently the system works. The system of work has adjusted to other changes — child labour laws, unions and laws that allow women time off to have children — and it can adjust to an open retirement age too.

Third, some people say that older workers take jobs from the young. Robert Atchley calls this the strongest argument for forced retirement. He says that in modern society we may have to put a time limit on work to give everyone a chance.[29] But a rule that retires older workers to create jobs for the young makes older people scapegoats: it uses them to patch up cracks in the economy instead of making basic changes. U.S. economist James Schulz writes that "we can provide jobs for younger and older people if we're willing to undertake the policies necessary to promote and ensure full employment while restraining prices."[30] It's just easier to blame unemployment on the older worker.

James Pesando, economics professor at McMaster University, writes that this kind of policy assumes "the 'lump-of-labour fallacy,' the mistaken notion that there exists a fixed number of jobs that must be allocated among competing workers."

The baby boom has led to a glut of workers and a shortage of jobs, but studies show that in time the economy can absorb new workers without getting rid of older workers. As these people find work in the next few years they will create a new demand for goods, and this in turn will create a demand for more workers. "The important point," Pesando says, "is that the postponement of retirement by elderly workers does *not* imply a corresponding reduction in the job opportunities available to [others]."[31]

Some people even argue that in the next few years, with the decrease in the birth rate and fewer young people in the work-force, we may need older workers to stay on at work. "Once the baby boom generation is absorbed [into the work-force]," the Croll Commission says, "a labour shortage could develop. At that time, the older population is more likely to be welcomed in the labour force than to be viewed with concern."[32] "As a matter of public policy," Roland Penner, Attorney General of Manitoba, says, "there is a need to retain experienced, skilled workers past the age of 65."[33]

Older people no longer have to apologize for working, and they have begun to challenge compulsory retirement rules. In 1981 Professor Imogene McIntire won an appeal against her forced retirement from the University of Manitoba.

"Age," she told *The Winnipeg Free Press* at the time, "is no criterion for the quality of wisdom or experience." She went on to say that she would work "as long as I'm productive and can contribute something."[34]

Professor McIntire's case has opened the way for other appeals. John Green, former safety co-ordinator of Brandon, Manitoba, told *The Winnipeg Free Press* he would like to go back to work right away. He said he would take his case to court and sell his house, if he had to, in order to fight for his right to work.

Aubrey Newport will also appeal his forced retirement from the Manitoba Civil Service. The Civil Service Superannuation Act provides for mandatory retirement at 65 unless a person gets special permission from the Civil Service Commission to stay on at work. Mr Newport intends to take his case to court.

These court cases and appeals have freed Manitobans from the threat of forced retirement, but they also set the stage for a Canada-wide change in retirement rules. In 1985 the new Charter of Rights will challenge all provincial laws that now allow for mandatory retirement at 65. Canadians who want to keep on working after age 65 will be able to do so.

Voluntary Retirement

Changes in the law will give people more choice as they reach
retirement age and will help many people avoid the shock of sudden retirement, but it will probably not change most people's decision to retire by the age of 65. A survey of retirement in Canada
conducted by the Department of Health and Welfare found that
37% of men had retired early, by age 64. "Of these," the report
says, "58% had retired because of ill-health and a further 10%
because of layoff." None of these people would have stayed at
work past 65.[35] Also, half of the workers who gave mandatory
retirement as their reason for leaving work said they were content
with the timing of retirement. Some said they would have retired
earlier if they had had more money.[36] Statistics Canada estimates
that an end to mandatory retirement would increase the percentage of older workers by only about 2% (from 15% in 1977 to 17%
today).

Gerontologist Bernice Neugarten writes, "people retire just as
soon as they feel they have enough money to do so. They either
choose to get out of the labour market or poor health forces them
out." Only a small percentage of workers (about 8% to 10%) fit
the stereotype of the faithful worker who is forced out of work.[37]

A 1981 Harris poll in the U.S. found that of those people 25 to
39 who planned to retire at age 65 or sooner 57% said they would
retire at 65 even if they could get higher pensions at age 68. And
72% of the workers 55-64 Harris talked to rejected the idea of
postponing retirement.[38] Canadians often say the same thing. Ed
Chaze, a Winnipeg bus driver, told *Free Press* reporter Glen
MacKenzie that he would need about $1,000 a month to live on
when he retires. But, he said, "if I could get $800 a month, I'd be
gone."[39]

Studies show again and again that most workers would not
choose to stay at work. Given the choice, they retire. "The debate
over abolishing mandatory retirement," Robert Atchley says, "or
raising the retirement age for mandatory retirement obscure[s] a

more important policy issue. . . . All sorts of evidence indicates that most workers retire as soon as it is financially feasible."[40]

In the U.S., for instance, when the Social Security system offered reduced benefits at age 62, the typical age of retirement dropped from 65 to 63.[41] Canadian studies show the same trend to early retirement. A Canadian Council on Social Development study in Canada found that "81 percent of those under age 65 and 62 percent over 65 thought the pensionable age should be lowered to 60 years."[42] An Ontario study found that 68% of workers opted for retirement earlier than 65 given the chance.[43] The Canadian Pension Plan Advisory Commission reports a "growing social pressure for early retirement."[44]

Wes Weston makes the best case I know for early retirement. After the war he went into the civil service. He worked for the Land Title's Office for seventeen years, then transferred to Mines and Resources and stayed there until he turned 63.

"I retired early," Wes says, "because I had sufficient funds to do the things I've always wanted to do. My work with the government was far from what I wanted to do. I wanted to be able to sit down and systematically while away my time with these." He points to a bookcase filled with philosophy books.

Wes gets four pension cheques each month — a small army pension, his OAS pension, the CPP and his civil service pension. The last three go up with increases in the cost of living, so Wes has no money problems. He and his wife live in a big three-bedroom apartment. They use one bedroom for Wes's study; the other has been fixed up as a den and TV room.

They use their living-room to entertain guests and as a music room. Wes had a piano and a full sized electric organ. "In retirement," he says, "I want to think, maybe write my memoirs. I also want to improve the little knowledge I have of music. I've got a number of works that I want to explore more thoroughly."

Wes has only one complaint: he's still too busy. He serves on the board of directors of three senior organizations. He works a few days a week at the Manitoba Society of Seniors (MSOS) headquarters. And he and his wife have designed a table-top golf game that he hopes will sell well enough to create a legacy for his grand-children.

"I'm busier than ever. We just opened an office to market our game. We're already getting orders from some ads we placed. We want to have it on the shelves for Christmas. And I still work for MSOS. Once the game gets going, though, I want to really retire. I'll cut back on my community work. Then I'll take a year or two off just to read and write."

The system today encourages more and more people to choose early retirement. Pension policies make it an attractive option. Some new private pension plans, for instance, encourage people to retire early. They give workers a lump of credit for past work, and when workers come into a large amount of retirement income all at once they tend to retire.[45]

Other pension plans in Canada allow early retirement on a reduced pension. Ninety-seven percent of pension plans covering 95% of their members offer this option. Some private and public plans even include a special rule allowing early retirement on an *unreduced* pension for a certain number of years of service or age plus service. The Advisory Commission on pensions reports that 12% of public sector plans covering well over half of their members and 3% of private plans covering 28% of their members offer this option.[46]

Finally, the Canada Pension Plan discourages people from staying at work past 65. It pays no higher benefits if a worker puts off retirement, so workers lose a year of benefits for every year they continue to work. This loss, and high taxes on a working income, can make retirement look like the most sensible option.

Better pension incomes lead people to retire at age 65 today. And although retirement receives bad press Robert Atchley reports that people 45 years old and over have "very positive" views of retirement, regardless of their age and sex.[47] The overwhelming majority of people he has studied are satisfied with retirement, and the better their health, the higher their education and the more money they have, the more satisfied they are.[48]

Popular myth leads us to believe that people feel lonely and resentful when they retire, but for many people retirement opens up a range of new options. Some people choose to work part time, others start new careers and others devote themselves to community service. Older people today have begun to explore all these options, and as they succeed in their retirement they may encourage even more people to retire in the future.

Changes in the System

Flexible Retirement

Classics professor Tom Larmond eased into retirement. He took his pension at 65 but continued to teach one course in his specialty, Greek theatre, for the next three years. At 68 he gave up his course to a young professor. He now has the title Professor Emeritus, and the university gives him an office that he shares with another retired professor. He comes in two or three times a week to do research, he gives guest lectures and he lunches in the faculty club to keep in touch with his colleagues.

Professor Larmond has adjusted to retirement without a hitch. Teachers and scholars like him can slide into retirement: they can leave work a little at a time over a period of a few years. Experts call this "flexible retirement." It offers an option to the sudden shock of mandatory retirement.

Other professionals also take retirement one step at a time. Doctors and lawyers, for instance, often choose flexible retirement. They don't have to leave their practices at any set age (though some hospitals do put an age limit on residency rights). They can cut back to half days, reduce the number of clients and take on only the cases they choose. They can eventually retire full time when and if they want to.

Given the choice most workers say they would prefer flexible retirement. The Harris study in the U.S., for instance, found that 37% of people between 55 and 64 preferred a gradual retirement option. And the majority of workers over 55 wanted some flexible form of retirement — three or four day weeks, job sharing or a freer work schedule after 65.[49] The Health and Welfare Canada retirement survey found that 35-40% of the people questioned favoured a part-time transition to retirement.[50] Today, however, no formal system of flexible retirement exists in Canada.

Sweden has set up a program that might work well here. In 1975 the government there passed the Partial Pension Insurance Act. Under this plan workers between 60 and 65 can switch to part-time work with almost no effect on their pre-retirement income.

To qualify for a partial pension workers have to reduce their work by at least an average of 5 hours a week (down to 35 full-time hours), and they can work as few as 17 hours. (A person has to work at least every second month, so a worker can't work six months and take six months off.) In 1977 10% of all workers 60-65 took partial pensions. Nearly all the workers who chose partial pensions went from a 40 hour to a 17-21 hour work week. A Swedish survey showed that another 10% might choose this option in the future.

The Swedish system allows workers a new freedom. It gives them the chance to structure a retirement that works for them and it creates better odds for making a successful switch to full retirement. "They've worked 40 or 50 years," a Swedish official with the National Social Insurance Board says. "They need time to calm down and adjust to retirement. . . . People should be able to stay on at work as much as they want and retire slowly . . . so they don't face the shock at 65."[51]

In Canada this plan might also alleviate the problem of sudden lay-offs for older workers. It would give employers as well as workers more choice.

Part-time Work

A recent Health and Welfare report says that "opportunities to work part time are very important for Canada's older workers." In 1981 24% of employed men aged 65-69 and 32% of those aged 70 and over held part-time jobs. Among female workers, 43% of those aged 65-69 and 47% of those aged 70 and over worked on a part-time basis.[52]

Many older people find they need to work part time after they retire — some because they need the money, others because they enjoy work and the chance it gives them to meet people. But not everyone has the same chance to work part time after they retire. "The choice of working after 65," according to the Canadian Council on Social Development, "is . . . available only to a minority."[53] Many older workers who want to work can't find jobs once they retire. Statistics Canada reports that when older workers lose their jobs it takes them 20% longer than a younger person to find work again.[54]

The Croll Commission's report comes back again and again to problems older workers face when they look for work. "Job opportunities for persons over 50 are not readily available and special qualifications are needed to overcome discriminatory attitudes." One Quebec study, for instance, found that people 65 and over made up only a tiny fraction (1.75%) of all the people who registered with Canada Employment. Still, only 8% of this small group found work.[55]

People with higher education and higher-income jobs have the best options for early retirement and for work after 65. Men over 65 with a university degree, for instance, have a four times greater labour force participation rate than men with less than grade five. And women with a university degree have a five times greater rate than women with less than grade five. People with higher education like doctors or lawyers have special skills that make them marketable. Also, the kinds of work they do "often allow them to continue beyond age 65 in academic, managerial, professional or consultative capacities." Less well-educated workers may have trouble getting back on the job ladder.[56]

People who retire but want to work often need help getting started again. In 1976 Age and Opportunity (A & O), a social service agency, surveyed retired people in Winnipeg. Thirteen percent of the people they talked to wanted work but couldn't find jobs, so A & O applied to the federal New Horizons program for funds to start a Senior Citizens Job Bureau. New Horizons granted them $8,000 for operating expenses, and the Department of Labour agreed to pay for a two person staff. In May 1978 A & O opened Canada's first job bureau for seniors.

Sheila Crawford, who has been with the Bureau from the beginning, still runs it six years later. Since 1978 the Bureau has helped about 2,500 people over age 60 find work. From May 1978 to November 1983, Mrs Crawford says, the Bureau has listed over 8,000 jobs and filled almost 7,000 of them. One thousand of these jobs led to permanent part-time work (10-12 hours or more a week). Almost 1,200 of these jobs came from the business community, the rest from people who need tradesmen on a daily, casual basis — carpenters, electricians, typists, bookkeepers, plumbers or painters.

"A widow, for instance, might need a leaky tap fixed," Mrs Crawford says. "A union plumber charges $12.50 to $25 just to come out, and then $8 to $12 an hour to do the work. A 5¢ faucet washer can end up costing $25. But a Job Bureau worker will charge a flat rate, say, $10. He may charge for gas if he has to come a long way, so he might make it $12, but he'll tell the person how much it'll cost before he starts. Sometimes he'll even give an estimate over the phone."

In one case a young married couple wanted to insulate their basement. The husband called the Job Bureau. "I've got all the tools and equipment," he said, "but I don't know where to begin." Mrs Crawford sent out one of her workers, he and the young man agreed on a price and they went to work on the job together. "We tell our workers to give a total figure when they estimate a job. That way people know how much it will cost them, no matter how long the job takes."

The Bureau has trouble finding enough tradesmen. Those people it finds, however, want to work. They made good money when they worked, but they may not have had a company pension or savings, so they work to keep up their standard of living.

Skilled secretaries, for instance, are often widows. They may have no private pension and have to live on OAS and Spouse's

Allowance payments. They need money, and the Job Bureau can get them placed for weeks at a time when a full-time secretary takes a vacation. Sometimes they stay on in a permanent job.

Mrs Crawford says that older workers often choose to work for more than money. They also want social contact. ''Idleness begins to affect their social lives. People want jobs where they'll meet people.'' The Bureau has the hardest time finding people to work alone as homemakers or housekeepers. Older workers would rather work in a retail store where they can meet customers, or in an office with other workers. ''We get calls for homemakers and babysitters everyday,'' Mrs Crawford says, ''but no one will take them.

''I have one employer who wants a husband and wife team to do industrial cleaning. It pays well, but no one will take it. I've called all our married couples. The husband says, 'I want to get *away* from her.' And the wife says, 'I don't want to work *with* him, I want to get him out from under my feet.' They want to meet new people at work.''

Even with unemployment in the area hovering around 9% in 1984, the Job Bureau filled 50% more jobs than in 1983. And more of these jobs went to women than ever before. To keep up the momentum, Mrs Crawford has produced a TV commercial about the Bureau, and she appears on radio talk shows to discuss the Bureau's work. But continuity, she says, is the key to the Bureau's success. ''We know our people. Sometimes they drop by on a day off to chat and have coffee. We also know the jobs. An older person sometimes calls us because they want another older person to do the work — someone they can trust. We get to know the people who need the work done.''

In 1983, for the first time, the Bureau received funding for two years as a Canada Employment and Immigration Outreach Program. Edmonton, Calgary and Ottawa also have Job Bureaus for Seniors, and in St John, New Brunswick, a number of community groups help older people find work. If the present trend to part-time work continues, these agencies will play an important role in the lives of older workers in the future.

Second Careers

Not everyone who retires wants to work at their old job — even part time. In a study of three large corporations, one marketing executive said he retrained himself as an insurance broker. Other executives became fishermen or started ranches. "At 75 years of age," one man said, "[I] spent most of last winter caring for 500 head of cattle and 400 head of hogs."[57]

The 1981 Harris poll found that 18% of 65-year-olds said they wanted to switch to a new kind of work when they retired. This figure jumped to 54% for 18-54 year olds.[58]

Sheila Crawford says that one man, a former school principal, refused to take any job teaching or working with children. He had other skills he wanted to sell. He'd remodelled his house over the years, knew carpentry, plumbing and painting and loved to putter around. Sheila found him a job in no time as a painter. "He's meticulous," she says. "You can't get a better job done."

Other people turn to community service work when they retire. Bernice Neugarten reports that "many business executives become engaged in community affairs in the last years of their employment and find it relatively easy to move into those areas after they retire."[59] For these people a second career means more than just an income: it means they can explore talents they never had time for when they worked full time.

Ed Arneson retired five years ago. He planned to sit back and relax, at least in the first year of retirement, but a few weeks after he retired someone asked him to help teaching a writing course at the local Y. He went down for the afternoon — and he's been teaching courses ever since.

Ed wrote for the CBC before the war. His first radio play aired when he was 15. Later he wrote fantasies and horror stories, many of them for children, but he gave up writing for the civil service when his family came along. "Writing is hard work," he says, "and the only reason I wrote was for the money. When I didn't need the money any more, I quit writing."

In retirement he found people could use his experience as a writer. Now he's president of three writers' workshops for seniors, teaches a ten-lesson writing course to people of all ages at the Y and edits the province's Senior Citizen newspaper.

Ed isn't paid for teaching, but he gets a lot of satisfaction from his work and that seems to be the important thing at the moment. Without planning it he has swung into a second career. "A second career," writes Swiss doctor and writer Paul Tournier, "is like a plant whose seed has been sown in the midst of a person's active life, which has taken root, which has developed tentatively at first, but which bears all its fruits in retirement."[60]

People who voluntarily take up a second career say they feel free from the daily demands of their previous work. They don't have to sit on committees or please their superiors, they don't have to boss others and they are free from the routine work that ate up their time.

Rev. John Wong found this kind of freedom once he recovered from the first shock of retirement. He found a new kind of fulfillment outside the system. "I don't think I was able to work to my potential when I was rector," he says after three years of retirement. "It's only when I was free from parish work that I developed."

Rev. Dr Wong now works at pastoral care and conducts services at the St Boniface nursing home in Winnipeg. He works with the older patients on a one-to-one basis and says he gets more pleasure from the work he does now than he ever got from fund-raising or preaching to a congregation — the kinds of jobs that took up most of his time as a rector.

He receives a small honorarium for his work, but like Ed he does it mainly because he enjoys it. He's so popular, he says, that half-a-dozen seniors have already booked him for their funerals. "They don't want anyone else. And it makes me feel useful, it's a sign of their appreciation." When he told his wife about these bookings, she laughed. "That's fine," she said, "but it all depends on who goes first, you or them."

Ann Carrier also gave her time to others when she retired. She worked as a bookkeeper in Vancouver for ten years after her second husband died, then learned that her niece in Quebec wanted to go back to school to finish her degree. The problem was that her niece had no one to care for her husband and four children. At 63 years of age Ann decided to give a year of her life to her niece.

She lived with the family for a year, doing all the housework, cooking, shopping and mothering while her niece studied. "I didn't know if I could do it," she says. "And I will say it was hard work. But it was the most exciting year of my life. I felt a great sense of achievement. And I have a very close relationship with the children."

Many older people move into a second career when they see someone in need or something that ought to be done. In some cases only they can do the job.

Joe Wilder, 89, a retired pharmacist, recently published his second book, *Lotions, Potions, and Liniments Pure*. When he retired at 75, he wanted something to do and found it when he started attending creative writing classes for seniors. After a while he began to publish some of his work in the local newspaper. "Then it dawned on me," he says. "Maybe I should write a story about my own family."

He called his first book *Read All About It: Reminiscences of an Immigrant Newsboy*. "In the first book, I go back to 1910 when I was selling newspapers on Main Street. I tell about the things that happened there, the hanky panky that went on — the fancy ladies, the bar rooms and exploitation of immigrants. I write as a chronicler for my children and grandchildren so they'll know their roots."

Older people like Joe who take up second careers also take on new roles in society. They become counsellors, historians and advisors who work outside the established hierarchy. But none of this happens automatically. For years gerontologists spoke of retirement and old age as a "roleless role." They meant that society doesn't prepare people for retirement. Instead, older people have to prepare for it themselves.

The Future

Whatever kind of retirement people choose — flexible retirement, part-time work, a second career or a life of leisure — they stand the best chance of success if they plan it in advance. Some people do this planning themselves and swing into retirement with no problems. Others need some guidance after forty years on the job.

"Many employees," according to the Warner-Lambert Company of Canada, "[are] totally unprepared for their retirement." Warner-Lambert offers a full pre-retirement counselling course for its workers — one of the few private companies in Canada to do so. They offer it because they find that workers sometimes see retirement as a "worrisome ordeal, with lots of financial problems, loneliness and confusion. . . ."[61]

Pre-retirement education (PRE) programs can ease some of this distress. Louis Harris found that 84% of people aged 55 to 64 in the United States supported the idea of programs to help workers learn about finances in retirement. Nearly 75% of people 55 and over supported programs to help people plan their personal lives. Seventy-seven percent of 55-64-year-olds thought these programs were important.[62]

Since the 1950s interest in PRE programs has spread across Canada. Forty percent of the people in a recent survey of workers said either they had taken part or would like to take part in a PRE program.[63] Workers throughout Canada can find programs where they work, through the government or at local community colleges and social agencies.

These programs vary. Some are short, intensive courses offered in one to three consecutive days. Others are offered in two or three hour classes once a week over several weeks. Some programs begin a few weeks or months before retirement, others start in middle age. But all of them have some basic goals in common.

First, they encourage the worker to prepare for retirement. PRE programs educate middle-aged workers about early retirement, investment options and pension benefits. Few of us know how to prepare for retirement or just what to expect: a course in middle age, when people are young enough to plan, can help them adjust smoothly later.

The Canadian Broadcasting Corporation, for instance, starts its program early. At age 45 workers take a one-day seminar on finances. Then, between ages 50 and 65, they take a three-day seminar that discusses different facets of retirement in detail. The CBC also offers workers a chance to try flexible retirement. "CBC adds an extra three weeks to the annual leave of people three years before retirement, an extra six weeks for those two years before, and an extra nine weeks in the final year."[64]

Second, PRE programs often work on more than just the use of time and finances. They also help workers and their spouses look at how retirement will change their relationship. Sheila Crawford, director of the Winnipeg Senior Citizens Job Bureau, says that when she counsels couples, she often finds that the men have no idea what their wives do all day. "I sit them down and I say, 'Bob, what does Mary do while you're at work?' 'Oh,' he'll say, 'she talks on the phone, does a little shopping. On Thursdays she plays bridge with the girls.' He really has no idea what she does. When he retires, he'll find that Mary's busy most days. She's got volunteer work, a class at the university or she may even go back to work part time. She's had to fill up her days for herself for years if she's never had a job before. And she'll keep busy after 65. Bob, who expects Mary to be around as his companion all day, may find himself left in limbo unless he prepares for retirement."

Barbara White, partner in Retirement Planning Consultants of Toronto, also has her clients discuss the role that each spouse will play after retirement. Without planning, she says, retirement can lead to divorce.[65]

Do PRE programs work? One study by Mark Greene and his colleagues at the University of Oregon shows that they do. In a survey of almost nine hundred workers from fifty-eight companies, all of whom had chosen chose early retirement, only a little more than half of those who could have taken PRE programs had taken them. Greene and his co-workers found that half the people with low retirement-adjustment scores had made no plans. On the other hand, when people felt prepared for retirement, they adjusted more smoothly: those who had made some plans showed medium or high adjustment.[66]

PRE programs allow workers to explore new roles and activities with other retirees. They also help reduce stress and negative attitudes.[67] One study found that whether a PRE program consisted of lectures or discussion, whether it was long or short, it improved workers' sense of satisfaction.[68]

More could be done in Canada to make PRE programs open to more people. Only 8% of retired men and 3% of retired women today say they have actually taken part in a PRE program.[69] People in some provinces have a better chance of finding a program than others: in 1982, for instance, more than seventy companies offered programs in the Toronto-Hamilton region, while in other parts of the country these programs did not exist at all. Ontario seems to be ahead of the rest of the country, but more and more courses will appear across the country if present trends continue.

"Much more should be done to devise and implement effective programs in this country," the Croll Commission recommends.[70] And for good reason. "Of all employees now aged 55 and working with an employer with a pension plan, 71% will never work past 65 . . . 15% will die before 65, 6% will be laid off and not find another job, and 50% will retire early, either because of early-retirement provisions or illness. . . ."[71] In the future, retirement will be a normal part of adult life.

What will this future be like? First, an end to mandatory retirement will make retirement a non-issue for some people. They will keep on working as long as they can do their jobs. Second, pre-retirement education will help people adjust to life after work. Third, retirement will mean more choice in the future. Some people will go on working, some will take early retirement, others will work part time. But one thing seems certain: all of us will have to prepare for retirement long before we reach the age of 65.

RECREATION AND LEISURE: A TIME TO REAP

What Do People Do in Old Age?

Andy Rooney calls one of his reports to America "Saturdays With the White House Staff." "Every Saturday morning," he says, "I make a list of Things to Do Today. I don't *Do* them, I just make a list. My schedule always falls apart, and I realize that what I need is the kind of support the President gets." With the White House staff on his side he figures he could get a decent breakfast (made by the kitchen staff), read the paper (pre-digested by a group of editors), take care of his mail (pre-sorted by a secretary), fix the sink, clean the storm gutters (with a little help from the maintenance staff), go to the barber, get the car washed and be back before noon to have a cup of coffee at home. With all the work done he could relax for the afternoon — watch a ball game or take a nap.[1]

He's dreaming of course. Saturdays don't work out like this. We all have too much to do, and not enough time to do it. Also, on our day off we'd rather relax than do all the work that's piled up and that we know we can't get done in one day anyway. So we spend a lot of our free time feeling guilty about not caulking the windows, cleaning the garage or fixing the faucet.

We all need more time. Studies show that middle-aged people spend at least half their waking hours at work. Add to this the time they take to shave, wash, dress, eat and commute, and on a weekday, according to one American study, the average person has only about four hours left for recreation.[2] Canadian studies report the same pattern. On the average day (including days off) people have only about six hours of free time.[3]

All this changes when a person retires. A study of 5,000 retired people in the U.S. found they had an average of 8.3 hours each day for leisure.[4] That comes to over 3,000 hours a year, or 60,000 hours over a 20-year retirement.

Farrell Fleming, former philosophy instructor and now executive director of Creative Retirement Manitoba, a seniors' education centre in Winnipeg, says that most people haven't given much thought to how they will use their time in retirement. "All through life," he says, "we use our free time to get ready for work, and when people retire they only have this model to fall back on. Basically, they retire to play, and they play as long and as hard as they can. Then when they can't play any more they wait. That's what the people in nursing homes are doing — they're waiting."

This model of leisure doesn't fit retirement today. People don't retire to rest up for more work. When people retire they move into a new phase of life. And most of them won't work again. Professor Joffre Dumazedier believes that leisure in retirement has a new purpose — the "realization of the individual for his own sake."[5]

Not many people see retirement as a time for self-realization or as a time to learn new skills and gain new knowledge, but some people have begun to explore new models of retirement. They've found new purpose and meaning in old age, and their life-styles and activities point the way to the future.

How, though, do most older people actually spend their time — and why?

To judge by the statistics older people don't do much. They show, for instance, less involvement in sports than any other age group. In 1974 13% of Canadians engaged in some sports activity, but only 2% of people over 65 took part in sports.[6] The same trend holds for men and women, in spectator sports as well as exercise.[7]

The Canada Health Survey "Physical Activity Index" found that the proportion of "very active" people in different age groups showed a steady decrease with age. Forty-six percent of men and 32% of women 15-19 years old were "very active", compared to only 11% of men and 5% of women after age 65.[8]

Other kinds of activity decrease too. "Almost invariably," Rolf Schliewen reports in a study for the Secretary of State's Office, "participation (in leisure activity) decreases with age. . . ."[9] People over 65, for instance, go to movies and visit cultural institutions less often than the young.[10] And it's not the cost that keeps older people away: a Statistics Canada study found that people over 65 went to cultural events less often than any other age group, whether the events cost money or not. The study also showed that while 5% of Canadians visited historical sites in 1972, only 1.6% of older people did.[11]

What do older people do, if they don't go to shows or take part in sports? More than 80% of retired people told Canada's Department of Health and Welfare they spent some of their time watching television.[12] Statistics Canada found that 40% of older people watch more than fifteen hours of television a week. Older people said they spent more time watching television than doing any other leisure activity.[13]

A Canadian Radio and Television Commission study found that older people spend a lot of time reading. Eighty-three percent of the older people in the study said they read the newspaper an average of one and a quarter hours on weekdays — twice as much time as the average in the study. Even people over 80 who reported hearing and eyesight problems spent more time than the average person reading the newspaper.[14]

Older people also visit a lot with friends and relatives.[15] In the U.S., Louis Harris found that 38% of older people spent "a lot of time" visiting.[16] A Canadian study found that 80% of older people had visited friends or relatives in the preceding week, and 40%

of retired people said they saw friends or relatives more than three times a week; 20% saw them daily.[17]

All the studies show the same trend: older people spend most of their time — 56% — on passive, "receptive" media-related leisure.[18] They spend a lot of this time at home or indoors with friends and relatives, and as they age they spend more and more time on solitary activities like watching television or reading.[19]

These facts and figures may not surprise you. They support a common view of old age as time of decline. Researcher Marc LaPlante, for instance, told a Quebec conference that "the golden age, the age of retirement, in spite of all one may think, remains the age of boredom and solitude for the vast majority of the people."[20] The Canada Healthy Survey characterizes this decrease in activity as inevitable, "to be expected in view of the general deterioration which is part of the aging process."[21]

Gerontologists have even created a theory to explain these facts. They call it "disengagement theory." Researchers Elaine Cumming and William Henry first described it in their book *Growing Old*. They wrote that as people aged they disengaged themselves from their middle-aged roles. This prepared them for death — the final disengagement — and it helped society fill these roles with younger people who could carry on after the old died. Cumming and Henry found that older people who disengaged reported high life satisfaction, and they concluded that disengagement works well for older people and society.[22] But not all the facts support the disengagement theory.

Bernice Neugarten, Robert Havighurst and Sheldon Tobin at the University of Chicago looked at the same research data as Cumming and Henry, but the Chicago team found many other patterns of aging. Some people who enjoy old age, they found, remain active. They "reorganize" their lives after retirement and turn to new activities to substitute for work. A second group the researchers called "focused." These people show a medium amount of activity: they select one or two roles and put all their energy into them. Both groups showed just as much life satisfaction as the disengaged group.[23]

Hundreds of research studies since the 1960s support the Chicago researchers. They show that no one pattern of aging leads to high life satisfaction. The research shows that how a person ages — whether they remain active or withdraw — depends on many things: wealth, income, social roles and the age group (young-old or old-old) to which they belong.

A close look at the Canada Health Survey, for instance, shows that the decline in activity after age 65 depends more on physical well-being than on age. The study divided people by age and then rated them in each age group according to how active they were. Among people 45-64 years old the survey rated 12% as "very active" and 19% as "sedentary." Among people 65 and over the survey ranked only 8% as "very active" and 29% as "sedentary" — a clear decline in activity with age.

But when the survey compared only the healthy people in each age group the figures gave a different picture. Of the healthiest 45-64 year olds, 13% ranked as "very active" and 18% as "sedentary." Of the healthiest people 65 and over, the same proportion — 13% — ranked as "very active." Moreover, only 15% ranked as "sedentary" — 3% less than the 45-64 year olds. Finally, the figures for healthy people 65 and over don't differ that much from the total population (20% "very active" and 14% "sedentary").[24] People in good health and with positive emotional well-being tend to remain very active, and, according to the Canada Health Survey, "this is particularly true of older people."[25]

Income and social status also make a difference in what people do. Barry McPherson, professor of sociology at the University of Western Ontario, found that older people who earn $20,000 a year or more show less interest in spectator sports compared to people with middle incomes. "Even within the same age cohort, life chances and life-styles vary because of differences in social status."[26] Other studies in Canada show that higher income and more education lead to more active leisure.[27]

Studies also find that gender influences activity level. Professor McPherson found that at all ages men are more active than women in sports.[28] The Canada Health Survey showed that older women had a lower fitness level than older men.[29] This may reflect the lack of opportunity women have had to participate in sports in the past, in which case the difference may disappear in the future. Today, for instance, women show the same amount of participation in exercise programs as men.[30]

Clearly, some older people remain more active than others, but recent studies show that as a group older people live more active lives today than older people in the past.

The Canada Survey of Leisure, for instance, found in 1978 that 37% of older people exercised. About 20% of them said they exercised for their health, but 30% said they exercised to feel good in general or because they enjoyed it.[31] A recent Canadian government study reported that one older person in five went out or participated in sports or exercise in the week of the survey.[32] Harris found that between 1974 and 1981 older people showed an increase in leisure-time activities ranging from going out to eat in a restaurant, to going to a recreation centre, to shopping, to going to the library. He also found that, compared to 1974, in 1981 a smaller proportion of older people reported a visit to a doctor or medical clinic in the preceding month.[33]

As new groups of people move into old age, research indicates that they will bring with them better income, more education, better health and more experience with the use of leisure time. They will remain active in old age, and they will find new ways to enjoy retirement. They will also find a recreation system that offers more options in retirement than ever before.[34]

The System Today

Leisure and recreation programs for seniors exist all across the country. In Saskatchewan seniors can get free fishing licences and free access to provincial parks. Manitoba, Saskatchewan and Quebec offer assisted travel tours. Quebec offers short vacations at countryside resorts. Nova Scotia runs fitness and recreation classes. Alberta has a recreation consulting service and promotes senior involvement in the theatre. Airlines, buses, theatres, restaurants and travel agencies across the country offer senior citizens discounts. All of these programs and services help older people stay active.

Most cities and towns across Canada also have senior centres. They form the closest thing to a nation-wide recreation system for older people. Some centres are in church basements, others in empty store-fronts, others in their own buildings. They offer places for older people to drop in, meet one another, play cards or take classes. Some centres also offer meals, medical care and counselling. The federal government calls senior centres "the most important source of recreation and cultural activity" for older people in Canada.[35]

The federal government has funded scores of senior groups across Canada through its New Horizons program. New Horizons was established in 1972 to help groups of seniors start their own recreation programs. The groups must have at least ten members, most of whom have to be over 60 years old and retired. New Horizons won't pay a salary for full-time staff except in special cases, and it won't give money to groups or agencies that perform services for seniors. All the money goes as direct contributions to older people to use for projects they design.

"In the first years of the program," Esther Korchynski, acting regional manager for New Horizons says, "people asked for almost nothing but recreation centres. I thought by now all the drop-in centres would be up, but more grant requests come in for them all the time. In every little community people seem to be getting together more. They hear that other groups have set up a recreation club or centre and they want one too.

"Also, in the city a lot of centres spring up with new housing. People want to get out of their apartments. They want to have some place to meet one another."

New Horizons may pay for rent, maintenance, utilities, furniture and equipment. "Every group wants a pool table," Esther says. "A shuffleboard table, card tables and carpet bowling are standard equipment. People also want craft supplies — ceramics, pottery, quilting and needlework equipment for the women."

New Horizons also pays for renovations, and it will grant money to help build a centre — up to $12,000 for each group. If a centre costs more than $12,000, New Horizons contributes the seed money, the seniors the rest. In Victoria, for instance, the "James Bay New Horizons Society" now meets in a $350,000 building. For its 1,200 members the centre offers more than fifty activities — seminars on painting, dance, writing, photography and languages. "We try to offer something for everyone," president Walter Fraser says.

The centre took months to set up. First, the group had to find a site. Then they had to involve three levels of government in funding the project. Then they waited years until the centre was built. The city owns the building, but Mr Fraser says "we were actively consulted at every stage of construction, we manage the building and we own everything in it."[36]

Victoria has so many seniors that this kind of project doesn't seem odd there. But centres like this have begun to spring up across the country, even in small towns. "One group of forty or fifty people began with a $12,000 contribution," Esther Korchynski says. "Then they raised $30,000 to build their own centre. Another club raised $120,000 for their centre from a start-up grant of $12,000."

Many people think of senior centres as kindergartens for older people, places where they come to pass the time and escape boredom, but centres do more than this. "As you visit the centres and talk to the people," Esther says, "you find that they form a tremendous support system.

"I had a prejudice against social-recreational clubs when I first started at New Horizons. But you have to look under the surface. The centres help people stay involved where they might not be involved in anything else."

"I know one man in Pearson, Manitoba, who's 84. He comes to

the centre every day from two to five. He'd be in an institution without that, but now he's making it on his own."

Some New Horizons-sponsored centres have professional staff to advise members and run programs. Most simply offer games, fellowship and a chance for people to get out of the house. These centres have one drawback: they have no common policy. And New Horizons sets no standards for the centres it funds.

In Winnipeg a non-profit agency called Age and Opportunity, Inc. (A & O), also runs a system of centres, which meet the strict standards set by the National Institute of Senior Centres. A & O opened its first centre in 1960 and now has seven neighbourhood centres.

A & O centres offer programs like bingo, billiards and folk dancing, but they also offer members financial and personal counselling and health care. They are open five days a week, every week, from 9 to 5. They all have boards of directors made up of members who make the major decisions about programs, fund-raising, and care for the centres. Most also have meal co-ordinators. And they all have full-time professional directors.

A formal *Working Arrangement* between the staff and the members states that the staff has "the *main* responsibility to ensure that social services such as counselling, educational and training programs, and other helping services are provided for centre participants and older persons in the community."[37] With the guidance of the members the staff sets up programs such as podiatry clinics, legal counselling sessions, financial planning and language classes. At one centre classes might include English as a second language, at another conversational French. Centres also offer lunch and supper meals.

"We see centres as more than recreation facilities," Dorothy Hardy, A & O's full-time gerontology consultant, says. "We see them as a pipeline for direct social services to older people in their own neighbourhoods."

In 1983, for instance, A & O served almost 25,000 meals to older people at five centres, an increase of 70% over 1981. The centres also gave information to almost 12,000 older people, a

53% increase over 1981. They also counselled and gave health information and screening to almost 8,000 people, up 77% from 1981.[38]

Not all members come to get something from the centres. Many of them also come to give.

"At our centres," says Dorothy Hardy, "the seniors plan all the programs and do a lot of the work. Our staff work with them where they need help, but we try to get them involved and active in running the centre. We want them to develop their talents and abilities." At the A & O Stradbrook Centre, for instance, members help make and serve the meals.

"When I come in in the morning," Bev Kyle, director of the centre, told me, "sometimes I find a group of the women waiting to get in to start lunch. Even very frail people come in to help.

"I tell them, 'Don't come before nine o'clock. You can't get in.' But they're there waiting anyway.

"One woman just got out of the hospital. She had no strength, her hands shook, but she came to do the dishes anyway. After a while she got her strength back and now she looks after another woman who's more frail than she is."

The Main Street Centre takes up part of the main floor of the North Point Douglas Manor — a senior citizens' high-rise — a half mile north of Jack's Hotel. It sits in the heart of Winnipeg's north end. The Croation Needle Crafts Shop stands across the street, the Ukrainian National Federation headquarters is on the next block and from the door of the centre you can see the silver dome of a new Ukrainian church on the next corner.

Each A & O centre has its own flavour. It depends on the people who use them. Stradbrook is a middle-class centre: people talk in low polite voices, they come for lunch or for programs like Art or French, then leave. The Main Street Centre, on the other hand, has the flavour of a European market. People hug and touch one another, talk and laugh in loud voices. And for many, the centre is the hub of their lives.

Ninety percent of the nearly three hundred members here are Ukrainian. Almost all speak English, but for many Ukrainian is still their first language. Some of them also speak Polish, Russian and some German as well as English. About eighty to a hundred people come on a normal day, a hundred and fifty or more show up for birthdays, when there's dancing and a three-piece band. The Main Street Centre is probably the only organization in the world with a ''Pierogie and Holupchi Sub-Committee.''

Not everyone stays at the centre all day. Some people come in at 8:30 a.m. to help the paid meal co-ordinator prepare lunch. Later in the morning people come for crafts — pottery or art class — and some of them stay for lunch. Other people come mainly for lunch: many of them can't cook for themselves any more. The centre serves meals to about twenty-five to thirty people a day. When I was there recently the sign said ''Meal Sold Out,'' and that is often the case. Some people stay after lunch to pass the afternoon. The men shoot pool, the women talk. Some people come for the supper meal on Wednesday.

When I got to the centre I met Mr Hreniuk, its president. He worked on the railway for forty years as a section man. Like most of the men here he has skin like leather, tanned from years of outdoor work. The members will celebrate his birthday today along with the other members who have birthdays in March. Mr Hreniuk is 75, about the average age for Main Street members.

Today the place is packed. The senior executive have invited their MLA, Maureen Hemphill, Provincial Minister of Education, to the birthday party. When they called to invite her, they told her assistant that they thought they should see their representative *between* elections, not just when she was looking for votes. She took the hint and agreed to come and speak at the party. A shrewd politician, she also donated the birthday cake.

Mr Hreniuk introduces me to everyone in sight: the entire centre executive, the tea convenor and the kitchen committee. I've managed to avoid two sticky political debates — one over the French-language issue, another about the federal election. I also get invited to stay for lunch and the birthday party. Mrs Kinski, the woman in charge of refreshments, says that she has already reserved a seat for me next to Ms Hemphill.

It won't do any good to say I have already eaten lunch or that I have a class to prepare for. "You have to stay," Mrs Kinski says, "and that's that." She also has made me promise to come back and speak to centre members about my research.

Mrs Kinski is secretary of the centre. She also works in the office on Tuesday afternoons, answering the phone and selling bus tickets. She says that she started working at the centre three years ago when she retired. "I worked for twenty-two years part-time at the Bay and I wanted to keep working with people. At the centre I found I could help with the crafts and carpet bowling. I help at meals. I help weak people carry their trays and chop up their food.

"Lots of the other members help too. We serve meals every day and members help make them. One man brings his own knife and cuts up vegetables for the salad, another man puts out the bread and another man sets the table. Men and women work together. One man loves to put the dishes in the dishwasher.

"We have a birthday convenor who plans the monthly birthday party. She goes out and buys all the food, then gets a team of women to help her make the lunch. One month we made eight roasters of cabbage rolls. We only have two ovens, so some of the members who live in the building volunteered to bake some in their stoves upstairs. Lots of people participate."

A centre like Main Street not only exists in a community, it also creates a community for older people. Life in a good centre like this one reflects the backgrounds and needs of the people who use it.

Changes in the System

New Directions

The Harris poll in the U.S. found that more people used senior centres in 1981 than in 1974, and a large number of people who didn't use centres said they would like to use one in the future. The demand for centres will grow, and so will the number of people who use them.

Harris also found, however, that 70% of college graduates did not attend a centre, a third of the people over 65 said they had no time to attend and 64% of people who earned $15,000 a year or more showed little interest in centres.[39] As more people come into old age with better incomes and more education many will choose places other than senior centres to spend their time.

Bob Stewart, executive director of Age and Opportunity, says he sees this trend already. "Many new retirees are not attracted to senior centres. The new faces are not 65 or 66. Instead we see more 70- and 75-year-olds. Part of this has to do with where we used to put our centres. We tended to put them in senior citizen housing like North Point Douglas Manor. Now ten years later the average age of the people who live there has gone up, and since many of them come to the local centre the age of centre members has gone up.

"But that's only part of the story. I see another trend here. People who come to use centres from outside the buildings won't want to become members or run the centres. They'll just want to use the services the centre offers."

Bev Kyle, director of the Stradbrook A & O Centre, agrees. She sees a trend in her centre away from membership, perhaps because Stradbrook attracts younger middle-class people.

"This centre isn't their lives," Bev says. "They come here for classes or for lunch, but they keep their personal lives to themselves, and often they have no interest in serving on the centre board or coming to meetings. They come for a program, then they're off somewhere else — to the university for classes, or the art gallery, or the symphony. These people don't just come from the neighbourhood around the centre, they come from all over the city. And they think of the centre as just one more place to go."

The figures support what Bev says. Stradbrook has 189 members, one of the smallest memberships of any centre. But about 200 non-members are enrolled in the centre's classes, and about 200 more drop in during the year to use the library or get information.

"Only about 100 people do any of the work," Bev says. "About 40 come to meetings. Most of the people just come for the programs."

Senior centres also face more competition today.

"There are some things we do well," Bev says, "and there are some things that others do better. We have a good art program, for instance, and people like our meal program, but people interested in exercise can get it other places, and they do. We may as well admit that. The centre will have to adapt."

The agency has already begun to make some changes. A & O has built its two newest centres free of senior high-rise housing. Bob Stewart says he hopes that these centres will have a higher community profile and attract more younger old people, as well as continue to serve those in their seventies and eighties.

"We also want to build a major downtown centre for people from all over the city," he says.

The agency has begun to move in this direction. A & O, the Job Bureau and two other senior groups have proposed that the city build a new senior administration centre downtown. This project would become a part of the city's new downtown redevelopment plan.

A large downtown centre will mean a shift in A & O practice. It is likely that many of the people who came to such a centre would not likely help run it. A large downtown centre with lavish facilities might also threaten the survival of smaller, more modestly equipped local centres.

Bob Stewart says he doesn't think this will happen because different types of people would use each of the centres.

"At some of our centres, like Stradbrook, people come from all over the city for the programs. We could offer more for these people in one central place. But our counselling often works best in the local centres. People who get referred to a counsellor downtown often don't come. Maybe they don't want to admit they need professional help, or maybe they prefer to talk to someone like Maria Rogers in a less formal way. We don't know. But the centres still have this counselling role to play. People also like to come to the local centres for meals. And last year we made seventy-five hundred Outreach contacts through the local centres — a 60% increase from 1982.

"These programs have grown, and we want them to stay strong and grow in the future. The local centres serve a certain group of older people. They stay sensitive to the neighbourhood and to local languages and issues. In the Notre Dame Centre, for instance, we've begun to see Southeast Asian older people show up for the first time. They're new immigrants with special needs. The local centres can adapt to this kind of change."

New Programs

A big downtown centre would help A & O find a new place for itself in the growing market for senior programs. Until a few years ago A & O ran the only high quality education and recreation programs for older people in the city. "Now," Bev Kyle says, "there are New Horizons groups springing up all over the place, and these programs draw people away from the local centres."

The young old want quality programs. They'll travel to find them: when they can't find them at a senior centre, they go elsewhere — or they invent them themselves. A look at the programs funded by New Horizons shows a trend away from dependence on senior centres.

"Initially," a report on New Horizons's first decade says, "[seniors] applied for grants to do the type of things society expected of them. They formed primarily social clubs for self-entertainment. Before long, however, they began branching out into activities which enabled them to acquire new knowledge and skills, to develop latent talents, and to maintain and improve their physical health. . . ."[40]

New Horizons reports, for instance, that more older people now belong to exercise groups than ever before. And more people join groups or start their own exercise programs all the time.[41]

Older people have also used New Horizons money to set up

bands, choirs and music groups across the country. A group in Newfoundland calls itself the "Silver Chord Singers and Players." They perform at benefits and shows throughout the province.

"I'm in my late seventies," one member says, "and singing with the group gets me out and makes me feel that I'm contributing." Most of the members have never sung in a choral group before: the Silver Chords has opened a new creative outlet for them.[42]

A New Horizons program in Winnipeg saved one of its members' life. Howard Birch, 67, had a heart attack in 1980. Six weeks later his wife died. "It took the guts out of me," he says. "I felt completely lost. I even contemplated suicide."

Howard is now master of ceremonies for a Winnipeg theatre group called Studio Two. I spoke to him backstage after a matinée show.

"I went to see someone at A & O to get something to do," he says, "but they had nothing at the time. Then one day the lady from A & O called me back. She told me about an ad in the paper for a male actor. I'd never acted before in my life. I worked as a bus driver for thirty-five years — what did I know about acting?

"I said, 'No thanks.' But she said, 'Go.' So I went, and I'm still here. I don't know where I'd be if I hadn't gotten mixed up in this thing."

This "thing," as Howard calls it, was started by director Will Dickson. Will calls it "readers' theatre." Studio Two puts on a one-hour show of light comedy. The actors use no props and wear no costumes or make-up. The four women in the cast wear brown skirts and cream-coloured blouses with bright scarves. Howard wears a black academic gown. He sits on a stool in one corner of the stage in front of a lectern. The women carry their scripts in their hands. They don't act so much as read to the audience, though they move around as they talk.

"Studio Two keeps to one principle," Will Dickson says. "We do everything with the utmost simplicity. We do everything ourselves. We don't have to worry about lighting or dressing rooms.

We can set up in no time. We can play anywhere — on a stage or in a classroom.''

Will started Studio Two in 1980 after he retired. Now Creative Retirement Manitoba sponsors the program. Will says it comes out of the kind of thing that Charles Laughton and Agnes Moorehead used to do in the 1930s and '40s. ''They used to sit on stools and read to the audience. We move around a little more, but we're reviving an old form.''

Will worked in the theatre in his spare time for over fifty years. He acted and directed in Winnipeg theatre groups in the 1940s. He studied acting at the American Academy of Dramatic Arts in New York and at Toronto's Royal Conservatory. In the 1950s he received the Canadian Drama Award ''for outstanding contribution to the development of Canadian drama.'' But Will never acted for pay. He had a career in Canadian Pacific's accounting department, and when CP offered workers early retirement at 60, he grabbed the chance.

''Don't get me wrong,'' he says. ''I liked my job. In the summer I'd get to audit the books at the Banff and Lake Louise hotels. And I got to learn about the latest data-processing techniques.

''But work took up so much time and energy that I had no time for the theatre. You can't call up thirty people a half-hour before a rehearsal and tell them you have to work late, so I dropped out of theatre work. When I had the chance to retire I had all kinds of things I wanted to do.''

When Will returned to Winnipeg from Montreal, where he'd worked, he looked around for a theatre group to join, but there was nothing in the city for older people.

''Young people could join the avant-garde theatre or go to university classes, but there was nothing for the older experienced non-professional actor. It was a shame there was no outlet. So I started Studio Two.''

Will called up some of the people he had worked with to see if they wanted to form a new group. Doris Benson, Sheila Maurer, Primrose Hopkins and Madge Murray Roberts all said they would join, and they are all still with it today. "These people brought enthusiasm and talent to the group," Will says. They also brought years of experience in the theatre: between them, Will and the four women had over 180 years of theatre background.

In its first year Studio Two mounted about ten performances of a show called "I Hate Poetry" in nursing homes and senior centres in Winnipeg. In 1983 a $4,500 New Horizons grant to pay for hotel, travel and food expenses enabled them to take their show on the road. That year they gave fifty-four performances all around the province.

"We played at Winnipeg's Centennial Concert Hall," Doris says. "There, they have plush dressing rooms with sublime mirrors. And we played in nursing homes and country schools. One time we had to change in a boiler room and another time in a broom closet."

They also made a film for the Alcoholism Foundation of Manitoba about alcoholism in old age. In 1984 they gave over ninety shows to all sorts of groups from kindergarten classes to high schools to pre-retirement education courses.

As word spreads the group receives more and more requests. "I'm afraid to answer the phone," Will says. "We don't advertise, but the requests keep coming. I don't know how much more we can handle.

"At the end of every show someone comes up and asks how they can join. They want to get on the stage — to be in front of people. But they don't realize how hard we work."

Will writes or borrows all the material Studio Two performs. He spends the summer hunting through libraries for songs, poems or concepts he can turn into skits for the revue.

He leans toward light, funny pieces. This year he adapted a Stanley Holloway routine called "Albert and the Lion," about two proper British parents who don't want to cause a fuss when their little boy Albert gets eaten by a lion at the zoo one Sunday. Older audiences remember the original, but it's funny even for someone who has never seen it before.

Will shows up in September with a rough script. The other

members come with ideas. "But," Primrose says, "Will does all the work." Then the rehearsals start. The players rehearse six to nine hours a week during the season (September to June), and they put in hundreds of hours before anyone ever sees the revue.

Will demands perfection from the actors. I went to one of their rehearsals to see how they get ready for a show. Will and I sat behind a long table, Howard and the women stood about fifteen feet away facing us.

The group had a show in two days at Lions Place, so Will suggested a full run-through. I stayed for about half an hour, but I only saw two skits: Will had them go over scenes again and again.

Rehearsals like this go on all through the year. "We often have to cancel other things we're doing to rehearse or give a show," Sheila says. "And when we go out of town we'll do twelve or thirteen shows in two or three days. That takes a lot of time and energy."

For all their work Studio Two players get no pay. "I could get a 1,000% raise," Howard says, "and I'd make the same as I do now. We do it because we have a lot of fun."

New Skills

The Studio Two cast brought their knowledge of the theatre with them into old age. All of them except for Howard worked in community theatre for years, and some of the women have appeared professionally on Winnipeg's Rainbow Stage and on CBC radio. But not everyone carries their pre-retirement activity into old age. Some people find a new talent or interest when they retire, something they couldn't have imagined themselves doing before.

Jack and Alice Randall, for instance, joined a massage class three years ago when they were both 75.

After a year of classes six of the students wanted to use their massage techniques on nursing home patients. They applied for and got a New Horizons grant, and when it came time to choose a president, Jack was elected.

Now the group visits two nursing homes, one in Red View, a suburb of Winnipeg, and another in Middlechurch, just outside of town. With its New Horizons grant the group bought three massage tables from the U.S. at a cost of about $1,000. They also hired teachers to help them perfect their skills.

"We're the only group we've ever heard of with professional massage tables." Jack says, "The people who come to teach us keep asking if they can borrow them.

"When we go to a home we take the tables with us. They're bulky but they fold up and fit in a van. Two of us work on one person. The six of us work on three people at a time for about twenty minutes each. One person massages the legs, feet, hands and arms. The other works on the back and neck.

"Sometimes the old people are so weak or crippled we have to help them onto the table. Many of them are frail, like a china cup. They're delicate, and you have to be gentle."

"The thing they like most," Alice says, "is the 'belly rub.' We finish with that. I call it dessert. We turn them on their backs, put our left hand on their forehead and rub their tummy from side to side. They all like that."

The people in the nursing homes don't have to come for massage if they don't want to. The homes run an exercise program at the same time.

"But the people who come all come back," Jack says.

"People sit all day in a wheelchair," says Alice, "they get a backache or a stiff neck. By the end of the massage their aches are gone. Also, they like us. The staff often don't have time to spend one-to-one with the patients. For twenty minutes they have our undivided attention."

"We benefit from the massage too," Jack says. "We use our hands and arms. It gives us some exercise, and that makes us feel better. You also feel you do some good for somebody."

Over the years New Horizons has found that more and more "groups . . . ventured into projects which provided service to others." They've gone in all directions — meals-on-wheels, foster grandparent programs, skills-exchange services, counselling and therapy. Programs like Studio Two and the Massage Team show that, given the chance, retired people "continue to be active, creative, and productive members of their communities."[43]

Personal Growth

On weeks when the massage team goes to Red View, a New Horizons-funded Personal Growth Group works with people at Middlechurch. Like the massage team, members of this group learned a batch of new skills — Tai Chi, Gestalt analysis, meditation — after they retired, then decided that they wanted to teach them to others.

The Personal Growth Group models its work on a program in the U.S. Gay Luce and Eugenia Gerrard, a psychologist and therapist in Berkeley, California, started the SAGE (Seniors' Actualization through Growth Explorations) program in January 1974. A brochure on the SAGE program calls it "an eclectic program of personal growth to enhance physical and mental health of older adults." The founders designed the program for people over 60 years old in the belief that people can grow in new ways as they age "if they are given skills, group support and ways of discovering sources of deep inspiration."[44]

SAGE uses a variety of techniques to promote a better self-image, trust, confidence and creativity in its members. The program includes art therapy, autogenic training (a relaxation technique), biofeedback training, Feldenkrais exercises, foot massage, Gestalt dream analysis, hatha yoga, meditation, music therapy, Tai Chi, progressive relaxation and deep breathing — anything that will improve the older person's health and self-esteem.

The program mixes mental, physical and spiritual exercises, eastern and western approaches to health, individual and group techniques. To some people it sounds like an odd mix, and Gay Luce admits that she wasn't sure older people would take to it.[45]

The first SAGE group consisted of twelve older people aged 63 to 77 and four younger people. They met once a week as a group for three to four hours, and once a week each older person came for a personal session. Some of the members had serious health problems like Parkinson's disease and hypertension, others were on tranquilizers or pain-killers. They ranged from foremen to union leaders, to political activists, to retired executives to house-wives. Most of them had never tried the SAGE techniques before, but they signed up for an eight-month trial program.

Ken Dychtwald, one of the program's first workers, says that in a short time people began to feel better. Herb Pillars, a 75-year-old SAGE member says he started the program with arthritis in his hands, backaches and a stiff neck. "I still have a little trouble with the arthritis, but the backache is gone, and I can now twist my head and see the traffic behind me on the road when I'm driving. Also, I used to smoke. You can't smoke and deep breathe at the same time!"[46]

"In my SAGE group," Ellie Korbach says, "I had a chance to work through some of my long-repressed grief about losing six people including my brother within a short period of time." Ellie is 73. She had cancer and suffers from high blood pressure and rapid heartbeat.

One day, she says, emotions started coming up and she began to cry during a deep-breathing exercise. "I wept bitterly for two hours, and I wept away a score of sorrows. And, finally, I started to laugh, thinking of all the people who have loved me all my life and still love me. . . ."[47]

Warden McDonald, another SAGE member, says, "Our vigour increased and the enthusiasm, love and faith of the SAGE staff began to rub of on us. . . . As our circulation improved so did our ego. We began to be more open, friendly and helpful to people of all ages."[48]

Word about SAGE spread and the SAGE staff began to offer workshops around the U.S. They also produced videotapes that other groups could use to start local SAGE programs.

The Personal Growth Group in Winnipeg applied for and got a New Horizons Grant to start a SAGE Group, buy the videotapes and begin to learn the SAGE techniques.

"It's given me a whole new life," Rose Champion, one of Winnipeg's first members, says. "I'm more aware of my body, more responsible for myself. There's so much more I can do. I feel much better than I did seven years ago."

"Retirement's been the most exciting time of my life," Elsie Singer, another Winnipeg member, says. "I was worried about retirement and what I'd do, but the Personal Growth Group has opened new doors for me. The deep breathing eases my fears. It gets me over anxiety."

Most of the people in the group report these kinds of changes, and after two years of classes members wanted to teach the techniques to others. Two of them took personal growth-related courses at the University of Southern California, while other members went to workshops sponsored by the School of Social Work at the University of Manitoba. In August 1982 they all went to an intensive five-day workshop on SAGE techniques in Winnipeg. Sessions include Gestalt training, a day-long study of therapeutic touch and a workshop on communication and friendship.

Soon they started a teaching team and some members now teach SAGE beginners' classes. Others visit nursing home patients too sick to come to classes downtown. These SAGE teachers have also taught staff members in nursing homes how to run SAGE classes for their patients.

I visited a SAGE class run by Rose and Elsie at the Middlechurch Home. The average age of residents at Middlechurch is 87. The home has a hostel care (level 1 and 2) wing for people who don't have a severe illness but can't live at home, and a nursing care wing (levels 3 and 4) where people need constant care. The SAGE program attracts half its members from each group.

Rose and Elsie hold their class at 10:00 a.m. in a small gym-sized room. Two storeys high, it has a balcony upstairs with a pool table, exercise equipment and a walkway. Off to one side green light filters in from a sun-room filled with plants. Rose put some Bach on the stereo to liven up the atmosphere.

A little after ten o'clock I see some of the staff wheeling people into the room in wheelchairs. Other people trickle in with walkers and canes. People look sleepy. No one talks, though one or two people smile at each other. Nineteen people show up this morning, all women. Two men watch from the balcony above.

Rose starts the session off by introducing herself and Elsie.

"The nurses say you had the bar open last night and everybody's tired," Rose says. "Have you been doing your exercises?" No one answers.

As she talks she and Elsie work their way around the group massaging people's shoulders. They make small talk with the women as they massage their backs.

"Where's Ida?" one woman asks.

"She had a meeting this morning," Rose says.

"You rotate coming?"

"Yes. But we'll come as long as you want us to."

"That'll be indefinitely."

Rose says they all like the massage and some come just for that. Now she sits down at the front of the group again with a microphone.

"Let's shake our hands." She shakes hers in front of her to show them what she means. "I understand you all have a hangover this morning," she says.

"I only had a ginger ale," one woman says. "That doesn't leave you much of a hangover."

"Didn't you have any wine?"

"Oh, the white wine. I forgot about that."

"Okay," Rose says, "now let's do some Do-in. You remember, tap your head with your fingers forward and back. Do it really hard. Now make a fist and start on your shoulders. Reach as far back as you can. Relax. Take a deep breath or two. Don't forget the inside of your arms. Now your legs."

When they finish tapping they close their eyes to get the feel of their bodies. "Do you feel any tingling?"

"That's hard work," one woman says.

"It is," Rose says. "Take your time. Maybe I rushed you this morning, but you can use it to wake up in the morning. You'll feel really good. Today I was feeling really tired. I did my stretching at home and I was wondering how many of you were doing yours.''

These people get little if any exercise outside the SAGE classes. The staff cooks their food and wheels them around in their wheelchairs, but they spend most of their day sitting. Their breathing becomes shallow. Eugenia Gerrard, founder of SAGE, says that people in nursing homes ''rarely get the benefit of a full breath.''[49]

Each session differs. There's no set routine. Rose and Elsie use whatever methods they think the group needs. Elsie admits to being discouraged sometimes. It often seems that the people in the home just come for entertainment, but whatever their reasons, deep-breathing and muscle-relaxation make them feel better.

''The personal growth classes aren't all physical,'' Elsie tells me later. ''They're intended to help people become aware of their feelings, too. Sometimes we discuss various feelings.''

With this group Rose and Elsie spend most of the time on physical movement. On the way out to Middlechurch in the car Elsie tells me why. ''Most of the people aren't mentally alert. They also don't have much practice in experiencing themselves. Our program depends on the group, and this group seems withdrawn. Some of them are confused. We try to get them involved by talking to them, but some of them don't even know what day it is.''

Still, she feels that even the worst cases get something out of the session, even if it's only a massage, and the less confused patients enjoy some of the visualizing exercises. Elsie tries one they like. ''Let's remember a favourite song,'' she says. ''Can you remember a song and what it meant to you? Close your eyes and try.''

''I remember 'The White Cliffs of Dover,''' one woman says.

''I remember 'It's a Long Way to Tipperary,''' says another. ''I remember my two brothers that went off to the war.''

''I remember 'Always' by Irving Berlin. My husband used to sing that. We danced to that before we got married.''

Rose finishes the session with an exercise called "Pow". The women pull their arms back, then shoot their hands out in front of them and shout "Pow!" as they breathe out. They all smile and laugh at that. And they all applaud. The group still looks tired but a lot brighter than when it came in.

"If anyone wants a hug on the way out," Rose says, "I'll give you one."

She says goodbye and hugs people as they go out. She and Elsie wheel some of the people back to their rooms.

Elsie and Rose have begun to teach some of the staff at the home the SAGE methods. I asked Judy Klos, one of their students and the assistant activity director at Middlechurch, how she feels about the program.

"Some people just come because it's so quiet in here, but most of them say they feel better and most of them come back. When I run the program I try to increase their awareness of their senses. One week I put an icicle in a box and passed it around. They had to feel it with their eyes closed and guess what it was. They liked that. But you have to be aware of their limits. You can't do much with hearing. Some of them have hearing problems and they miss what you're trying to do.

"I'd say it gives most of them a more positive attitude to themselves. You can't always tell what it's doing. We didn't think Mrs Fowles knew where she was: she's 103 and confused a lot of the time. One week I went to get her. I said, 'Do you want to come to SAGE?' 'Oh yes,' she said, 'that's the one that makes me feel good.'"

I asked Judy if I could talk to some of the group members, and we visited a few of the hostel care patients in their rooms.

"I didn't think much of it the first time," Mrs Jones, 87, says. "I thought it was nuts. I came back because I'm open-minded. I like the eye exercise with SAGE and the neck exercise where you roll your head."

Only two men come out for SAGE. Judy took me to talk to Mr Hadji. "Oh, SAGE definitely helps," he said, "only there's not enough time. Now I do some self-massage at night. It helps my arm where I have some muscle problems. It seems better than before.''

Mrs Bingham, 84, has been coming to the SAGE classes for four months. ''I love it,'' she says. ''I don't find ordinary exercises interesting, but SAGE brightens me up. I especially like the Tai Chi. I never did this sort of thing before. I should have, I guess — it gets you kind of limbered up in the legs and arms. After SAGE the arthritis in my legs doesn't feel as bad, and the tapping helps too. There should be more people attending SAGE. It would help everybody.''

Even people who need heavy care can grow a bit, sometimes in astounding ways. One woman at Middlechurch who had never left the home began meditation as part of the SAGE program. Eventually she took a trip to California by herself. People who used to become depressed every year at Christmas sailed through it after the SAGE program began.

Like the massage program, SAGE does as much for the teachers as it does for the students.

''At first,'' Rose says, ''I was scared. What did I know about working with people in a nursing home. But now I feel useful. I have a purpose to keep on going. I see the people in the wheelchairs. They start smiling. They purr under your hands when you massage their backs or necks. One day I got carried away with 'The Blue Danube.' I was massaging one woman's back and she started shouting, 'Enough already, enough.' It's very rewarding work. I just have to hug them when I go.''

''We give them a little love,'' Elsie says, ''and we get it all back.''

Ida Fontaine, who works at Middlechurch every other week, says that teaching the SAGE course has opened new doors for her. ''I worried about retirement. Now I have no time for work at home. These people in nursing homes feel forgotten. They don't know what they can do. One week a woman said, 'I can't do that,' meaning a head massage. Then after I did it for her she liked it and her hands went up to do it for herself. I get a lot out of going there.''

The patients at Middlechurch identify with their older teachers in a way they don't with younger activity workers. It's one thing to see someone 25 or 30 dancing around or doing Tai Chi, but when they see someone their own age doing it, they know that it's possible for them too.

Ken Dychtwald, one of the founders of the SAGE program in California, predicts that programs like SAGE will change our ideas about aging. Healthy older people, he says, "present an entirely different image of the later years. . . . We discover that with the right preparation, attitude, attention, and meaningful involvement, growing older holds the potential for being a full and thoroughly rewarding maturation process, not unlike the ripening of a fine wine or musical instrument."

Like a fine wine or instrument, older people need the care to nurture their growth. Groups like SAGE, the Massage Team and Studio Two have begun to explore this kind of care and also what older people need to learn to bring out the best that old age has to offer.

The Future

What passes for the facts about leisure in retirement today simply tells us what is, not what will, or can, be.

Norman Cousins, writer and teacher, makes this point in a story about Pablo Casals. Cousins visited the cellist at his home when Casals was almost ninety. Casals couldn't dress himself, had trouble walking and suffered from emphysema and probably rheumatoid arthritis. Cousins describes a morning scene at Casals's house.

"He came into the living room on Marta's [his wife's] arm. He was badly stooped. His head was pitched forward and he walked with a shuffle. His hands were swollen and his fingers were clenched."

In spite of his illnesses, Casals played the piano before breakfast every day, and Cousins says that at the keyboard Casals became a new man. His fingers stretched, he sat up straight, he breathed more freely. Then he began to play. He played Bach's "Well-Tempered Clavier." He hummed as he played. He said Bach spoke to his heart.

"Then he plunged into a Brahms concerto and his fingers, now agile and powerful, raced across the keyboard with dazzling speed. His entire body seemed fused with the music; it was no longer stiff and shrunken but supple and graceful and completely freed of its arthritic coils."

When he finished he got up and went to have breakfast. He ate, talked and then went for a walk on the beach.[51]

I don't know any story that more clearly shows the meaning of recreation. When people hear the word they often think of play, something people do to fill up time until they go to work again. But recreation also means "re-creation," rejuvenation, and the story about Casals shows that true recreation can restore vigour and life even in late old age.

Casals's talent may have been extraordinary but the effect of re-creation on him isn't so rare. Many of my students who work with older people see "miracles" like this all the time, and they have convinced me that true re-creation can take place at any age.

Patty Mehan runs a day centre for older people who are unable to care for themselves at home. A driver picks them up at their houses and brings them to the centre for five hours a day. They have a hot lunch, then get a ride home in the afternoon.

Patty tries to get everyone involved in the centre's activities, but one group of women wouldn't do anything. All of them had come from the Ukraine as young women and lived on farms most of their lives. They kept to themselves, sat back and watched other people carpet bowl or play bingo, but never took part.

One day a friend of Patty's, a choreographer, asked if any of the women in her centre knew any Ukrainian songs and dances. He wanted to put together a show of authentic Ukrainian music but was having trouble finding material. Patty said she would ask, and she took a tape recorder to the centre and asked the Ukrainian women if they would sing Ukrainian songs that meant something special to them. The response was immediate.

"One of the women grabbed the microphone out of my hand. She almost swallowed it. And she began to sing her wedding song. As she sang she started to cry. Then other people began to sing songs — birthday songs, work songs, songs for children. The women cried and sang all afternoon. One woman got up to lead everyone in a Ukrainian version of 'Happy Birthday.' She waved her arms and swayed like a conductor to get everyone into the act. The next day they came back with more songs and with stories about life in the Ukraine."

These women had no interest in games and play, but they did have a need to share their ethnic roots through oral history and song. Like Pablo Casals they needed to feel useful. And they needed a time and place to express their creativity. Patty Mehan's program gave them both.

Today and in the future, people will need help finding worthwhile activities and interests to engage them in old age. Carl Jung, psychoanalyst and writer, suggested "colleges for forty-year-olds which prepare them for their coming life and its demands as the ordinary colleges introduce our young people to a knowledge of the world and of life."[52] Some colleges like this have started up already, and more will appear in the future. They show that old age can be as interesting and worthwhile as any other time of life.

8

EDUCATION: LEARNING TO GROW OLD

Education for What?

Farrell Fleming, 40-year-old director of Creative Retirement Manitoba, bounces back and forth in front of the blackboard. He is explaining that for a Buddhist, suicide doesn't create a moral problem.

"But it's not right for people to kill themselves," insists a well-dressed woman in her sixties at the front of the room.

"Who says it's not right," says a man on my left. "It just doesn't seem right to you because that's what you've been taught."

The class is involved. They're thinking, calling into question their values and beliefs. Most classes at Creative Retirement are like this. The people who come to them don't sit like sponges: they listen, they think about what they hear and if they don't agree they say so.

Farrell Fleming taught philosophy at the University of Manitoba before he came to Creative Retirement. He finds work with older people more of a challenge. "Don't get me wrong," he says, "I had pretty good luck at the university when I was there, and I thought it would be a downer to work with older people. But

I found that older people brought more energy, more happiness, more general good humour . . . also more knowledge or at least more wisdom to class than younger people did.''

When Farrell invited me to attend this class, ''Buddhist Philosophy and Retirement,'' I expected to find a small group around a seminar table. When I arrived, however, I found the room packed with about thirty-five older people. Farrell says that enrolment in his philosophy classes grows every year.

''Last year we did Indian philosophy, the year before last we did the Stoics.'' Most of the people who come have no formal training in philosophy. Some have little formal schooling at all. But older people treat philosophical questions as real problems.

''When I taught existentialism to undergrads,'' Farrell says, ''we had to treat the questions of life and death, responsibility for your actions, or how to live a good life as theoretical issues. Most of the students still lived at home with their parents, who paid the bills, put the food on the table and told them when to come in at night. For these people existential questions were exercises in the imagination. But older people are ready for this kind of question.''

Today many older people have come back to school. They don't come to get credits or degrees or to compete for marks on tests. They come for personal development, to find meaning in later life.

The bulk of writing on education, however, doesn't say much about older students. And most schools today serve the functions Emile Durkheim, a French sociologist and educator, described in the 1890s: they teach children to become adults, and they prepare young people for specific jobs in society.

''According to this view,'' writes Professors John Myles and Monica Boyd of Carleton University, ''investment in education is an investment in human capital, just as investment in plant and machinery is an investment in physical. Society should expect to reap the rewards of such investment in the form of expanded wealth and economic growth.''

Since society can't expect this kind of return on its investment when it educates older people, education for seniors receives almost no financial support from government or schools. ''In a society which evaluates things and people in terms of their exchange value in the market," Myles and Boyd say, "there is little room for education for its own sake."[1]

Canada's aging population will challenge this view. "As far into the future as we can see," says Ernest Boyer of the Carnegie Foundation for the Advancement of Teaching, "the shape of American higher education is going to reflect a much older student."[2] Education that tests and grades students or that prepares them for jobs won't appeal to older learners.

Professor Myles reports that, in a study conducted with Dennis Forcese of Carleton University, even tuition waivers didn't attract older people to university classes. He believes that the style and approach to education at universities doesn't meet the older person's needs.

Some schools have begun to change their programs to attract older students, and older people have begun to set up new education programs of their own — like Creative Retirement Manitoba. The facts are forcing the system to change.

In the 1960s and '70s universities sprang up like mushrooms after a rain storm. Fuelled by the baby boom, schools like Carleton University, York University and Simon Fraser University grew up and expanded almost overnight. The government gave grants to universities based on enrolments, and the number of students grew each year. From 1961 to 1981 Canada's post-secondary aged group (18-24) grew from 9.4% to 13.8% of the population.

At the same time grade schools found themselves with empty classrooms. From 1951 to 1971 the proportion of elementary school-aged children in Canada's population grew from 14.4% to 17.2%, but by 1976 the proportion dropped to 14.4% again. Experts predict it will drop to under 12% by 1991.[3] The baby boom has grown up.

Schools built for the baby boomers in the 1940s and 1960s stand empty. Some schools have become warehouses for used textbooks, others administration office buildings. One Ontario professor has suggested that the province turn empty schools into apartments or nursing homes for older people.

The shortage of students in the grade schools should have alerted the universities to coming trouble, but no one paid much attention. By the late 1970s and early 1980s the number of students had dropped, and so had government grants based on enrolment.

Money spent on schools from 1970 to 1975 (by all levels of government) dropped from 21% of the government's budget to 16.72%. Myles and Boyd pinpoint 1982 as the first year of crisis for post-secondary education. Prospects for the future look even worse. Professor Z. Zsigmond, in a study for Statistics Canada, predicts that post-secondary aged students will drop from a high of 13.8% of Canada's population in 1981 to only 9.91% in 1991.[4]

Post-secondary schools have three ways to meet this crisis. First, they can offer more services to young students (18-24 years old). Second, they can reduce services and frills to cut costs. And third, they can woo new clients. Universities have tried all three routes, but the third route — the attempt to draw in new students — has led universities to look for older clients.[5]

Older people have time for education. There are more of them today, and, Professor Myles says, "we know [older people] tend to have a stronger interest in cultural, political and social affairs than do the young. . . ."[6]

Also, Statistics Canada reports that new generations of older people will have more education. In 1981 24% of older people had a high school education or better, but 39% of people 45-64 had more than a high school diploma and 64% of people 25-44 had at least a high school education.[7] These people will tend to keep on learning as they age.

Harris found in the U.S., for instance, that the proportion of people 65 and over enrolled in education courses doubled from 2% to 5% from 1974 to 1981. He also found that the higher the education of the person, the more likely they were to take a course. Only 2% of older people with less than a high school diploma took education courses in 1981, but 16% of older people with university degrees took courses that year.[8]

The System Today

The education system will have to adapt in at least three ways if it hopes to attract older learners. First, it will have to make education more accessible to older adults. Second, schools and teachers will have to adapt their methods to suit the older learner. And third, schools will have to make subjects relevant to mature people who return to school with a lifetime of experience.

Access

Access doesn't just mean lower fees. It means making a person feel welcome. One handicapped student made this point: "It's no use putting ramps on the buildings so I can get inside, if, when I get in, I still feel you don't want me there." Universities may do away with fees for older students, but they still give all sorts of signals that they don't want them on campus.

Professors Myles and Boyd made up the case of Mrs Smith to show the kinds of problems older people face. Mrs Smith arrives at her local university to find "classes dispersed over a large campus with limited facilities for getting around." She goes to the Student Centre to relax, but the noise and loud music give her a headache. She likes her younger classmates, but they have different interests and different reasons for coming to school. She finds she can't form any deep friendships with most of the people she meets.

Add to this the fact that Mrs Smith may have to travel forty-five minutes each way during rush hour on three different days just to take one course, and you get some idea why university classes don't appeal to her. "For the elderly to participate in such institutions, they must accommodate themselves to the typical social patterns, concerns, and life-styles of the young. The result is that their participation in such institutions is minimal."[9]

Some students like Mrs Smith only feel out of place. Others are actually intimidated. One woman I know took two years just to find the courage to fill out an application. The first year she picked one up at the Registrar's office, but the crowds and paperwork frightened her so much that she put off going to classes until the next year.

J. Roby Kidd, a pioneer in the field of adult education, believes that adults often link schools with failure. "Though they might subscribe to the notion that 'school days are the happiest days of life,' [they] still carry some feelings about the school they attended that range from mild dissatisfaction to hatred and loathing."[10]

Adults often need help getting over these fears before they can start learning in schools again. Mavis Turner, a member of the University of Winnipeg Counselling Department, says that "more than anything else, the older student needs encouragement." Mavis herself has been on the other side of the counsellor's desk. She got her Master's degree in Continuing Education at age 55 — after a twenty-four-year break in her education.

"I had three years of a home economics degree finished when I got married," she says. "I'd planned a career as a textile chemist. But then the war started and my husband got transferred East. We moved and then we started a family. I didn't come back to school until 1967, after my husband died.

"It took me two years to get any kind of confidence when I went back to school. I know how the older students feel. A lot of them come in and they think, 'What sort of freak am I?' They need someone to talk to, and when they see me they say, 'Thank goodness you're not a 20-year-old. I couldn't talk to a younger person.' They feel comfortable talking to me, and I can use myself as an example of someone who has overcome the same problems."

If people can't get to schools, or if they feel threatened by them, they won't go. Someone like Mavis can make life easier for older students, as can a more acute awareness of why older people come back to school. For instance, few older people come back to school for job training or a degree. Most come for their own enjoyment. Seventy percent of the older people in Harris's study in the U.S. said they came back to school to expand their knowledge, make good use of their time or be with other people. Schools need to adapt their methods to these goals.

Styles of Learning

Older people may not see the point of multiple choice, fill-in-the-blank or short-answer tests, and they have much less practice than younger people in these kinds of tests. This makes it difficult for older people to prove what they know about the subjects they are studying.

Older students, for instance, make more mistakes on test problems than do the younger ones, and they take longer to see the goal of a problem. They also tend to repeat the same problem-solving methods even if they don't work.[11] If they are going to do as well as younger students on tests, older people need a chance to learn the skills the tests require. "When given sufficient opportunity to develop their skill and gain additional experience with unfamiliar tasks and problems, [older people] improve their performance without outside intervention."[12]

Special classes can teach these skills and give older people test-taking practice. Also, teachers can help older students do better by giving them extra time to work on tests and designing work with the older student's situation in mind. For instance, the rate of memory intake increases if a teacher can reduce the number of things that need to be reviewed at one time. If teachers have to give tests they can reduce the stress on older students by testing them more often. Also, they should write clear instructions that take the older learner through the work one step at a time. This helps improve recall.

Teachers can help older students improve their memories. Mnemonic aids such as key words, alphabetized lists, associations between new facts and things people already know help.

Teachers should also know that a class of older students will differ more among themselves than a class of younger students. Some people will learn quickly. Energetic, active, task-oriented people learn better no matter what their age.[13] Other people need more time. "I slow the pace of delivery a fraction," says Eamon McPhee, an adult educator for over fifty years. "I don't rush things. If I get into names and places, I stick them up on the board. I use yellow chalk on a green board so people can see better. And big handwriting. Some people lip-read a little as their hearing goes without even knowing it, so I don't wander around too much or they lose half the lecture.''

This sounds like common sense. But few teachers know or use these methods. Older students often have to struggle to keep up with a lecturer. They may blame this on their age, but they suffer more from a lack of familiarity with schools than from aging.

''When they come back to school,'' Mavis Turner says, ''many of them don't know how to write an essay. They don't know how to take notes efficiently. They don't know how to study. Time after time I find that people have guilt feelings about writing in books. They were taught to revere books, and it's hard for them to let go of that idea and write in the margins or underline a text. They feel they desecrate the written word. I have to teach them to treat the books as tools. I show them my books — that makes them feel a little better — but I also have to teach them concrete skills like shorthand notetaking. And how to study.

''Retention is the worst problem. They say, 'I've read it over four times and I still can't remember it.' They get discouraged and they put it down to age. They think their brains are failing.

''But it's just a lack of practice. The more they use their memories, the better they get. It's like a machine that you don't use: it rusts. In everyday life you don't have to retain information. If I go shopping, I make a list. Then I take the list *with* me. I don't leave it home. But on tests you have to recall specific, detailed information. Older students aren't used to that. With practice, though, that skill gets honed up again.''

A few years ago Mavis and a learning-skills instructor offered a learning-skills course for older students. About thirty people signed up for the ten-session program, half of which dealt with skills and half with an orientation to student life. ''Students from the class still drop in to see me today,'' Mavis says, ''not just with their problems, but to say how they're doing. Without that course many say they would have dropped out.

"The people who stick with it do well. The older students work hard. They're keen to learn, and they have more time to spend on their courses. The mature students — say, the middle-aged mothers — who come back to school have a lot of problems. They don't have the time to study. Older students have the time. You just have to keep them encouraged."

Relevance

Older students can adapt to the system. They can learn mnemonics, study and test-taking skills. They can learn to jump through the same hoops as younger students. But why should they? Why shouldn't the system adapt itself to the needs of the older learner?

The "tell 'em-and-test 'em" methods used in schools today assume that the students know nothing. Some people call this the bucket theory of education. In this model the teacher is a big, full bucket, the students small, empty buckets. The teacher teaches by pouring knowledge into the little buckets. At the end of the term he or she tests the students to see how much they each have in their buckets.

This method demeans the older student. It discounts what people bring to the classroom. It assumes that only the teacher has something worthwhile to say. A normal university lecture consists of one person talking to a silent audience for one to three hours. "I'd never get through the subject matter if I let them ask questions," one of my colleagues told me.

"But nothing could be worse than this attitude in a class of adults," says Eamon McPhee, who began teaching adults in 1929. I asked him what a teacher should keep in mind when teaching older students.

First, he says, a teacher should know what the students have to offer to the class.

"I use the first six hours of the course to find out what each student has that no one else has. That's a lot of time, and I do it publicly by talking with each of them in class. I tell them that if the discussion turns to a topic they know about, the class will feel free to call on them. I also tell them that interruptions and observations are highly welcomed.

"One time, I recall, I started to discuss the growth of the Workers' Educational Association in Britain. I saw one of the chaps in the class smiling to himself. He said, 'I happen to be in your class because of the inspiration and training I got in higher education through the WEA.' 'Well,' I said, 'what am I doing trying to tell you about it? You can come right up here and take over this class, because you've forgotten more than I know.' So up he came, and he did a lovely job."

This method takes a lot of trust. A teacher has to respecct the students before it can work, but this respect turns adults into better learners because it draws them into the learning process. Roby Kidd, calls this "engagement" and puts it at the centre of adult education.

"Children," he writes in his classic study *How Adults Learn*, "expect to have to learn things, whether or not they see any meaning in learning; adults are much less ready to accept learning without clear relevance . . . satisfaction must be felt in terms of the learner's own expectations and needs."[14]

Adults learn "horizontally." They link what they learn in school to what they already know, and they try to apply what they learn to their own lives. "Vertical learning" of abstract facts to pass tests doesn't make sense to them.[15]

Society set up the school system to test the young, but when older students come back to school, *they* test the system. Is the knowledge useful? Does it help me make better sense of my life and the world around me? Does it help me live more fully, enjoy my life more? These are the kinds of questions older people ask of the schools.

Changes in the System

Older students bring new challenges to educational institutions.

Schools will have to change their ideas about the length of courses, the times they offer them, the types of tests (if any) they use and the kinds of social supports they give to students. Some of these changes are already happening.

Elderhostel

One of the fastest growing programs in the world is called Elderhostel. It combines university education with European hosteling.

Marty Knowlton, a social activist and educator, started the program in New Hampshire in 1975. He designed a high-grade intellectual program for older people and then arranged for them to live on a university campus.

Elderhostel accepts students over the age of sixty and their husbands or wives. It doesn't matter how much education a person has had in the past: if you're interested in a course or subject, you can sign up.

Elderhostel, Inc., runs out of a central office in Boston. The office publishes catalogues (the Summer 1983 Catalogue, for instance, takes up 112 newspaper pages), promotes the program and enrols people in courses around the world. Each school in the system designs its own courses, hires its own faculty and provides extra-curricular activities as well as room and board for the students.

Most programs put students up in university dorms, so Elderhostelers share the common joys and frustrations of campus life. On some campuses people have to share rooms, often they have to share bathrooms and they all eat in the university dining hall. Sometimes things get a little more rugged. The Yosemite Institute in Yosemite National Park in California describes its quarters like this: the "rustic bunkhouse consists of two rooms, each with 25 beds. Mattresses without linens are provided. The bathhouse has toilet facilities and two showers. Participants must clean tables, floors, kitchen and dishes after meals, and clean the bunkhouse and bathhouse on Friday."[16]

Programs last one week — from Sunday night to the following Saturday. Elderhostel tries to keep the class size small: most programs take in from thirty-five to forty-five people at a time. In 1983 the total fee for the week — including food, rooms, course fees and costs for extra-curricular tours and activities — came to $180 U.S. ($190 in Alaska and Hawaii).

How do older people respond to this simple life? They rave about it. "With Elderhostel," says Pat Ferris, 64, "you are able to relax, have a good holiday and at a very reasonable cost — I couldn't believe you could have such wonderful food and accommodation at such a low rate."[17]

"It's a pretty fine deal," David Etheridge, national co-ordinator for Elderhostel Canada, says, "— a great way to travel cheaply, enjoy the stimulation of participating in college-level courses and, perhaps most importantly, meeting people."[18]

People come to the courses from all over the world. A class in Florida might include local people as well as students from Canada, England, France and California. Some people travel from campus to campus throughout the year taking courses.

William Bandy, an Elderhosteler, says he and his wife have taken courses at eight universities. *The Wall Street Journal* reported on Mr Bandy while he was attending a University of California Elderhostel program. "I'm signed up for Dundee University in Scotland, London University in London and Brighton Polytechnic on the south coast of England," he told reporter Ray Vicker. "After I come back I'll look up a few more colleges in the United States."[19]

The year Elderhostel began (1975), 200 older people enrolled in the program in five schools in New Hampshire. Eight years later over 80,000 older people had signed up at over 600 schools. By 1984 the program had grown to over 100,000 people at schools in more than a dozen countries. Elderhostel now offers courses in 900 schools in England, Scotland, Wales, Mexico, Bermuda, all the Scandinavian countries, Germany, the Netherlands, France, and Italy as well as North America.

The Elderhostel head office does not expect a slowdown in growth. The 1981 annual report stated that the "demand for the program continued to exceed availability by a significant amount

— even in a year of 80% expansion! There is no indication that this is a short-term situation."[20]

Last year Elderhostel turned away 15,000 people because there was no more room in the program. The summer programs are usually filled by the first of April. Elderhostel now also offers a winter program, and these sessions make up one of the fastest growing parts of the Elderhostel system.

Older people can now choose from hundreds of courses as well as the time of year they want to take them and the school or part of the world they wish to study in. Someone who wants to visit California, for instance, can take a summer course at the University of San Francisco, on the edge of Golden Gate Park. Courses there focus on the Far East and include "The Far East: Its Places, Peoples and Politics"; "Religions of the Far East"; and "Foods of the Far East." In the last course, students prepare and sample dishes from Japan, China, the Phillippines, Vietnam and Indonesia. They get recipes to take home with them. The Elderhostel brochure advises "bring aprons."

If the high country suits you, you might sign up for a course at Colorado Mountain College — Timberline Campus, Leadville, Colorado. The school sits ten thousand feet up in the Rocky Mountains. Courses include "Body Talk: Biofeedback and You"; "Leadville: the Magic City's History"; and "Environmental Protection for the High Country." They offer students a chance to use biofeedback equipment, take walking tours of the city and hike in the mountains during free time.

If you'd rather be in Rome, Elderhostel runs courses from mid-May to late June. The two-week program cost $620 U.S. in 1983 — not including air fare. The program, sponsored by Trinity College, Hartford, Connecticut, meets in a renovated convent. Courses (all given in English) include "History, Art and Architecture of Ancient Rome"; "Renaissance and Baroque Art of Rome"; and a course in "Modern Italy." Students take walking tours, visit the Roman Forum and Hadrian's villa and visit churches to view the painting and sculpture of Michelangelo, Raphael and other masters.

For people who would rather see Canada first, the Canadian branch of Elderhostel opened its first program at the University of New Brunswick in 1980. The Canadian programs have expanded quickly. From 1980 to 1981 the number of participants in Ontario more than doubled, and growth in the Maritimes programs jumped from only one program in New Brunswick in 1980 to programs in all four provinces in 1981.[21]

Elderhostel now offers courses in all provinces. The University of Ottawa, for instance, offers two different programs — one in English and one in French. The Memramcook Institute in New Brunswick, near Moncton, has offered one-week courses that started in early July and ran to the end of August. Topics included "Particularities of the Acadian History and Culture"; "Pencil Sketching"; and "Music and the Cinema." Keyano College, north-east of Edmonton, has offered a look at local ecology. Courses included "Heavy Equipment Operation"; "Tars and Technology"; and "A Practical Look at Forestry in Northern Alberta." For this last course the brochure said "bring boots, rain coats".

How do Canadians like Elderhostel? I asked Robert Williston, one of the first people to promote Elderhostel in Canada. He visited the course at Keyano College last year. "I talked with one 97-year-old woman," he says, "who'd just climbed down from a twenty-ton tractor-crawler. 'My husband drove one of those for twenty years before he died,' she said. 'I've always wanted to have a hand at it myself, but he'd never let me. Now I know what he did all those years.'"

Robert is sold on Elderhostel and wants to see it grow in Canada.

"Let me give you an example of why I like the programs so much," he says. "My mother always wanted to vist Georgia, but she doesn't like going places alone, so she signed up for the Elderhostel program there. She took the train down by herself, but once she got there the program staff had a place for her to stay on the university campus. She ate in the dining halls — the same spaghetti, rubber chicken and hamburgers the students got — and she loved it. She took three courses and she met lots of new people. She says it's the greatest vacation she's ever had.''

Universities value Elderhostel as much as the participants, because the program uses university facilities during slow times of the year — summers and holidays. And with declining enrolments at some schools, Elderhostel fills empty dorms during the winter.

Older people on campus also enrich campus life. Some professors have set up intergenerational classes by arranging to have Elderhostel students join regular summer classes for a week or two. At the University of New Hampshire, writer Gayle Kloosterman says, the graduate students invite Elderhostelers to late-afternoon Happy Hours. One young student told director Marty Knowlton about meeting one of the older students. "She's terrific — she knows so much! Why isn't my grandmother like that?" Knowlton suggested that the student give his grandmother a chance and talk to her as he had talked to this woman — as a colleague and equal. These meetings, Knowlton says, help bridge the generation gap in students' families.[22]

Faculty and staff gain too. They learn to work with older students, and they gain a new positive view of old age. In Canada, Robert Williston says, faculty fight to teach Elderhostel classes, even at half the normal pay.

Borden Painter, who teaches "Tudor England" at Trinity College in Hartford, Connecticut says that while younger people take university life for granted, Elderhostelers have "a wonderful sense . . . of discovery, a kind of sense of what a privilege it is for them to be at a place like Trinity College with an opportunity to learn and meet people and really soak it all up.''

Older students also bring their life experiences to the classroom. "Occasionally," Painter says, "you can have people who are almost ready to take over the class — they're so active." He finds Elderhostel students more mature and better able to relate their experience to the course, "whether it's in literature or art or history of . . . contemporary events.''[23]

Another teacher, Jim Halstead, teaches "Current Economic Issues: Behind the Headlines" at Occidental College in Los

Angeles. He says he enjoys the older students because of their energy and interest. "There's never a dull moment with these people. It's tremendous . . . I clearly think that I benefited more from this than the average student in the Elderhostel class. . . ."[24]

At a time when education programs face cutbacks all across North America, Elderhostel has grown stronger and more independent. It has attracted more students each year since it began, and more students have meant a more efficient central office. From 1979 to 1982, the cost per student has gone from $30 to about $20 in spite of inflation. In 1983 Elderhostel also began a drive to ask its alumni for donations. This, according to the 1982 annual report, "should provide an important supplementary source of support."

Elderhostel takes no money from the government, nor does it ask for any. "To the contrary," the 1981 annual report says, "Elderhostel represents the very best in successful private initiative in the non-profit sector."[25]

A University Day Program for Seniors

Elderhostel gives older people a taste of university life, but one criticism levelled at it is that it segregates older students. "It's subject to the accusation of being separate, but not quite equal," says Gordon Hancock, program co-ordinator of continuing education at the University of Manitoba. "It appears to be based on the same segregative attitudes that plague older persons elsewhere in society."[26]

Mr Hancock, who has recently finished a study of senior education programs in Canada and the U.S., says that most programs for older people don't give them a chance to get a degree or even to get into degree courses. Of the sixteen schools he visited, all with centres of gerontology, only one school, Boston University, offers "access to mainstream education for the older person."[27] Programs for older people offer mostly short-term, unrelated courses which lack continuity and substance.

"Older people want education the same as anyone else," Mr Hancock says. "I'd like to see older people with younger people in schools. We in continuing education want to see older people as part of the warp and weave of society.''

In Canada, the University of Winnipeg Senior Education Program goes a long way toward this goal. It had one of the first programs in North America that allowed older people to take regular undergraduate classes for credit. The university also offers a series of non-credit courses as a community service. Students can start with these and move up to audit credit courses or take them for credit as their confidence increases. Senior students pay no tuition, only a $3.00 fee to get a library and identification card.

The senior education program started in 1972. In 1980 450 students signed up for five non-credit courses. This figure jumped to 800 in 1982, and to over 1,500 people in eleven courses in 1984.

''We're not sure exactly how many people come,'' says Barb Spence, co-ordinator of the senior education program, ''because not all of them enroll. A lot of them come and then bring a friend. The university doesn't mind as long as the classes don't get too full. Then I have to go around and ask if they're all registered.''

A list of the most popular courses this year includes: ''Man and Landscapes in Western Canada'' (250 students); ''Contemporary World Issues'' (550 students in two sections); ''Introduction to Investing'' (90 students); ''Microcomputers'' (155 students in four sections) and six sections of ''Conversational French'' at three levels (125 students).

The key to the program's success? First, the university tries to make it as easy as possible for people to take classes. It puts all the classes in two time slots — mid-morning and early afternoon. That way people don't have to fight the rush-hour to get to or from class. Classes run two hours, long enough to cover a topic in depth but not so long that people get tired.

Second, the university has made registration easy. It has special registration forms with big print for seniors. To make registration less painful the university sets aside a special day, place and time for seniors to register and adds extra staff to give the seniors special attention. No one has to stand in line.

Third, the university involves seniors in planning the program.

Each year the Division of Continuing Education and Community Service and the university president hold a spring luncheon with senior representatives at which the seniors suggest new courses. The administration uses these ideas to plan the next year's program. As the program grows the administration is finding other ways to get senior input.

"I go around to all the classes in the winter term," Barb Spence says. "I ask the classes what they're interested in, what they'd like to see as well as what courses they liked this year. I also get new ideas from other places. This year I heard of a course called "Chapter and Verse: Lectures on Poets and Poetry." It sounds good, so I'll try to use it."

Is there a philosophy or a set of principles behind the program? "Based on input from the seniors," Barb says, "we try things we think will work. We know that people want social stimulation. The courses give them a chance to get out, to be together. They also want good quality courses. They want to learn something about a new topic or to get some interesting information. Our microcomputer course, for instance, really took off this year."

Some courses work so well that people come back year after year. Professor Tim Ball teaches the most popular course in the program, a geography course called "Contemporary World Issues." In 1981 his class had over 400 people enrolled, so the university opened a second section. The class now has close to 600 students.

Professor Ball keeps the class lively by dealing with issues right out of that day's newspaper. I attended one class at which he discussed an Australian plan to tow icebergs to Australia for fresh water. He also talked about world climate change, population and other topics students raised.

"I'm amazed," he says, "that they're so interested in the future." But Professor Ball sees this as the start of a trend. "The young used to learn from the old," he says, "now we all learn together. . . ."[28]

Another course, "Writing and Journalism," encourages older people to "use as content their memories of social, technological and cultural change as they have experienced it, particularly as it relates to the history of Western Canada.''[29]

Eric Wells, a broadcaster, journalist and former editor of *The Winnipeg Tribune*, teaches the course. The class writes to a deadline each week, and Mr Wells edits the copy. Then the student rewrites until both teacher and student are happy with the results.

Some of the students have sold their writing to magazines and newspapers. Margaret Cantelon, a retired teacher who sold a recent article to *Western Producer*, told *Inside Info*, the university newsletter, that the course has led her to ''see things from a different point of view. . . . You can't sit around [in retirement]. Having an interest revitalizes a person. It keeps you alive.''[30]

In 1984, with the help of a grant from Imperial Oil, Ltd., the class published a book called *Through the Gateway to Yesteryear*. ''I had no idea it would be feasible,'' Eric Wells says, ''but every student produced a publishable story. Not one stuck out.'' The book is a collection of short stories, poems and research articles by the seniors about their early years in Canada, and the university will send it to libraries and schools throughout the province.

People not only come to the non-credit program to acquire knowledge, they also come to socialize. The university is downtown across from the Bay and on most of the major bus routes. This makes access easy for most people even in winter. Students often meet at noon for lunch or coffee at the university, then go to their afternoon classes.

After a year or two some of the non-credit students move on to take credit courses. And the university encourages them to sign up for any course it offers including special credit courses for seniors. They pay no fee for any of these courses.

Why do older people take credit courses?

''Most of the people who take the courses are women,'' Mavis Turner says. ''About ten or twelve women to every man. Men don't seem to have the same need to achieve. They've achieved at work and they're glad to retire. Most of the women grew up during the Depression. They never had the chance to go to university, only the boys went. Some of them put their brothers through school. They always wanted to go, but couldn't. Now they say, 'Here's my chance.'''

One of the credit students, Margaret Perry, graduated in 1983 with a B.A. in English. She was 89 at the time. Mrs Perry says she likes the discipline of credit courses — she thinks of the essays and tests as a part of learning.

She would have gotten the degree sooner, she says, but when the seniors' program first began, older students could take only one half-course each year. Now that she has her degree, she has some new plans. She wants to work for her doctorate. "Anyone who knows me, knows . . . I always have to be learning something," she says. "You know my age, so you'll know I don't have too long to get my doctorate degree. But it's not out of my reach. Life is a learning process that never stops."[31]

The University of Winnipeg may have one of the oldest and largest programs in Canada, but other universities and colleges across the country also offer degree and non-degree courses for seniors. Most schools allow them to enroll for free or for only a small fee.[32]

Creative Retirement Manitoba
Programs like that of the University of Winnipeg or Elderhostel try to adapt traditional university courses to older people. While they do often consult older people about the course offerings, it is the administration that hires the staff and arranges the courses. The older student only comes to use the service.

At Creative Retirement Manitoba older people design courses and programs for themselves. A nineteen-member board of directors made up of retired people sets policy, hires staff and handles the finances. A curriculum committee of the board plans the schedule of courses. Senior volunteers also run the office, work at registration and do odd jobs around the place.

Creative Retirement grew out of a program started by Age and Opportunity, Inc. A & O started a senior education program called the Institute for Continuous Learning in 1973, but by 1978 it found the program too expensive. The organization agreed to pay the cost of office help and mailing for two more years, but it wanted to pull out all support by 1980. The Winnipeg Foundation agreed to pay for staff salaries from 1978 to 1980. After that, the Institute would have to find its own funds. A & O hired Farrell Fleming, the current director, to start up the new Institute.

The new program grew quickly. In 1979-80 600 seniors enrolled in 37 courses. Many of the courses had waiting lists. Also, over 1,200 seniors attended the Institute's Open Forum lecture series. The Institute also co-sponsored a successful summer Elderhostel-style program with the University of Manitoba. In 1981 the Institute became an independent non-profit educational centre and changed its name to Creative Retirement Manitoba.

New Horizons granted funds to Creative Retirement to pay for equipment and, in a rare move, a director's salary. New Horizons has also helped fund some new programs at Creative Retirement — the Massage Team and the Personal Growth Group to name only two.

Expert senior volunteers teach nearly all the courses. Some of these teachers started out here as students. Others received their training in traditional programs, then brought their skills to Creative Retirement.

June Eastham went back to the university when her husband died. "I took two courses the first year," she says, "a course on food preparation the first term and one on nutrition the second term." She went on to take a range of home economics courses, and now she teaches cooking and nutrition classes at Creative Retirement.

Arthur Leeds, a retired classics professor and past president of Creative Retirement, teaches two courses, one based on his slide collection of ancient Greece and Rome, the other based on slides he has taken over the years in Britain. He also lectures in Creative Retirement's Distinguished Professor series.

Creative Retirement runs several related but distinct programs. First, there is a program of twenty-eight courses offered throughout the week. Students pay five dollars for the first course they take, three dollars for each extra course. Creative Retirement also asks students to buy a five-dollar membership to cover mailing. People who can't pay the fees may have them waived.

A list of some of Creative Retirement's courses for the winter of 1984 gives an idea of the program. Classes include:

> Creative Dress Design for Mature Women
> Feldenkrais-Awareness through Movement
> Memory and Aging
> Acupressure Massage (*Shiatsu*)
> Cuisine Naturelle
> Intermediate Creative Writing
> Death — Transition to Life
> Tai Chi (Beginners, Continuing, Intermediate)
> Interesting Older People (a lecture series)
> Distinguished Professor Lecture Series
> My Favourite Recipes ($1 extra to pay for the food)
> Calligraphy

The Curriculum Committee tries for a mix of courses. Some deal with the mind, some with the body. Health-related courses like foot massage, Tai Chi and nutrition draw a good crowd, as do courses on stress reduction, hypnotism and memory. "The most popular courses," Farrell Fleming says, "teach people to care for themselves. People take these classes because they don't want to be a burden on others."

A course in holistic health drew forty-five people one year. So did a class on heart attack first-aid. A reflexology class, one of the first self-help courses, drew a record sixty-five people when it first started.

Academic courses also attract students. The Distinguished Professor Lecture Series — the biggest course in the program — drew fifty students in 1982. The second biggest course, Farrell Fleming's "Philosophy: Life's Greatest Questions," drew forty-six.

Almost anything Farrell offers draws a good crowd. This year when he offered a course called "Death — Transition to Life," thirty people signed up. I asked Ray Michaels, one of the students, why he took the course. ''Farrell was teaching it,'' he said. ''That was the main reason. Oh, I have an interest in the subject. Most people do. But the main reason was Farrell. I'll take anything he teaches.'' Ray has taken all Farrell's philosophy courses — Hindu philosophy, Buddhist philosophy, Muslim philosophy.

''Most of the people in the course,'' Farrell says, ''felt relief to be able to talk about death in a normal way. Other cultures make death more a part of life. When we talked about death in other cultures, like Canadian Indian culture, the people said the ideas fit with their own. They began to feel at home with their own way of seeing death, and they began to see that around the planet a tradition of wisdom about death and dying exists. This gave people a wider framework for their own views and beliefs. It made perfect sense to them. This knowledge seems to be useful for older people. It helps them function in an optimal way. And this may be the prime time of life to teach and learn this kind of thing.''

Creative Retirement gives older people a chance to explore new, non-traditional subjects, and the students welcome the chance. A course on self-hypnosis called ''Talk to Yourself'' drew sixty-five students in 1981 — the biggest class that year. Reg Killeen, 72, taught the class between sessions of taping his television show and talking to students at a local high school. I asked him how he felt about the students at Creative Retirement. ''Some of the best,'' he says. ''We have preconceived ideas about older people — that they're set in their ways. This just isn't true. They're wonderful to work with ''

Each term the curriculum committee at Creative Retirement experiments with new courses. Sometimes they work, sometimes they don't. A few years ago a course called ''You and Your Aging Parent'' for seniors with very old parents drew only two people. A course called ''Death and Dying'' drew only six students. When a course doesn't work out the committee tries something else.

Sometimes a course catches on right away. Calligraphy met with a good response from the start. Now Creative Retirement offers two sections — advanced and intermediate — to over forty people. Sometimes a course, like Farrell's course about death takes on a second life and does well. By trying new courses and continuing old ones that work, Creative Retirement has built a strong core program, one that attracts new students each year.

In 1984, 992 students took classes in the winter program — not including about 100 people in courses in personal care homes and 120 people who attended an Open Forum slide and lecture series each week. This makes Creative Retirement one of the biggest (if not the biggest) independent senior education centres in North America.

Who are the students? A 1982 survey of students found that most were between 65 and 75 years old, retired and in good health.

About three times as many women come out for courses as men. About a third of the students are married, a third widowed and a third single (separated, divorced or never married). Almost 80% of the students have some high school education, while about 10% have done university graduate work. (Only about 24% of people over 65 in Canada had a high school diploma or better in 1981). About half of the couples had an annual income between $6,000 and $12,000. A third reported income of over $12,000 a year. Single people had a lower income, 84% of them reporting an income below $9,000 a year.

In short, some of Creative Retirement's students live below the poverty line, while others have middle-class incomes. Most are in good health and are relatively well educated. This fits what we know about adult education. People who have the most education come back for more; those with the least education don't go on.[33] People with little education miss the chance to learn after they retire.

Creative Retirement tries to meet the needs of these people in two ways. First, its general program provides a non-threatening way for older people to return to school. Creative Retirement describes itself as ''an educational institution strictly for older people and carried out in a way which makes people feel quickly at home and at ease.''[34]

Second, Creative Retirement runs a Core Area Initiatives Program that takes classes into the community. Co-sponsored by municipal, provincial and federal governments, the program began in 1983 with the goal of reaching people who wouldn't come to class on their own. It now has its own full-time co-ordinator, Doug Wasyliw, who designs and promotes new courses.

Through the Core Area program Creative Retirement has started three new Open Forum Series — one in English downtown, one in French in St Boniface and another given in Winnipeg's north end in Ukrainian. The Ukrainian Open Forum features talks on Ukrainian dancing, embroidery, literature, music and history. The French program offers lectures in French on foreign countries and a demonstration of jigging by Les Danseurs de la Rivière Rouge.

The Core Area program also works with other groups in the city. Doug Wasyliw plans to start courses in massage and fitness as well as financial planning for blind elderly people. (The Canadian National Institute for the Blind will co-sponsor the latter.) Doug says he wants to expand the program to include Feldenkrais exercises — techniques that make people more aware of their bodies and of movements and balance.

Doug has also helped start a fitness and exercise class for Native people at the Indian and Métis Friendship Centre. "Exercise is a concept foreign to Native culture," Doug says. "For them exercise means work. Jumping around to work up a sweat doesn't make any sense. During the classes people go off to do other things, then come back in later. You have to explain the value of exercises to them as you run the program.

"It's been touch and go to get it started. Now some of the younger native social workers want to learn exercise methods for older people so they can teach the classes. Creative Retirement will help design a fitness leadership workshop just for them."

The Core Area program has also designed a program for older women. The Women's Employment Centre and the Women's Health Action Centre have both set up classes. "These groups see many women in their mid 50s," Doug says, "so we said, 'Do you want us to do some information sessions on aging?' They said alright. We talk to groups of women about retirement planning, widowhood and health.''

Nearly 900 people took part in Core Area programs in 1983-84. And the Core Area's First annual report says the program will design new courses in 1984-85 in languages other than French, English and Ukrainian. It will also offer three new pre-retirement programs at no cost.

''We'll provide information or programs on aging to any group in the Core Area,'' Doug says. ''If no one's doing it, we will. We'll try any program that might be useful and educational for older people.''

A Senior Volunteer project is Creative Retirement's third major program. Farrell Fleming says he would like Creative Retirement to become a place where people can ''start to do things not strictly for themselves, but also for others.'' As an example he cites the Personal Growth Group that visits the Middlechurch Home. He also mentions a new volunteer project that supplies older people as resources to teachers in public schools. The seniors visit classes to offer students specific skills or insights.

I visited Chancellor Public School one morning along with Farrell and a team of six senior volunteers. We visited a fifth-grade class of gifted children who had started a project on the future of Canadian society.

''We need to learn about the past before we can learn about the future,'' Vicki Krasner, one of the students, said when I asked her why they wanted to talk to old people. The children had already interviewed their parents and grandparents for practice.

''I wanted them to talk to some non-family members,'' Renata Fischer, their teacher, says, ''to learn some new things and get the experience of seeing what other older people are like.''

Renata arranged for teams of three students to talk with each older person. The children had their questions planned in advance, and each group sat at a table with a tape recorder. To make their guests feel at home the students set up some rules. ''You don't have to answer if you don't want to," one boy said. "Just shake your head no, then it won't come out on the tape recorder."

The seniors came prepared to talk about the past. Rita Arledge, a former teacher, brought in some spellers and readers dating from the Thirties. June Eastham brought in pictures of the family farm she lived on as a girl. All the students in her group had a list of questions to ask June.

"What job opportunities did your parents have?"

"What did you want to grow up to be?"

"What was your favourite activity?"

When the young interviewers exhausted their list of questions after about ten minutes June kept talking. She told them how her father had sown straight rows of grain by putting up a flag at the end of the field and keeping his eye on the flag as he plowed. She told them about churning butter and how on Saturdays her mother used to sell butter and eggs in town to buy other food. She described ten- and twelve-foot-high snow-drifts and riding to school in a horse-drawn cutter with blankets and footwarmers to prevent frost-bite. She told them about sowing grain in the spring from the back of a tractor and how she caught her finger in the machinery one year. She held up her hand like a relic and showed them the scar on her finger to prove it.

One of the girls lived on a farm too, and it turned out that everyone in the group — young and old — had suffered two common plagues: piano lessons and younger sisters.

The students then took their guests on a tour of their school, a new, open-concept building that fans out like a wheel around a hub. The library, music room and gym stand at the centre, the classes on the rim. The seniors asked about the noise in the open areas, about new teaching methods and about art projects on the walls.

As the tour progressed it became clear that the older guests were as interested in exploring the school as the students were in learning something about life B.M.J. — Before Michael Jackson.

"This program has begun to grow," says Farrell Fleming. "It could get huge. I can see that in a year we may need a full-time staff member just to co-ordinate the volunteers and the schools. This began as just a part of our Core Area Initiatives grant, but now we have at least four services we offer to schools.

"First we have the Studio Two drama program. They've done shows for all grades — shorter ones for kindergarten, the full show for high school classes.

"Second, we do a local history unit with the schools that includes guided tours of parts of the city. We bring in old photos, maps, that sort of thing.

"Third, we do the sort of thing you see here today. We've never done just this kind of thing before. But we have all sorts of expertise that the schools could call on. Sybil Shack, for instance, is a writer and former school principal and past president of the Manitoba Teachers' Society, and could do some work with the kids on writing. Jean Carson could talk about political action. We have a wealth of talent the schools could use.

"Fourth, we want to work with the schools to develop a section on aging in the Family Life program. We could talk about what it's like to get older or to be old. Soon we'll be starting to do in-services with teachers, with whole school staffs, to get them more aware of the issue of aging and to show them how they could use older people in the classroom."

Farrell believes that Creative Retirement's potential is almost unlimited. "The need for an independent not too large, highly personal educational institution for seniors," he wrote in a Creative Retirement annual report, "will increase as the senior population increases. This population will have increasing amounts of formal education, and will demand more 'meaning' in its activities than that presently supplied by some current senior programs. So far, the main educational institutions, universities, colleges and schools, have not shown themselves particularly adaptable to the special needs of seniors. . . . Creative Retirement believes the kind of programming flexibility it possesses is making, and will continue to make, a significant contribution to the well-being of seniors in the Province."[35]

The Future

All the figures indicate that older people in the future will have more education than the old today, and people with education tend to want more of it. The growth of new educational programs and the expansion of existing programs all point in this direction.

But "in the field of education," writes Robert Atchley, "we see perhaps the ultimate in the withdrawal of support from older people." Education, he says, serves the young. It prepares people for jobs. Even adult education serves mainly to help people get better jobs, new careers or promotions. "Only a very tiny portion of formal education . . . is devoted to the skills involved in the enjoyment of living. . . . There is some question how relevant education is for the young, but there can be no question that most formal education programs have been irrelevant for older people."[36]

Some changes have begun to take place in senior education. New programs designed for older people have begun to spring up, but Atchley is right about the lack of support. In the U.S. in the early 1970s, for instance, higher education received fifty times more financial support per student than basic adult education.

Professor David Radcliffe at the University of Western Ontario found that Britain shortchanges adult education too. From 1958 to 1980, he reports, real expenditures on education in Britain jumped 85% to 90%, but most of this money went to people under 25. Adult education expenditures fell from 0.5% of the total budget in 1975 to 0.4% in 1981 — a 20% decrease.[37]

In Canada all education programs have faced cutbacks, and like everyone else seniors have felt the pinch. Gordon Hancock's study of senior education in North America found that in 1983, "Where programs for older citizens did exist in a center [on aging], they are being curtailed or dropped as a result of financial restraint."[38]

Until a year ago, an older person could take any course they wanted at the University of Winnipeg for a simple $3.00 fee. Now, with overcrowded classes and staff cut-backs, older students can only take a course if there is room after all the younger students have signed up. This makes older students second class citizens in the university unless they want to pay full tuition, but tuition has risen this year and many older people can't afford the cost.

Senior groups can, however, obtain short-term funding to start up experimental programs. New Horizons grants run from 18 to 36 months; corporations sometimes give start up money to groups; organizations like the Winnipeg Foundation offer money to buy furniture or equipment. But if a group relies on this kind of funding it will face trouble before long. Many worthwhile projects fade away because they can't find stable sources of income.

A successful program called Grandfriends in Winnipeg folded a few years ago because no funding agency would pay for a program co-ordinator. The program placed seniors in local public schools as teachers' aides, but someone had to match up the seniors with the schools and keep track of the schools' and older helpers' needs — including transportation for the helpers. The city agreed to pay expenses, but not the salary of a co-ordinator. Within a year the program lost 90% of its volunteers and closed.

Creative Retirement's Core Area program has revived the Grandfriends idea, but it has funding for only two more years — just enough time to get the program started before it falls apart again?

The Core Area's parent program, Creative Retirement Manitoba, has limped along for over ten years on short-term grants. As I write this, CRM technically has no money left to pay its executive director in spite of its grants for programs.

Farrell Fleming, the executive director and spirit behind Creative Retirement, sometimes has had to take severe cuts in pay or no pay at all to get through times when funds ran out. Short-term grants also keep him writing grant applications and reports to granting bodies instead of running Creative Retirement's program. In December 1983 the provincial government granted

Creative Retirement $10,000. This helped, but it fell far short of Creative Retirement's needs: salary for staff came to about $70,000 in 1983. The government's commitment to adult education appears to mean promises but no money.

Senior education programs have few choices. Elderhostel has worked to free itself from short-term grants. When it first began it got funds from Exxon, the Atlantic Richfield Foundation and AT&T, to name just a few donors, but Elderhostel wants financial independence and it is not far from reaching this goal.

In 1979 Elderhostel depended wholly on grant income. In 1981 67% of its income came from grants. In 1982 only 40% of its income came from grants. By 1983 it planned to earn almost 90% of its income from interest on savings and tuition fees. Elderhostel has also refused all government support.

Most groups will opt for a mix of grants, government funds and fees. They can also pursue donations, bequests and creative financing. The finance committee at Creative Retirement has suggested that the organization sponsor a casino night to raise money quickly (a suggestion the Creative Retirement Board has rejected in the past).

If senior education is to have a future, government must help — and not just with short-term grants. Long-term plans to fund and support education for older people make the most financial sense. "Seniors with active, alert and questioning minds are healthy people, and can be most useful to society and the community in which they live."[39] Programs like the University of Winnipeg program for seniors, Elderhostel and Creative Retirement serve as models of learning and good aging for the future.

9

POLITICS

A Poetry Reading

We all showed up, like parents at a school play, to watch the birth of Manitoba's first senior citizen political organization — the Manitoba Society of Seniors (MSOS). Yhetta Gold, then executive director of Age and Opportunity (now director of the National Advisory Council on Aging), was there — A & O had donated staff and office-help to study the need for a Seniors' Society. Farrell Fleming was there — he had worked as A & O's paid advisor to the study group that founded MSOS. Gordon Kroeker from Health and Welfare Canada and Eric Lubosch from the provincial Department of Health and Welfare had come as guests and friends of the new group. Thirty seniors — half from the city of Winnipeg, half from rural regions — came as representatives to form the society.

At ten a.m. on February 22, 1978, Jim Mullan, interim chairman of MSOS, welcomed us to the meeting. Then he read a piece of poetry which he dedicated "to the Seniors' Movement." He called it "Together." I reprint parts of the poem here with his permission.

With muscle-powered tools at hand,
we hoped and dreamed, we schemed and planned;
with work and sweat, we built this land —
   Together.

Now younger shoulders, lithe and strong,
carry the load of work along,
leaving us free to sing this song —
   Together.

Free from responsibility,
now is the time for you and me.
to relish our own society —
   Together.

Each of us, singly, is old and weak;
united, we are a force unique;
provided we join, to stand and speak —
   Together.

Marathoners in life's long run,
completing our race in the setting sun,
let's show that seniors can get things done
(and in the process still have fun) —
   Together.

What is striking about this poem is not its quality or its sentiments but the fact that it was read at all. In spite of a lifetime of attending all sorts of meetings and belonging to all kinds of groups, I cannot think of a single political group that convened its inaugural session with a poem, and I think this says something about senior politics today.

Much of the research on senior political action has focused on voting trends, lobbying tactics and advocacy groups, and most of it concludes that seniors do not wield significant political power and will not in the future in spite of their growing numbers.

This research, however, misses an important truth about senior political action. Sometimes, it is true, older people want and need power, because programs like a national health care system and a government pension plan require political clout to get started and to keep going. But seniors also have wider concerns. They have less interest in power for its own sake than younger age groups. Given decent services and a fair income, most seniors would rather turn to poetry, education and community service than to power politics. It is a mistake to judge the value of senior politics entirely by the size of senior groups or the commitment of their members to militant action.

"I'd rather read and write poetry," Jim Mullan told the group when he had finished his reading, "than dicker with the government." So would most of us, but some older people feel a responsibility to their fellow seniors in need. And this moves them to political action.

Senior political action also goes beyond lobbying, vote-getting, power-broking and deal-making. It includes advocacy for wider social change. It includes seniors serving as advisors to government and industry. It includes community service and volunteer work. And it includes the discovery of new life-styles and alternatives to old age as we know it today.

"In politics, perhaps more than in any other institution," writes Robert Atchley, "the older person is still able to play the role of sage." One American study shows, for instance, that older people play a larger role at political nominating conventions than one would expect from their numbers. They also serve as public officials in greater number than their proportion in the population would suggest.[1] Presidents, cabinet ministers and judges, for instance, often get their posts in their late 50s and keep them well into their 60s. In 1975 over 20% of State Representatives and almost 40% of Senators in the U.S. were over 60 years old, and 3% of Representatives and 15% of Senators were over 70 years old. This pattern has remained the same for the last six sessions of Congress.[2]

In Canada a random sample of ninety Ministers of Parliament

in 1982 found that they averaged 49 years old. Almost 10% were over 60.[3] Five of the last ten Canadian prime ministers were 60 or older. Prime Minister Pierre Trudeau resigned from office at the age of 63.

Older people remain active in politics in other ways too. A greater proportion of older than younger people vote. In the U.S., 18-year-olds as a group show the poorest voter turn-out. The turn-out increases as people age: recent American research shows that 75% of people over 70 voted in the 1980 presidential election, compared to 60% of 25-year-olds, and a greater portion of people in their 80s voted than people in their 20s.[4] Older people in the U.S. constitute 20% of the voting public (as opposed to only 10% of the general population), and researchers predict their percentage as voters will increase in the future.[5]

Some of the first studies done in Canada also found that young people voted least. Voting seemed to peak among 50-year-olds and then dropped off in older groups.[6] A more recent study, however, compared different age groups with the same income, education, occupation, region, community size, marital status, sex and language group. James Curtis and Ronald Lambert of the University of Waterloo found no drop in voting or political interest among older groups once they looked at people with the same background. Instead, they found that interest, voting and affiliation with political groups increased even past the age of 70. "We are struck," they write "with our failure to detect any clear evidence for a reduction in reported organizational involvement or affiliation with age once controls are made. . . . So far as voting and political interest are concerned, there is either no drop-off with age or even some modest increases."[7]

Studies also indicate that older people tend to follow political campaigns more closely than younger people and are "at least disposed to political action," if they see their interests served through politics.[8]

This makes older people a potential power block in society. In Canada about 10% of the population was over 65 in 1981, and the median voting age was 42. By 2031 the older population could grow to as much as 21% of the population, raising the median voting age to 48 years. Statistics Canada predicts that from 1981 to 2021 the percentage of voters over 65 will rise from 13.4% to 21% of the total voting public.[9]

Given the growing numbers of older people and the high proportion of people over 65 who vote, Professor Gifford of the School of Social Work at Dalhousie University believes "It is . . . therefore evident that if seniors were to tend to vote en bloc (as they probably did in the Diefenbaker 'pension increase' landslide of 1958) they could be a significant electoral factor."[10]

A powerful senior vote could bring about sudden social change, and some experts believe that if older people use their votes to pass laws and create policies for their own interests at the expense of the middle-aged, they will set off an intergenerational conflict. Professors Joseph Tindale and Victor Marshall, for instance, predict increased tension between older and younger age groups over the cost of programs for the elderly.[11]

Will we see the growth of senior voting power in the next few years? Will younger groups revolt against such power? Most researchers do not believe this will happen.

First, they say, older people do not vote as a bloc. They differ as much from one another as they do from younger people. Educated, urban, white-collar voters, for instance, don't vote the same way as less educated, rural, blue-collar voters. Voters also vary by region of the country and ethnicity.[12]

John Duffey, a senior activist in Canada, believes that older people lack a group-consciousness. They seem more individual and less group centred than the young. "Grey Power," he writes, ". . . is a myth. . . . The truth is that [seniors] do not speak with one voice, nor are they likely to do so in the foreseeable future."[13]

Second, most older people do not feel the need to organize because they do not see the political system as unfair or unresponsive to their needs.[14] A study of leaders of senior organizations in Canada in 1982 found that they were not angry with the system. "While all were advocating improvement in particular programs or policies affecting seniors," Professor Gifford writes in his report on this study, "many at the same time expressed the sentiment that 'seniors never had it so good.'"[15]

Third, seniors' votes may not affect policy as much as other forms of political action do. The policy system, according to A. Paul Pross, "tends to be characterized by superficial public deliberations and by the assignment of major responsibility for policy development to the political executive, the administrative arm, and *recognized* pressure groups."[16] The extent of senior influence, Professor Kenneth Kernaghan of Brock University says, "will depend significantly on the recognition these groups are granted in the policy-making process, especially by federal and provincial public servants."[17]

Seniors will not be able to force policies on younger age groups, but they have begun to receive the recognition Professor Kernaghan says they need in order to bring about change. Provincial and federal government departments, for instance, have turned to older people more and more for advice on senior issues. Senior provincial advisory councils have become partners with the government in setting up new programs, and different levels of government have funded scores of new grass-roots senior groups across the country, groups which now sometimes work with varying degrees of success to change government policy.

The System Today

Before he retired in 1974 Cas Carter, now 70 and president of the Manitoba Society of Seniors, worked full time in the Excise and Duty department of the federal government and also did some freelance work as dance and music critic for *The Winnipeg Free Press*. He speaks enthusiastically about the goals of MSOS.

"Other seniors' organizations," Cas says, "are involved in education or providing hobbies for older people. . . . But we at the MSOS are the ones who organize the seniors to act. . . . Seniors must be organized to speak with a united voice."

MSOS started in 1979. By 1981 900 people held individual

memberships and forty-two clubs with a total of 3,000 members belonged. MSOS also has a board made up of members from the province's eight regional councils. These regions have a total of seven hundred clubs, making MSOS the largest senior group in the province.

MSOS raises money to support its work through raffles, dues and donations, but most of its program funds come from the provincial and federal governments. The provincial government, for instance, pays for a full-time executive director. The federal New Horizons program supports specific projects like the Manitoba Senior Citizens Games — a province-wide competition that includes quilting as well as nine-hole golf, five-pin bowling, swimming, horseshoes and photography.

Groups like MSOS exist all across the country. Professor Gifford of Dalhousie University reports that about forty senior social action groups exist in seven provinces, most of them west of Quebec.[18] To name a few: in Quebec la Fédération de l'Age d'Or du Québec boasts 165,000 members; Canadian Pensioners Concerned now has twenty branches in three provinces; and Ontario's United Senior Citizens has a membership of 250,000.

According to Professor Gifford, about one older person in three belongs to some kind of senior organization, usually a senior club or centre, and these 3,700 clubs are often part of national federations or provincial regional councils.

Few of the local clubs, however, participate in political advocacy, and most of their members are not involved in political action. The clubs leave advocacy to national and regional groups like MSOS. At best, clubs pass motions or bring local and regional issues to the provincial and national groups. Once a year, for instance, the National Federation of Pensioners and Senior Citizens, Canada's largest senior group, meets to pass resolutions which they then bring before the government.

Do these groups make any difference? Most of them claim they do.

The National Senior Citizens Federation, for instance, lobbied in 1963 and 1965 and helped set up a better federal pension plan.[19]

In Quebec, la Fédération de l'Age d'Or du Québec reports its successes, in its newsletter *La vie nouvelle*. "Almost every issue," Professor Gifford says, "is able to report on some government action, or on actions by stores and restaurants in establishing discounts, which can be attributed to [their] advocacy."[20]

The Alberta Council on Aging (ACA) also reports success in its work. In 1982 the Council raised the issue of rising crime against seniors. In October of that year the Alberta government appointed a commission to look into the issue.

MSOS succeeded this year in keeping bus fare increases for seniors to five cents (the city had proposed a ten-cent raise). They also protested a raise in home heating gas prices, and although John Brott, a member of MSOS, says he doubts that gas prices will stay down, he adds that the gas company involved had to pay for part of their appeal.

When seniors intervened in hearings in the past, they had to pay the costs. But many seniors do not have that kind of money. Now, through the efforts of the MSOS, the government says that an applicant for a raise — in this case the gas company — has to pay part of the cost of a challenge. Cas Carter feels that the MSOS has won a victory for everyone by getting aid for its legal counsel. "Automatically," he says, "this decision has set a precedent and other groups in society will benefit from it."

Senior groups also promote an awareness among seniors and the public about new life-styles in old age.

The Alberta Council on Aging publishes a magazine each quarter called *Foresight: The Magazine for Retirement Planning*. The Royal Canadian Legion helps fund the magazine, which has no political content. It runs articles on food, sports and fitness, travel, finances and time-management. In 1982 it won the Sir Frederick Haultain Award for "outstanding contribution in the field of education." Forty-five companies now use *Foresight* to help their workers plan for retirement.

The ACA also helps older people remain active. In 1981, with the aid of a New Horizons grant, it set up a consultative service called "Project Involvement." This program made senior volunteers available to boards of directors, training programs and community groups throughout the province. Now Project Involvement will become a permanent service sponsored by the ACA and four government departments.[21]

The Manitoba Society of Seniors also offers services to its members. It runs a photocopy service (partly subsidized by New Horizons), an income tax advice service and a travel service. In 1981 MSOS offered low-cost tours to Spain, Las Vegas and Vancouver, and in 1982 it ran a Florida-cruise package tour.

MSOS publishes the quarterly *Manitoba Seniors Journal* and a monthly newsletter called *Dateline* to keep members up to date on MSOS action. Members are also encouraged to write their MLAs and to put pressure on the government when it's needed.

Most groups like the ACA, MSOS and the National Federation of Pensioners and Senior Citizens work within the system. They report on issues their members raise, advise the government on policy and play a useful part in the political process. For the most part they receive the courteous and interested attention of politicians.[22]

They do, however, face some problems.

First, most seniors do not appear to be interested in becoming involved in political issues.[23] Fred Grayston, Vancouver senior activist, writes that 63,000 of British Columbia's 320,000 seniors live in Vancouver, "yet they are almost invisible. Our greatest problem in our every endeavour is motivation of Seniors in their own interests."[24]

Mr Grayston believes that most seniors hesitate to act because they "have an ingrained fear of authority."[25] Other writers suggest that older people are self-reliant and don't like to join groups.[26] It is even possible that some people won't join a seniors' group because they don't want to admit their age. One group had to change its name because they first called themselves Options for Life Development (OLD). Even people over 75 wouldn't join a group called OLD.[27]

Second, senior groups in Canada lack organization. New Horizons has helped set up scores of new groups since 1972, but

few of them have contact with one another. No national group —
like the American Association of Retired People in the U.S., with
over nine million members, or the National Council of Senior
Citizens in the U.S., with over three million members — speaks
for all of Canada's seniors. Differences in language and culture
prevent English and French groups from acting together, but even
within Quebec or Ontario major groups rarely work together.

Class differences also keep groups apart. Professor Gifford's
research indicates that National Federation leaders tend to come
from the working class while French association leaders come from
the middle class — most have worked as social service professionals. Other groups scattered around the country draw their
leaders from an upper middle class background.[28]

This lack of contact between groups has begun to change. The
Alberta Council on Aging, for instance, reports the foundation of
the Inter-Agency Council on Aging which met for the first time in
February 1983. It will draw together non-government groups
interested in aging to establish a common stand on basic issues.
British Columbia already has a Council of Senior Citizens'
Organizations. And in New Brunswick, the St Thomas University
School of Social Work, the New Brunswick Senior Citizens
Federation, the New Brunswick Gerontology Association and the
Province of New Brunswick Social Services Department plan to
hold the first Canadian national conference of non-governmental
senior organizations in Fredericton in 1985. A steering committee
for the conference met in 1984, and the Samuel and Saidye Bronf-
man Family Foundation has agreed to help fund the meeting. The
federal government also supports this plan. The theme of the conference: ''A National Consultation of Networking for Seniors in
Canada.'' Topics of the consultation will include networking,
advocacy, self-help, community development, public relations and
fund-raising.[129]

Seniors *have* begun to organize, but this won't solve a third
problem they face. Policy changes have not generally come from
seniors working alone but from the joint efforts of the old with
other groups or of groups ''on behalf of older people.''[30]

Professor Trela, gerontologist and student of senior politics, believes that American senior interest groups have not had much success.[33] At best pressure groups of older people make issues visible. Then a "cause" is picked up by other groups — unions or politicians. Adult children, for instance, support policies that help the aged — often their own older parents. This allows them to shift the burden of their care to the state, which perhaps explains why politicians receive wide support for social security and medical care policies.

Older people do best politically when they can link their concerns with those of other groups, and they will have to forge stronger links if they want more political power. Some of the newest senior political groups have done just this, setting up coalitions with other groups and with young people. This signals a change in the thrust of senior politics.

Changes in the System

Jim Mullan, first president of MSOS, and his wife Phyllis moved into a new high-rise for seniors just after he retired. It was a new building, clean and well designed. The other tenants were interested in acquiring some furniture and equipment for their recreation room, and when Jim, the president of the tenants' association, heard about a new federal program called New Horizons he applied for a grant for some chairs, couches, a piano and card-tables. A few days later the local New Horizons representative came over to talk to the tenants about their needs.

The representative quibbled and hedged and tried to trim their request. She asked how many people would use the equipment, and why they wanted each item. When they asked for a typewriter, she asked why they couldn't write their newsletter out by hand. In the end the grant request met her needs, not theirs.

Jim and the tenants felt humiliated, but they kept quiet. When it came time to send in their formal request, Jim wrote a letter instead, but not just any letter — it took the form of a poem called "up-beat." He sent it to everyone he could think of — to the local head of New Horizons, to the national head of New Horizons, to the premier of the province, to his local Member of Parliament, to the cabinet minister in charge of New Horizons and even to the Prime Minister. Here is an excerpt from his poem:

> We planned our New Horizons, believing the printed lines
> Which said that we, ourselves, knew best the shape of our designs
> And Hope that great uplifter, quickened our Up-Beat heart,
> For we had here, or so we thought, the chance for a brand-new start.
>
> But our dream of a New Horizon was only a dream, no more;
> And dreamers when they waken are much as they were before;
> Make do with cast-off records; make do with cast-off books;
> Be glad for the scarred piano, no matter how cheap it looks!
>
> But: Thanks to New Horizons — for a dream — though it faded fast!
> Thanks for pricking the bright balloon of escape from the want of the
>   past!
> Thanks for approving the second-hand, when we hoped so much for
>   the new;
> And Thanks, we hope, for a free-er hand when retirement comes to you.

A few days later Jim received a call from the local chief of New Horizons, who seemed anxious to meet with him and discuss the tenants' needs.

"Can we get a new piano," Jim asked, "and some more crafts for the ladies?"

"Mr Mullan," the man said, "you'll get *anything* you ask for."

Jim used a different approach here than that used by MSOS or other lobby groups which work as partners with government. He got action by stinging some bureaucratic flesh.

The Gray Panthers in the United States have raised this technique to a fine art. "Their approach to nursing-home reform, for example, was to stage a street play at the AMA Convention in Atlantic City in which a doctor sold patients to the Kill 'Em Quick

Nursing Home; doctors' wives were reported to have glared in disapproval at what the old folks were doing.'' The Panthers also monitor sales practices. In December 1973 they joined with Ralph Nader's Retired Professionals Action Grou (RPAF) to investigate pensions. And they run a Panthers' Media Watch that ''stalks the networks in an effort to blot out the presentation of old age as 'disease or naptime' and extracted from CBS at least a promise to do better.''[32]

Maggie Kuhn, Gray Panther leader, founded the organization in 1972 with six other retirees when her company forced her to retire. Together they made a commitment to use their retirement years for public service. She says the Panthers work for change in three ways.[33] First, they set up coalitions with other interest groups. They joined with the American Association of University Women, for instance, to lobby for the right of seniors to audit university courses across the country. They set up a coalition of senior groups in Philadelphia to study the transport system and report to the government.[34] And in Long Beach, California, and Washington, D.C., they ''succeeded in getting free checking accounts for the elderly. . . .''[35]

Second, the Panthers act as social critics. They challenge the power structure of society as ''elders of the tribe.''[36] They helped set up a new apprenticeship program at Kodak that retains older workers who would otherwise be retired to train the young. They encourage seniors to ''monitor public bodies, such as the courts, commissions, the city councils, and learn what public responses are. Learn to shadow the people who are elected and who are accountable.''[37]

Third, the Panthers test new models of aging and new life-styles for the aged. Maggie Kuhn says they ''try on the future for size.''[38] They have set up multi-age co-op housing and food co-ops and they run leadership workshops for older people.

In Philadelphia they have set up multi-age consciousness-raising groups. Twenty to thirty people from teenagers to retirees, meet on Saturday mornings to discuss their life experiences and to help one another with problems. These sessions, the Panthers say, increase members' self-esteem and break down age stereotypes. Also, as people listen to one another they sometimes come to see the social causes of their problems. The groups help members direct anger, frustration or self-pity into action that brings about change.

The Panthers have also worked with Temple University medical school students on a "Health Block" project. The project locates "health builders" on a block in the city — natural leaders who form the core of a neighbourhood health network. The project assigns a "health team" of medical school students to the block. The team gives care where it is needed and shows people how to prevent illness. The project also includes an advisory group to evaluate the strengths and weaknesses of the program.

The Panthers claim that this kind of program leads to better health. But it also serves as a new form of medical school education for the students. Students begin to see medicine as a way to create health, not just as a technique to cure illness.[39]

When they can, the Panthers get young and old working together. The Panther motto is "age and youth in action." "Using the experience and survival knowledge of old people and the idealism and energy of young people to change attitudes and social policy," Maggie Kuhn says, "our long range goals are directed toward social change and in the direction of a more humane and just society. . . ."[40]

No group like the Gray Panthers exists in Canada, although one senior activist, Tom Alsbury, former mayor of Vancouver, wants to follow Maggie Kuhn's lead. Mr Alsbury has used Panther-style tactics before. In 1972 he called a public meeting to protest legislature members' pay increases in British Columbia while many older people lived in poverty. The meeting drew 1,000 people and resulted in the start of Vancouver's Pensioners' Action Now. Within six months the group had between 15,000 and 16,000 members.

Mr Alsbury also directed a campaign against the Social Credit government's policies in 1981. The government had promised a denticare plan for that year but decided to postpone the program.

At the same time it announced a plan to increase the cost of automobile insurance for seniors. Alsbury's campaign in the media alerted the public to the government's plan and the government was forced to back down.[40]

Mr Alsbury now says he wants to expand senior action to help other groups. He plans to start a branch of the Gray Panthers and "enlist intelligent, active young people. We'll be youth and age attacking the social problems, not only of the seniors but of young people. . . . I'm going to try to broaden the base of our operation," he told the Canadian Press in Vancouver. "Bad as conditions are for the millions of seniors, there are young families, young women left with children, whose income is infinitely lower than seniors . . . I'm going to try to organize the seniors to fight for them, because their need is greater than ours."[41]

Seniors like Maggie Kuhn and Tom Alsbury have found new ways to serve society. They work as educators, social critics, social historians, advocates and explorers of new social forms. Older people also serve as mediators and advisors to the young.

Switzerland, for instance, has created a commission to foster this kind of service. Officially called the "Good Offices Commission" it is popularly known as the "Committee of Four Wise Men." It consists "of men who in fact have the authority that is conferred upon them by their age, their experience, and their independence of mind." These men hold no office. They have no power to act. They serve only to advise. They "have no decisions to make, but only a mission of study."[42] This role suits many older people who have already held public office and are now ready to move into a new advisory role.

In Canada Justice Emmett Hall has played this role of advisor many times since he retired in 1973. In a recent profile of Hall, Elaine Dewar writes that "his phone rang with requests for service" almost as soon as he got back to Saskatoon. "In 1973 he arbitrated a nasty national railway strike. Then it was a commission on Saskatchewan universities, then another on the province's justice system. In 1976 it was another railway dispute."

In 1977 David Crombie called on Hall to review Medicare. "To squash the name-calling he needed facts,'' Dewar writes. "But who could ferret for them? His gaze fell upon 'the father of medicare,' Emmett Hall, a man whose credentials were beyond question. . . ."[43]

There was a time when Justice Hall could have been dismissed as being one in ten thousand, but more older people than one might think have taken on this type of advisory role. Some of them work singly, some in groups.

Jessie Ford, for instance, aged 73, spends part of her time talking to groups of younger women about women's rights.

"My primary goal,'' she says, ''is justice. When I see injustice I have to do something about it. That's why I have such a big interest in the women's movement.''

Jessie has taken her message to the government too. "A few years ago,'' she says, ''in Manitoba we got the best family law in Canada, and that's because the women in this province piled into it. We lobbied every member of the Conservative caucus, every Minister. The Attorney General listened to us. He still does. And in the end we got a better lot.''

Jessie has also started work on a new project called the "Senior Citizens' Think Tank'' which consists of a dozen creative, articulate, intelligent seniors. Some of them have worked as teachers, others have worked with government or in social service jobs. Most of the members are women. The Think Tank has advised the government more than once about future policies and programs.

The Think Tank first came together in 1982 to write a report for the United Nations World Assembly on the Aging in Vienna. At the time, neither the World Assembly Committee nor the government in Ottawa had asked for any senior input to the conference. They had planned a conference by experts, for experts, about old people. Seniors had no part to play except as objects of study.

The Think Tank members decided to write a report for the conference anyway, and they met twice a month from October 1980 to December 1981 to talk about and plan their report. During that time the Canadian government and the United Nations began to see the need for senior input, and the National Advisory Council on Aging in Canada sent out a set of questions for senior groups to answer so that it could make their views part of its report in Vienna.

In early 1982 the Think Tank wrote a ten-page response to the National Advisory Council's questions. Their paper called on the government to assure a decent income for all older people, to create more nursing homes and better home care and to put an end to social isolation of older people.

"Emphasis should be placed on self-help and mutual-help programs rather than on 'do-for' programs. Many thousands of elderly are being 'done good for' at considerable cost when they themselves or cooperative contemporaries could supply the necessary services. . . . Programs for the elderly should provide opportunities for active participation . . . [and] study groups should be formed and centred around community problems with the aim of preparing papers and briefs to be presented to the appropriate authorities."[44]

Jean MacCrae, a retired school principal, took the Think Tank report to a conference in Ottawa sponsored by the National Advisory Council in February 1982. The conference brought together about a hundred seniors from across the country to share their views with the government. But the government, Jean says, didn't seem to care much about senior's views. "The whole set up was casual, unimportant. We saw the Minister of Health and Welfare, Monique Begin, on the first day and then didn't see her again.

"The government planned no social functions for us. We had no chance to get together. They scheduled every minute of the meetings. Our working group, for instance, met for fifty-seven minutes, and we had to follow a schedule — three minutes for this, two minutes for that. We had one coffee break, but the coffee was so far from our meeting room that we didn't have time to get any and still get back for the rest of our meeting. So we skipped the coffee. It was all done without much regard for the seniors who attended. I felt it was just a gesture."

The media treated the conference poorly too. The government had invited some of the healthiest, best educated older people in the country to the conference. On the dais at the opening session sat some of the most intelligent, active seniors anywhere. Jean remembers, however, that when she got back to her hotel she was shocked at the six o'clock news report on the meeting.

"The narrator spoke about the conference, alright, but meanwhile on the screen they flashed pictures of decrepit, destitute older people. They showed an old man picking up cigarette stubs, an old lady shuffling down the street. All of them were wrecks. They didn't show any up-and-coming seniors walking briskly down the street with their heads up, even though those were the kind of people at the conference. All they had to do was show pictures of the people sitting at the head table."

Jean came back from the conference annoyed at the way the government had treated the conference members. "The seniors," she says, "took the chance to meet seriously. The Think Tank, for instance, had a solid report and other people reacted to it. I think the reports of the Think Tank and the working groups at the conference surprised the government."

The Think Tank kept up its work in spite of the government's token interest. The group took part in a series of public forums on aging at the University of Winnipeg in 1982, spoke to university classes about senior issues that fall, appeared on television, wrote articles on senior issues for the Manitoba Seniors Journal and held a panel discussion at the Canadian Association of Gerontology meetings in November 1982.[45]

In October 1983 the government held another conference in Ottawa. Jean went back again as the Think Tank representative. Over three hundred people attended this second conference, and "there was a big difference between the two conferences in every way. The government seemed to take the whole thing more seriously. We had outstanding speakers at the plenary sessions. The government made a noticeable attempt to get experts to the meetings. The head of the Canadian Pharmaceutical Society was in my group, and so was the head of the Canadian Dietetic

Society. Older people were more visible too. In many cases expert speakers were seniors themselves.

"We also had more opportunity to socialize. For example we had a banquet where four excellent seniors spoke to us about their own lives. And we started the beginnings of a seniors' network. The whole thing showed a real regard for older people.

"With the first meeting the government had just made a gesture. We felt we were unimportant. But I think we had shown what seniors could do, and this time seniors did most of the talking. I think the government has learned that if you want something done for seniors, get the seniors to do it."

Groups like the Think Tank will always have their limits. For one thing, they will never appeal to masses of people. But even with its small numbers, an elite group like this can improve the quality of government programs for older people.

In their book about American business, *In Search of Excellence*, Thomas Peters and Robert Waterman, Jr., describe the small group in the best companies as being "critical to effective organizational functioning" even though it may be overlooked in favour of larger, more visible divisions.

The small group or task force, according to Peters and Waterman, "is an exciting, fluid, ad hoc device in the excellent companies. It is virtually the way of solving and managing thorny problems, and an unparalleled spur to practical action."[46] The small groups or task forces that Peters and Waterman found in the best companies look just like the Think Tank.

First, they don't have many members — five to ten people in most cases. The Think Tank had twelve members but only about seven, the ideal number for a small group, showed up at any meeting.

Second, only the busiest and most able people join these groups. Busy people don't have time to waste: they want to get work done and go on to other things. Most of the people in the Think Tank belonged to a long list of committees and other working groups. None of them had time for the Think Tank, but they found the time and when they got together they got down to work.

Task forces tend to enlist able people because only the most able people can decide on issues and act on their views. The Think Tank did not try to include representatives from other senior groups nor did it attempt to include varied types of people. It simply selected the most capable people it could find to do the job. This meant educated, politically aware, articulate older people who could think issues through in a way the government would respect and express their views in writing.

Third, members volunteer and set their own goals. People only joined and stayed on if they wanted to. No one committed themselves to the Think Tank for any length of time, but even though they didn't have to come most members came back week after week.

Like the task forces in the best businesses, the Think Tank set its own goal — to produce a report to the Canadian government and the United Nations. They made up the job for themselves, and perhaps because no one had asked for this report the Think Tank members committed themselves to creating as thorough and forceful a report as they could.

Fourth, task forces meet to do a job, then disband. The Think Tank worked as a team through most of 1982, produced their report for the government and then disbanded. Now the Manitoba government has planned its first provincial conference on aging for the spring of 1985, and it has invited Jean MacCrae and Jessie Ford to serve as the Think Tank's representatives on the planning committee. The group will meet again to determine whether it has any role to play in this conference.

Last, Peters and Waterman say, the task force (or Think Tank) needs the right context or climate to work in. Members need to talk to each other often. They need to share their ideas. And they need to work in a larger organization that respects this kind of work.

Think Tanks can't make the government listen to their reports. They can't claim to speak for a large number of voters. And they can't play power politics or lobby for change. The provincial and national federations do this best. But to the extent that the government asks for and listens to the advice of thoughtful older people, small groups like this can effect change.

Small groups like the Think Tank add to the range of seniors' political options. And they do more than produce reports on what older people need. Ivan Illich, writer and social critic, says groups like this display "conviviality" — the "autonomous and creative intercourse among persons, and the intercourse of persons with their environment. . . ." People need more than goods and services. "They need above all the freedom to make things among which they can live, to give shape to them according to their own tastes, and to put them to use in caring for and about others."[47]

The Future

The seniors' movement will gain momentum in the next few years. First, as more people come into old age with higher education, white-collar jobs and middle-class incomes they will turn to political action to express themselves.[48] This has already started to happen in Canada. In a study of senior leaders Professor Gifford found that half had incomes between $10,000 and $20,000 a year in 1982, and about half had worked as supervisors, professionals or managers.[49]

These activist seniors have begun to speak out on issues, and they will "raise the consciousness of the elderly and other segments of society to the needs and concerns of the aging population. . . ."[50]

Second, the provincial and federal governments and private foundations have begun to support senior political action. Gifford reports that "special interest groups of seniors continue to emerge, including social action groups."[51]

A government report called *New Horizons: The First Decade* cites New Horizons's impressive record of involvement in forming "seventy-eight major regional groups which are affiliated with approximately twenty-five provincial organizations. These in turn are affiliated with one of several national federations."[52]

The Special Senate Committee on Retirement Age Policies also encouraged more senior action. It recommended that retired people "organize, protest and show militancy in order to improve their chances of achieving dignity, obtaining higher incomes as well as medical and other services and finding useful work."[53]

And a British Columbia study group called "The Group of 10 + 2," sponsored by New Horizons, found that the young old "themselves wish to be an intrinsic and valuable part of the larger society and wish to participate in policy making and planning action." They found that many older people believe seniors "must individually and collectively take initiative in acting on their own interests."[54]

Third, the baby-boom generation knows a lot about political action. Many of its members took part in civil rights and anti-war protests in their youth. They are used to the idea of changing society through politics, and, as they enter old age, they are likely to use their numbers and the political methods they have learned to reshape society to meet their needs in the future.

Older people may never have the power to force changes, but they can and will bring the problems and concerns of the elderly to public awareness. To this extent they have already begun to play an important role in Canadian politics.

10

DISCOVERING A GOOD AGE[1]

The Secret of Good Aging

The interview had gone well and I was relaxed and unprepared when the host of a morning talk show in Vancouver asked me a final question. ''Professor, on the basis of your research, what would you say is the secret of a good old age?''

The secret? For a moment I went blank. Was this how Ponce de León felt when the king asked him where he had found the fountain of youth? With several hundred thousand listeners waiting for my next words, I was stumped. What is the secret of a good old age?

I have thought about this question a lot since that show, but the answer I gave then still holds true. There is no secret, no magic formula. A good old age doesn't come about from some special talent or as a secret gift. It comes about when, given a basic income, reasonable health, good self-esteem and a little energy, a person sets out to discover a meaningful life for him- or herself. And I believe that Canada today provides more people than ever before with the basic needs which will enable them to make their discoveries.

We have one of the best health care systems in the world. We have nursing homes for the frail elderly and for younger old people who can't live on their own. Most of these institutions give high quality health care. They also offer recreation programs and a sense of community to people who otherwise would be isolated in their own homes.

Some people believe that we institutionalize too many people, and most provinces have set up home care programs — from Meals on Wheels to visiting nurse and homemaker services — to help people stay at home. These programs will help keep people out of institutions, as will respite care programs that give families relief from the pressures of care, and day programs that bring people into hospitals or nursing homes a few days a week. These programs give people hot meals, a chance to socialize and medical care if they need it.

Our health care system also offers fitness programs and diet advice, encourages medical check-ups. And it offers recreation programs. All of these programs help people stay well so that they come into late old age in better health.

Most older people want to live on their own in their apartments or houses, and both the federal and provincial governments have tried to meet this need. Since the 1950s they have built thousands of units of safe, affordable housing throughout the country. Many of these units have dining-rooms, beauty parlours, medical and shopping services. They do more than just house people: they add to the quality of older people's lives.

In general older people don't mind high-rise or apartment living, but some want to stay in houses they own. Tax rebate programs, home repair grants and services that help older people with heavy chores (like putting up storm windows) help people stay in their own houses. So do programs that will pay to remodel a house so that a person in a wheelchair can live there and get around by themselves.

Some public housing offers new options. Lions Place in Winnipeg and many other senior housing blocks offer education and recreation programs. They have trained staff members who design programs just for the residents. These enriched housing blocks help people remain active and involved as they age.

The OAS and GIS programs and provincial supplements ensure that most older people live above the poverty line. The Spouse's Allowance program gives benefits to spouses under 65, even if their spouse has died. And the Canada (and Quebec) Pension Plan pays out more money to more older people than ever before.

Many people have decided to protect themselves from poverty by saving for old age in their middle years. The government supports this idea by offering tax breaks for RRSP savings, and more and more people have started to make use of this program. This will ensure a better old age in the future for those who plan ahead.

New pension laws like those passed in Manitoba and better private pension plans will also help ease the financial pinch of retirement in the future. New laws will allow workers to hold on to their pension funds even if they change jobs and to keep the full amount in their fund (their portion *and* their employer's portion) in less time than in the past. The new laws will also give women a better chance to build up pension funds.

Still, some more work needs to be done here. Single older people often fall below the poverty line, and many of the oldest old people (most of them single women) have the lowest incomes in the country. The Canadian Sociology and Anthropology Association and other concerned groups have urged the government to raise the incomes of these people immediately. This must become a national priority.

All the above developments will give more people than ever before the option to retire.

Some people will take up that option at 65. Others may decide to retire early. Still other people may want to work past 65. New laws that forbid age discrimination will open the way for more choice about retirement. Some people will work part time after they retire — to keep active or to make extra money. Some people will start second careers. Others will turn to volunteer work. People will tailor retirement to meet their own, their family's and their community's needs.

Retirement no longer means loss of meaning and self-esteem. Older people now see it as a chance to grow. They take classes at the university. They join art, music and dance groups. They learn public speaking, poetry-writing and massage. And they often use their work skills in new ways to help others — as advisors to government, industry and community service groups.

Seniors' political groups have lobbied the government to achieve many of these benefits, and senior groups will continue to advise the government on seniors' needs. They will rely on the government to play a major role in meeting the older people's needs in the future. Government will improve health care, housing, pensions and retirement for older people. And it will support new options in recreation, education and leisure: it has already begun to do so.

Government, however, can only encourage a good old age. It can keep people out of poverty, ensure basic health care, provide decent housing and protect older people from abuse and discrimination. But it cannot create a good old age.

Once older people have met their basic needs, they have to create a good old age for themselves. And many older people have begun to do just that. They are pioneers of a new old age. And they can teach the rest of us the "secrets" of good aging.

Facing Old Age

Kurt Jager has the charm of a European courtier and the wisdom of a Supreme Court judge. His mild Austrian accent and soft voice create an instant warmth, and his mane of white hair and beard give him the appearance of a biblical sage.

Now in his mid-fifties, he is an eminent professor at a well-known business school. And he has begun to prepare for his retirement: last year when his youngest child left home he and his wife

Helga decided to make some changes. "There were no excuses any more," he says. "I didn't have to keep working for the kids or the family."

I have travelled nearly two thousand miles to Toronto to hear Kurt's views on good aging. We're sitting at the dining-room table in his home after dinner. Helga is with us. The talk turns to whether or not they ought to move from their inner-city house to a piece of land they own in the country.

Over the years their house has gone up in value. They bought it cheap and paid it off long ago. Now the neighbourhood is in demand among young professionals. "Just selling the house," Kurt says, "we can live on the interest. It's crazy. Unbelievable."

But they're not rushing into a quick sale. For one thing they wonder if they can stand the isolation of country life. Their daughter and son-in-law already live on the land, but Helga is an artist and she feels that she needs some contact with other artists. Would her work dry up without people to share her ideas? And what about the friends they'll leave behind? And the city they love?

As we talk their dream mixes with their fears. They're not sure they want to let go, so they hesitate. Fantasy draws them on, the need for security holds them back.

They're both testing their dreams, looking at their fears, trying out plots and scenes of what might be. They don't need my advice. But they need to talk to hear the questions again.

As I go upstairs to bed I wonder what is eating my two friends. Why the sudden urge to move? Why jump to take this new risk? Why not just sit back and enjoy their new freedom?

In retrospect I should have gotten a clue when Kurt said, "There are no excuses any more." But it wasn't until I had talked to many more people about what it's like to move into later life that I realized that Kurt and Helga were meeting a challenge — a challenge to fulfill their dream now or give it up forever.

When I left Kurt and Helga the next day they hadn't decided anything, but six months later when we met again Kurt was building a new house out of the old barn on his land in the country. He showed me a book full of pictures.

That summer Kurt lived on the land. He stayed in the house as it was being built, working alongside the carpenter and the old stonemason they had hired. "I read at night until the sun went down," he says. "Then in the morning I'd get up to mix mortar and build with stone. . . .

"Younger people should be envious. It's the greatest time of life. Of course, it's scary too. You find yourself without excuses. Face to face with yourself, with the challenge to live your life as you want to and with no reason not to.

"It's not just a new *stage*," he says. "I'm put off by the ideas of stages, as though life was nothing but endless change. No. This is a time for bringing things together. It's a time to discover wholeness."

That, after all, is what the house is all about.

Kurt is finding this wholeness in many ways, bringing together parts of himself that he had almost forgotten existed. After years of intellectual work — teaching, writing, going to meetings — at last he is working with his hands. Now he plans to buy some sheep, and he has picked out a spot on the shoreline where he can sit and watch the sailboats in summer. . .

He isn't just a dreamer, though. He's trying to ease into this new life. For instance, he didn't quit his job all at once: he's on leave from his old school and has taken a one year post at a college near the new house. He and Helga are going to try it for a year, one step at a time. "And then. . ." Kurt says, "then we'll see."

Kurt has taken his first steps into a new phase of life. He's scared, partly because he has to give up so much to move on, partly because he doesn't know what's ahead. For years he put off the writing he wanted to do. Teaching, committee work and family life all took up his time. Now he has the chance to write. But, he wonders, does he have anything to say? That's why he calls his retirement a "wager." It's a risk, but one he has to take.

He's not alone — either in his fear or in seeing that later life poses a challenge to his mid-life routine. When I asked the many people I spoke with how they got to where they are now, they have all said a good old age didn't just come to them one day. They worked for it. They had to discover it for themselves.

No two people tell the same story, and yet this path of discovery appears to have a definite shape to it. This pattern holds for nearly all the people I talked to who now enjoy old age, regardless of their ethnic background, sex or income. What I have found is a clear series of stages that define a positive movement from mid-life to old age.

Looking for a Good Old Age

I set out to study good aging in the fall of 1980 with the support of the Social Sciences and Humanities Research Council of Canada. I wanted to talk to the healthiest, happiest, most fulfilled older people I could find to learn how they had gotten to where they are now.

I began with a group of about three hundred older volunteers who all lived in the community, said they were in good health and were enjoying a good old age.

I asked them all to fill out a basic questionnaire giving their age, sex, marital status, etc. And I also asked them to fill out Everett Shostrom's *Personal Orientation Inventory* (POI).[2] This test measures self-actualization. Self-actualizing people, Robert Knapp, psychologist, says, "[use] their talents and capabilities more fully than the average person, live in the present rather than dwelling on the past or the future, function relatively autonomously, and tend to have a more benevolent outlook on life and human nature than the average person."[3] The POI includes measures of inner-directedness, time-competence and self-acceptance, as well as spontaneity and self-regard, traits which have all been related to good aging by other researchers.

I used the scores on this profile's two main scales — time-competence and inner-directedness — to select my final sample.

All the people I selected showed an above-average tendency toward self-actualization, and I used this as a sign of good aging. These scores allowed me to sift from the large sample of three hundred a precise small group of twenty-five people for further study.

I interviewed all of them in their homes in interviews lasting from one-and-one-half to several hours, then had all the interviews transcribed verbatim from tapes. In the end I had on file for each person a set of basic demographic data, a personality profile, an in-depth interview, and notes on their home decor and appearance that I jotted down while we talked.

Who were these people? What were they like? As I said all of them scored well on the POI. All of them lived on their own or with their husbands or wives. They were all friendly and in good spirits.

Their ages ranged from 55 to 85 years. None of them were very rich, but none of them were very poor either. More than half of them were women. They ranged from housewives to lawyers, from social workers to pharmacists, from teachers to secretaries, from civil servants to nurses. Many of them had held white-collar jobs. Most of them were retired or semi-retired.

One key point: all of them were able to meet their basic needs for food, shelter, health, income, self-esteem and a sense of belonging. And they were all active, though in different ways. I didn't pick these people because they were normal or average. As I said, I tried to pick the most fulfilled, content, intelligent, creative older people I could find.

"Isn't this a biased sample?" you might ask. Of course. But I had a good reason for choosing it. I wanted to learn what aging is like for people who have met their basic needs, who show a high degree of psychological well-being in later life and who say they are living a good old age. I wanted an optimal sample of older people because I was asking a specific question: I wanted to know what a good old age looks like today and I wanted to know how people got there. Only people living a good old age could help me answer these questions.

There is also another important reason to study this group.

They are at the forefront of a trend. They're better educated, healthier, more active and have more options than any past generation of older people, and in these respects they most closely resemble the current forecasts of what aging will look like in the years to come.

What *does* it take to age well? How do people discover a good age?

Writers in the past have seen aging as a time to turn inward.[4] Carl Jung, for instance, says that "aging people should know that their lives are not mounting and unfolding, but that an inexorable inner process forces the contraction of life."[5] Erik Erikson, one of the keenest students of the life cycle, sees old age as a time to sum life up, a time to look back over the past, tie up loose ends and see life as good. Integrity — the sign of a good age, he says — requires "the acceptance of one's one and only life cycle as something that had to be and that, by necessity, permitted of no substitution."[6]

Psychoanalytic theory describes old age as a time to look back. But it ignores the fact that older people go on living. More recent work has begun to correct this narrow view of old age. Robert Butler, for instance, takes issue with the idea that a person in old age can only accept who they are and what they have been. "People are locked in by such a theory," he says. They may look healthy from Erikson's point of view, but they suffer because they are trapped by their work, marriage or life-style. "Excessive or exaggerated identity seems clearly to be an obstacle to continued growth and development through life and to appreciation of the future. . . . Human beings need the freedom to live with change, to invent and reinvent themselves a number of times throughout their lives."[7]

My own conversations with highly self-actualized older people support Butler's view. The people I talked to did not live serene, content, closed lives in old age. Instead they lived thoughtful, issue centred, active lives, open to the future. In every case they remained engaged in the discovery of who they were, not by looking into the past but by facing specific challenges that came as they aged. Sometimes these challenges came from within, like Kurt's need to give up his teaching job and move to the country. Sometimes they came from outside: widowhood and retirement force people to rethink who they are. The most actualized older people in every case faced and took up these challenges, and this led the way to further growth as they aged.

After talking to dozens of these people a pattern began to take shape. I found that self-actualized older people discovered a good age through a series of stages. First, they faced a problem or moment of crisis — a *challenge*. Second, they saw that this problem demanded some response from them — I call this the stage of *acceptance*. Finally, they responded to this challenge and moved into the future — I call this *affirmation*. These three stages in the passage to later life all take place in the face of *denial*. As I use the word here, it simply means that a person wants to remain the same. A person engaged in denial tries to hold on to what is or has been.

Discovering a Good Old Age

Denial

For years the experts have known that people deny their age. Many studies show that even into their seventies people still maintain they're middle-aged. Those in their eighties frequently express their contempt for "old folks" — meaning individuals either older or less healthy than they are. Older people also tend to see themselves as younger than their age mates.

Some writers have suggested that these people don't want to identify themselves with the low status of the aged: by denying their age they escape the label of being old. There is probably something to this, given the public attitude to aging. But denial isn't always a conscious choice. People deny their age without even knowing it, and everything seems to support their retreat.

For one thing people immerse themselves in routines. They lose themselves in roles, careers and duties. They find ready-made niches. They fit in, and society gives its rewards to those who conform.

In adolescence, Ernest Becker says, "life sucks us up into standardized activities." Society defines goodness, success and right action, and people conform to these standards. They shape their lives to please their parents and teachers. They become what others expect them to be. "Instead of working our inner secret, we gradually cover it and forget it, while we become purely external men, playing successfully the standardized hero-game into which we happen to fall by accident, by family connection, by reflex patriotism, or by the simple need to eat and the urge to procreate."[8]

Above all, this system gives a person safety and security. It says that you are doing what's right, good, true and just. With this guarantee you need never think again. Becker says this better than anyone else I know:

> Man is protected by the secure and limited alternatives
> his society offers him, and if he does not look up from
> his path he can live out his life with a certain dull
> security.[9]

Society, Becker says, maps out forms of safe heroism that people can fit into to get the sense of importance they need without too much risk or danger. The roles of middle age offer safety and security from doubt. They give a person a sense that they are doing well, that everything is as it should be. But, this "dull security" exacts its price, sometimes with interest.

Sociologist Zena Smith Blau, who has studied the transition to later life, says that "a great many adults, become *too well adjusted* to society's expectation and insufficiently attuned to their own nature and needs."[10] This shell can be broken all at once in later life when the secure and routine roles of mid-life fall away. Nature causes some of this loss. Children grow up and start their own families. A spouse may die. Illness may force a person to pull back from social contacts. No one can avoid these losses when they come, and most people adapt to them.[11]

Society also causes role-loss. People are more mobile today.

Children sometimes have to move away to find jobs. Neighbour-hoods are less stable. Longtime friendships break up. And then there's forced retirement. Zena Smith Blau calls this a form of social "banishment."[12]

When role loss strikes in old age people can find themselves in limbo without meaning or purpose. A case from my files will show what this means.

In a middle-class suburban high-rise, I talked with Mr Roth, a healthy man with enough money to live well. Since his wife's death, however, he has begun to live like a recluse.

I first met Mr Roth when he came to the university to be a part of my study on successful aging. He wore a tweed sport jacket and light brown slacks. He had perfectly trimmed silver-white hair. On the chair next to him sat a brown shopping bag.

"Oh I see you've just come from shopping," I said. "I hope there's nothing that will spoil."

"No," he said, "I haven't been shopping. I've brought these things to show you."

While the other people who had answered my ad for subjects began filling out their forms, I sat with Mr Roth. First he took out a collection of yellowed news clips and faded pictures of a smiling, youthful Mr Roth with jet black hair. One news story told about his trip to Miami for a socialist convention when he was 20 years old. Then he took out pictures of his wife, of their vacations together, of his store in a nearby town. Then more news clips about awards he'd won from the Chamber of Commerce.

I was embarrassed. I had asked people to come to fill out some forms in a group, and I planned to contact them later if they scored well. But Mr Roth wanted me to become involved with his life — and not even with his present life but with the past, with his youth and his early married years.

I apologized. Here he had brought me his life and all I wanted were his answers to some questions on a paper and pencil test. He deserved more than I was ready to give him just then. I asked him to fill out the forms, then I set up a time for us to meet at his home.

On my way to visit him I looked over his test scores and saw that he'd scored low on time competence (a measure of how well a person integrates the past and future with the present). But what did that mean? I wondered about this as I rode the elevator to the ninth floor.

Mr Roth met me at the door. Again he wore a sport jacket and freshly pressed slacks, though this time his white shirt was open at the neck. I had noticed on his form that he was widowed, but he hadn't spoken of Mrs Roth. Now, as he showed me around his apartment, he stopped in the bedroom near an 18×24 oil portrait of his wife.

"Her eyes follow you wherever you go," he sighed.

As we entered the living-room I noticed that pictures lined the top of the television, the coffee tables and the walls — pictures of a younger Mr Roth and his wife, sometimes just the two of them, sometimes with friends. Each picture had a date pasted on it. As we sat down to talk he again took out snapshots and newspaper clippings of the past.

He and his wife had lived in a small town for most of their married years. He had a dry goods business, and although they were never rich, they had managed. He was a respected member of the community, well liked and happy.

At 65 he retired, sold his business and moved into the city to be closer to family. He and his wife looked forward to a comfortable retirement and the joy of just being together. Then Mrs Roth died of cancer.

As he described these events tears welled up in his eyes and he began to sob, clutching my arm for control. Each time he talked about his wife and their life together he broke down.

Now he lives alone. He has no close friends, no work to do, no interests. He belongs to a lodge where he helps with duties like planning meetings and get-togethers, but this only covers his loneliness.

As for his family, he only has a sister and her family left. He pays her to cook him his meals, but he feels cut off from close contact with her. She's tired of babying him, and she thinks it's about time he stopped mourning and got on with life. Mr Roth thinks his brother-in-law is a bore, and the feeling appears to be mutual. On the whole he gets little pleasure from his family. Instead he spends most of his time staring at the walls.

"Maybe you could try volunteer work?" I said.

"No, I don't want to visit people. It's too hard to do, and it's not making use of my intelligence."

"Maybe the university then. You could take some courses?"

"Yes. Maybe. But the big classes — there's no chance to say what you really think."

At last I gave up. We both knew he wouldn't try any of these things. As I left Mr Roth he gave me a gift, a Parker ballpoint pen.

"Come back again. Please come back," he said, "just to talk for a little while."

Don't people like Mr Roth see what's happening to them? Aren't the losses in old age — of roles, friends, spouse, career — among the most predictable changes in life?

The answer is simple. No one is so blind as the person who *will not* see. Old age comes as a shock because people always look elsewhere. Routine keeps a person from thinking about where they are going. It gives a feeling of security and importance, a feeling that "I can do it again" as I've always done it — forever.[13]

In later life, however, some doubts do creep in. The body may give a first clue: it doesn't work as well as it used to. Then changes take place in the world around us: children grow up, friends die, suddenly the roles and rules of mid-life seem to narrow and we become aware that time is running out. In light of the realization that there's only so much time left a person can feel a sudden urge to break out. That is why Kurt and Helga couldn't wait to set up a new life in the country: for them it was literally now or never.

To succeed up to mid-life a person has to narrow themselves to fit society's mould. This brings some happiness, but it also puts strong limits on personal growth. Family and work can become a trap.

"The better we have succeeded in entrenching ourselves in our personal standpoints and social positions," Carl Jung writes, "the more it appears as if we had discovered the right course and the right ideals and principles of behavior. For this reason we suppose them to be eternally valid and make a virtue of unchangeably clinging to them. We wholly overlook the essential fact that the achievements which society rewards are won at the cost of a diminution of personality."14

Jung goes on to say that "We can't live in later life using the rules of youth and middle age. For what was great in the morning will be little at evening, and what in the morning was true will at evening become a lie."15

When the roles of the middle years drop away a crisis can result, and modern society doesn't give much guidance to the older person experiencing such crises. Discovering a new role for oneself in later life becomes a vital task, vital in the sense that life itself can hinge on the outcome.

The older people I have met were no more prepared than anyone else to meet the challenge of later life, but somehow they have been able to make something worthwhile out of a time that scares most of us to death. In each case they have taken up the challenge of aging, set out to discover new meaning for themselves. Above all they have refused to be banished from life and society just because they're over 65.

The Challenge

It would be fine to pretend you weren't aging if denial did not demand more and more energy as people age. After all, we can't "do it again" forever, and this pretence at omnipotence only blinds us to the fact that we are aging. Life will not go on forever as it has in middle age, and the cost of denial is that when it happens aging comes as a shock.

Marcel Proust relates how the awareness of his own age came to him suddenly while visiting some friends he had once known well. His friends, he says, now looked old, and they made him "aware of the time that had passed for them; this had never happened to me before, and I was overwhelmed by the revelation that time has passed for me too. . . . We did not see our own appearance, our own age; but each like a facing mirror, saw the other's."16

"We did not see our own appearance," Proust says, and now we know why. Unless a person is shocked out of their normal way of seeing, they carefully screen themselves from the knowledge that they are aging.

Let me give an example of this process.

I am sitting on a sofa sipping tea with Joanna in her living-room high above the city, in one of the wealthiest sections of town.

From where I sit I can see into the guest-room. Since Joanna lives alone, the second bedroom of this two-bedroom suite is pure luxury. It serves as a study and a guest-room when her children or grandchildren come to stay. Here she has hung an enormous acrylic painting of daisies. "I happen to like it, so I bought it," she says, as if to apologize for its size and bright colour. I happen to like it too, and I tell her so.

Joanna's comment about the daisies tells me in an offhand way that she intends to be her own person, now that she has found herself again after the years of turmoil following her husband's death. Once again she is beginning to discover who she is, and her home, her activities, her likes and dislikes, all say, "This is who I am. Take it or leave it. But don't ask me to live by your rules."

She tried living by someone else's rules after her husband's death twelve years ago. They had lived a comfortable middle-class life — two cars, a cottage, a house, children and friends. They were involved in everything.

Then he became ill with cancer of the brain. "Well," she says, "it was a matter of carrying on. I was going to stop working in real estate and be with my husband when he was sick, but I didn't. My supervisor thought it wasn't a good thing to dwell on it, to be at home a lot. He was right. So I carried on with my job. Of course, I had to do it well. It's part of the picture. You have to do it all well. It has to be perfect.

"I seemed to have this idea that I was going to carry it all on, that I could do it. I did for two years, and I ran myself into the ground, running up to the hospital at noon and helping him with his lunch, going up again after work and then at night just sacking out so I could go on with another day. It was very hard."

This rigid adherence to an idealized picture of what she should be eventually had a serious effect on Joanna.

"I think all this running up to the hospital constantly wasn't really genuine. I did it. I cared for his suffering. But I was human. I wished someone else could be doing it. So I was not being true to myself. I think that led to a lot of things later.

"Also, the year my husband died I got my master's degree. I took my oral exam when he was already in the hospital. My advisor suggested that we postpone it due to the circumstances, but I said no and I did it. I did everything. Everything. It was unbelievable."

Even after her husband died she was determined to carry on as though nothing had happened.

"I was so determined that nothing like my husband's death was going to throw me, and I didn't allow myself a grievance time.

"After his death, I travelled. At Christmas I went to Spain, Hawaii or wherever. At Easter I went somewhere. I went to Europe. There was never a day — I didn't allow myself any time at all. Do you get the picture? No time to breathe."

To any committee that wanted her she said yes. Then, of course, she would take on the chairmanship. She was running to meetings as well as doing things for the real estate board.

"It was unbelievable," she says, looking back. To keep herself going, she eventually turned to drugs and alcohol.

"No wonder I needed something. I didn't want to lean on people. I think I got hooked on a sleeping pill every night when my husband was sick, plus I drank a bit. Well, for a year after he died I was hospitalized off and on. I was using different kinds of pills. The doctor would change prescriptions, but I wouldn't discard the old ones. I took more alcohol than I'd like to admit along with the pills. I was, a very, very confused person.

"That was my way of coping, my way of standing the pain. I needed some kind of anaesthetic."

Meanwhile her world was collapsing.

"Two days after the funeral I went back to work because I knew I had to get out of this, get away from it, get back to work. And I think that was a good thing to do. But the next day I broke my arm. I was hurrying to get caught up with my work, and I slipped running for the car and a few bones snapped. Meanwhile I was still coping with a couple of courses at the university. Then three weeks after my husband died my daughter and her husband broke up. I think she was waiting until after he died to tell me.

"It all came down on me right then. But it still took two years till I gave in. I was going to deal with it all. I was going to cope with it all. Nothing thrown at me was going to blind me. You finally have to get floored to realize you can't do it alone.

"Well, I finally got floored. The last time I drove my car I drove right into a restaurant — right through the window.

"I had the car washed that day. And I was parked in front of this pizza parlour having a cup of coffee. I thought the sidewalk was quite a distance from the front of the car. I didn't want it sticking out so I put it in low and just eased it up. I drove right through the window.

"I just stepped out of the car — over these shards of plate glass, big pieces of plate glass on the road — and I said, 'I'd like a cup of coffee.' 'Lady,' said the owner, 'you get back in that car.' He was quite certain I was out of my tree. But I didn't get back. I just sat in the booth until the police came.

"That's the last time I drove. That was getting near the end."

For Joanna denial led to a dive into frenetic action. What was she denying? Her loneliness? Her loss? Her fear of her own death? Probably all these feelings drove her at that time.

At the same time it led her to a challenge. "I realized, 'Hey, you're going nowhere but down'. . . . And that's when I turned it around."

Acceptance

The first stage of the movement into old age, then, is the challenge that comes with the dawning knowledge that one is aging, that one is mortal, that life can't go on as it has.

Arthur Miller starts his play *Death of a Salesman* at just this moment of awakening. Willy Loman, the leading character, is in the process of losing his connection with the life he has built in middle age. As the play opens, he arrives home after cutting short a routine business trip and tries to explain to his wife why he is back early.

> I was driving alone, you understand? And I was fine. I was even observing the scenery. . . I opened the windshield and just let the warm air bathe over me. And then all of a sudden I'm going off the road. I'm tellin' ya, I absolutely forgot I was driving."

In the end Willy kills himself because he can't face failure, aging or death. Denial, as Miller shows, turns aging into agony. The alternative is to accept what the coming of age has to tell us, and this is the second phase of growth into later life.

Joanna says this in her own way. "I had to get floored," she says, "before I could stop running." After the car crash she finally took a year off from work, and for the first time her district manager said he agreed with the idea. "I don't know if I did very good work the last year," she says. "Looking back, the strain must have been showing.

"Then I went to A.A. I still go occasionally. They have this theme of surrender to win, and there was a great deal in that. Surrender to win. Yes, let go."

Acceptance may sound like defeat, like giving up, but nothing could be further from the truth. Acceptance does mean a turn *away* from the goals and projects of mid-life, but it also means a turn *toward* an alternative way of being.

In his book *Learning to Grow Old*, Paul Tournier distinguishes between acceptance and resignation. When someone accepts life, he says, they "say yes to life in its entirety . . . The adult who cannot accept growing old, or the old person who cannot accept his old age, or who accepts it grudgingly, 'because he's got to,' is in the same difficulty, blocked in his evolution against the stream of life."[18]

Oddly, acceptance of aging does not usually lead to a dread of death or decrepitude. The transition may create anxiety but it does not lead to disaster any more than the growth to adulthood leads to the destruction of the adolescent. In fact, it can lead to very positive realizations and the end of potentially harmful fantasies.

"At the time when I had my breakdown," Joanna says, "I thought I was going to get back to real estate. That was my goal when I took a year's leave of absence — to get back there. Because I was the highest paid agent, I got a good salary plus commission, with all these awards, you know. And that was a status claim. I was going to get back.

"Now I'm so glad that I got away from that and got involved in these marvelous things I'm doing now. When I finally retired I found so many things that were more important than sales."

What was the transition like at the time?

"It was terrifying, terrifying. That beautiful job let go. The house too — it was as if the house were sustaining me. I resisted, actually. I resented. And I blamed a lot of people because I had to do these things.

"And it was so hard for me to do that turn around that I did. I think actually the alcohol and the pills that created that collapse really helped because they made it catastrophic. I had to do something or terminate. Getting off them was sort of critical.

"When I went to Alcoholics Anonymous they taught me to find a new pattern. I didn't feel that I belonged anywhere. I felt so out of place everywhere, because I was responding in ways that weren't acceptable, I guess. A.A. was a terrific help. They carry you when there's no one else left. Everyone sort of backed off. I was left alone. I had to get away from the pills every night and the liquor. They carried me until I found a new way up, a new pattern.

"I was, well, inactive for two years, just trying to learn a new way, like learning to walk again. And I disposed of everything — the house, the cottage, the cars (two cars), snowmobiles, boats, everything. And it was like starting again with a bus pass."

"Let me tell you about that, because it's sort of typical of what I was going through. I had never ridden a bus and I didn't trust them. I'd go to the bus shelter and I'd wait, then I'd say to myself, 'It probably won't come. I think I'll call a cab.'

"At my age I had to learn how to ride a bus and to make a connection. I had to learn what bus to take to get to the park or what connection to the St James Hospital. I found it works beautifully. You know, it all fits."

"It was marvellous. Buses are such social places. I used to tend to depression. If I stay in too much I still do. But if I get dressed, get out of here, get on a bus, I'm all right. You get on the Broadway bus, it's a social club. And the West Clarke bus, they're all very serious. Very righteous, probably going to do some very laudable activity. Every bus is different. Good God. It's great fun. Much better than riding in my air-conditioned Lincoln.

"All of a sudden I was thrown into that, and I bought blue jeans and parkas and things for the weather. It didn't matter anymore what I looked like.

"When I was working I used to have my hair back-combed. 'Done.' And then after it was done I'd wear a thing around it at night so it would hold its shape for a week. Now I say, 'Oh the hell with my hair.' It used to be more trouble than it was worth. I just got it cut like this — short, in a pixie cut. I wash it and I blow it, and it feels good.

"Before I was always afraid. I remember one day I was shaking out a new duster and it floated to the balcony on the floor below. I wouldn't go down and get it. That's a very small thing, but I was afraid. Now I'd think nothing of going down and saying, 'Hey, my duster's on your balcony.' I don't know why I would be afraid. I just was.

"I guess for me the change had to come in the form of a crisis. That's the only way I would accept it. I resist change, especially change imposed on me. Now, if I had to let it all go, I know I could do it. I have something here [pointing to herself] that I can be comfortable with."

Joanna speaks about the courage to age. Like Paul Tillich's

"courage to be," it requires that a person face the non-being of aging — the loss of beauty, strength, wealth, power, friends, a spouse and, in the end, life itself. Just as a person grows into adulthood, so they grow into old age. And the key word in both phrases is "growth." The coming of age sets up the condition for this growth. It presents a person with a challenge to affirm life in spite of its limits.[19]

A good age begins when a person first accepts the claim of aging. Only then can they affirm this new stage of life.

Affirmation

And now? "Oh, now I feel a new freedom," Joanna says. "A new happiness. It's a new life. I wish I'd done it before. I'm so glad I finally retired instead of waiting.

"At first I took a leave of absence, but then I didn't go back. Instead I took a second year. After that I left for good. They gave me a lovely letter saying I'd done a very good job and the company president said I could come back any time I chose. But I didn't.

"I began to volunteer at our local school a couple of afternoons a week. I worked with either slow learners or very fast children. I liked the very fast children. I like to see the movement. I guess because I move like that too."

All of this was part of Joanna's attempt to find a new pattern for her life.

"I was keeping my day filled with other things, slowly and painfully trying to fill my life. I found that physical exercise is a must for me, so I joined a health spa and I go there two or three times a week. I also joined a golf club and started golfing. These physical things, along with a lot of meetings, going back to school and working as a volunteer, all helped.

"That took about two years. And after that all of a sudden I found a lot of people wanted my services because I have a lot of training. And I started these two senior citizens' Toastmasters clubs. There are three of them going now. I'm doing youth leadership work in Riverside with fast learning kids. I teach them public speaking, talking on your feet, that sort of thing. I do a couple of those courses every year.''

Joanna also sits on the board of directors of a seniors' education centre. She still attends meetings and she still loves to travel.

From the outside her life looks almost the same as before she retired: She is busy, active, involved. But it's not the same. The meaning of life is different for her today.

Paul Tournier speaks of an ''inner revolution'' in later life. He says that ''really to accept retirement is to accept that one no longer gives the orders, that one is no longer in authority. It is to accept that one is no longer a part of the hierarchical society. It means taking part in a different game.''[20]

But what game? What are its rules? And most important of all, what is the purpose of playing?

Today Joanna works hard as one of the district lieutenant-governors for Toastmasters International. She visits twenty-four clubs in her district. Two of them, as she said earlier, she started herself.

''It's good fun,'' she says. ''Some are like a poor man's university. Others have lawyers and professors as members. Every club has a different kind of person. I find that very interesting.''

I asked her if she planned to go further in the Toastmasters organization.

''I'm thinking no,'' she says, ''that I don't want to do it, because it would be a very time-consuming thing and that's not what I want. It's not a status thing anymore, to be the head guy.

''The year I finally quit real estate I was elected head of the district real estate board, which is really the pinnacle.'' She smiles at the irony. ''I refused that and said, 'No, I can't do anything for a while.'

''I realize now I don't want that at all. It's more the getting there, isn't it? The journey that we like. The journey and not the destination. And once you get there — well — you ask, 'Is this all there is?' ''

For Joanna and all the other people I have talked to, neither status nor position matter much in their lives. When I asked people, "What's most important to you today?" in nearly every case they answered "people."

Martin Buber, philosopher and writer, said something like this late in his life. The last chapter of his autobiography he titled — "Books and Men." There he says that in his youth he preferred books to people. But, as he aged, ". . . this has become less and less the case. . . . I knew nothing of books when I came forth from the womb of my mother, and I shall die without books, with another human hand in my own."[21]

But how can people maintain this human bond today in the face of social forces that threaten to tear family and friends apart? Joanna maintains it by caring for others. In addition to her Toastmasters and volunteer work, she has developed a special bond with her teen-age granddaughter.

"My relationship with her is very close," she says, "very open. When she was fifteen, she started having sex with boys, and she told me, not her mother. We talked it through and I got her to go to the clinic for pills. I got her to tell her mother eventually. Now she comes to me with anything. I think it's because I'm not judgmental.

"With my own children I worried too much about their making it in every way. I seemed to think, 'Oh dear, I don't want them to make the mistakes I did.' I was trying too hard and not letting them do their own suffering.

"With my grandchildren, though, I give them a lot more freedom — even the fellow four years old — to let them make their own decisions instead of thinking I know better.

"I say to them, 'How do I know what's right for you? How can I tell you what path to take?' So my grandchildren confide in me where they won't in their own parents. Sometimes I know I can't help them. Very often we'll talk for an hour and I don't do anything. After that hour they'll come to a decision . . . I guess I can be a listener, and I think that's something I owe to my fellow human beings."

I asked Joanna to sum up her life today.

"The grandchildren are wonderful," she says. "I love them dearly. But what really gives my life meaning now is inside. It's not external anymore. I have my inner resources — I always had them, but I didn't use them.

"Now I don't have to run around any more. I'm not at the centre. And death? I don't fear it. I think about it and I think, 'Oh, twenty years from now I won't even be here.' And it's sort of 'What the hell. Who do I think I am?' And it's really great.

"For me getting older was very painful at first because I resisted change. Now I'm changed, and it's okay. I would say I have a new freedom. My granddaughter tells me she's mature at 17. Well, I tell her I'm still maturing. I'm still at it. I thought I had no limits, but for me a great learning was recognizing my limits. It was a complete turnover, almost like a rebirth.

"I guess I've learned we're all weak really. At least we should accept that — being weak — and realize, 'Hey. I'm only a fragile human being.'" Now Joanna can admit her own limits. This was the great lesson aging taught her. She can now affirm her life in spite of loss and change. And she can now move on to a new challenge: to help younger people find meaning for themselves.

The Age of Discovery

A few years ago a debate raged among experts over two theories of good aging. One group said that a good old age was due to disengagement while the other claimed that it was due to activity. But neither of these theories were based on studies of the most self-actualized older people. With older people who are self-actualized, the split between activity and disengagement doesn't make sense. Did Joanna disengage from her mid-life roles? Or did she re-engage in new roles? Is she active? Or is she withdrawn? Does it make sense to define her life now in terms of social roles at all?

The most fulfilled older people, I found, do withdraw from life in one respect. Kurt, Joanna and most of the other people I talked with value their time alone.

"I don't do the things I don't want to do anymore," Joanna says. "I've learned to say no. Today I'm going to the lake. I bought this house there and I'm going with two rolls of wallpaper. I may paper the kitchen. I'll play my records and tapes. There's satellite TV there if I want to watch a show. I may go to bed, I may not. It's very cozy there, very warm.

"Now I know when I need to get away, when I need to back off. Yesterday the most important thing was to go out and ski for an hour. Isn't that funny? It should be the least important really."

Yet, Joanna also spends a lot of her time teaching young people and working for Toastmasters. And though Kurt now lives on his farm, he still criss-crosses the country many times a year to speak to professionals in business and government.

These people remain active but their activity isn't a goal in itself: it is only the outward sign of a deeper process. K. Warner Schaie calls this the process of "reintegration." For these "selected older individuals who exemplify what folk myth describes as the 'wisdom of old age,'" he says, "activity requires meaning and purpose."[22]

Activity alone — playing golf, taking courses or travelling — may be important for some people, but for others it may only be a surface sign that covers over a lack of meaning. These activities can cover up the void of old age and keep people from coming to grips with the challenge of living beyond middle age. Meaningless action can short-circuit the chance to discover a good age.

The best older people display what psychoanalyst Rollo May calls "intentionality." "It refers," he says, "to movement toward something."[23] Intentionality from the Latin root *tendre* — to stretch — refers to a reaching out to the future.

"And you cannot understand the overt behavior," May says, "except as you see it in relation to, and as an expression of, its intention. Meaning has no meaning apart from intention. Each act of consciousness *tends toward* something, is a turning of the person toward something and has within it, no matter how latent, some push toward a direction for action."[24]

The most actualized older people have made this intention conscious. They display what Victor Frankl calls the "will to meaning."[25] They see old age as a time for self-discovery and a time to share their talents with others.

There is a unique set of values at work here and these people know it. They are not trying to win fame or fortune. They have been through that phase of life and are now discovering new meaning in life. They speak about silence, thinking, caring, devotion, a concern for others and a desire to remain self-sufficient as they age. They are busy and involved, active and committed. But they are also withdrawn and quiet, thoughtful and reserved. Above all they are responding to the challenges aging poses for them, and in the process they are discovering how to grow old.

Today, as always, a good old age does not just happen. People must discover it for themselves. Whether or not they learn how to age well depends in part on what they expect old age to be and how they meet its challenges.

In the past researchers too often studied the hardships of old age. For every one account of good aging, volumes and volumes of studies exist describing the misery of old age. The lack of balance points to our deep prejudice and fear of aging, and as long as we look only at sick and troubled people and at the problems that come with age, we shall never create an ideal of good aging to which we can all aspire.

Today we can fulfill the basic needs of most older people in our society, and more people than ever before have the chance to live a good old age. We can now work to create the best possible old age, and there is no better place to begin than with ourselves.

APPENDIX

Thousands of seniors' organizations, groups and government agencies to serve seniors exist throughout the country. It would take a small book to list them all. The Office on Aging in Ottawa and the Canadian National Council on Aging have computerized lists that are kept up to date. You should contact them if you need a more complete listing than I give here. Below I offer only a small sample of the many groups you could contact to learn more about older people.

I have noted with the following code numbers the main purpose of each group: (1) general service or information; (2) health care; (3) housing; (4) income; (5) retirement; (6) education and leisure; (7) politics.

Government Agencies for the Elderly

Federal

Many federal government agencies (e.g. Canada Mortgage and Housing Corporation, New Horizons, Health and Welfare Canada, etc.) have offices in cities across the country. Check your phone book for offices in your area.

Canada Mortgage and Housing
Corporation (3)
Canadian Housing Information
Centre
Ground Floor, Annex
Montreal Road
OTTAWA, Ontario
K1A 0P7

Health Promotion Directorate (2)
Health Services and Promotion
Branch
Health and Welfare Canada
OTTAWA, Ontario
K1A 1B4

Income Security Programs Branch (4)
Health and Welfare Canada
Room 1304
Brooke Claxton Building
OTTAWA, Ontario
K1A 0L4

National Advisory Council
on Aging (1)
Room 1264
Jeanne Mance Building
Tunney's Pasture
OTTAWA, Ontario
K1A 0K9

National Council of Welfare (4)
Brooke Claxton Building
OTTAWA, Ontario
K1A 0K9

New Horizons Program (6)
Health and Welfare Canada
6th Floor
Brooke Claxton Building
OTTAWA, Ontario
K1A 1B5

Office on Aging (1, 2)
Health and Welfare Canada
Room 1132
Brooke Claxton Building
OTTAWA, Ontario
K1A 0K9

Secretariat on Fitness and the Third
Age (6)
c/o Canadian Parks and Recreation
333 River Road
VANIER, Ontario
K1L 8B9

Statistics Canada (1)
User Services Division
Central Inquiries
Main Floor
R.H. Coats Building
Holland Avenue
OTTAWA, Ontario
K1A 0T6

Provincial

Newfoundland and Labrador
Department of Health (2)
Confederation Building
ST JOHN'S, Newfoundland
A1C 5T7

Department of Social Services (1)
Services to Senior Citizens
P.O. Box 4750
ST JOHN'S, Newfoundland
A1C 5T7

Recreation and Sports Services (6)
Workers Compensation Building
146-148 Forest Road
ST JOHN'S, Newfoundland
A1A 1E6

Prince Edward Island
Department of Health and Social
Services (2)
Community Based Services for
the Elderly
P.O. Box 2000
CHARLOTTETOWN,
Prince Edward Island
C1A 7N8

Division of Youth, Fitness and
Recreation (6)
Department of Education
P.O. Box 2000
CHARLOTTETOWN,
Prince Edward Island
C1A 7N8

Nova Scotia
Department of Health (2)
Joseph Howe Building
P.O. Box 488
HALIFAX, Nova Scotia
B3J 2R8

Department of Recreation (6)
Bank of Montreal Tower
P.O. Box 864
HALIFAX, Nova Scotia
B3J 2V2

Department of Social Services (1)
Family Benefits Division
Senior Citizens Financial Aid
Programs
Johnston Building
Prince Street
P.O. Box 696
HALIFAX, Nova Scotia
B3J 2T7

Health Services and Insurance
Commission (1)
Box 760
HALIFAX, Nova Scotia
B3J 2V2

Senior Citizens Commission (1)
5182 Prince Street
Box 696
HALIFAX, Nova Scotia
B3J 2T7

Old Age Security and Guaranteed
Income Supplement (4)
Suite 740, Barrington Street Tower
Scotia Square
HALIFAX, Nova Scotia
B3J 3J5

Senior Citizens Secretariat (1)
Sixth Floor
Dennie Building
1740 Granville Street
P.O. Box 2065
HALIFAX, Nova Scotia
B3J 2Z1

New Brunswick

Department of Social Services (1)
Community Based Services for Senior
Program
P.O. Box 6000
FREDERICTON, New Brunswick
E3B 5H1

Québec

Haut-Commissariat à la jeunesse,
aux loisirs et aux sports (6)
1035, rue de la Chevrotière
7e étage
QUÉBEC, Québec
G1R 5A5

Ministère des affaires sociales (1)
Service des politiques aux adultes
et personnes âgées
1075, chemin Ste.-Foy
3e étage
QUÉBEC, Québec
G1S 2M1

Ontario

Advisory Council on Senior Citizens
(1)
700 Bay Street
Room 203
TORONTO, Ontario
M5G 1Z6

Health Research and Development
Council of Ontario (2)
Ministry of Health
Eighth Floor, Hepburn Block
Queen's Park
TORONTO, Ontario
M7A 1R3

Ministry of Community and Social
Services (1)
Att: Seniors' Programs Supervisor
2197 Riverside Drive
Room 701
OTTAWA, Ontario
K1H 7X3

Provincial Secretariat for Social
Development (1)
Provincial Co-ordinator for Senior
Citizens
Third Floor
700 Bay Street
TORONTO, Ontario
M5G 1Z6

Sports and Fitness Division (6)
Ministry of Culture and Recreation
77 Bloor Street West
Fifth Floor
TORONTO, Ontario
M7A 2R9

Manitoba

Council on Aging (1)
175 Hargrave Street
Seventh Floor
WINNIPEG, Manitoba
R3C 3R8

Department of Fitness, Recreation
and Sport (6)
200 Vaughan Street
Second Floor
WINNIPEG, Manitoba
R3B 1T5

Department of Health (2)
Administrative Services Division
Medical Supplies and Home Care
Equipment
1500 Regent Avenue
WINNIPEG, Manitoba
R2C 3A8

Department of Health (2)
Community Health Programs Division
831 Portage Avenue
WINNIPEG, Manitoba
R3G 0N6

Department of Health (2)
Provincial Gerontologist
Seventh Floor
175 Hargrave Street
WINNIPEG, Manitoba
R3C 0V8

Saskatchewan

Department of Social Services (1, 2)
1920 Broad Street
REGINA, Saskatchewan
S4P 3V6

Home Care (2)
1920 Broad Street
REGINA, Saskatchewan
S4P 3V6

Senior Citizens' Provincial Council (1)
Room 540, Avord Tower
2002 Victoria Avenue
REGINA, Saskatchewan
S4P 3V7

Alberta

Department of Social Services and
Community Health (2)
Seventh Street Plaza
10030 - 107 St.
EDMONTON, Alberta
T5J 3E4

Financial Counselling Division (4, 5)
Alberta Consumer and Corporate
Affairs
9945 - 50 Street
EDMONTON, Alberta
T6A 0L4

Health Care Extended Benefits (2)
Box 1376
EDMONTON, Alberta
T5J 2Y6

Health Care Insurance (2)
Box 1360
EDMONTON, Alberta
T5J 2N3

Home Conversion Program (3)
Third Floor, One-Twelve Professional
Centre
10050 - 112 Street
EDMONTON, Alberta
T5K 1L9

Provincial Senior Citizens' Advisory
Council (1)
c/o Senior Citizens' Bureau
Ninth Floor, Seventh Street Plaza
10030 - 107 Street
EDMONTON, Alberta
T5J 3E4

Recreation Services to Special Groups
(6)
Department of Recreation and Parks
10363-108 Street
EDMONTON, Alberta
T5J 1L8

British Columbia

Medical Services Commission (2)
1515 Blanshard Street
VICTORIA, B.C. V8W 3C8

Ministry of Health (2)
Support Services Centre
Att: Manager, Administrative Services
836 Roderick Street
VICTORIA, B.C. V8X 3Z6

Ministry of Human Resources (1)
Senior Citizen Counsellor Program
Parliament Buildings
VICTORIA, B.C. V8V 1X4

Provincial Gerontologist (1)
Planning and Support Services
Ministry of Health
1515 Blanshard Street
VICTORIA, British Columbia
V8W 3C8

Sports and Fitness Division (6)
Ministry of Recreation and
Conservation
Parliament Buildings
VICTORIA, British Columbia
V8V 1X4

Northwest Territories/Yukon

Recreation Division (6)
Department of Natural and Cultural
Affairs
Government of the N.W.T.
YELLOWKNIFE, N.W.T.
X0E 1H0

Recreation Branch (6)
Department of Education
P.O. Box 2730
WHITEHORSE, Yukon Territory
Y1A 2C6

Non-Government Organizations for the Elderly

National

Advisory Council on the Status
of Women (1)
Box 1541, Station "B"
OTTAWA, Ontario
K1P 5R5

Canadian Association for Adult
Education (6)
29 Prince Arthur Avenue
TORONTO, Ontario
M5R 1B2

Alzheimer's Society of Canada (2)
185 Bloor Street East
Suite 222
TORONTO, Ontario
M4W 3J3

Canadian Association for Health,
Physical Education and Recreation
(2, 6)
355 River Road
VANIER, Ontario
K1L 8C1

The Arthritis Society (2)
920 Yonge Street
Suite 420
TORONTO, Ontario
M4W 3J7

Canadian Association of Gerontology
(1)
238 Portage Avenue
WINNIPEG, Manitoba
R3B 2A7

Association of Canadian Pension
Management (4)
2 Bloor Street West
Suite 503
TORONTO, Ontario
M4W 3E2

Canadian Long Term Care
Association (2)
77 Metcalfe Street
Room 306
OTTAWA, Ontario
K1P 5L6

Canadian Pension Conference (4)
67 Mowat Avenue
Suite 537
TORONTO, Ontario
M6K 3E3

Canadian Pensioners Concerned, Inc.
(4, 5)
24 - 830 McLean Street
HALIFAX, Nova Scotia
B3H 2T8

Canadian Society of Geriatric
Medicine (2)
Parkwood Hospital
81 Grand Avenue
LONDON, Ontario
N6C 1M2

Elderhostel Canada (6)
P.O. Box 4400
FREDERICTON, New Brunswick
E3B 5A3

Fitness Canada (6)
Journal Building
365 Laurier Avenue West
Eleventh Floor
OTTAWA, Ontario
K1A 0M5

Institute for Research on Public
Policy (1)
275 Slater Street
Fifth Floor
OTTAWA, Ontario
K1P 5H9

Canadian Association of Pre-
Retirement Planners (4, 5)
10 Chemin Starr
YARMOUTH, Nova Scotia
B5A 2T1

Canadian Council on Social
Development (4)
55 Parkdale Avenue
P.O. Box 3505, Station "C"
OTTAWA, Ontario
K1Y 4G1

Canadian Geriatrics Research Society
(2)
Geriatric Study Centre
351 Christie Street
TORONTO, Ontario
M6G 3C3

Canadian Institute of Religion and
Gerontology (6)
Suite 203
40 St. Clair Avenue East
TORONTO, Ontario
M4T 1M9

Canadian Institute of Senior Centres
(6)
c/o Bernard Bertel Centre
1003 Steeles Avenue West
WILLOWDALE, Ontario
M2R 3T6

Inuit Cultural Institute (1)
ESKIMO POINT, N.W.T.
X0E 0L0

National Pensioners and Senior
Citizens Federation (4,5)
3505 Lake Shore Boulevard West
TORONTO, Ontario
M8W 1N5

Native Council of Canada (1)
170 Laurier Avenue West,
Fifth Floor
OTTAWA, Ontario
K1P 5V5

Victorian Order of Nurses for Canada
(2)
5 Blackburn Avenue
OTTAWA, Ontario
K1N 8A2

Provincial

Newfoundland and Labrador

Newfoundland and Labrador
Association for the Aging (1)
Memorial University of Newfoundland
ST JOHN'S, Newfoundland
A1C 5S7

Newfoundland and Labrador
Association on Gerontology
100 Forest Road
ST JOHN'S, Newfoundland
A1A 1E5

Newfoundland and Labrador
Association of Nursing Homes (2)
P.O. Box 789
BONAVISTA, Newfoundland
A0G 1B0

Newfoundland and Labrador
Pensioners and Senior Citizens
Federation (7)
121 Newton Road
ST JOHN'S, Newfoundland
A1B 3A9

Prince Edward Island

Nursing Home Association of Prince
Edward Island (2)
338 Grafton Street
CHARLOTTETOWN,
Prince Edward Island
C1A 1L5

Senior Citizens Federation (7)
382 Queen Street
CHARLOTTETOWN,
Prince Edward Island
C1A 4E1

Nova Scotia

Associated Homes for Special Care (2)
P.O. Box 3095
Dartmouth East P.O.
DARTMOUTH, Nova Scotia
B2W 4Y3

Canadian Pensioners Concerned, Inc.
(4,5)
(Nova Scotia Division)
Tower 1, Suite 103
Halifax Shopping Centre
7001 Mumford Road
HALIFAX, Nova Scotia
B3L 2H9

Canadian Association of
Pre-Retirement Planners (5)
10 Chemin Starr
YARMOUTH, Nova Scotia
B5A 2T1

Elderhostel (Atlantic Canada) (6)
Kathryn Rice
Continuing Education
Dalhousie University
6100 University Avenue
HALIFAX, Nova Scotia
B3H 1W7

Nova Scotia Association of Health
Organizations (2)
Suite 600, 5991 Spring Garden Road
Halifax Professional Centre
HALIFAX, Nova Scotia
B3H 1Y6

Federation of Senior Citizens and
Pensioners of Nova Scotia (7)
720 Glace Bay Road
RESERVE MINES, Cape Breton,
Nova Scotia
B0A 1V0

Nova Scotia Federation of Senior
Citizens and Pensioners (7)
25 Palmer Street
TRURO, Nova Scotia
B2N 4E8

Gerontology Association of Nova
Scotia (1)
c/o Mount Saint Vincent University
1600 Bedford Highway
HALIFAX, Nova Scotia
B3M 2J6

Senior Citizens Information and
Service Centre (1)
Suite 203
Barrington Street
HALIFAX, Nova Scotia
B3J 2A1

New Brunswick

New Brunswick Association of
Nursing Homes, Inc. (2)
132, rue Principale
FREDERICTON, New Brunswick
E3A 1C7

New Brunswick Senior Citizens
Federation, Inc. (7)
Suite M
567 St George Boulevard
MONCTON, New Brunswick
E1E 2B9

New Brunswick Gerontology
Association (1)
130 University Avenue
SAINT JOHN, New Brunswick
E2K 4K3

Université du Troisième Âge (6)
University of Moncton
MONCTON, New Brunswick
E1E 2B8

Québec

Association québécoise pour la défense
des droits des retraités et pre-retraités
(5)
1800, rue Bercy, suite 103
MONTRÉAL, Québec
H2K 4K5

Certificat de gérontologie (6)
Université de Montréal
Chemin Queen Mary
C.P. 6128, Succursale "A"
MONTRÉAL, Québec
H3C 3J7

Comité d'action gérontologique
Association des anciens de
l'Université Laval (1)
Jean-Louis Delisle
Pavillon Lacerte
Université Laval
STE FOY, Québec
G1K 7P4

Elderhostel (Québec) (6)
Roland Doyon
Directeur de programmes
Université Laval
2379 Pavillon Bonefant
QUÉBEC, Québec
G1K 7P4

Ontario

Baycrest Centre for Geriatric Care (2)
3560 Bathurst Street
TORONTO, Ontario
M6A 2E1

Canadian Council of Retirees
(C.L.C.)
(Ontario Section)
Room 204, 15 Gervais Drive
DON MILLS, Ontario
M3G 1Y8

Canadian Pensioners Concerned, Inc.
(4, 5)
(Ontario Division)
51 Bond Street
TORONTO, Ontario
M5B 1X1

Catholic Office of Ministry to the
Elderly (1)
3377 Bayview Avenue
WILLOWDALE, Ontario
M2M 3S4

Fédération de l'âge d'or du Québec (7)
1415 est, rue Jarry
MONTRÉAL, Québec
H2E 2Z7

Groupe multidisciplinaire de
recherche en gérontologie (1)
Université de Sherbrooke
SHERBROOKE, Québec
J1K 2R1

Laboratoire de gérontologie de
l'Université Laval
Pavillon de Roninck
Chambre 2467
Cité universitaire
QUÉBEC, Québec
G1K 7P4

Elderhostel (Ontario) (6)
Remo Brassolotto
Continuing/Community Education
Humber College
P.O. Box 1900
REXDALE, Ontario
M9W 5L7

Gerontology Research Centre (2)
University of Guelph
GUELPH, Ontario
N1G 2W1

Gerontology Research Council
of Ontario (1)
88 Maplewood Avenue
HAMILTON, Ontario
L8M 1W9

Help the Aged (1)
Suite 311A
44 Eglinton Avenue West
TORONTO, Ontario
M4R 1A1

Office on Aging (1)
Togo Salmon Hall
McMaster University
1280 Main Street West
Room 308
HAMILTON, Ontario
L8S 4M2

Older Adult Centres' Association
of Ontario (6)
Suite 509
250 Consumers Road
WILLOWDALE, Ontario
M2J 4V6

Ontario Gerontology Association
Association (2)
c/o Department of Statistics
University of Waterloo
WATERLOO, Ontario
N2L 3G1

Ontario Social Development Council,
Inc. (1)
Committee on Aging
Suite 404
1240 Bay Street
TORONTO, Ontario
M5R 2A7

Manitoba
Age and Opportunity, Inc. (1)
304 – 323 Portage Avenue
WINNIPEG, Manitoba
R3B 2C1

Alzheimer's Family Resource Centre
(2)
B – 170 Hargrave Street
WINNIPEG, Manitoba
R3C 3H4

Programme in Gerontology (1)
University of Toronto
Room 407
455 Spadina Avenue
TORONTO, Ontario
M5S 1A1

RAISE (2)
Home Support Service for the Elderly
230 East Avenue
KITCHENER, Ontario
N2H 1Z4

Seniors' Employment Bureau of
Ottawa-Carleton (4, 5)
Suite 307
Sparks Street
OTTAWA, Ontario
K1P 5A6

Third Age Learning Associates
(TALA) (6)
Glendon College
Bayview Avenue
TORONTO, Ontario
M4N 3M6

United Senior Citizens of Ontario,
Inc. (7)
3505 Lake Shore Boulevard West
TORONTO, Ontario
M8W 1N5

Centre on Aging (1)
University of Manitoba
338 Isbister Building
WINNIPEG, Manitoba
R3T 2N2

Commission on Aging (1)
Jewish Community Council
Second Floor
370 Hargrave Street
WINNIPEG, Manitoba
R3B 2K1

Creative Retirement Manitoba (5, 6)
21st Floor
185 Smith Street
WINNIPEG, Manitoba
R3C 3G4

Pension Commission of Manitoba
(4, 5)
401 York Street
WINNIPEG, Manitoba
R3C 0P8

Long Term Care Council (2)
Manitoba Health Organization
377 Colony
WINNIPEG, Manitoba
R3B 2P5

Senior Citizens' Job Bureau (4, 5)
Room 300, Dayton Building
323 Portage Avenue
WINNIPEG, Manitoba
R3B 2C1

Manitoba Association of Gerontology
(1)
320 Sherbrook Street
WINNIPEG, Manitoba
R3B 2W6

University of Manitoba (6)
Continuing Education Division
Study Canada — Summer Program
WINNIPEG, Manitoba
R3T 2N2

Manitoba Society of Seniors (7)
1102 Childs Building
211 Portage Avenue
WINNIPEG, Manitoba
R3B 2A2

University of Winnipeg (6)
Continuing Education Division
515 Portage Avenue
WINNIPEG, Manitoba
R3B 2E9

Saskatchewan

Saskatchewan Association of Special
Care Homes (2)
2 - 150 Albert Street
REGINA, Saskatchewan
S4P 2S4

Saskatchewan Gerontology
Association (1)
1920 Broad Street
REGINA, Saskatchewan
S4P 3V6

Saskatchewan Coalition for Women's
Pensions (4)
R.R. #5
SASKATOON, Saskatchewan
S7K 3J8

Saskatchewan Health-Care
Association (2)
1445 Park Street
REGINA, Saskatchewan
S4N 4C5

Saskatchewan Co-Ordinating Council
on Social Planning (1)
314 - 220 Third Avenue South
SASKATOON, Saskatchewan
S7K 1M1

Saskatchewan Seniors Association,
Inc. (7)
P.O. Box 1027
NIPAWIN, Saskatchewan
S0E 1E0

Senior Citizen "Action Now"
Association (7)
Suite 219, Ross Block
SASKATOON, Saskatchewan
S7K 1L5

Senior Citizens' Service (1)
1517 - 11th Avenue
REGINA, Saskatchewan
S4P 0H3

Alberta

Alberta Association on Gerontology
(1)
810 General Services Building
University of Alberta
EDMONTON, Alberta
T6G 2H1

Canadian Pensioners Concerned
(Alberta Division)
907, 4440 - 106 Street
EDMONTON, Alberta
T6H 4X1

Alberta Council on Aging (7)
Room 390, First Edmonton Place
10665 Jasper Avenue
EDMONTON, Alberta
T5J 3S9

Foresight Magazine (6)
Alberta Council on Aging
Room 390, First Edmonton Place
10665 Jasper Avenue
EDMONTON, Alberta
T5J 3S9

Alberta Pensioners and Senior
Citizens Organization (7)
1119 12th Street South
LETHBRIDGE, Alberta
T1K 1R2

University of Alberta, Edmonton (6)
Community Relations Office
423 Athabasca Hall
EDMONTON, Alberta

Alberta Senior Citizens Sports
and Recreation Association
722 - 16th Avenue Northeast
CALGARY, Alberta
T2E 6V7

University of Calgary (6)
Faculty of Fine Arts
2500 University Drive Northwest
CALGARY, Alberta
T2N 1N4

British Columbia

British Columbia Health Association
(2)
440 Cambie Street
VANCOUVER, British Columbia
V6B 2N6

Committee on Gerontology (1)
University of British Columbia
VANCOUVER, British Columbia
V6T 1W5

British Columbia Long Term Care
Association (2)
321 - 1675 8th Avenue West
VANCOUVER, British Columbia
V6J 1V2

The Council of Senior Citizens'
Organizations of British Columbia
(COSCO) (7)
5115 Frances Street
BURNABY, British Columbia
V5B 1T2

Gerontology Association of British
Columbia (1)
c/o 411 Seniors' Centre
411 Dunsmuir Street
VANCOUVER, British Columbia
V6B 1X4

Gerontology Centre (1)
Simon Fraser University
BURNABY, British Columbia
V5A 1S6

Old Age Pensioners of B.C. (7)
514 - 1200 W. 73rd Avenue
VANCOUVER, British Columbia
V6P 6J8

Senior Citizen "Action Now"
Association (7)
6575 Cypress Street
VANCOUVER, British Columbia
V6P 5L9

Senior Citizens' Association of British
Columbia (1)
P.O. Box 10, R.R. #1
HALFMOON BAY, British Columbia
V0N 1Y0

Seniors' Alcoholism and Drug
Rehabilitation Society (2)
Fourth Floor
411 Dunsmuir Street
VANCOUVER, British Columbia
V6B 1X4

Social Planning and Review Council
of British Columbia (1)
Committee on Aging
109 - 2182 West 12th Avenue
VANCOUVER, British Columbia
V6K 2N4

Vancouver Homesharers' Society
(for Seniors) (3)
810 - 2045 Nelson Street
VANCOUVER, British Columbia
V6G 1N8

Victoria Institute of Gerontology (1)
841 Fairfield Road
VICTORIA, British Columbia
V8V 3B6

Northwest Territories/Yukon

The Elders Association (1)
c/o Inuit Cultural Association
ESKIMO POINT, N.W.T.
Y1A 2J3

Yukon Council on Aging (1)
4 Lewes Boulevard
WHITEHORSE, Yukon
Y1A 2J3

NOTES

CHAPTER 1

[1] *Peege* (Phoenix Films: 1970).

[2] Robert Butler, *Why Survive? Being Old in America* (New York: Harper & Row, 1975), xi.

[3] Robert Atchley, *The Social Forces in Later Life,* 3rd ed. (Belmont, California: Wadsworth, 1980), 256.

[4] A small sample of these studies would include: Carol Seefelt, et al., "Using Pictures to Explore Children's Attitudes Towards the Elderly," *The Gerontologist* 17 (1977): 506-512; Carl Eisdorfer and J. Altrocchi, "A Comparison of Attitudes Toward Old Age and Mental Illness," *Journal of Gerontology* 16 (1961): 940-943; Tom Hickey, et al., "Children's Perceptions of the Elderly," *Journal of Genetic Psychology* 112 (1968): 227-235.

[5] Harris, Louis, et al., *Myth and Reality of Aging in America* (Washington, D.C.: National Council on Aging, 1975).

[6] Milton Orris, *Factors Which Contribute to the Social and Economic Independence of People Over 60* (Saskatoon: The Joint Advisory Committee on Aging, 1970), 6.

[7] Daniel Koenig, et al., *The Golden Years in British Columbia: How They Are Seen by Senior Citizens* (Victoria, B.C.: Department of Human Resources Province of British Columbia, 1977), 109.

[8] Herbert Northcott, "The Best Years of Your Life," *Canadian Journal on Aging* 1, nos. 3-4 (December 1982): 77.

[9]William Thomas, "The Expectation Gap and The Stereotype of the Stereotype: Images of Old People," *The Gerontologist* 21, no. 4 (1981): 403, 405.

[10]Susan Green, "Attitudes and Perceptions About the Elderly: Current and Future Perspectives," *International Journal of Aging and Human Development* 13, no. 2 (1981), 101.

[11]Erdman Palmore, "Facts on Aging: A Short Quiz," *The Gerontologist* 17 (1977): 315.

[12]Robert Butler, "Age-Ism Another Form of Bigotry," in S. Zarit, ed., *Readings in Aging and Death* (New York: Harper and Row, 1982), 185.

[13]Robert Butler and Myrna I. Lewis, *Aging and Mental Health* (St. Louis: C.V. Mosby, 1973), 127.

[14]Simone de Beauvoir, *Old Age* (Harmondsworth, England: Penguin, 1978), 10.

[15]Harris, *Myth*, reported in *American Association of Retired Persons Bulletin* 15, no. 10 (November 1974).

[16]*Seniors Tell All* (Toronto: Ontario Advisory Council on Aging, 1980), 1.

[17]Erik Erikson, "The Eight Ages of Man," in his *Childhood and Society*, 2nd ed. (New York: W.W. Norton, 1963).

[18]Ann Fales, et al., *Contexts of Aging in Canada* (Toronto: OISE Press, 1981), 55.

[19]National Center for Health Statistics, *Health Characteristics of Persons with Chronic Activity Limitation*, series 10, no. 112, Washington: USGPO, 1974), cited in E. Palmore, "Facts on Aging" in S.H. Zarit, ed., *Readings in Aging and Death* (New York: Harper and Row, 1982), 3.

[20]Health and Welfare Canada, *The Health of Canadians* (Ottawa: Minister of Supply and Service Canada, 1981), 125.

[21]Jon Hendricks and C. Davis Hendricks, *Aging in Mass Society*, 2d ed. (Cambridge, Massachusetts: Winthrop, 1981), 173.

[22]Palmore, "Facts", 316, citing Matilda Riley and A. Foner, *Aging and Society*, vol. 1 (New York: Russell Sage, 1968).

[23]D. Bromley, *The Psychology of Human Aging*, 2d ed. (Harmondsworth, England: Penguin, 1974), 182.

[24]Paul Baltes and K. Schaie, "Aging and IQ — Twilight Years," in Zarit, *Readings*, 98.

[25]Bromley, *Psychology*, 201.

[26]Aristotle, *Rhetoric* 2.13 (1389b–90a), in *The Basic Works of Aristotle*, ed. Richard McKeon (New York: Random House, 1941).

[27] Bernice Neugarten, ed., "Aging in the Year 2000: A Look at the Future," *The Gerontologist* 15, no. 1 (February 1975), Part II.

[28] David Fischer, *Growing Old In America*, expanded ed. (Oxford: Oxford University Press, 1978), 147.

[29] Hendricks, *Aging,* 274-75.

[30] Health and Welfare Canada, *Fact Book on Aging* (Ottawa: Minister of Supply and Services, 1983), 68-69.

[31] Hendricks, *Aging,* 306.

[32] Palmore, "Facts", 316, citing James Birren, ed., *Handbook of Aging and the Individual* (Chicago: University of Chicago Press, 1959).

[33] Jordan Tobin, "Normal Aging — The Inevitability Syndrome," in Steven Zarit, ed., *Readings in Aging and Death* (New York: Harper and Row, 1977), 44.

[34] W. Masters, and V. Johnson, *Human Sexual Response* (Boston: Little, Brown, 1966).

[35] Alex Comfort, *A Good Age* (New York: Simon and Schuster, 1976), 192.

[36] Frank Clemente and Michael B. Kleiman, "Fear of Crime Among the Aged," *The Gerontologist*, 16 (1976): 207-210.

[37] Hendricks, *Aging*, 349.

[38] Criminal Justice and the Elderly, "Elderly Duped No More Often, But Harmed More, by Consumer Fraud," *Criminal Justice and the Elderly Newsletter,* Summer 1979, 3.

[39] Louis Harris, *Aging in the Eighties: America in Transition* (Washington, D.C.: National Council on the Aging, 1981), 8.

[40] Barry McPherson, *Aging as a Social Process* (Toronto: Butterworth, 1983), 294.

[41] R. Yin, "Fear of Crime Among the Elderly: Some Issues and Suggestions," *Social Problems*, 27, no. 4 (1980): 492-504.

[42] Vasilikie Demos and Ann Jache, "When You Care Enough: An Analysis of Attitudes Toward Aging in Humorous Birthday Cards," *The Gerontologist* 21, no. 2 (1981): 214.

[43] Patrick Babin, *Bias in Textbooks Regarding the Aged, Labour Unionists and Political Minorities* (Ontario: Ministry of Education, 1975).

[44] W. Gantz et al., "Approaching Invisibility: The Portrayal of the Elderly in Magazine Advertising," *Journal of Communications* 30, no. 1 (1980), 56-60.

[45]G. Gerbner, et al., "Aging with Television: Images on Television Drama and Conceptions of Social Reality," *Journal of Communications* 30, no. 1 (1980): 38.

[46]Robert Rosenthal and Lenore Jacobson, *Pygmalion in The Classroom* (New York: Holt, Rinehart and Winston, 1968).

[47]*Priorities for Action* (Ottawa: National Advisory Council on Aging, 1981), 13.

[48]Comfort, *A Good Age*, 32-33.

[49]Green, "Attitudes," 100.

[50]T. Hickey and R. Kalish, "Young People's Perceptions of Adults," *Journal of Gerontology* 23 (1968).

[51]M. Seltzer and R. Atchley, "The Conceptions of Old: Changing Attitudes and Stereotypes," *The Gerontologist* 11 (1971): 226-230.

[52]E. Thomas and K. Yamamoto, "Attitudes Towards Age: An Exploration in School Age Children," *International Journal of Aging and Human Development* 6, no. 2 (1975): 117.

[53]Green, "Attitudes," 111-112.

[54]Atchley, *Social Forces*, 259.

[55]W. Achenbaum, *Images of Old Age in America — 1790 to Present* (Michigan: Institute of Gerontology, 1978).

[56]Fischer, *Growing Old*.

[57]Bernard Strehler, "A New Age for Aging" in Zarit, *Readings,* 63-69.

CHAPTER 2

[1]George Burns, in Rex Reed, *Valentines and Vitriol* (New York: Delacorte, 1977), 88-89.

[2]Health and Welfare Canada, *Fact Book on Aging in Canada* (Ottawa: Minister of Supply and Services, 1983), 16.

[3]Health and Welfare Canada, *Retirement Age* (Ottawa: Health and Welfare Canada, 1979), table II, B1.

[4]Health and Welfare Canada, *Canadian Government Report on Aging* (Ottawa: Minister of Supply and Services, June 1982), ix.

[5]Harold Sheppard and S. Rix, *The Graying of Working America: The Coming Crisis in Retirement — Age Policy* (New York: Free Press, 1977).

[6]Quoted by Val Ross, "The Coming Old Age Crisis," *Maclean's*, 17 January 1983, 25.

[7]*Ibid.*, 24.

[8]David Broder cited in James Schulz, *The Economics of Aging*, 2d ed. (Belmont, California: Wadsworth, 1980), 2.

[9]Leroy Stone and M. MacLean, *Future Income Prospects for Canada's Senior Citizens* (Toronto: Butterworth, 1979), 33.

[10]Lewis Auerbach and A. Gerber, *Perceptions 2: Implications of the Changing Age Structure of the Canadian Population* (Ottawa: Supply and Services Canada for The Science Council of Canada, July 1976), 3.

[11]Statistics Canada, *Canada's Elderly* (Ottawa: Minister of Supply and Services, 1979), Introduction.

[12]Ronald Blythe, *The View in Winter* (Harmondsworth, England: Penguin, 1979), 5.

[13]F. Leacy, ed., *Historical Statistics of Canada*, 2d ed. (Ottawa: Minister of Supply and Services, 1983), Series A 78-93.

[14]Statistics Canada, *The Elderly in Canada* (Ottawa: Minister of Supply and Services, April 1984), table 6.

[15]Statistics Canada, *Canada Year Book 1980-81* (Ottawa: Minister of Supply and Services, 1981), 111.

[16]Leacy, *Historical Statistics*, Series A 125-163.

[17]Auerbach and Gerber, *Perceptions 2*, 15.

[18]Department of Social and Family Services, *Cultural Differences Among the Aged in Ontario* (Toronto: Dept. of Social and Family Services, 1969).

[19]Jacob Bronowski, *The Ascent of Man* (London: BBC Publishing, 1976), 268.

[20]Jon Hendricks and C. Davis Hendricks, *Aging in Mass Society*, 2d ed. (Cambridge, Massachusetts: Winthrop Publishers, 1981), 39.

[21]*Ibid.*, 45.

[22]Fernand Braudel, *The Structure of Everyday Life*, vol. 1, tr. Siân Reynolds (New York: Harper and Row, 1978), 88.

[23]David Hacket Fischer, *Growing Old in America* (Oxford: Oxford University Press, 1978), 278, table V.

[24]Daniel Kubat and D. Thornton, *A Statistical Profile of Canadian Society* (Toronto: McGraw-Hill Ryerson, 1974), 50, table D-1.

[25]Thomas McKeown, *The Role of Medicine: Dream, Image or Nemesis?* (Princeton, N.J.: Princeton Univ. Press, 1979), 91; René Dubos, *Mirage of Health* (New York: Harper and Row, 1971), 20.

[26]John McWhinnie and B. Ouellet, "Health Trends," in David Coburn et al., eds., *Health in Canadian Society* (Toronto: Fitzhenry and Whiteside, 1981), 34.

[27]McKeown, *Role of Medicine,* 92.

[28]Lewis Thomas, "Medicine Without Science," *The Atlantic,* April 1981, 41.

[29]Ivan Illich, *Limits to Medicine* (Harmondsworth, England: Penguin, 1976), 29, citing G. Gortvay and I. Zoltan, *I. Semmelweis, His Life and Work* (Budapest: Akademiai Kiado, 1968).

[30]Jacob Bronowski, *The Ascent of Man* (London: BBC Publishing, 1976), 279.

[31]Leacy, *Historical Statistics,* Series B 51-58; Statistics Canada, *Vital Statistics,* 1: *Births and Deaths* (Ottawa: Statistics Canada, 1981) #84-204 (Annual), table 1.

[32]Leacy, *Historical Statistics,* Series D 65-74; Statistics Canada, *Population Projections for Canada and the Provinces, 1976-2001,* #91-520 (Occasional), table 3.

[33]Bronowski, *Ascent,* 279.

[34]Illich, *Limits,* 29; Braudel, *Structures,* 26-28.

[35]McKeown, *Role of Medicine,* 105.

[36]Statistics Canada, *Vital Statistics,* #84-203 (Annual).

[37]Leacy, *Historical Statistics,* Series B51-58; Statistics Canada, *Vital Statistics,* 1: *Births and Deaths,* #84-204 (Annual), table 22.

[38]Braudel, *Structures,* 90.

[39]Morton Puner, *Vital Maturity* (New York: Universe Books, 1979), 25.

[40]Terry Copp, *The Anatomy of Poverty* (Toronto: McClelland and Stewart, 1974), 25.

[41]George Torrance, "Introduction" in Coburn et al., *Health in Canadian Society,* 18.

[42]Alan Artibise, *Winnipeg: An Illustrated History* (Toronto: Lorimer, 1977), 104.

[43]Statistics Canada, *Canada Year Book 1980-81,* 150.

[44]Statistics Canada, *Canada Year Book 1980-81,* 116; Statistics Canada, *Population Projections,* #91-520 (Occasional), table 3.

[45]Warren Kalbach and Wayne McVey, *The Demographic Bases Of Canadian Society* 2d ed. (Toronto: McGraw-Hill Ryerson, 1979), 96; Statistics Canada, *Canada Year Book 1980-81,* section 4.5.1, 121.

[46]Statistics Canada, *Technical Report on Population Projections for Canada and the Provinces, 1976-2001,* #96-516 (Occasional), table 65.7.

[47]Statistics Canada, *Canada Update,* 1983 Bulletin (based on 1981 Census data).

[48]Statistics Canada, *Perspective Canada III* (Ottawa: Minister of Supply and Services, 1980), 3.

[49]Edmund Murphy, and D. Nagnur, "A Gomperz Fit that Fits: Applications to Canadian Fertility Patterns," *Demography* (1972): p. 46; Lory Laing and P. Krishnam, "First Marriage Decrement Tables for Males and Females in Canada 1961-1966," *Canadian Review of Sociology and Anthropology* 13, (1976): 222.

[50]John Kettle, *The Big Generation* (Toronto: McClelland and Stewart, 1980), 202.

[51]Health and Welfare Canada, *Fact Book,* 24-25.

[52]Auerbach and Gerber, *Perceptions 2,* 9.

[53]Blythe, *The View in Winter,* 5.

[54]Health and Welfare Canada, *Fact Book on Aging,* 18.

[55]Statistics Canada, *The Elderly* (1984), table 2.

[56]Betty Havens, "Differentiation of Unmet Needs Using Analysis by Age/Sex Cohorts," in Victor Marshall, ed., *Aging in Canada* (Toronto: Fitzhenry and Whiteside, 1980), 220-21.

[57]Health and Welfare Canada, *Government Report on Aging,* 3; Health and Welfare Canada, *Health of Canadians,* 109-114.

[58]Ann Fales, et al., *Contexts of Aging in Canada,* (Toronto: OISE Press, 1981), 55.

[59]Ira Rosenwaike, et al., "The Recent Decline in Mortality of the Extreme Aged: An Analysis of Statistical Data," *American Journal of Public Health* 70 (1980): 1074-80.

[60]Statistics Canada, *Canada's Elderly,* chart 3.

[61]Leroy Stone and S. Fletcher, *A Profile of Canada's Older Population* (Montreal: Institute for Research on Public Policy, 1980), 14.

[62]Health and Welfare Canada, *Government Report,* chart 2.

[63]Leslie Amster and H. Kraus, "The Relationship Between Life Crises and Mental Deterioration in Old Age," *International Journal of Aging and Human Development* 5, no. 1 (1974): 52.

[64]Statistics Canada, *The Elderly,* table 2.

[65]Health and Welfare Canada, *Fact Book,* 28.

[66] Linda Gerber, "Ethnicity Still Matters: Socio-Demographic Profiles of the Ethnic Elderly in Ontario," *Canadian Ethnic Studies* 15, no. 3 (1983): 72.

[67] Kwok Chan, "Coping With Aging and Managing Self-Identity: The Social World of the Elderly Chinese Women, *Canadian Ethnic Studies* 15, no. 3 (1983): 47.

[68] Department of Social and Family Services, *Cultural Differences Among the Aged in Ontario* (Toronto, 1969), 18, citing Robert Kneem, "Sample Study of Estonian Old Age Population in Toronto" (unpublished paper, 1963).

[69] Gerber, "Ethnicity," 68-76.

[70] Bernice Neugarten, "Acting One's Age: New Rules for Old," *Psychology Today*, April 1980: 78.

[71] Rafael Salas, "Aging: A Universal Phenomenon," *Populi* 9, no. 4 (1982): 4.

[72] Health and Welfare Canada, *Report on Aging,* chart 1; John Myles and M. Boyd, "Population Aging and the Elderly," in D. Forcese, ed., *Social Issues* (Scarborough, Ontario: Prentice-Hall, 1982), 271.

[73] Salas, "Aging," 4.

[74] *The Globe and Mail*, 11 July 1983, 88.

[75] Frank Denton and B. Spencer, "Canada's Population and Labour Force, Past, Present, and Future," in Victor Marshall, ed., *Aging in Canada: Social Perspectives* (Toronto: Fitzhenry and Whiteside, 1980), 22-25.

[76] Stone and Fletcher, *Profile*, 16.

[77] Auerbach and Gerber, *Perceptions 2,* 3.

[78] Stone and Fletcher, *Profile,* 17.

[79] Health and Welfare Canada, *Report on Aging,* ix.

[80] Myles and Boyd, "Population," 259.

[81] Denton and Spencer, "Canada's Population," 25.

CHAPTER 3

[1] Louis Harris and Associates, *The Myth and Reality of Aging in America* (Washington, D.C.: The National Council on Aging, June 1975), 31.

[2] Health and Welfare Canada, *Canadian Governmental Report on Aging* (Ottawa: Minister of Supply and Services, 1982), 92 and 43; Health and Welfare

Canada, *The Health of Canadians* (Ottawa: Minister of Supply and Services, 1981), 169.

[3] Ethel Shanas, "The Status of Health Care for the Elderly," in Gari Lesnoff-Caravaglia, ed., *Health Care of the Elderly* (New York: Human Sciences Press, 1980), 173.

[4] James Bennett and J. Krasny, "Health Care in Canada," in D. Coburn, et al., eds., *Health and Canadian Society* (Toronto: Fitzhenry and Whiteside, 1981), 49.

[5] Statistics Canada, *Perspective Canada* (Ottawa: Office of the Senior Advisor on Integration, 1980), 49.

[6] Lewis Auerbach and A. Gerber, *Perceptions 2* (Ottawa: Minister of Supply and Services Canada, 1976), 44.

[7] Bennett and Krasny, "Health Care," 60.

[8] Frank Denton and B. Spencer, "Population Aging and Future Health Costs in Canada," *Canadian Public Policy* 9, no. 2 (1983): 157.

[9] Bennett and Krasny, "Health Care," 47.

[10] George Torrance, "Introduction: Socio-Historical Overview: The Development of the Canadian Health System," in Coburn, et al., eds., *Health*, p. 28.

[11] Bennett and Krasny, "Health Care," 43.

[12] Coburn, et al., *Health*, 441.

[13] Bennett and Krasny, "Health Care," 40-43.

[14] *Ibid.*, 56.

[15] Denton and Spencer, "Population," 156.

[16] Statistics Canada, *Perspective Canada* (Ottawa: Office of the Senior Advisor on Integration, 1977), 37, table B.18.

[17] S.W. Martin, *Health Care for the Aged* (Toronto: Ontario Council of Health, 1978), 2; Bennett and Krasny, "Health Care," 46.

[18] Bennett and Krasny, "Health Care," 44.

[19] J. Clark and N. Collishaw, *Canada's Older Population* Staff Papers, Long Range Health Planning, (Ottawa: National Health and Welfare, 1975), 14-16.

[20] Health and Welfare Canada, *The Health,* 113-114.

[21] Statistics Canada, *Perspective* (1980), 50.

[22] John McWhinnie and B. Ouellet, "Health Trends," Coburn, et al., eds., *Health*, 35.

[23] Daniel Kubat and D. Thornton, *A Statistical Profile of Canadian Society* (Toronto: McGraw-Hill Ryerson, 1974), 54; Statistics Canada, *Perspective* (1977), 63; George Torrance, "Introduction," in Coburn, et al., eds., 10.

[24] Health and Welfare, *The Health* 112.

[25] Bennett and Krasny, "Health Care," 47.

[26] J. Nash and S. Wymelenberg, "Slow, Steady and Heart breaking," *Time,* 11 July 1983, 46.

[27] Adrian Ostfeld and D. Gibson, eds., *Epidemiology of Aging* (Maryland: Dept. NEW, 1972), 132.

[28] J. Woodard, "Alzheimer's Disease in Later Adult Life," *The American Journal of Pathology* 49 (1966): 1157-65.

[29] W. Hughes, "Alzheimer's Disease," in *Brain Structure and Aging,* ed. E. Wright, et al. (New York: MSS Information, 1974), 164.

[30] Bennett and Krasny, "Health Care," 47-48.

[31] Statistics Canada, *Perspective* (1980), 49.

[32] Cope Schwenger and M. Gross, "Institutional Care and Institutionalization of the Elderly in Canada," in Victor Marshall, ed., *Aging in Canada* (Toronto: Fitzhenry and Whiteside, 1980), 248-56.

[33] Torrance, "Introduction," 12.

[34] Marc Lalonde, *A New Perspective on the Health of Canadians* (Ottawa: Dept. of National Health and Welfare, 1974), 60.

[35] Joan Eakins Hoffman, "Care of the Unwanted: Stroke Patients in a Canadian Hospital," in Coburn, et al., eds. *Health*, 292.

[36] Ibid., 293.

[37] Howard Weaver, et al., *Geriatrics Reports* (Vancouver: Regional Hospital District, 1975), 39.

[38] Hoffman, "Care," 294.

[39] *The Winnipeg Free Press*, 28 September 1983.

[40] Martin, *Health Care*, 6.

[41] Auerbach and Gerber, *Perceptions 2,* 39-49.

[42] Daniel Baum, *Warehouses for Death* (Toronto: Burns and MacEachern, 1977), introduction and 18-19.

[43] Robert Kahn, "Excess Disabilities," in S. Zarit, ed., *Readings in Aging and Death* (New York: Harper and Row, 1977), 228-29.

[44] Schwenger, "Institutional Care," 256.

[45] *Ibid.*, 251, 256.

[46] Auerbach and Gerber, *Perceptions 2,* 107.

[47] Baum, *Warehouses,* 8.

[48] Health and Welfare, *Canadian Government Report,* 43, 92.

[49] Auerbach and Gerber, *Perceptions 2,* 106, citing N. Markus, "Home Care for the Aged," *On Growing Old,* 12 (February 1974): 6-7.

[50] L. Wilson, *Programs for the Aged in Europe* (Ottawa: Health and Welfare Canada, 1971), 12-13.

[51] Baum, *Warehouses,* 72.

[52] Community Care Services, Inc., *A Brief to the Ontario Cabinet* (Toronto: Community Care Services, Inc. [Metropolitan Toronto], 1978), 18.

[53] Ontario Advisory Council on Senior Citizens, *Through the Eyes of Others* (Toronto: Ontario Advisory Council on Senior Citizens, 1978), 15.

[54] Community Care Services, *Brief,* 10.

[55] Auerbach and Gerber, *Perceptions 2,* 42.

[56] McWhinnie and Ouellet, "Health Trends," 39.

[57] Lalonde, *A New Perspective,* 12.

[58] Health and Welfare, *The Health,* 114.

[59] Statistics Canada, *Perspective* (1977), 63.

[60] *Ibid.*

[61] Lewis Thomas, *The Lives of a Cell* (New York: Bantam, 1974), 35-36.

[62] Lewis Thomas, *The Medusa and the Snail* (New York: Viking, 1974), 170.

[63] Coburn, *Health,* 444, citing M. Freidman and R. Rosenman, *Type A Behavior and your Heart* (New York: Knopf, 1974).

[64] Bennett and Krasny, "Health Care," 48-49.

[65] Statistics Canada, *Perspective,* (1980), 48.

[66] Lalonde, *A New Perspective,* 15.

[67] Bennett and Krasny, "Health Care," 48-49.

[68] *American Journal of Public Health* (October 1984) as reported in *The Winnipeg Free Press,* "Healthy Lifestyle After 65 Discounted," 6 October, 1984.

[69] Lalonde, *A New Perspective,* 52.

[70] Herbert De Vries, "Physiology of Exercise and Aging," in Gari Lesnoff-Caravaglia, ed., *Health Care of the Elderly* (New York: Human Sciences Press, 1978), 208-09.

[71] *Ibid.,* 114.

CHAPTER 4

[1] Ontario Advisory Council on Senior Citizens, *Through the Eyes of Others* (Toronto: 1978), 5; Ontario Advisory Council on Senior Citizens, *Seniors Tell All* (Toronto, 1980-81), 18.

[2] Lawrence Crawford, "New Ways — Old Ways," in Blossom Wigdor and Louise Ford, eds., *Housing for an Aging Population: Alternatives* (Toronto: University of Toronto Press, 1980), 113, citing Bernice Neugarten.

[3] John Miron, "Household Formation Among the Elderly," in Wigdor and Ford, eds., *Housing,* 26.

[4] Alan Backley, "Social Policy Issues," in Wigdor and Ford, eds., *Housing,* 102.

[5] Health and Welfare Canada, *Fact Book on Aging* (Ottawa: Minister of Supply and Services, 1983), 68-69.

[6] Statistics Canada, *The Elderly in Canada* #88-932, (Ottawa: Minister of Supply and Services, 1984), table 4.

[7] D. Fraser, *Defining the Parameters of a Housing Policy for the Elderly* (Canada Mortgage and Housing Corporation, 1982), 86.

[8] Health and Welfare Canada, *Fact Book,* 78.

[9] *Ibid.,* 80.

[10] Ontario Advisory Council on Senior Citizens, *Seniors,* 50.

[11] Health and Welfare Canada, *Canadian Governmental Report on Aging* (Ottawa: Minister of Supply and Services, 1982), 67.

[12] G. Gutman, *The Long Term Impact of Multi-Level, Multi-Service Accommodation for Seniors,* Senior Citizen Housing Study Report No. 3 (Canada Mortgage and Housing Corporation, 1983), table 12.

[13] Fraser, *Defining,* 69.

[14]Canadian Council on Social Development, *Housing the Elderly* (Ottawa: CCSD, 1976), 111.

[15]Albert Rose, "Social Policy Issues for Housing an Aging Population," in Wigdor and Ford, eds., *Housing*, 78.

[16]Health and Welfare Canada, *Governmental Report*, 66.

[17]*Ibid.*, 65; Claude Bennett, "Introductory Remarks," in Wigdor and Ford, eds., *Housing*, 1.

[18]Health and Welfare Canada, *Fact Book*, 70; Statistics Canada, *The Elderly*, table 3.

[19]Health and Welfare Canada, *Fact Book*, 74-75.

[20]Salem Alaton, "Playing for Time," *The Globe and Mail*, 9 June 1984.

[21]*Ibid.*

[22]Barry McPherson, *Aging as a Social Process* (Toronto: Butterworth, 1983), 301.

[23]Bruno Gelba, "Creating a Human Bond," in Steven Zarit, ed., *Readings in Aging and Death* (New York: Harper and Row, 1977), 239.

[24]Ontario Ministry of Health, *Annual Report,* 1983; also Alaton, "Playing for Time."

[25]Salem Alaton, "There's No Place Like Home," *The Globe and Mail*, 16 June, 1984.

[26]*The Winnipeg Free Press*, 30 October 1981.

[27]*The Winnipeg Free Press*, 17 June 1981.

[28]*The Winnipeg Free Press*, 22 June 1981.

[29]Fraser, *Defining,* 99.

[30]*Ibid.*, 88.

[31]Health and Welfare Canada, *Governmental Report*, 61, 70, citing Statistics Canada, *Family Expenditure Survey*, 1978.

[32]Fraser, *Defining,* 102-03.

[33]Rose, "Social Policy Issues," 75.

[34]Jane Bryant Quinn, "On Reverse Mortgages," in *Newsweek,* 30 March, 1981, 75.

[35]Health and Welfare Canada, *Governmental Report*, 71.

[36]*Ibid.*, 72.

[37]*The Winnipeg Free Press*, citing Henry Bartel and Michael Daly in *Au Courant,* (Economic Council of Canada).

[38]Quinn, "On Reverse Mortgages," 75.

[39]Fraser, *Defining,* 107.

[40]Health and Welfare Canada, *Governmental Report,* 62.

[41]Fraser, *Defining*, 102-03.

[42]*Ibid.*, 101.

[43]Ontario Advisory Council on Senior Citizens, *Through the Eyes of Others*, 57.

[44]*Today Magazine*, 17 January 1981, 9.

[45]Wendy Smith, *Single Old Men on Main Street: An Evaluation of Jack's Hotel,* (Winnipeg: 1979), 7, citing the 1976 Census of Canada.

[46]J. Tindale, "Identity Maintenance Processes of Old Poor Men," in V. Marshall, ed., *Aging in Canada* (Toronto: Fitzhenry and Whiteside, 1980), 91-92.

[47]City of Toronto Planning Board, *Report on Skid Row* (Report of the Research and Overall Planning Division, November, 1977), 9.

[48]Smith, *Single Old Men,* 5.

[49]*Ibid.,* 12-13.

[50]*Ibid.,* 9, quoting John Rogers, Executive Director of the Main Street Project, 23 June 1978.

[51]Tenant demographic data, supplied by Jack's Hotel manager, from files, 1 November 1983.

[52]Smith, *Single Old Men,* 14-15.

[53]*Ibid.*, 10, 16.

[54]*Ibid.,* 13.

[55]Canadian Council on Social Development, quoted in *Lions Place Functional Program,* 1980, 10.

[56]Betty Havens, "Differentiation of Unmet Needs Using Analysis by Age/Sex Cohorts," in Marshall, ed., *Aging in Canada*, 218-20.

[57]Manitoba Council on Aging, *Report of the Manitoba Council on Aging,* (Winnipeg: 1981), 5.

[58]Havens, "Differentiation," 219.

[59]Leroy Stone, "Some Issues Regarding Housing Design and Affordability Arising from the Living Arrangements of Canada's Senior Citizens," in Wigdor and Ford, eds., *Housing*, 57.

[60]Rose, "Social Policy Issues," 87.

[61]G. Gutman, "Issues and Findings Relating to Multi-Level Accommodations for Seniors," *Journal of Gerontology* 33 (1978):592-600 and personal communication on the subject.

[62]Canadian Council on Social Development, *Beyond Shelter* (Ottawa, 1973), 389-97.

[63]Lions Place brochures and *Lions Place Functional Program* (1980).

[64]Rose, "Social Policy Issues," 87.

[65]Health and Welfare Canada, *Fact Book*, 76.

[66]Stone, "Some Issues," 61.

[67]Douglas Rapelje, "Alternatives: How Do We Make Them Happen," in Wigdor and Ford, eds., *Housing*, 215.

[68]Crawford, "New Way — Old Ways," 119-20.

[69]Mary Alice Kellogg and Andrew Jaffee, "Old Folks Commune," in Zarit, ed., *Readings in Aging and Death*, 247.

[70]Cheryl Payne and Wayne Bona, "Dartmouth S.H.A.R.E. — Senior Housing at Reduced Expenses," from abstract of paper presented at the Canadian Association of Gerontology Meetings, 1984.

[71]Douglas Rapelje, "Home Sharing," from abstract of paper presented at the Canadian Association of Gerontology Meetings, 1984.

[72]Maggie Kuhn, Gray Panthers Project Fund Letter, 29 September 1980.

[73]Health and Welfare Canada, Governmental Report, 61; John Burkus, "Social Policy Issues," in Wigdor and Ford, eds., *Housing*, 99.

CHAPTER 5

[1]Leroy Stone and Michael MacLean, *Future Income Prospects for Canada's Senior Citizens* (Toronto: Butterworth, 1979), 11, xiii.

[2]Louis Harris and Associates, *Aging in the Eighties: America in Transition* (Washington, D.C.: National Council on Aging, 1981), 12, 66.

[3] John Oughton, 'We Can't Get No Satisfaction — True or False?'' *Today Magazine,* 1981.

[4] David Cheal, "Altruism and the Adult Life Cycle," paper presented at a seminar at the Centre on Aging, University of Manitoba, November 25, 1983, 5.

[5] David Cheal, "Intergenerational Family Transfers," in *Journal of Marriage and the Family* 45, no. 4 (1953):6.

[6] Cheal, "Altruism," 5.

[7] Cheal, "Intergenerational," 8.

[8] Stone and MacLean, *Future,* xiii.

[9] Leroy Stone and Susan Fletcher, *A Profile of Canada's Older Population* (Montreal: The Institute for Research on Public Policy, 1980), 87; Stone and MacLean, *Future,* 24-25.

[10] Stone and MacLean, *Future,* 22.

[11] Ontario Advisory Council on Senior Citizens, *Through the Eyes of Others* (Toronto: Ontario Advisory Council on Senior Citizens, 1978), 36.

[12] Health and Welfare Canada, *The Incomes of Elderly Canadians in 1975,* Social Security Research Report No. 6 (Ottawa: Policy Research and Strategic Planning Branch, February 1979), 34.

[13] Health and Welfare Canada, *Fact Book on Aging in Canada* (Ottawa: Minister of Supply and Services, 1983), 42.

[14] National Council of Welfare, *Poverty in Canada* (Ottawa: NCW, 1982), table 5, page 2.

[15] Gail Lem, "CLC Adamant About Upgrading Pensions," in *The Globe and Mail,* 30 May 1983.

[16] Monique Begin, "Notes for an Address by the Hon. Monique Begin at the Annual Conference of the Alberta Council on Aging," 29 May 1981, 7.

[17] Barbara Amiel, "Trouble in Tomorrowland," *Maclean's,* 13 April 1981, 45.

[18] Gail Lem, "Business Not Convinced Total Overhaul is Necessary," *The Globe and Mail,* 30 May 1983.

[19] Health and Welfare Canada, *Fact Book,* 46.

[20] Monique Begin, "Notes for an Address by the Hon. Monique Begin to the National Pensioners and Senior Citizens Federation," presented in Lethbridge, Alberta, 25 September 1980, 2.

[21] Statistics Canada, *The Elderly in Canada* (Ottawa: Minister of Supply and Services, 1984), tables 9 and 10.

[22] National Council of Welfare, *A Pension Primer* (Ottawa: Minister of Supply and Services, April 1984), 6, 11.

[23] Health and Welfare Canada, *Retirement Age* (Ottawa: Minister of Supply and Services, April 1979), 104.

[24] Health and Welfare Canada, *Canada Pension Plan: Report for the Year Ending March 31, 1982* (Ottawa: Minister of Supply and Services, 1983), 22-26.

[25] National Council of Welfare, *A Pension Primer*, 16, 23.

[26] Monique Begin, "The Aging Society: Implications for Federal Social Policy," notes for an address by the Hon. Monique Begin to the 1981 Thematic Seminar of the Regina Regional Group of the Institute of Public Administration of Canada, 2 March 1981, 5.

[27] National Council of Welfare, *A Pension Primer*, 43.

[28] Health and Welfare Canada, *Fact Book,* 47.

[29] Amiel, "Trouble," 46.

[30] Diane Francis, "Ottawa's Pension Blues: The Country's Largest Nest Egg Could Be Going Broke," *Quest Magazine*, May 1983, 14-18.

[31] Health and Welfare Canada, *Fact Book*, 47.

[32] National Council of Welfare, *Financing the Canada Pension Plan* (Ottawa: NCW, 1982), foreword.

[33] National Council of Welfare, *A Pension Primer*, 3, 6.

[34] National Council of Welfare, *1984 Poverty Lines* (Ottawa: Minister of Supply and Services, 1984), 6.

[35] Health and Welfare Canada, *Better Pensions for Canadians* (Ottawa: Minister of Supply and Services, 1982), 57.

[36] Begin, "Notes for an Address," 25 September 1980, 1.

[37] Kenneth Bryden, *Old Age Pensions and Policy-Making in Canada* (Montreal: McGill-Queen's University Press, 1974), 76.

[38] Health and Welfare Canada, *Better Pensions for Canadians: Highlights* (Ottawa: Minister of Supply and Services, 1982), 9.

[39] Louise Dulude, *Women and Aging: A Report on the Rest of Our Lives* (Ottawa: Advisory Council on the Status of Women, 1978), 50.

[40] The National Council of Women of Canada, *The Financial Situation of Older Women: A Study Guide* (Ottawa: National Council of Women, 1978), 14.

[41] Monique Begin, "A Fair Deal from Private Pensions," notes for an Address to the West Island Senior Citizens Enterprises, 2 May 1979, 4.

[42] Begin, "The Aging Society," 5.

[43] Begin, "Notes for an Address," 25 September 1980, 4.

[44] Special Senate Commission on Retirement Age Policies, *Retirement,* 62.

[45] Dulude, *Women and Aging*, 56, citing the Economic Council of Canada, *People and Jobs,* 90-91.

[46] Special Senate Commission on Retirement Age Policies, *Retirement Without Tears* (Hull, Quebec: Canadian Government Publishing Centre, 1979), 65.

[47] National Council of Welfare, *Women and Poverty* (Ottawa: NCW, 1979), 48.

[48] Special Senate Commission on Retirement Age Policies, *Retirement*, 65.

[49] Pat Armstrong and Hugh Armstrong, *The Double Ghetto* (Toronto: McClelland and Stewart, 1978), 38.

[50] National Council of Welfare, *Poverty in Canada* (Ottawa: NCW, 1982), table 1.

[51] *Ibid.*, 33.

[52] *Ibid.,* 19.

[53] Dulude, *Women and Aging,* 52.

[54] Special Senate Commission on Retirement Age Policies, *Retirement,* 89.

[55] Dulude, *Women and Aging,* 52-53.

[56] Dulude, *Women and Aging*, 52-53; Special Senate Commission on Retirement Age Policies, *Retirement,* 89.

[57] Armstrong and Armstrong, *The Double Ghetto,* 16.

[58] Health and Welfare Canada, *Fact Book*, 47.

[59] Special Senate Commission on Retirement Age Policies, *Retirement,* p. 65.

[60] National Council of Welfare, *Women and Poverty,* 52.

[61] Dulude, *Women and Aging,* 38, 40.

[62] *Ibid.,* 38.

[63] Begin, "A Fair Deal," 3.

[64] Dulude, *Women and Aging,* 40.

[65]Begin, "Notes for an Address," 29 May 1981, 6.

[66]Special Senate Commission on Retirement Age Policies, *Retirement,* 59.

[67]National Council of Welfare, *Women and Poverty*, 32.

[68]*Ibid.,* 31.

[69]Health and Welfare Canada, *Better Pensions for Canadians: Focus on Women* (Ottawa: Minister of Supply and Services, 1982), 6-7.

[70]Begin, "A Fair Deal," 2.

[71]Dulude, *Women and Aging,* 57.

[72]Health and Welfare Canada, *Better Pensions,* 33.

[73]*Ibid.*

[74]Health and Welfare Canada, *Better Pensions . . . Focus on Women,* 8.

[75]Leroy Stone, "Interest Group Coalitions and Confrontations as Factors in the Design of Form of Support Systems: General Theory," paper presented to Aging Seminar at the University of Manitoba, 1 November 1983, 2.

[76]*Ibid.,* 3.

[77]Health and Welfare Canada, *Better Pensions,* 38.

[78]Health and Welfare Canada, *Better Pensions for Canadians: Highlights,* 9; Task Force on Retirement Income Policy, *The Retirement Income System in Canada: Problems and Alternative Policies for Reform,* vol. 1 (Ottawa: Minister of Supply and Services, 1980), 110.

[79]Neena Chappell, "Social Policy and the Elderly," in Victor Marshall, ed., *Aging in Canada: Social Perspectives* (Toronto: Fitzhenry and Whiteside, 1980), 41.

[80]Health and Welfare Canada, *Better Pensions . . . Highlights*, 15.

[81]Health and Welfare Canada, *Better Pensions,* 38.

[82]The Pension Commission of Manitoba, "Amendments to the Manitoba Pension Benefits Act," Information Circular, Special Bulletin, 1983, unpaginated.

[83]Norman Provencher, "First Steps to Reform Pension System Near," *The Globe and Mail*, 30 May 1983, R1.

[84]Health and Welfare Canada, *Better Pensions . . . Highlights*, 15-16.

[85]Amiel, "Trouble," 46.

[86]Stone and MacLean, *Future,* 84.

[87]Francis, "Ottawa's Pension Blues," 14.

[88] National Council of Welfare, *Financing the Canada Pension Plan* (Ottawa: NCW, December 1982), 7.

[89] National Council of Welfare, *Financing*, 5.

[90] Frank Denton, A. Leslie Robb and Byron Spencer, *The Future Financing of the Canada and Quebec Pension Plans: Some Alternative Possibilities* (Ottawa: Minister of Supply and Services, 1980), 27.

[91] Stone and MacLean, *Future*, 92.

[92] John Myles, "Some Implications of a Changing Age Structure," in Gloria Gutman, ed., *Canada's Changing Age Structure: Implications for the Future* (Burnaby, B.C.: SFU Publications, 1982), 43.

[93] National Council of Welfare, *Women and Poverty*, 31.

[94] National Council of Women, *The Financial Situation*, 5, 9.

[95] Amiel, "Trouble," 46.

[96] Health and Welfare Canada, *Better Pensions*, 53.

CHAPTER 6

[1] Robert Atchley, *The Sociology of Retirement* (New York: Schenkman, 1976), 87.

[2] Gordon Streib and Clement Schneider, *Retirement in American Society* (Ithaca, N.Y.: Cornell Univ. Press, 1971), 74-79.

[3] Susan Haynes, et al., "Survival After Early and Normal Retirement," *Journal of Gerontology* 33:269-78.

[4] Atchley, *The Sociology of Retirement*, 87, 91.

[5] Health and Welfare Canada, *Retirement Age* (Ottawa: Minister of Supply and Services, April 1979), 53.

[6] James Schulz, *The Economics of Aging* (Belmont, California: Wadsworth, 1976), 58.

[7] White House Conference on Aging, *Background Paper on Research in Gerontological and Social Sciences* (Washington, D.C.: USGPO, 1960), 25.

[8] Louis Harris, "Pleasant Retirement Expected," *Washington Post,* 28 November 1965.

[9] Elizabeth Heidbreder, "Factors in Retirement Adjustment: White Collar/Blue Collar Experience," *Industrial Gerontology* 12 (1972):69-79.

[10]Streib and Schneider, *Retirement,* 144.

[11]Renate Lerch, "Keeping Days Full Makes for Fulfilling Retirement," *Financial Post,* 17 April 1982, 24.

[12]Health and Welfare Canada, *Canadian Governmental Report on Aging* (Ottawa: Minister of Supply and Services, 1982), 32-33.

[13]Statistics Canada, *Canada's Elderly* (Ottawa: Minister of Supply and Services, 1979), chart 9.

[14]Health and Welfare Canada, *Retirement Age,* figure V.A.1.

[15]*Ibid.,* 53.

[16]James Schulz, *The Economics of Aging,* 2d ed. (Belmont, California: Wadsworth, 1980), 199.

[17]Bernice Neugarten, "Acting One's Age: New Rules for Old," an interview by Elizabeth Hall, *Psychology Today,* April 1980, 72.

[18]Health and Welfare Canada, *Governmental Report,* 32-33.

[19]*Ibid.,* 34.

[20]Statistics Canada, *Canada's Elderly,* chart 9 – commentary.

[21]Canadian Council on Social Development, *Statement on Retirement Policies* (Ottawa: CCSD, March 1976), 8.

[22]Health and Welfare Canada, *Retirement Age,* 40.

[23]Louis Harris and Associates, *Aging in the Eighties: America in Transition* (Washington, D.C.: National Council on Aging, 1981), 49.

[24]Special Senate Committee on Retirement Age Policies, *Retirement Without Tears* (Hull, Quebec: Canadian Government Publishing Centre, 1979), 128.

[25]Erdman Palmore, "Facts on Aging," in Steven Zarit, ed., *Readings in Aging and Death,* 2d ed. (New York: Harper and Row, 1982), 2-3.

[26]Matilda Riley and A. Foner, *Aging and Society,* vol. 1 (New York: Russell Sage, 1968); Robert Atchley, *The Social Forces in Later Life,* 3d ed. (Belmont, California: Wadsworth, 1980), 155.

[27]Atchley, *The Social Forces,* 157.

[28]*Ibid.,* 155.

[29]Atchley, *The Social Forces,* 168.

[30]Schulz, *The Economics of Aging,* 2d ed., 200.

[31]J. Pesando, *The Elimination of Mandatory Retirement: An Economic Perspective*

(Toronto: Ontario Economic Council, 1979), 21-22.

[32]Special Senate Committee on Retirement Age Policies, *Retirement,* 50.

[33]Roland Penner, cited in Canadian Association of University Teachers *Bulletin,* 1981, no. 1:1.

[34]*The Winnipeg Free Press,* 12 January 1981.

[35]Canadian Pension Plan Advisory Commission, *Retirement Ages* (Ottawa: Minister of Supply and Services, June 1980), 17.

[36]Pesando, *The Elimination of Mandatory Retirement,* 7.

[37]Neugarten, "Acting One's Age," 72.

[38]Harris and Associates, *Aging in the Eighties*, xiv.

[39]Glen MacKenzie, "Boredom a Major Problem, Seminar on Retirement Told," *The Winnipeg Free Press*, 7 April 1981.

[40]Atchley, *The Social Forces*, 169.

[41]Richard Barfield and James Morgan, *Early Retirement: The Decision and the Experience* (Ann Arbor, Michigan: University of Michigan, Institute of Social Research, 1969); Lenore Bixby, "Retirement Patterns in the United States: Research and Policy Interaction," *Social Security Bulletin*, 39, no. 8:3-19.

[42]Canadian Council on Social Development, *Statement,* 5, citing Gosette La Framboise, *A Question of Need* (Ottawa: CCSD, 1975).

[43]Canadian Council on Social Development, *Statement,* 5, citing a study by L. Crawford and Jean Matlow, "Some Attitudes Toward Retirement Among Middle-aged Employees in a Longitudinal Study, 1959-1978," *Industrial Relations Quarterly Review* 27, no. 4:616-31.

[44]Canadian Pension Plan Advisory Commission, *Retirement Ages,* 12-13.

[45]J. Pesando and S. Rea, *Public and Private Pensions in Canadian Economic Analysis* (Toronto: University of Toronto Press, 1977), 119-121.

[46]Canadian Pension Plan Advisory Commission, *Retirement Ages*, 12-13, 15.

[47]Atchley, *The Social Forces*, 163, citing results of research published in "The Meaning of Retirement," *Journal of Communications* 24:97-100.

[48]Atchley, *The Social Forces*, 180; Harold Strauss, et al., "Retirement and Perceived Status Loss: An Inquiry into Some Objective and Subjective Problems Produced by Aging," in Jaber Gubrium, ed., *Time, Roles and Self in Old Age* (New York: Human Sciences Press, 1976), 226.

[49]Harris and Associates, *Aging in the Eighties,* 94.

[50]Health and Welfare Canada, *Retirement Age*, 50.

[51]Harriet Miller, "Flexible Retirement — Will Sweden Make It Work?" in *Dynamic Maturity* (Washington, D.C.: AIM Division, AARP, March 1976), reprinted in Steven Zarit, ed., *Readings in Aging and Death*, 1st ed. (New York: Harper and Row, 1977), 44.

[52]Health and Welfare Canada, *Fact Book*, 38-39.

[53]Canadian Council on Social Development, *Statement,* p. 3.

[54]Health and Welfare Canada, *Fact Book,* 40-41.

[55]Special Senate Committee on Retirement Age Policies, *Retirement,* 122.

[56]Health and Welfare Canada, *Governmental Report*, 34.

[57]Dean Morse and Susan Gray, *Early Retirement — Boon or Bane?* (Montclair, New Jersey: Alanheld, Osmund, 1980), 91.

[58]Harris and Associates, *Aging in the Eighties*, 94.

[59]Neugarten, "Acting One's Age," 74.

[60]Paul Tournier, *Learning to Grow Old* (London: SCM Press, 1972), 125.

[61]Special Senate Committee on Retirement Age Policies, *Retirement,* 118.

[62]Harris and Associates, *Aging in the Eighties*, 101.

[63]Health and Welfare Canada, *Retirement Age,* 137.

[64]Lerch, "Keeping Days Full," 25.

[65]*Ibid.*, 24.

[66]Health and Welfare Canada, *Retirement Age,* 138.

[67]H. Cox and A. Bhak, "Symbolic Interaction and Retirement Adjustment: An Empirical Assessment," *International Journal of Aging and Human Development* 9, no. 3:279-86; M. Kaplan, *Leisure: Lifestyles and Lifespan* (Philadelphia: W.B. Saunders, 1979).

[68]R. Barfield and J. Morgan, *Early Retirement: The Decision and the Experience and a Second Look* (Ann Arbor, Michigan: Institute for Social Research, 1974).

[69]Health and Welfare Canada, *Retirement Age*, 137.

[70]Special Senate Committee on Retirement Age Policies, *Retirement,* 119.

[71]Giles Gherson, "Retirement 'a Moral, Not an Economic Issue,' " in *Financial Post*, 8 March 1980.

CHAPTER 7

[1]Andrew Rooney, "Saturday Mornings with the White House Staff," in *And More by Andy Rooney* (New York: Atheneum, 1982), 207.

[2]Sebastian de Grazia, *Of Time, Work and Leisure* (Garden City, N.Y.: Anchor Books, 1964), table 3.

[3]Department of the Secretary of State, *Citizens Participation in Non-Worktime Activities,* vol. 1 (Ottawa: Citizenship Branch, Secretary of State, 1974), 80, table 6.7, citing study by S. Meis and W. Scheu (Vancouver, 1970).

[4]Joffre Dumazedier, "Cultural Mutations in Post-Industrial Societies" in *Leisure and the 3rd Age* (Paris: International Center of Social Gerontology, 1972), 14.

[5]*Ibid.*, 31.

[6]Statistics Canada, *Perspectives Canada: A Compendium of Social Statistics* (Ottawa: Information Canada, 1974), 102.

[7]C. Hobart, "Active Sports Participation Among the Young, the Middle-aged and the Elderly," *International Review of Sports Sociology* 10, nos. 3-4:27-40.

[8]Statistics Canada, *Perspective on Health* #82-540E (Ottawa: Minister of Supply and Services, February 1983), 32.

[9]Rolf Schliewen, *A Leisure Study — Canada 1975* (Ottawa: Minister of Supply and Services, 1977), 60.

[10]*Ibid.,* 74-77.

[11]Statistics Canada, *Perspectives,* 102, table 5-6.

[12]Health and Welfare Canada, *Retirement Age* (Ottawa: Minister of Supply and Services, April 1979), 67.

[13]Statistics Canada, *Perspective Canada II* (Ottawa: Minister of Supply and Services, 1977), 77.

[14]Environics Research Group, *Reaching the Retired: A Survey of the Media Habits, Preferences and Needs of Senior Citizens in Metro Toronto* (Montreal: Information Canada, 1974), 117-118.

[15]*Ibid.*, 31; also Health and Welfare Canada, *Fact Book on Aging in Canada* (Ottawa: Minister of Supply and Services, 1983), 86.

[16]Louis Harris and Associates, *Aging in the Eighties: America in Transition* (Washington, D.C.: National Council on Aging, 1981), 21.

[17]Health and Welfare Canada, *Fact Book*, 86.

[18]Environics Research Group, *Reaching the Retired*, 34-36.

[19]Barry McPherson, *Aging As a Social Process* (Toronto: Butterworths, 1983), 418.

[20]Marc LaPlante, "Leisure in Canada by 1980," position paper for Health and Welfare Canada, *Leisure in Canada*, proceedings of the Montmorency Conference on Leisure (Ottawa: Information Canada, 1969), 21.

[21]Statistics Canada, *Perspective on Health*, 32.

[22]Elaine Cumming and W. Henry, *Growing Old: The Process of Disengagement* (New York: Basic Books, 1961).

[23]Bernice Neugarten, et al., "Personality and Patterns of Aging," in *Middle Age and Aging,* ed. Bernice Neugarten (Chicago: University of Chicago Press, 1968), 175.

[24]Health and Welfare Canada, *The Health of Canadians* (Ottawa: Minister of Supply and Services, 1981), 79-80.

[25]B. Milton, *Social Status and Leisure Time Activities: National Survey Findings for Adult Canadians,* monograph 3 (Montreal: Canadian Sociology and Anthropology Associates, 1975), 56-57, 73.

[26]Barry McPherson and Carol Kozlik, "Canadian Leisure Patterns: Disengagement, Continuity of Ageism," in V. Marshall, ed., *Aging in Canada* (Toronto: Fitzhenry and Whiteside, 1980), 115-117.

[27]Secretary of State, *Citizen Participation*, 83-84; also Milton, *Social Status*, 56-57 and 102; and Hobart, "Active Sports Participation," 38.

[28]McPherson and Kozlik, "Canadian Leisure Patterns," 116-117.

[29]Statistics Canada, *Perspective on Health*, 35.

[30]McPherson and Kozlik, "Canadian Leisure Patterns," 116-117.

[31]Statistics Canada, *Culture Statistics 1976, Recreational Activities*, #87-5010cc (Ottawa: Ministry of Industry, Trade and Commerce, November 1978), 41.

[32]Health and Social Welfare Canada, *Fact Book*, 86.

[33]Harris and Associates, *Aging in the Eighties*, 23.

[34]Marc-André Delisle, "Elderly People's Management of Time and Leisure," *Canada's Mental Health* 30, no. 3:32; McPherson, *Aging as a Social Process*, 417; Parks Canada, CORD Technical Note No. 22, "Trends in Participation in Outdoor Recreational Activities" (Ottawa: National and Historic Parks Branch, Parks Canada, 1973).

[35]Health and Welfare Canada, *Canadian Governmental Report on Aging* (Ottawa: Minister of Supply and Services, 1982), 113-114.

[36] Health and Welfare Canada, *New Horizons: The First Decade* (Ottawa: Minister of Supply and Services, 1982), 13.

[37] Age and Opportunity, Inc., ''Working Arrangements Between Staff and Senior Centre Membership Organizations'' (Winnipeg: Age and Opportunity, 1983), 3.

[38] Age and Opportunity, Inc., *Annual Report*, (Winnipeg: Age and Opportunity, 1983), unpaginated.

[39] Harris and Associates, *Aging in the Eighties*, 25-27.

[40] Health and Welfare Canada, *New Horizons*, 7-8.

[41] Health and Welfare Canada, *New Horizons*, 8.

[42] *Ibid.*, 65.

[43] *Ibid.*, 8.

[44] SAGE, *A Workshop in Successful Aging* (Berkeley, California: SAGE, undated).

[45] Gay Luce, *Your Second Life* (New York: Delacorte Press, 1979), 4.

[46] Ken Dychtwald, ''The SAGE Project . . . A New Image of Age,'' *Journal of Humanistic Psychology* 18, no. 2:70.

[47] *Ibid.*

[48] Carol Powell, ''SAGE — Reshaping Attitudes About Aging,'' *Second Spring*, August/September 1978, quoting from *An Old Guy Who Feels Good.*

[49] SAGE, ''The Coming of Age,'' videotape produced and distributed by the SAGE Program, Berkeley, California.

[50] Ken Dychtwald, ''Humanistic Services for the Elderly,'' *Journal of Humanistic Psychology* 21, no. 1:45.

[51] Norman Cousins, *Anatomy of an Illness as Perceived by the Patient* (New York: Norton, 1979), 71-74.

[52] Carl Gustav Jung, ''The Stages of Life,'' in his *Modern Man in Search of a Soul*, tr. W. Dell and Cary Baynes (New York: Harcourt, Brace and World, 1933), 108.

CHAPTER 8

[1] John Myles and Monica Boyd, ''Population Aging and the Elderly,'' in Dennis Forcese and Stephen Richer, eds., *Social Issues* (Scarborough, Ontario: Prentice-Hall Canada, 1982), 272.

[2] "Grownups on Campus," *Newsweek*, 21 December 1981, 72.

[3] Myles and Boyd, "Population Aging," 270, citing table adapted from Z. Zsigmond et al., *Out of School into The Labor Force: A Summary of Findings* (Ottawa: Statistics Canada, 1979), 86.

[4] *Ibid.*

[5] W. Clark, et al., *The Class of 2001* (Ottawa: Statistics Canada, 1979), 71.

[6] Myles and Boyd, "Population Aging," 271.

[7] Health and Welfare Canada, *Fact Book on Aging in Canada* (Ottawa: Minister of Supply and Services, 1983), 84.

[8] Louis Harris and Associates, *Aging in the Eighties: America in Transition* (Washington, D.C.: National Council on Aging, 1981), 83.

[9] Myles and Boyd, "Population Aging," 271.

[10] J. Kidd, *How Adults Learn* (1959; New York: Association Press, 1973), 95.

[11] Robert Atchley, *Aging: Continuity and Change* (Belmont, California: Wadsworth, 1983), p. 62.

[12] Leonard Giambra and David Arenberg, "Problem Solving, Concept and Learning and Aging," in Leonard Poon, ed., *Aging in the 1980's* (Washington, D.C.: American Psychological Association, 1980), 256.

[13] James Fozard, "The Time for Remembering," in Poon, ed., *Aging in the 1980's*, 282.

[14] Kidd, *How Adults Learn*, 108-109, 131.

[15] Peter Siegle, "The Adult Learner," *Adult Leadership* 3, no. 9, cited in J. Kidd, *How Adults Learn*, 172.

[16] Elderhostel, *Summer Catalogue* (Boston: Elderhostel, 1983), 17.

[17] Chris Morris, "Over-60s Taking Advantage of Elderhostel Program," *Star-Phoenix* (Saskatoon), 6 August 1983.

[18] *Ibid.*

[19] Ray Vicker, "More and More Students Aged 60 and Up Take One Week Courses at Colleges Here and Abroad," *The Wall Street Journal*, 12 April 1983.

[20] Elderhostel, *Annual Report*, 1981, 4.

[21] *Ibid.*, 4.

[22] Gayle Kloosterman, "Educational Hosteling: Elderhostel," *Perspective on Aging*, May/June 1977, 19-20.

[23] Elderhostel, *Annual Report*, 1982, 5.

[24] *Ibid.*, 6.

[25] Elderhostel, *Annual Report*, 1981, 4, and *Annual Report*, 1982, 3.

[26] *University of Manitoba Bulletin* 18, no. 16 (1984):7; also personal interview.

[27] Gordon Hancock, *A Study of Gerontological Activities and Centres of Gerontology on University Campuses in the U.S. and Canada* (Winnipeg: Centre on Aging, University of Manitoba, 1983), 31.

[28] University of Winnipeg, *Inside Info* 11, no. 1:14.

[29] University of Winnipeg, *Calendar*, 1981-82, 22.

[30] University of Winnipeg, *Inside Info*, 10, no. 7:17-18.

[31] Barry Mullin, "Yearning for Learning Motivates Senior," *The Winnipeg Free Press,* 22 October 1983.

[32] Health and Welfare Canada, *Canadian Governmental Report on Aging* (Ottawa: Minister of Supply and Services, 1982), 115.

[33] Brian Milton, *Social Status and Leisure Time Activities: National Survey Findings for Adult Canadians* (Montreal: CSAA Monograph Series, 1975), 74.

[34] Institute for Continuous Learning, *Report*, 1980, 2-3.

[35] *Ibid.*, 7-8.

[36] Robert Atchley, *The Social Forces in Later Life,* 3d ed. (Belmont, California: Wadsworth, 1980), 32-33.

[37] David Radcliffe, "Education and the Elderly in The United Kingdom," in *A UNESCO Report*, citing House of Commons debate, 16 February, 1981, 11.

[38] Hancock, *A Study*, 31.

[39] Institute for Continuous Learning, *Report*, 1980, 8.

CHAPTER 9

[1] Robert Atchley, *The Social Forces in Later Life*, 3d ed. (Belmont, California: Wadsworth, 1980), 298.

[2] *Ibid.*, citing *Statistical Abstract of the United States: 1976* (Washington, D.C.: United States Government Printing Office, 1976).

[3] Government of Canada, *Parliamentary Guide* (Ottawa: Supply and Services, 1982-83), 298-422.

[4] Atchley, *Social Forces*, 101.

[5] Jon Hendricks and C. Davis Hendricks, *Aging in Mass Society*, 2d ed. (Cambridge, Massachusetts: Winthrop, 1981), 382, 389.

[6] William Mishler, *Political Participation in Canada* (Toronto: Macmillan of Canada, 1979), 102-103.

[7] James Curtis and Ronald Lambert, "Voting, Election Interest, and Age: National Findings for English and French Canadians," *Canadian Journal of Political Science* 9, no. 2:305-6.

[8] Atchley, *Social Forces*, 294.

[9] Statistics Canada, *Population Projections for Canada and the Provinces*, (Ottawa: Supply and Services, 1979), 215, 255, 468, cited in Kenneth Kernaghan, "Politics, Public Administration and Canada's Aging Population, *Canadian Public Policy* 8, no. 1:72.

[10] C. Gifford, "Senior Power in Canada," poster presentation typescript, presented at the Canadian Association of Gerontology Meetings, 1982, 1.

[11] Victor Marshall and Joseph Tindale, "A Generational Conflict Perspective for Gerontology," in Victor Marshall, ed., *Aging in Canada* (Toronto: Fitzhenry and Whiteside, 1980), 45-50.

[12] James Trela, "Status Inconsistency and Political Action in Old Age," in Jaber Gubrium, ed., *Time, Roles and Self in Old Age* (New York: Human Sciences Press, 1976), 143.

[13] John Duffey, "Grey Power — Is It a Myth?," *Prime Time Magazine* 1, no. 3:1.

[14] Trela, "Status Inconsistency," 142-43.

[15] C. Gifford, "Social Characteristics of Seniors Organization Leaders in Canada," paper presented at the Canadian Association of Gerontology, Winnipeg, 7 November 1982, 11.

[16] A. Pross, "Canadian Pressure Groups in the 1970's: Their Role and Their Relations with the Public Service," *Canadian Public Administration* 18 (Spring):121-135.

[17] Kernaghan, "Politics," 75.

[18] Gifford, "Social Characteristics," 2.

[19] Kenneth Bryden, *Old Age Pensions and Policy-Making in Canada* (Montreal: McGill-

Queen's University Press, 1974), 194-197, cited in Kernaghan, "Politics," 74-75.

[20]C. Gifford, "Senior Politics," *Policy Options* (September 1983):15.

[21]Alberta Council on Aging, *Annual Report 1983-1984* (Edmonton: ACA, 1984), 1.

[22]Gifford, "Senior Politics," 13.

[23]Gifford, "Social Characteristics," 12.

[24]Fred Grayston, letter to Art Kube, President of the British Columbia Federation of Labor, 23 August 1983.

[25]Fred Grayston, letter on the Solidarity Movement in British Columbia, 16 August 1983.

[26]Trela, "Status Inconsistency," 144.

[27]Duffey, "Grey Power," 1.

[28]Gifford, "Social Characteristics," 12.

[29]Fred Grayston, personal correspondence, April 29, 1984.

[30]Atchley, *Social Forces*, 301.

[31]Trela, "Status Inconsistency," 144.

[32]David Hapgood, "The Aging Are Doing Better" in Ronald Gross, et al., eds., *The New Old* (Garden City, New York: Anchor Press, 1978), 353.

[33]Margaret Kuhn, "What Old People Want for Themselves and Others in Society," in Paul Kerschner, ed., *Advocacy and Age* (Los Angeles, California: University of California Press, 1976), 93-96.

[34]Margaret Kuhn, "Learning by Living," *International Journal of Aging and Human Development* 8, no. 4:363.

[35]Hapgood, "The Aging Are Doing Better," 354.

[36]Kuhn, "What Old People Want," 93-96.

[37]Kuhn, "Learning by Living," 365.

[38]Kuhn, "What Old People Want," 93-96.

[39]Rein Selles, "Maggie Kuhn: Portrait of an Elder Advocate," interview in *Foresight* 1, no. 2:35.

[40]Kuhn, "What Old People Want," 88; also Kuhn, "Learning by Living," 360.

[41]*The Winnipeg Free Press*, "Seniors' Activist Fights for Young."

[42]Paul Tournier, *Learning to Grow Old* (London: SCM Press, 1972), 145.

[43]Elaine Dewar, "Doctoring Medicine," *Today Magazine,* 7 February 1981, 6-8.

[44]Think Tank, "Report of the Senior Citizens Think Tank to the Canadian Government," 6 January 1982, 8-9.

[45]Edwin Eagle, "Seniors Think Tank," *Manitoba Seniors Journal* 5, no. 2:6.

[46]Thomas Peters and Robert Waterman Jr., *In Search of Excellence: Lessons from America's Best Run Companies* (New York: Harper and Row, 1982), 126-132.

[47]Ivan Illich, *Tools for Conviviality* (New York: Harper and Row, 1973), 11.

[48]Trela, "Status Inconsistency," 136-38.

[49]Gifford, "Social Characteristics," tables 11a and 11c.

[50]Barry McPherson, *Aging as a Social Process* (Toronto: Butterworth, 1983), 256.

[51]Gifford, "Senior Power in Canada," 2.

[52]Health and Welfare Canada, *New Horizons: The First Decade* (Ottawa: Minister of Supply and Services, 1982), 8.

[53]Special Senate Committee on Retirement Age Policies, *Retirement Without Tears* (Ottawa: Minister of Supply and Services, 1979), 115.

[54]Fred Grayston, "Draft Statement: The Summary Position of the Group of Ten Plus 2," 17 October 1983.

CHAPTER 10

[1]Parts of this chapter appeared in *Winnipeg Magazine*, May 1981, under the title "Launching a Good Old Age," and, under the title "Discovering a Good Age," in *The International Journal of Aging and Human Development* 16, no. 3 (1983).

[2]Everett Shostrom, *Personal Orientation Inventory* (San Diego, California: Educational and Industrial Testing Service, 1963).

[3]Robert Knapp, *Handbook for the POI* (San Diego, California: EDITS, 1976), 2.

[4]Robert Butler, *Why Survive? Being Old in America* (New York: Harper and Row, 1975); E. Erikson, *Childhood and Society*, 2d ed. (New York: W.W. Norton, 1963); C.G. Jung, "The Stages of Life," in *The Portable Jung*, ed. Joseph Campbell and tr. R. Hull, 1933; Harmondsworth, England: Penguin, 1976); Bernice Neugarten, Robert Havighurst and Sheldon Tobin, "Personality and

Patterns of Aging,'' in Bernice Neugarten, ed., *Middle Age and Aging* (Chicago: University of Chicago Press, 1968).

[5] Jung, ''The Stages of Life,'' 109.

[6] Erikson, *Childhood and Society*, 268.

[7] Butler, *Why Survive?*, 400-401.

[8] Ernest Becker, *The Denial of Death* (1973: New York: Free Press, 1975), 82.

[9] *Ibid.*, 74.

[10] Zena Blau, *Old Age in a Changing Society* (New York: New Viewpoints, 1973), 185.

[11] Robert Havighurst, Bernice Neugarten and Sheldon Tobin, ''Disengagement and Patterns of Aging,'' in Neugarten, ed., *Middle Age and Aging*, 170-171.

[12] Blau, *Old Age*, 215.

[13] Alfred Schutz, *Collected Papers* 2d ed. (The Hague, Martinus Nijhoff, 1962) 1:247, 249.

[14] Carl Gustav Jung, ''The Stages of Life,'' in *Modern Man In Search of a Soul*, tr. W. Dell and Carey Baynes (New York: Harcourt, Brace and World, 1933), 104.

[15] *Ibid.*, 108.

[16] Marcel Proust, cited in Simone de Beauvoir, *Old Age* (1970; Harmondsworth, England: Penguin Books, 1978), 290.

[17] Arthur Miller, *Death of a Salesman*, (1949; New York: Viking Press, 1967), 14.

[18] Paul Tournier, *Learning to Grow Old* (London: SCM Press, 1972), 178.

[19] Paul Tillich, *The Courage to Be* (1952; London: Fontana Library, 1962).

[20] Tournier, *Learning*, 140-41.

[21] Martin Buber, *Meetings,* ed. Maurice Friedman (La Salle, Illinois: Open Court, 1973), 59-61.

[22] Warner Schaie, ''Adult Cognitive Development,'' *International Journal of Aging and Human Development,* 8, no. 2:135.

[23] Rollo May, *Love and Will* (New York: Dell, 1969), 229.

[24] *Ibid.*, 230.

[25] Victor Frankl, *The Doctor and the Soul*, Richard Winston and Clara Winston, tr. (New York: Alfred Knopf, 1957), x; and Victor Frankl, *The Will to Meaning* (New York: New American Library, 1970), 41.

BIBLIOGRAPHY

Achenbaum, W., *Images of Old Age in America — 1790 to Present* (Michigan: Institute of Gerontology, 1978).

Age and Opportunity, Incorporated, *Ad Hoc Institute Review Committee Report: Institute for Continuous Learning* (Winnipeg: 1980).

Age and Opportunity, Incorporated, *Working Arrangements Between Board, Staff, and Senior Centre Membership Organizations* (Winnipeg: Age and Opportunity, Inc., 1983).

Alberta Council on Aging, *Annual Report 1983-84* (Edmonton: ACA, 1984).

Amiel, Barbara, "Trouble in Tomorrowland," *Maclean's* 13 April 1981: 44-46.

Amster, Leslie, and H. Kraus, "The Relationship Between Life Crises and Mental Deterioration in Old Age," *International Journal of Aging and Human Development,* 5, no. 1, 1974: 51-55.

Arendt, Hannah, *The Human Condition* (Garden City, New York: Doubleday, Anchor, 1959).

Aristotle, *Rhetorica, The Basic Works of Aristotle* ed. Richard McKeon (New York: Random House, 1941).

Armstrong, Pat, and Hugh Armstrong, *The Double Ghetto* (Toronto: McClelland and Stewart, 1978).

Artibise, Alan, *Winnipeg: An Illustrated History* (Toronto: Lorimer, 1977).

Atchley, Robert, *Aging: Continuity and Change* (Belmont, California: Wadsworth, 1983).

Atchley, Robert, *The Social Forces in Later Life* 3d ed. (Belmont, California: Wadsworth, 1980).

Atchley, Robert, *The Sociology of Retirement* (New York: Schenkman, 1976.

Atchley, Robert, "The Meaning of Retirement," *Journal of Communications*, 24, 1974: 97-101.

Auerbach, Lewis, and A. Gerber, *Perceptions 2: Implications of the Changing Age Structure of the Canadian Population* (Ottawa: Supply and Services Canada, 1976).

Babin, Patrick, *Bias in Textbooks Regarding the Aged, Labour Unionists and Political Minorities* (Toronto: Ontario Ministry of Education, 1975).

Backley, Alan, "Social Policy Issues," in Blossom Wigdor and Louise Ford, eds., *Housing for an Aging Population: Alternatives* (Toronto: University of Toronto Press, 1981.)

Baltes, Paul, and K. Schaie, "Aging and IQ — Twilight Years", in Steven Zarit, ed., *Readings in Aging and Death: Contemporary Perspectives,* 2d ed. (New York: Harper and Row, 1982).

Barfield, Richard, *Early Retirement: The Decision and the Experience and a Second Look* (Ann Arbor, Michigan: Institute of Social Research, 1974).

Barfield, Richard, and James Morgan, *Early Retirement: The Decision and the Experience* (Ann Arbor, Michigan: University of Michigan, Institute of Social Research, 1969).

Baum, Daniel, *Warehouses for Death* (Toronto: Burns and MacEachern, 1977).

Becker, Ernest, *The Denial of Death* (New York: Free Press, 1975).

Begin, Monique, "The Aging Society: Implications for Federal Social Policy," notes for an address by the Hon. Monique Begin to the 1981 Thematic Seminar of the Regina Regional Group of the Institute of Public Administration of Canada, 2 March 1981.

Begin, Monique, "Notes for an Address by the Hon. Monique Begin at the Annual Conference of the Alberta Council on Aging," 29 May 1981.

Begin, Monique, "Notes for an Address by the Hon. Monique Begin to the National Pensioners and Senior Citizens Federation," presented in Lethbridge, Alberta, 25 September 1980.

Begin, Monique, "A Fair Deal from Private Pensions," notes for an address by the Hon. Monique Begin to the West Island Senior Citizens Enterprise, 2 May 1979.

Bennett, James, and Jacques Krasny, "Health Care in Canada," in David Coburn, Carl D'Arcy, Peter New and George Torrance, eds., *Health and*

Canadian Society. (Toronto: Fitzhenry and Whiteside, 1981).

Birren, James, ed., *Handbook of Aging and the Individual* (Chicago: University of Chicago Press, 1959).

Bixby, Lenore, "Retirement Patterns in the United States: Research and Policy Interaction," *Social Security Bulletin* 39, no. 8: 3-9.

Blau, Zena, *Old Age in a Changing Society* (New York: New Viewpoints, 1973).

Blythe, Ronald, *The View in Winter* (Harmondsworth, England: Penguin, 1979).

Botwinick, J., *Cognitive Processes in Maturity and Old Age* (New York: Springer, 1967).

Braudel, Fernand, *The Structure of Everyday Life* 1, Sian Reynolds, tr. (New York: Harper and Row, 1978).

Bromley, D., *The Psychology of Human Aging,* 2d ed. (Harmondsworth, England: Penguin, 1974).

Bronowski, Jacob, *The Ascent of Man* (London: BBC Publishing, 1976).

Bryden, Kenneth, *Old Age Pensions and Policy-Making in Canada* (Montreal: McGill-Queen's University Press, 1974).

Buber, Martin, *Meetings,* Maurice Friedman, ed. (La Salle, Illinois: Open Court, 1973).

Burkus, John, "Social Policy Issues," in Blossom Wigdor and Louise Ford, eds., *Housing for an Aging Population: Alternatives* (Toronto: University of Toronto Press, 1980).

Butler, Robert, "Age-Ism: Another Form of Bigotry," in Steven Zarit, ed., *Readings in Aging and Death: Contemporary Perspectives*, 2d ed. (New York: Harper and Row, 1982). pp. 185-187.

Butler, Robert, *Why Survive? Being Old in America* (New York: Harper & Row, 1975).

Butler, Robert, and Myrna Lewis, *Aging and Mental Health* (St. Louis: C.V. Mosby, 1973).

Canadian Association of University Teachers, "McIntire Ruling Makes Waves," *CAUT Bulletin*, 1981, no. 1: 1.

Canadian Council on Social Development, *Beyond Shelter* (Ottawa: CCSD, 1973).

Canadian Council on Social Development, *Statement on Retirement Policies* (Ottawa: CCSD, 1976).

Chan, Kwok, "Coping With Aging and Managing Self-Identity: The Social World of Elderly Chinese Women," in *Canadian Ethnic Studies*, XV, no. 3 (1983): 36-50.

Chappell, Neena, "Social Policy and the Elderly," in Victor Marshall, ed., *Aging in Canada* (Toronto: Fitzhenry and Whiteside, 1980).

Cheal, David, "Altruism and the Adult Life Cycle," paper presented at a seminar at the Center on Aging, University of Manitoba, 25 November 1983.

Cheal, David, "Intergenerational Family Transfers," *Journal of Marriage and the Family*, 45, no. 4 (1983): 805-813.

Clark, J., and N. Collishaw, *Canada's Older Population* (Ottawa: National Health and Welfare, 1975).

Clark, W., M. Devereaux and Z. Zsigmond, *The Class of 2001* (Ottawa: Statistics Canada, 1979).

Clemente, Frank, and Michael Kleiman, "Fear of Crime Among the Aged," *The Gerontologist*, 16 (1976): 207-210.

Comfort, Alex, *A Good Age* (New York: Simon and Schuster, 1976).

Community Care Services (Metropolitan Toronto), *A Brief to the Ontario Cabinet* (Toronto: Community Care Services, 1978).

Copp, Terry, *The Anatomy of Poverty* (Toronto: McClelland and Stewart, 1979).

Cousins, Norman, *Anatomy of an Illness as Perceived by the Patient* (New York: Norton, 1979).

Cox, H., and A. Bhak, "Symbolic Interaction and Retirement Adjustment: An Empirical Assessment," *International Journal of Aging and Human Development*, 9, no. 3: 279-86.

Crawford, L., and Jean Matlow, "Some Attitudes Toward Retirement Among Middle-aged Employees in a Longitudinal Study, 1959-1978," *Industrial Relations Quarterly Review*, 27, no. 4: 616-631.

Crawford, Lawrence, "New Ways — Old Ways," in Blossom Wigdor and Louise Ford, eds., *Housing for an Aging Population: Alternatives* (Toronto: University of Toronto Press, 1980).

Criminal Justice and the Elderly, "Elderly Duped No More Often, But Harmed More, by Consumer Fraud," *Criminal Justice and the Elderly Newsletter* Summer 1979: 3.

Cumming, Elaine, and W. Henry, *Growing Old: The Process of Disengagement* (New York: Basic Books, 1961).

Curtis, James, and Ronald Lambert, "Voting, Election Interest, and Age: National Findings for English and French Canadians," *Canadian Journal of Political Science*, 9, no. 2: 293-307.

de Beauvoir, Simone, *Old Age* (Harmondsworth, England: Penguin, 1978).

Delisle, Marc-André, "Elderly People's Management of Time and Leisure," *Canada's Mental Health*, 30, no. 3: 30-32.

de Grazia, Sebastian, *Of Time, Work and Leisure* (Garden City, New York: Anchor Books, 1964).

Demos, Vasilikie, and Ann Jache. "When You Care Enough: An Analysis of Attitudes Toward Aging in Humorous Birthday Cards," *The Gerontologist* 21, no. 2 (1981): 215-219.

Denton, Frank, "Canada's Population and Labour Force, Past, Present, and Future," in Victor Marshall, ed., *Aging in Canada* (Toronto: Fitzhenry and Whiteside, 1980).

Denton, Frank, and Byron Spencer, "Population Aging and Future Health Costs in Canada," *Canadian Public Policy* IX, no. 2 (1983): 155-163.

Denton, Frank, A. Leslie Robb, and Byron Spencer, *The Future Financing of the Canada and Quebec Pension Plans: Some Alternative Possibilities* (Ottawa: Minister of Supply and Services, 1980).

Department of the Secretary of State, *Citizens' Participation in Non-Worktime Activities* I (Ottawa: Citizenship Branch, Secretary of State, 1974).

Department of Social and Family Services, *Cultural Differences Among the Aged in Ontario* (Toronto: Department of Social and Family Services, 1969).

Dewar, Elaine, "Doctoring Medicine," *Today Magazine* 7 February 1981: 6-8.

De Vries, Herbert, "Physiology of Exercise and Aging," in Gari Lesnoff-Caravaglia, ed., *Health Care of the Elderly* (New York: Human Sciences Press, 1980).

Dubos, Rene, *Mirage of Health* (New York: Harper and Row, 1971).

Duffey, John, "Grey Power — Is It a Myth?," *Prime Time Magazine* 1, no. 3: 1.

Dulude, Louise, *Women and Aging: A Report on the Rest of Our Lives* (Ottawa: Advisory Council on the Status of Women, 1978).

Dumazedier, Joffre, "Cultural Mutations in Post-Industrial Societies," in *Leisure and the Third Age* (Paris: International Center of Social Gerontology, 1972).

Dychtwald, Ken, "Humanistic Services for the Elderly," *Journal of Humanistic Psychology* 21, no. 1: 39-56.

Dychtwald, Ken, "The SAGE Project . . . A New Image of Age," *Journal of Humanistic Psychology* 18, no. 2: 70-74.

Eagle, Edwin, "Seniors Think Tank," *Manitoba Seniors Journal* 5, no. 2: 6.

Eisdorfer, Carl, and J. Altrocchi, "A Comparison of Attitudes Toward Old Age and Mental Illness," *Journal of Gerontology* 16 (1961).

Elderhostel, *Annual Report 1981* (Boston: Elderhostel, 1981).

Elderhostel, *Annual Report 1982* (Boston: Elderhostel, 1982).

Elderhostel, *Summer Catalogue* (Boston: Elderhostel, 1983).

Environics Research Group, *Reaching the Retired: A Survey of the Media Habits, Preferences and Needs of Senior Citizens in Metro Toronto* (Montreal: Information Canada, 1974).

Erikson, Erik, *Childhood and Society*, 2d ed. (New York: W.W. Norton, 1963).

Fales, Ann, D. MacKeracher and D. Vigoda, *Contexts of Aging in Canada* (Toronto: OISE Press, 1981).

Fischer, David, *Growing Old in America* (Oxford: Oxford University Press, 1978).

Freidman, M., and R. Rosenman, *Type A Behavior and your Heart* (New York: Knopf, 1974).

Fozard, James, "The Time for Remembering," in Leonard Poon, ed., *Aging in the 1980's* (Washington, D.C.: American Psychological Association, 1980).

Francis, Diane, "Ottawa's Pension Blues: The Country's Largest Nest Egg Could Be Going Broke," *Quest Magazine*, May 1983: 14-18.

Frankl, Viktor, *The Will to Meaning* (New York: New American Library, 1970).

Frankl, Viktor, *The Doctor and the Soul*, Richard Winston and Clara Winston, tr. (New York: Alfred Knopf, 1957).

Fraser, D., *Defining the Parameters of a Housing Policy for the Elderly* (Ottawa: Canada Mortgage and Housing Corporation, 1982).

Gantz, W., H. Gartenberg, and C. Rainbow, "Approaching Invisibility: The Portrayal of The Elderly in Magazine Advertising," *Journal of Communications*, 30, no. 1 (1980): 56-60.

Gelba, Bruno, "Creating a Human Bond," in Steven Zarit, ed., *Readings in Aging and Death* (New York: Harper and Row, 1977).

Gerber, Linda, "Ethnicity Still Matters: Socio-Demographic Profiles of the Ethnic Elderly in Ontario," *Canadian Ethnic Studies*, XV, no. 3 (1983): 60-80.

Gerbner, G., L. Gross, N. Signorell and M. Morgan, "Aging with Television: Images on Television Drama and Conceptions of Social Reality," *Journal of Communications* 30, no. 1 (1980): 37-47.

Giambra, Leonard, and David Arenberg, "Problem Solving, Concept and Learning and Aging," in Leonard Poon, ed., *Aging in the 1980's* (Washington, D.C.: American Psychological Association, 1980).

Gifford, C., "Senior Politics," *Policy Options*, September 1983: 12-15.

Gifford, C., "Senior Power in Canada," poster presentation typescript, presented at the Canadian Association of Gerontology Meetings (Winnipeg: November 1982).

Gifford, C., "Social Characteristics of Seniors' Organization Leaders in Canada," paper presented at the Canadian Association of Gerontology Meetings (Winnipeg: November 1982).

Green, Susan, "Attitudes and Perceptions About the Elderly: Current and Future Perspectives," *International Journal of Aging and Human Development* 13, no. 2 (1981): 99-119.

Ronald Gross, Beatrice Gross, and Sylvia Seidman, eds., *The New Old* (Garden City, New York: Anchor, 1978).

Gutman, Gloria, *The Long Term Impact of Multi-Level, Multi-Service Accommodation For Seniors*, Senior Citizen Housing Study Report no. 3 (Ottawa: Canada Mortgage and Housing Corporations, 1983).

Gutman, Gloria, "Issues and Findings Relating to Multi-Level Accommodations for Seniors," *Journal of Gerontology*, 33 (1978): 592-600.

Hancock, Gordon, *A Study of Gerontological Activities and Centres of Gerontology on University Campuses in the U.S. and Canada* (Winnipeg: Centre on Aging, University of Manitoba, 1983).

Hapgood, David, "The Aging Are Doing Better" in Ronald Gross, Beatrice Gross and Sylvia Seidman, eds., *The New Old* (Garden City, New York: Anchor Press, 1978).

Harris, Louis, et al., *Aging in the Eighties: America in Transition* (Washington, D.C.: National Council on Aging, 1981).

Harris, Louis, *Myth and Reality of Aging in America* (Washington, D.C.: National Council on Aging, 1975).

Havens, Betty, "Differentiation of Unmet Needs Using Analysis by Age/Sex Cohorts," in Victor Marshall, ed., *Aging in Canada* (Toronto: Fitzhenry and Whiteside, 1980).

Havighurst, Robert, Bernice Neugarten and Sheldon Tobin, "Disengagement and Patterns of Aging," in Bernice Neugarten, ed., *Middle Age and Aging* (Chicago: University of Chicago Press, 1968).

Haynes, Suzanne, A. McMichael and H. Tyroler, "Survival after Early and Normal Retirement," *Journal of Gerontology* 33 (1978): 269-278.

Health and Welfare Canada, *Better Pensions for Canadians: Focus on Women* (Ottawa: Minister of Supply and Services, 1982).

Health and Welfare Canada. *Better Pensions for Canadians: Highlights* (Ottawa: Minister of Supply and Services, 1982).

Health and Welfare Canada, *Canada Pension Plan: Report for the Year Ending March 31, 1982* (Ottawa: Minister of Supply and Services, 1983).

Health and Welfare Canada, *Canadian Governmental Report on Aging* (Ottawa: Minister of Supply and Services, 1982).

Health and Welfare Canada, *Fact Book on Aging in Canada* (Ottawa: Minister of Supply and Services, 1983).

Health and Welfare Canada, *The Health of Canadians* (Ottawa: Minister of Supply and Services Canada, 1981).

Health and Welfare Canada, *The Incomes of Elderly Canadians in 1975*, Social Security Research Report no. 6 (Ottawa: Policy Research and Strategic Planning Branch, February, 1979).

Health and Welfare Canada, *New Horizons: The First Decade* (Ottawa: Minister of Supply and Services, 1982).

Health and Welfare Canada, *Retirement Age* (Ottawa: Minister of Supply and Services, 1979).

Health and Welfare Canada, *Retirement Ages* (Ottawa: Minister of Supply and Services, 1980).

Heidbreder, Elizabeth, "Factors in Retirement Adjustment: White Collar/Blue Collar Experience," *Industrial Gerontology*, 12 (1972): 69-79.

Hendricks, Jon, and C. Davis Hendricks, *Aging in Mass Society*, 2d ed. (Cambridge, Massachusetts: Winthrop Publishers, 1981).

Hickey, T., and R. Kalish, "Young People's Perceptions of Adults," *Journal of Gerontology*, 23 (1968): 215-219.

Hickey, Tom, L. Hickey and R. Kalish, "Children's Perceptions of the Elderly," *Journal of Genetic Psychology*, 112 (1968): 227-235.

Hobart, C., "Active Sports Participation among the Young, the Middle-aged and the Elderly," *International Review of Sport Sociology*, 10, no. 3-4: 27-40.

Hoffman, Joan. "Care of the Unwanted: Stroke Patients in a Canadian Hospital," in D. Coburn, C. D'Arcy, P. New, and G. Torrance, *Health and Canadian Society: Sociological Perspectives* (Toronto: Fitzhenry and Whiteside, 1980).

Hughes, W., "Alzheimer's Disease," in E. Wright, J. Spink, W. Andrew et al., *Brain Structure and Aging* (New York: MSS Information, 1974).

Illich, Ivan, *Limits to Medicine* (Harmondsworth, England: Penguin, 1976).

Illich, Ivan, *Tools for Conviviality* (New York: Harper and Row, 1973).

Jung, Carl, "The Stages of Life," in Joseph Campbell, ed., *The Portable Jung* (Harmondsworth, England: Penguin, 1976).

Jung, Carl, "The Stages of Life," in *Modern Man In Search of a Soul*, W. Dell and C. Baynes, tr. (New York: Harcourt, Brace and World, 1933).

Kahn, Robert, "Excess Disabilities in the Aged," in Steven Zarit, ed., *Readings in Aging and Death: Contemporary Perspectives* (New York: Harper and Row, 1977).

Kalbach, Warren, and Wayne McVey, *The Demographic Bases of Canadian Society* 2d ed. (Toronto: McGraw-Hill Ryerson, 1979).

Kaplan, M., *Leisure: Lifestyles and Lifespan* (Philadelphia: W.B. Saunders, 1979).

Kastenbaum, Robert, and N. Durkee, "Young People View Old Age," in R. Kastenbaum, ed., *New Thoughts on Old Age* (New York: Springer, 1964).

Kellogg, Mary Alice, and Andres Jaffee, "Old Folks Commune," in Steven Zarit, ed., *Readings in Aging and Death: Contemporary Perspectives* (New York: Harper and Row, 1977).

Kernaghan, Kenneth, "Politics, Public Administration and Canada's Aging Population," *Canadian Public Policy* VIII, no. 1: 69-79.

Kettle, John, *The Big Generation* (Toronto: McClelland and Stewart, 1980).

Kidd, J.R., *How Adults Learn* (New York: Association Press, 1973).

Kloosterman, Gayle, "Educational Hosteling: Elderhostel," *Perspective on Aging* May/June 1977: 18-20.

Knapp, Robert, *Handbook for the POI* (San Diego, California: EDITS, 1976).

Koenig, Daniel, C. Doyle and P. Debeck, *The Golden Years in British Columbia: How They are Seen by Senior Citizens* (Victoria: B.C.: Department of Human Resources, Province of British Columbia, 1977).

Kubat, Daniel, and D. Thornton, *A Statistical Profile of Canadian Society* (Toronto: McGraw-Hill Ryerson, 1974).

Kuhn, Margaret, "Learning by Living," *International Journal of Aging and Human Development,* 8, no. 4 (1977): 359-365.

Kuhn, Margaret, "What Old People Want for Themselves and Others in Society," in Paul Kerschner, ed., *Advocacy and Age* (Los Angeles: University of California Press, 1976).

La Franboise, Gosette, *A Question of Need* (Ottawa: Canadian Council on Social Development, 1975).

Laing, Lory, and P. Krishman, "First Marriage Decrement Tables for Males and Females in Canada 1961-1966," *Canadian Review of Sociology and Anthropology* 13, no. 2 (1976): 218-225.

Lalonde, Marc, *A New Perspective on the Health of Canadians* (Ottawa: Department of National Health and Welfare, 1974).

LaPlante, Marc, "Leisure in Canada by 1980," Proceedings of the Montmorency Conference on Leisure, *Leisure in Canada* (Ottawa: Information Canada, 1969).

Leacy, F., ed., *Historical Statistics of Canada,* 2d ed. (Ottawa: Minister of Supply and Services, 1983).

Luce, Gary, *Your Second Life* (New York: Delacorte Press, 1979).

McKeown, Thomas, *The Role of Medicine: Dream, Image or Nemesis?* (Princeton, N.J.: Princeton University Press, 1979).

McPherson, Barry, *Aging as a Social Process* (Toronto: Butterworth, 1983).

McPherson, Barry, and Carol Kozlik, "Canadian Leisure Patterns: Disengagement, Continuity of Ageism," in Victor Marshall, ed., *Aging in Canada* (Toronto: Fitzhenry and Whiteside, 1980). pp. 113-122.

McWhinnie, John, and B. Ouellet, "Health Trends," in David Coburn, C. D'Arcy, P. New and G. Torrance, *Health and Canadian Society: Sociological Perspectives* (Toronto: Fitzhenry and Whiteside, 1980).

Manitoba Council on Aging *Report of the Manitoba Council on Aging* (Winnipeg: MCA, 1981).

Markus, N., "Home Care for the Aged," in *On Growing Old,* 12 (February 1974): 1-8.

Marshall, Victor, and Joseph Tindale, "A Generational Conflict Perspective for Gerontology," in Victor Marshall, ed., *Aging in Canada* (Toronto: Fitzhenry and Whiteside, 1980).

Martin, S.W., *Health Care for the Aged* (Toronto: Ontario Council of Health, 1978).

Masters, W., and V. Johnson, *Human Sexual Response* (Boston: Little, Brown, 1966).

May, Rollo, *Love and Will* (New York: Dell, 1969).

Miller, Harriet, "Flexible Retirement — Will Sweden Make It Work?" in Steven Zarit, ed., *Readings in Aging and Death: Contemporary Perspectives* (New York: Harper and Row, 1977).

Milton, B., *Social Status and Leisure Time Activities: National Survey Findings for Adult Canadians,* Monograph 3 (Montreal: Canadian Sociology and Anthropology Associates, 1975).

Miron, John, "Household Formation among the Elderly," in Blossom Wigdor and Louise Ford, eds., *Housing for an Aging Population: Alternatives* (Toronto: University of Toronto Press, 1981).

Mishler, William, *Political Participation in Canada* (Toronto: Macmillan of Canada, 1979).

Morse, Dean, and Susan Gray, *Early Retirement — Boon or Bane?* (Montclair, New Jersey: Alanheld, Osmund, 1980).

Murphy, Edmund, and D. Nagnur, "A Gomperz Fit that Fits: Applications to Canadian Fertility Patterns," *Demography* 9, no. 1 (1972): 35-50.

Myles, John, "Some Implications of a Changing Age Structure," in Gloria Gutman, ed., *Canada's Changing Age Structure: Implications for the Future* (Burnaby, B.C.: SFU Publications, 1982).

Myles, John, and Monica Boyd, "Population Aging and the Elderly," in Dennis Forcese and Stephen Richer, eds., *Social Issues* (Scarborough, Ontario: Prentice-Hall Canada, 1982).

National Advisory Council on Aging, *Priorities for Action* (Ottawa: NACA, 1981).

National Center for Health Statistics, *Health Characteristics of Persons with Chronic Activity Limitation*, Series 10, no. 112 (Washington, USGPO, 1974).

National Council of Welfare, *1984 Poverty Lines* (Ottawa: Minister of Supply and Services, 1984).

National Council of Welfare, *Financing the Canada Pension Plan* (Ottawa: NCW, 1982).

National Council of Welfare, *Measuring Poverty: 1981 Poverty Lines* (Ottawa: NCW, 1981).

National Council of Welfare, *A Pension Primer* (Ottawa: Minister of Supply and Services, April 1984).

National Council of Welfare, *Poverty in Canada* (Ottawa: NCW, 1982).

National Council of Welfare, *Women and Poverty* (Ottawa: NCW, 1979).

National Council of Women of Canada, *The Financial Situation of Older Women: A Study Guide* (Ottawa: National Council of Women, 1978).

Neugarten, Bernice, "Acting One's Age: New Rules for Old," *Psychology Today* April 1980: 66-80.

Neugarten, Bernice, ed., "Aging in the Year 2000: A Look at the Future," *The Gerontologist* 15, no. 1 (1975): 4-9.

Neugarten, Bernice, Robert Havighurst and Sheldon Tobin, "Personality and Patterns of Aging," in Bernice Neugarten, ed., *Middle Age and Aging* (Chicago: University of Chicago Press, 1968).

Northcott, Herbert, "The Best Years of Your Life," *Canadian Journal on Aging* 1, no. 3-4 (1982).

Novak, Mark, "Discovering a Good Age," *The International Journal of Aging and Human Development* 16, no. 3 (1983): 231-239.

Novak, Mark, "Launching a Good Old Age," *Winnipeg Magazine* May 1981: 23-35.

Ontario Advisory Council on Aging, *Seniors Tell All* (Toronto: Ontario Advisory Council on Aging, 1980).

Ontario Advisory Council on Aging, *Through the Eyes of Others* (Toronto: Ontario Advisory Council on Aging, 1978).

Ontario Ministry of Health, *Annual Report* (Toronto: Ontario Ministry of Health, 1983).

Ontario Welfare Council, *Alternatives to Institutional Residential Care for Seniors* (Toronto: Ontario Welfare Council, 1977).

Orris, Milton, *Factors Which Contribute to the Social and Economic Independence of People Over 60* (Saskatoon: Joint Advisory Committee on Aging, 1970).

Ostfeld, Adrian, and D. Gibson, ed., *Epidemiology of Aging* (Maryland: Department of Health, Education and Welfare, 1972).

Palmore, Erdman, "Facts on Aging," in Steven Zarit, ed., *Readings in Aging and Death: Contemporary Perspectives*, 2d ed. (New York: Harper and Row, 1982).

Palmore, Erdman, "Facts on Aging: A Short Quiz," *The Gerontologist*, 17, no. 4 (1977): 315-320.

Parks Canada, "Trends in Participation in Outdoor Recreational Activities,"

CORD Technical Note no. 22 (Ottawa: National and Historic Parks Branch, Parks Canada, 1973).

Payne, Cheryl, and Wayne Bona, "Dartmouth S.H.A.R.E. — Senior Housing at Reduced Expense," from abstract of paper presented at the Canadian Association of Gerontology Meetings, 1984.

Pension Commission of Manitoba, "Amendments to the Manitoba Pension Benefits Act," *Information Circular, Special Bulletin* (Winnipeg: PCM, 1983).

Pesando, James, *The Elimination of Mandatory Retirement: An Economic Perspective* (Toronto: Ontario Economic Council, 1979).

Peters, Thomas, and Robert Waterman, *In Search of Excellence: Lessons from America's Best Run Companies* (New York: Harper and Row, 1982).

Peterson, David, "Life-Span Education and Gerontology," *The Gerontologist*, 15 (1975): 436-441.

Powell, Carol, "SAGE — Reshaping Attitudes about Aging," *Second Spring* August/September 1978: 3-7.

Pross, A., "Canadian Pressure Groups in the 1970s: Their Role and Their Relations with the Public Service," *Canadian Public Administration*, 18 (Spring 1975): 121-135.

Puner, Morton, *Vital Maturity* (New York: Universe Books, 1979).

Quinn, Jane Bryant, "On Reverse Mortgages," *Newsweek*, 30 March 1981: 75.

Rapelje, Douglas, "Alternatives: How Do We Make Them Happen?" in Blossom Widgor and Louise Ford, eds., *Housing for an Aging Population: Alternatives* (Toronto: University of Toronto Press, 1981).

Rapelje, Douglas, "Home Sharing," from abstract of paper presented at the Canadian Association of Gerontology Meetings, 1984.

Riley, Matilda, and A. Foner, *Aging and Society, Volume One* (New York: Russell Sage, 1968).

Rooney, Andrew, "Saturday Mornings With the White House Staff," in *And More by Andy Rooney* (New York: Atheneum, 1982).

Rose, Albert, "Social Policy Issues for Housing and Aging Population," in Blossom Wigdor and Louise Ford, eds., *Housing for an Aging Population: Alternatives* (Toronto: University of Toronto Press, 1981).

Rosenthal, Robert, and Lenore Jacobson, *Pygmalion in The Classroom* (New York: Holt, Rinehart and Winston, 1968).

Rosenwaike, Ira, N. Yaffe and P. Sagi, "The Recent Decline in Mortality of the

Extreme Aged: An Analysis of Statistical Data," *American Journal of Public Health*, 70 (1980): 1074-1080.

Ross, Val, "The Coming Old Age Crisis," *Maclean's* 17 January 1983: 24-29.

Salas, Rafael, "Aging: A Universal Phenomenon," *Populi* 9, no. 4 (1982): 3-7.

SAGE, *A Workshop in Successful Aging* (Berkeley, California: SAGE, undated).

Schaie, Warner, "Toward a Stage Theory of Adult Cognitive Development," *International Journal of Aging and Human Development* 8, no. 2 (1977-78): 129-138.

Schliewen, Rolf, *A Leisure Study — Canada 1975* (Ottawa: Minister of Supply and Services, 1977).

Schulz, James, *The Economics of Aging* (Belmont, California: Wadsworth, 1976).

Schulz, James, *The Economics of Aging*, 2d ed. (Belmont, California: Wadsworth, 1980).

Schutz, Alfred, *Collected Papers, Volume I* (The Hague: Martinus Nijhoff, 1962).

Schwenger, Cope, and J. Gross, "Institutional Care and Institutionalization of the Elderly in Canada," in Victor Marshall, ed., *Aging in Canada* (Toronto: Fitzhenry and Whiteside, 1980).

Seefeldt, Carol, R. Jantz, A. Galper and K. Serock, "Using Pictures to Explore Children's Attitudes Towards the Elderly," *The Gerontologist* 17 (1977): 506-512.

Segall, Mary, *Report of the Personal Growth Explorations Groups* (Winnipeg: Creative Retirement Manitoba, 1983).

Selles, Rein, "Maggie Kuhn: Portrait of an Elder Advocate," *Foresight* 1, no. 2: 33-35.

Seltzer, M., and R. Atchley, "The Concept of Old: Changing Attitudes and Stereotypes," *The Gerontologist* 11 (1971): 226-230.

Shanas, Ethel, "The Status of Health Care for the Elderly," in Gari Lesnoff-Caravaglia, ed., *Health Care of the Elderly* (New York: Human Sciences Press, 1980).

Sheppard, Harold, and S. Rix, *The Graying of Working America: The Coming Crisis in Retirement-Age Policy* (New York: Free Press, 1977).

Shostrom, Everett, *Personal Orientation Inventory* (San Diego, California: Educational and Industrial Testing Service, 1963).

Siegle, Peter, "The Adult Learner," *Adult Leadership* 3, no. 9, 16-18.

Smith, Wendy, *Single Old Men on Main Street: An Evaluation of Jack's Hotel* (Winnipeg: Canada Mortgage and Housing Corporation, 1979).

Special Senate Committee on Retirement Age Policies, *Retirement Without Tears* (Hull, Quebec: Canadian Government Publishing Centre, 1979).

Statistics Canada, *Canada Update* (Ottawa: Minister of Supply and Services, 1983).

Statistics Canada, *Canada Year Book 1980-81* (Ottawa: Minister of Supply and Services, 1981).

Statistics Canada, *Canada's Elderly* (Ottawa: Minister of Supply and Services, 1979).

Statistics Canada, *Culture Statistics 1976, Recreational Activities* no. 87-5010 (Ottawa: Ministry of Industry, Trade and Commerce, 1978).

Statistics Canada, *The Elderly in Canada* (Ottawa: Minister of Supply and Services, 1984).

Statistics Canada, *Perspective on Health*, no. 82-540E (Ottawa: Minister of Supply and Services, 1983).

Statistics Canada, *Perspectives Canada: A Compendium of Social Statistics* (Ottawa: Information Canada, 1974).

Statistics Canada, *Perspectives Canada II* (Ottawa: Minister of Supply and Services, 1977).

Statistics Canada, *Perspectives Canada III* (Ottawa: Minister of Supply and Services, 1980).

Statistics Canada, *Population Projections for Canada and the Provinces, 1976-2001* 91-520 (Occasional) (Ottawa: Minister of Supply and Services, 1983).

Statistics Canada, *Technical Report on Population Projections for Canada and the Provinces: 1972-2001* 91-516 (Occasional) (Ottawa: Minister of Supply and Services, 1983).

Statistics Canada, *Vital Statistics, Volume I: Births and Deaths* no. 84-203 and 204 (Annual) (Ottawa: Minister of Supply and Services, 1983).

Stone, Leroy, "Some Issues regarding Housing Design and Affordability Arising from the Living Arrangements of Canada's Senior Citizens," in Blossom Wigdor and Louise Ford, eds., *Housing For an Aging Population: Alternatives* (Toronto: University of Toronto Press, 1981).

Stone, Leroy, and M. MacLean, *Future Income Prospects for Canada's Senior Citizens* (Toronto: Butterworth, 1979).

Stone, Leroy, and M. MacLean, *Future Income Prospects for Canada's Senior Citizens* (Toronto: Butterworths, 1979).

Strauss, Harold, Bruce Aldrich and Aron Lipman, "Retirement and Perceived Status Loss: An Inquiry into Some Objective and Subjective Problems Produced by Aging," in Jaber Gubrium, ed., *Time, Roles and Self in Old Age* (New York: Human Sciences Press, 1976).

Streib, Gordon, and Clement Schneider, *Retirement in American Society* (Ithaca, N.Y.: Cornell University Press, 1971).

Task Force on Retirement Income Policy, *The Retirement Income System in Canada: Problems and Alternative Policies for Reform, Volume I* (Ottawa: Minister of Supply and Services, 1980).

Thomas, Lewis, *The Lives of a Cell* (New York: Bantam, 1974).

Thomas, Lewis, "Medicine Without Science," *The Atlantic* April 1981: 40-42.

Thomas, Lewis, *The Medusa and the Snail* (New York: Viking, 1974).

Thomas, E., and K. Yamamoto, "Attitudes toward Age: An Exploration in School Age Children," *International Journal of Aging and Human Development* 6, no. 2 (1975): 117-129.

Thomas, William, "The Expectation Gap and the Stereotype of the Stereotype: Images of Old People," *The Gerontologist*, 21, no. 4 (1981): 402-407.

Tillich, Paul, *The Courage to Be* (London: Fontana Library, 1962).

Tindale, J., "Identity Maintenance Processes of Old Poor Men," in Victor Marshall, ed., *Aging in Canada* (Toronto: Fitzhenry and Whiteside, 1980).

Tobin, Jordan, "Normal Aging — The Inevitability Syndrome," in Steven Zarit, ed., *Readings in Aging and Death: Contemporary Perspectives* 1st ed. (New York: Harper and Row, 1977).

Toronto Planning Board, *Report on Skid Row* (Toronto: Report of the Research and Overall Planning Division, November 1977).

Torrance, George, "Introduction: Socio-Historical Overview: The Development of the Canadian Health System," in D. Coburn, C. D'Arcy, P. New and G. Torrance, eds., *Health and Canadian Society: Sociological Perspectives* (Toronto: Fitzhenry and Whiteside, 1981).

Tournier, Paul, *Learning to Grow Old* (London: SCM Press, 1972).

Trela, James, "Status Inconsistency and Political Action in Old Age," in Jaber Gubrium, ed., *Time, Roles, and Self in Old Age* (New York: Human Sciences Press, 1976).

Weaver, Howard, Margaret McPhee, and Paul Lambert, *Geriatrics Reports* (Vancouver: Regional Hospital District, 1975).

White House Conference on Aging, "Background Paper on Research in Gerontological and Social Sciences" (Washington: U.S. Government Printing Office, 1960).

Wilder, Joseph, *Lotions, Potions and Liniments Pure* (Winnipeg: Prairie Publishing, 1982).

Wilson, L., *Programs for the Aged in Europe* (Ottawa: Health and Welfare Canada, 1971).

Woodard, J., "Alzheimer's Disease in Later Adult Life," *The American Journal of Pathology*, 49 (1966): 1157-1165.

Yin, R., "Fear of Crime among the Elderly: Some Issues and Suggestions," *Social Problems*, 27, no. 4 (1980): 492-504.

Zsigmond, Z., W. Clark and M. Devereaux, *Out of School into the Labour Force: A Summary of Findings* (Ottawa: Statistics Canada, 1979).

OTHER SOURCES

WHEN I FIRST looked at the literature on aging I found a mountain of research reports, books and texts. A list of sources in *The Journal of Gerontology* alone ran to 40 pages with 30 sources to a page — 1200 sources in all — and that was only a list for a three month period. It included books, doctoral dissertations, government reports, articles and book reviews, and the journal warned that its list was incomplete. I would have to read 40 sources a day just to keep up with the latest writings in the field, and that would only get me ready for the new list in the next issue. I felt depressed and confused. Where should I begin?

To help you avoid this confusion I suggest here a few of the most current, accurate, stimulating, informative and *readable* sources I know. Not a complete list by any means, but if you browse through these sources you'll come across excerpts from other good writings on aging. You can then choose the works that appeal to you most and track them down for a closer look.

General

These books discuss aging in general — not specifically aging in Canada.

Alex Comfort. *A Good Age*. New York: Simon and Schuster, 1976.

> Although Comfort is best known for the *Joy of Sex*, he was a gerontologist before he became a sexologist. This book gives advice and information on a variety of topics from ageism to wrinkles. Comfort arranged the topics alphabetically for easy reference. In the margins of the text, Comfort includes a series of beautiful aquatint portraits of familiar older people — May West, Arthur Rubenstein, Grandma Moses, Charles de Gaulle. Easy to read, caustic and witty. One of the best general books on the market. Something you'll want to pass on to others after you've read it.

Steven H. Zarit, ed. *Readings in Aging and Death: Contemporary Perspectives.* 2d ed. New York: Harper and Row, 1982.

Zarit designed this as a reader for college students. All of the readings would however appeal also to non-academic readers who want to know more about aging. I've even known students to read articles I didn't assign. Some of the articles come from magazines, and Zarit has included pictures and cartoons to break up the text. Most people say they enjoy the articles about the long-lived people of the Caucasus, about sex and the single grandparent and about life after death.

Ronald Gross, Beatrice Gross and Sylvia Seidman, eds. *The New Old.* New York: Anchor Press, 1978.

Upbeat readings on a range of topics. Gerontologists like Bernice Neugarten have written some of these pieces. Others come from older people themselves. There are pieces by Maggie Kuhn and U.S. Senator Charles Percy and excerpts from Shura Saul's wonderful book *Aging: An Album of People Growing Old.* The book also contains lists of programs run for and by older people. It has a list of books, magazines and organizations you can write to. The book is a little dated and not at all Canadian. It may be hard to get. Still, like the Zarit reader, it's a lively smorgasbord of writings on old age.

Simone de Beauvoir. *Old Age.* Harmondsworth, England: Penguin, 1977.

A classic. The author traces the way writers have treated old age from antiquity to the present, and concludes that older people have received worse treatment as time has gone by. Today old people get little respect. Her sociological facts are out of date and somewhat biased. Still, she gives one of the best reviews of world literature on aging.

Ronald Blythe. *The View in Winter.* Harmondsworth, England: Penguin, 1980.

The title hints at the book's slant, the sorrow of old age. Like de Beauvoir, Blythe reviews literary sources to learn about old age. He finds it a tragic time. He reports how older people in England age today, by presenting accounts of aging by the older people in their own words. These priceless stories make old age come alive as a time of joy and fulfilment as well as sorrow.

The Gerontologist
The Journal of Gerontology
The International Journal of Aging and Human Development

These three journals focus exclusively on the elderly. They print high-quality articles and the most up-to-date research reports. Not light reading, but a must for anyone doing research on aging.

Canadian Sources

Victor Marshall, ed. *Aging in Canada*. Toronto: Fitzhenry and Whiteside, 1980.

    The first Canadian reader on aging. A collection of scholarly articles on subjects ranging from income to age dependency, health care to housing. Again, not light reading, but a good research source. Some of the articles are getting dated, but here you'll find the names of the best-known gerontologists in the country. You can get their more recent work by writing to them. You'll also find a bibliography at the back that will put you on to more sources.

Gloria Gutman, ed. *Canada's Changing Age Structure*. Burnaby, B.C.: Simon Fraser Publications, 1981.

    Papers from a research symposium held at Simon Fraser University in August 1981. Many of these same writers appear in Marshall, although this book has more up-to-date information. Again, the papers have a scholarly tone; they'll appeal mostly to readers doing research on aging.

Blossom Wigdor, ed. *Canadian Gerontology Collection, Vols. I, II and III*. Winnipeg: Canadian Association of Gerontology, 1981.

    Collections of papers presented at the sixth through ninth meetings of the Canadian Association of Gerontology (1977 to 1980). Not all Canadian content, although the brightest stars in the Canadian gerontological galaxy appear. This is a collection of scholarly writings best used as a starting point for serious research. The CAG plans a fourth volume for the Spring of 1984. The CAG also puts out proceedings of special meetings, a directory of research in Canada and a current bibliography of Canadian sources on aging. Write for a list of publications. (See Appendix for address.).

The Canadian Journal on Aging (Canadian Association of Gerontology)

    Articles in this journal deal with the biology, health, psychology, sociology and social welfare of aging. This journal started in 1981, replacing *Essence*, a journal that dealt with aging and death and dying. University libraries will probably have the new *Canadian Journal on Aging* and back issues of *Essence*.

Government Sources

Statistics Canada

    Statistics Canada, the best single source of research information in the country, puts out a steady stream of reports based on census data and other surveys. The reports break the population down by age, so, on almost any topic, you can see how older people compare with other age groups. University libraries usually carry the full line of Stats Can publications.

The reference librarian will help you find reports on the topics you want to study. He or she will show you how the library files Stats Can reports and how you can look them up. Once you learn how, it's easy. Then you can browse through the files on your own. You'll get the most up-to-date information from these sources. And if you're doing a report for school, work or a community group, you'll impress your reader with hard, accurate figures.

Stats Can also puts out special reports on aging. These reports give summaries of census data that would take the average person months to compile.

The Elderly in Canada. Ottawa: Statistics Canada, 1984.

This most recent summary report on aging in Canada is based on the 1981 Census. It gives figures, graphs and an easy-to-read summary of topics like population aging in Canada, housing, ethnicity and marital status. Not as dry as it sounds and much easier to use than the massive census reports themselves, it is a good quick source of accurate figures. Stats Can offices have this and other reports. Or you can order it by mail from Publication Sales and Services, Statistics Canada, Ottawa, Ontario, K1A 0T6. You can also call Stats Can toll-free from anywhere in the country. Check your phone book or call information.

Health and Social Welfare Canada. *Fact Book on Aging in Canada*. Ottawa: Minister of Supply and Services Canada, 1983.

Printed for the Second Canadian Conference on Aging in 1983. It gives more facts than *The Elderly in Canada* and it uses more sources, including the Canada Health Survey, the National Nutrition Survey and the Labour Force Survey. This is a helpful book, easy to read and use. Check here first if you're writing something or giving a talk on aging.

National Advisory Council on Aging, *Writings in Gerontology*.

A series of reports put out by the National Advisory Council. The Council has taken professional papers or reports and reworked them for easy reading. Titles so far include, "The Economic Impact of Canada's Retirement Income System," "Family Role and the Negotiation of Change for the Aged," "Aging: Live and Let Live" and "Coping and Helping with Alzheimer's Disease." The Council plans to put out more reports in the future and will send you these and any future reports for free (we pay for them with our taxes). Just write to the National Advisory Council on Aging (see Appendix for address). You might also ask for their annual reports and any other reports they put out. Have them put your name on their mailing list.

National Council of Welfare. *Sixty-five and Older*. Ottawa: Minister of Supply and Services, 1984.

A close look at the income of Canada's elderly. Like all of the Council of

Welfare's papers, this one is well-researched, well-written, and makes the point that we need to do more for our older people. It's hard to praise the Council of Welfare's studies enough. A look at their 1982 study *Financing the Canada Pension Plan* will make you a believer too. It's the most readable report on the Canada pension plan anywhere and well worth a look if you're trying to understand pensions in Canada.

The Council of Welfare also puts out a *Pension Primer*. No doubt they are preparing other reports. For free copies, write to The National Council of Welfare (see Appendix for address). Be sure to get on their mailing list. That way you'll get all the latest reports as they come out.

These reports, and the others I mentioned before, all refer to other studies, and those refer to still more. Use each report as a guide to more information on a subject. Check the footnotes and reference lists for other useful sources. You can get a lot of government information for free and you can get it quickly at almost any university library. Provincial sources of data are also very useful.

Government of Manitoba. *Aging in Manitoba.* 1971, 1976, 1983.

A classic series of studies of aging in Manitoba. Betty Havens, former president of the Canadian Association of Gerontology and now Provincial Gerontologist of Manitoba, directed these studies. They give an overview of social services for the older people. The first report came out in 1971 in ten volumes, and focuses on older people's health and health needs. It also looks at topics like transportation and life satisfaction. It's become world famous for its accuracy and the breadth of questions it asks and answers.

In 1976 the province collected a second smaller sample of data. In 1983 the province redid the first survey with changes and improvements. These studies allow researchers to look at changes in the older population over a 12-year period. The first reports from the 1983 study should be out soon. Contact the office of the Provincial Gerontologist of Manitoba for more information about the study (see Appendix for address).

Other provinces also produce reports on older people. A talk with someone who does research for your province's department of health and social welfare should put you on to local sources. If you have a special question on a topic like housing, then go to that government office — provincial or federal. CMHC for instance, puts out and keeps track of studies on housing. Many of those studies discuss the needs of older people.

The Greatest Resource of All: People

One thing I've found — from the first day I started studying aging ten years ago to the last few days when I've been finishing up this book — there's no more enjoyable way to learn about aging than by talking to people who work in the field. People who work with and for the elderly are the most generous people in the world. They'll help you track down a source, they will pile your arms high with reports, papers and bibliographies. They will always take time to talk to you and answer your questions. Don't be afraid to ask.

Most of us in the field of aging love to talk about our work, and some of what you'll learn from experts in your talks, you can't learn any other way. As a bonus they will send you away with a touch of the enthusiasm they all feel for working with and for older people.

One last source. In my view, the best sources of all are older people themselves. I never would have started my work, if the older people I met hadn't been so friendly and open. They seemed to have escaped the ''I can't be bothered'' or ''what are you really after'' attitude some people take toward researchers. Talk to them. Let them tell you what it's like to be old. It's not the only way to learn about aging, but its surely the most fun.

Contemporary Family Issues

OTHER TITLES IN THIS SERIES

THE CHILD CARE CRISIS
The real costs of day care
for you—and your child
Fredelle Maynard

WOMEN & CHILDREN FIRST
Michele Landsberg

35/